THE DOCTRINE OF CONVENTIONALITY CONTROL

THE DOCTRINE OF CONVENTIONALITY CONTROL

Between Uniformity and Legal Pluralism in the Inter-American Human Rights System

Pablo González-Domínguez

intersentia
Cambridge – Antwerp – Portland

Intersentia Ltd
Sheraton House | Castle Park
Cambridge | CB3 0AX | United Kingdom
Tel.: +44 1223 370 170 | Fax: +44 1223 370 169
Email: mail@intersentia.co.uk
www.intersentia.com | www.intersentia.co.uk

Distribution for the UK and Ireland:
NBN International
Airport Business Centre, 10 Thornbury Road
Plymouth, PL6 7PP
United Kingdom
Tel.: +44 1752 202 301 | Fax: +44 1752 202 331
Email: orders@nbninternational.com

Distribution for Europe and all other countries:
Intersentia Publishing nv
Groenstraat 31
2640 Mortsel
Belgium
Tel.: +32 3 680 15 50 | Fax: +32 3 658 71 21
Email: mail@intersentia.be

Distribution for the USA and Canada:
International Specialized Book Services
920 NE 58th Ave. Suite 300
Portland, OR 97213
USA
Tel.: +1 800 944 6190 (toll free) | Fax: +1 503 280 8832
Email: info@isbs.com

The Doctrine of Conventionality Control. Between Uniformity and Legal Pluralism in the Inter-American Human Rights System

ISBN 978-1-78068-627-1
D/2018/7849/30
NUR 828

GPRC
Guaranteed
Peer Reviewed
Content

British Library Cataloguing in Publication Data. A catalogue record for this book is available from the British Library.

FOREWORD

One of the greatest and most persistent challenges of constructing a global system for the protection of human rights has always been how to bring international norms into a sustainable, healthy relationship with domestic constitutional systems.

It is self-evident that without strong domestic law and institutions, no global system of human rights protection could even aspire to be effective. Just as human rights pervasively get undermined and violated at local levels, so it is that they need to be protected and brought to life "in the small places, close to home," as Eleanor Roosevelt noted. And it is equally clear that international norms and institutions by themselves, cannot simply substitute for and displace the structures and institutions and habits of local communities in the protection of human rights. Distant, limited in scope and capacity, and detached from the social contexts in which the rule of law and the protection of human rights must take root if they are to be made real, international norms and institutions alone, cannot be the guarantors of human dignity everywhere and for everyone.

Yet, since the mid-twentieth century the nations of the world and their citizens have not been content to leave the demands of human dignity to the uncertain and inconsistent vagaries of domestic authorities. Rather, we have dedicated ourselves to drawing up universal norms of human rights, translating them into positive law backed by institutions, and struggling to establish adherence to and respect for them. The experience of human wrongs, of the most egregious violations of human rights, has taught us all too clearly that local communities, even under the most favorable conditions of the constitutional rule of law, always bear within them temptations to tyranny and abuse. For their own viability and strength, they need the accountability and the constraints that can come from recognized universal standards of human rights.

This inescapable tension has played itself out over the last seven decades in the drafting of treaties and the creation of international courts no less than in the halls of constitutional assemblies and the jurisprudence of high courts around the world. It is necessarily a tension that is permanent and structural to the global protection of human rights. It is constantly open to revision and renegotiation, as dynamic as the shifting sands of law, politics and culture. In each era we need to judge anew the conditions of the proper relationships between the transnational and domestic dimensions of human rights protection.

So it has been in the Inter-American human rights system. As the hemisphere has evolved from its high-water mark of criminal regimes, which used massive and systematic violations of human rights as intentional instruments of policy, to a predominance of constitutional democratic regimes (however endemically weak they may be in terms of political institutions and social inclusion, in many cases), so have the role of and the needs for the supranational human rights institutions changed with respect to domestic constitutional systems. We have witnessed the work of the Inter-American Commission and Court of Human Rights evolve from a primary concern for gross and systematic violations of non-derogable rights and *jus cogens* norms to more complicated and debatable questions of the balancing of multiple constitutional rights and liberties in the give-and-take of pluralistic democratic politics. We should not expect that the respective roles of international courts and domestic courts, and the interrelationship between them, could or should remain static under those conditions of epochal change.

This is the context in which the Inter-American Court's judicially-created doctrine of "conventionality control" must be situated. Originating in the Court's efforts to bring about a greater accountability for gross and systematic human rights violations at the end of an era dominated by dictatorships (as ably demonstrated by Pablo González-Domínguez here), it is now being debated and defined in relation to the proper responsibilities and prerogatives of constitutional courts in democratic polities. How it will evolve from here involves, on the one hand, nothing less than the core institutional legitimacy and effectiveness of international tribunals, and on the other hand, the political integrity of self-governing democracies.

To its most fervent proponents, conventionality control is an obvious and unproblematic logical aspect of the international protection of human rights. Obligations assumed by States oblige all of the separate powers of the States, and domestic law has never and should never excuse noncompliance with international obligations. Human rights as "universal" norms ought to have priority over other conflicting law. And judicial supremacy, extended into the international sphere, is as necessary to the interpretation and protection of human rights as adjudication is to the rule of law in any other context.

To its detractors, instead, conventionality control is an arrogant and brazen power grab by an Inter-American Court bent on "constitutionalizing" the Inter-American system by arrogating to itself the same sort of supremacy and direct control of domestic judiciaries that the European Court of Justice used to constitutionalize the European Union. It lacks any grounding in the text or intent of the American Convention on Human Rights, and it is fundamentally antidemocratic in its orientation.

The Inter-American Court cannot, on its own, mediate between those poles. Its jurisprudence on conventionality control, as we can see in this book, is shifting and not entirely consistent or clear. More fundamentally, the complex relationship between domestic and international juridical orders that conventionality control aims to capture and shape is precisely that: a *relationship.* No attempt to impose it in a one-sided way, without dialogue and exchange, conflict and compromise, among the relevant institutional actors, could work.

Without sustained dialogue that is supported by rigorous, balanced reflection and analysis, the uncertain experiment that conventionality control represents will fail. We must acknowledge honestly that conventionality control is not just an obvious and uncontroversial application of existing principles. It is, indeed, a new and bold way of approaching the entrenched challenge of relating domestic and international legal orders, a way that offers both peril and promise. Dictated from above, or substantively collapsing into a crude assertion of international judicial control and supremacy over constitutional systems, it would only be likely to backfire and provoke a justified but destructive resistance to the entire regional enterprise. But pursued with a sophisticated and intelligent sensitivity to the respective virtues and limitations of democratic self-governance, constitutionalism, and universal norms, it has the potential to serve as a source of integrative strength for human rights in the Western Hemisphere and beyond. Its promise, present in potential but still far from being realized, is to contribute an important building block to the emergence of an authentically global *Jus Commune* of human rights that our fragmented world sorely needs. Whether it is capable of realizing that potential, remains to be seen in the evolution of the theory and practice of the doctrine, in courts (international and domestic), in political life, and in scholarly reflection.

So it is essential to approach it with care – that is, with both openness and critical realism, and without polemic – as this book seeks to do. The threshold difficulty in forming an adequate judgment about conventionality control is to take a non-reductive approach. It requires an understanding of the distinctive perspectives and principles of *both* constitutional law *and also* public international law; embracing *both* the aspirational universality of human rights *and also* the irreducible importance of the local and particular in making human rights real; appreciating *both* the essential need for proper judicial control in the field of human rights *and also* the dark side of juristocracy for democratic politics and institutional legitimacy; being aware of *both* the strengths and achievements of global constitutionalism *and also* the value of constitutional identity, pluralism, and tolerance on the global stage.

Underlying this book's approach to conventionality control is the appeal to the principle of subsidiarity as an overarching theoretical key within which to harmonize those different and often contrasting elements that have to be kept in play and in balance. The principle of subsidiarity is not a magic bullet; it provides no formulaic solutions to the puzzle of conventionality control. But in contrast to the relatively sterile and dualistic understanding of the problem that emerges from sovereignty-based frameworks, subsidiarity does at least begin by addressing international and domestic law in terms of promoting "*both … and*" rather than "*either … or.*" It favors the building of a universal common good, genuinely oriented toward fostering a common understanding of the dignity of every human being, but lived out concretely in the specificities of local communities, including the diversity and integrity of their distinctive constitutional systems and traditions. That is a challenge that anyone who cares about the future of human rights ought to think about and be engaged in.

Paolo G. Carozza
University of Notre Dame

ACKNOWLEDGMENTS

Special thanks are due to Professor Paolo G. Carozza, to Judge Eduardo Ferrer Mac-Gregor Poisot and to Professor Douglass Cassel for their invaluable intellectual and moral guidance and their encouragement to write this book. Thanks are also due to Judges Eduardo Vio Grossi and Humberto Sierra Porto, and to Pablo Savedra Alessandri and Alexei Julio Estrada, for their intellectual and professional guidance during my time in the Inter-American Court of Human Rights, which was extremely helpful to gaining a better understanding of the theory and practice in the Inter-American Human Rights System.

I am extremely grateful to my friends and colleagues that supported me along the way, especially to those in the J.S.D. Program and in the University of Notre Dame Law School: Pier Pigozzi, Andrés López, Soledad Bertelsen and Samuel Tilahun; and to those in the Inter-American Court who commented on my work or helped me to refine arguments and perspectives on human rights questions: Bruno Rodriguez, Alfredo Ortega, Jorge Errandonea and Romina Sijniensky. Most importantly, I wish to thank my family and Ginny for all their constant and unconditional love and support throughout this exciting and enriching academic, professional and personal journey. I will be always deeply grateful to you.

I am deeply grateful to Tom Scheirs and to the editorial team of Intersentia for all their diligent work on this book. I am also grateful to the anonymous reviewers of the book proposal and for their critical comments.

Finally, I am deeply appreciative of the generous support for this project provided during my time at the University of Notre Dame by the Center for Civil and Human Rights, the Kellogg Institute for International Studies, the National Council of Science and Technology (Conacyt), the Rowe Fund of the Organization of American States, the Inter-American Court of Human Rights and the Legal Research Institute of the National Autonomous University of Mexico.

CONTENTS

LIST OF CASES AND OPINIONS

INTER-AMERICAN COURT OF HUMAN RIGHTS

CASES

OPINIONS

CONCURRING AND DISSENTING OPINIONS

INTERNATIONAL COURT OF JUSTICE AND THE PERMANENT COURT OF INTERNATIONAL JUSTICE

EUROPEAN COURT OF HUMAN RIGHTS

EUROPEAN UNION COURTS

INTERNATIONAL CRIMINAL TRIBUNALS

NATIONAL JURISDICTIONS

LIST OF TREATIES, INSTRUMENTS AND DOCUMENTS

TREATIES

INTER-AMERICAN SYSTEM

TREATIES IN GENERAL

CONSTITUTIONS AND STATUTES

NON-BINDING INTERNATIONAL INSTRUMENTS AND OFFICIAL REPORTS

GENERAL INTRODUCTION

1. OVERVIEW

Over the last two decades, there has been a tendency in the States parties to the American Convention on Human Rights, and in the institutions of the Inter-American System of Human Rights, to create rules and principles that allow domestic authorities – especially judges – to increase the effectiveness of the American Convention and other sources of international law at the domestic level. Several States have "opened the door" of their domestic legal systems, through constitutional amendments, or by decisions of their highest courts, to allow an ample incorporation of the human rights standards of the Inter-American System.[1] The Inter-American Court of Human Rights has followed a similar tendency, ordering States to amend laws and to change practices that have been identified as structural causes of human rights violations.[2] The States parties to the American Convention, as well as the Inter-American Court, apparently start from what could be called a truism for our times: that the effectiveness of the rights and freedoms recognized in international human rights law must lie primarily in the action of domestic institutions, not of international institutions.

The doctrine of conventionality control is one of the Inter-American Court's most recent efforts to increase the influence and effectiveness of the different sources of law in the Inter-American System at the domestic level. Although it is still an idea in progress, conventionality control can be defined as an international legal obligation that requires all the authorities of the States

---

1 *See*, Héctor Fix-Zamudio, *El derecho internacional de los derechos humanos en las Constituciones latinoamericanas y en la Corte Interamericana de Derechos Humanos*, 1(1) Revista Latinoamericana de Derecho 141 (2004); Allan R. Brewer-Carías, *Constitutional Protection of Human Rights in Latin America. A Comparative Study of Amparo Proceedings*, pp. 83, 87–162 (Cambridge University Press, 2009); Rodrigo Uprimny, *The Recent Transformation of Constitutional Law in Latin America: Trends and Challenges* 89 Tex. L. Rev. 1587 (2010–2011).

2 *See generally*, Sergio García Ramírez, *The Relationship Between Inter-American Jurisdiction and States (National Systems): Some Pertinent Questions*, 1(1) Notre Dame Journal of International and Comparative Law 124 (2015); Laurence Burgorgue-Larsen and Amaya Úbeda de Torres, *The Inter-American Court on Human Rights. Case Law and Commentary*, pp. 243–269 (Oxford University Press, 2011).

parties to the American Convention to interpret domestic law in accordance with the Inter-American *Corpus Juris*, which is integrated by the American Convention, treaties of similar nature (i.e. the Inter-American Convention to Prevent and Punish Torture), the interpretations of these treaties made by the Inter-American Court (in the exercise of its contentious or advisory jurisdiction) and other sources of soft law in the Inter-American System (i.e. the Inter-American Democratic Charter). In accordance with this doctrine, State authorities must avoid the enforcement of anti-conventional laws in case that no consistent interpretation is legally possible, although they must always act within their competences and the corresponding procedural regulations as defined by domestic law.[3]

The Inter-American Court introduced the doctrine of conventionality control to its case law in the decision of *Almonacid Arellano and others v. Chile* (2006).[4] In this case, the State of Chile was found internationally responsible for the enactment and enforcement of an amnesty law adopted in 1978, which resulted in the violation of the right to access to justice, truth and reparation for the next of kin of Luis Alfredo Almonacid Arellano, who was executed by police officers on September 16, 1973 during the first days of Augusto Pinochet's regime. The Inter-American Court followed its precedents created in the landmark case of *Barrios Altos v. Peru* (2001), declaring the nullity *ab initio* of the Chilean amnesty law.[5] But this time it went one step beyond previous cases connected with transitional justice, and determined that domestic judges are obligated by international law to ensure that anti-conventional laws do not adversely affect the provisions of the American Convention.[6] Therefore,

> the Judiciary must exercise a sort of "conventionality control" between the domestic legal provisions that are applied to specific cases and the American Convention on Human Rights. To perform this task, the Judiciary has to take into account not only the treaty, but also the interpretations thereof made by the Inter-American Court, which is the ultimate interpreter of the American Convention.[7]

---

3 *See*, Eduardo Ferrer Mac-Gregor Poisot, *Control de Convencionalidad (sede interna)*, in Eduardo Ferrer Mac-Gregor Poisot, Fabiola Martínez Ramírez and Giovanni Figeroa Mejía (Eds.), *Diccionario de Derecho Procesal Constitucional y Convencional*, Vol. I, p. 233 (Poder Judicial de la Federación, Consejo de la Judicatura Federal, Universidad Nacional Autónoma de México & Instituto de Investigaciones Jurídicas, 2014).

4 *See*, *Almonacid Arellano et al v. Chile*. Preliminary Objections, Merits, Reparations and Costs Judgment, Inter-Am. Ct. H.R. (Ser. C) No. 154 (Sep. 26, 2006) §124.

5 *See*, *Barrios Altos v. Peru Case*. Judgment, Inter-Am. Ct. H.R. (Ser. C) No. 75 (Mar. 14, 2001) §44.

6 *See generally*, Douglass Cassel, *El fallo Almonacid de la CIDH, y las obligaciones que de allí emanan para el Estado de Chile*, in Paulina Veloso (Ed.), *Justicia, Derechos Humanos y el Decreto Ley de Amnistía*, p. 81 (PNUD, 2010).

7 *Almonacid Arellano et al. v. Chile Case*, *supra* n. 4, §124.

The doctrine of conventionality control evolved in subsequent cases after *Almonacid*,[8] progressively constituting one of the most relevant topics in the recent jurisprudence of the Inter-American Court.[9] The relevance and strength of this doctrine can be observed in the fact that it has been used by the Court in more than 25 contentious cases and in three Advisory Opinions since 2006;[10] in the various concurrent opinions of several current and former judges of the Inter-American Court, who have discussed this topic in great detail;[11] in the continuous publication of legal articles and books written by prestigious judges and scholars of Latin America and other regions,[12] particularly by

---

8 *See generally, Dismissed Congressional Employees (Aguado-Alfaro et al.).* Preliminary Objections, Merits, Reparations and Costs Judgment, Inter-Am. Ct. H.R. (Ser. C) No. 158 (Nov. 24, 2006) §128; *Boyce et al. v. Barbados.* Preliminary Objection, Merits, Reparations and Costs Judgment, Inter-Am. Ct. H.R. (Ser. C) No. 158 (Nov. 20, 2007) §78, 79; *Radilla Pacheco v. Mexico.* Preliminary Objections, Merits, Reparations and Costs Judgment, Inter-Am. Ct. H.R. (Ser. C) No. 209 (Nov. 29, 2009) §339–340; *Gelman v. Uruguay.* Preliminary Objections, Merits, Reparations, and Costs Judgment, Inter-Am. Ct. H.R. (Ser. C) No. 221 (Feb. 24, 2011) §193, 239; *Andrade Salmón v. Bolivia.* Merits, Reparations and Costs Judgment, Inter-Am. Ct. H.R. (Ser. C) No. 330 (Dec. 1, 2016) §93.

9 *See*, Laurence Burgorgue-Larsen, *Chronicle of a Fashionable Theory in Latin America. Decoding the Doctrinal Discourse of Conventionality Control*, in Yves Haeck, Oswaldo Ruiz-Chiriboga and Clara Burbano-Herrera (Eds.), *The Inter-American Court of Human Rights: Theory and Practice, Present and Future*, p. 676 (Intersentia, 2015) (in the words of the French scholar: "What is sure is that, though doctrinal production on conventionality control, the Inter-American system today is at the centre of democratic discussions in the Americas. In this regard, it is more vigorous than ever.").

10 *See generally*, Claudio Nash Rojas, *Control de Convencionalidad. Cuadernillo de la Corte Interamericana de Derechos Humanos No. 7* (Inter-American Court of Human Rights & Ministerio de Relaciones Exteriores de Dinamarca, 2015) and Silvia Serrano Guzmán, *El control de convencionalidad en la jurisprudencia de la Corte Interamericana de Derechos Humanos* (Comisión Nacional de los Derechos Humanos, 2013).

11 *See, Dismissed Congressional Employees (Aguado-Alfaro et al.) v. Peru Case, supra* n. 8, Reasoned Concurrent Opinions of Sergio García Ramírez and A.A. Cançado Trindade; *Cabrera Garcia and Montiel Flores v. Mexico.* Preliminary Objections, Merits, Reparations and Costs Judgment, Inter-Am. Ct. H.R. (Ser. C) No. 220 (Nov. 26, 2010). Reasoned Concurrent Opinion of Judge Eduardo Ferrer Mac-Gregor Poisot; *Gender Identity, and equality and non-discrimination with regard to same-sex couples. State obligations in relation to change of name, gender identity, and rights from a relationship between same-sex couples (interpretation and scope of Articles 1(1), 3, 7, 11(2), 13, 17, 18 and 24, in relation to Article 1, of the American Convention on Human Rights.* Advisory Opinion OC-24, Inter-Am. Ct. H.R. (Ser. A) No. 14 (Nov. 24, 2017). Dissenting Opinion of Judge Eduardo Vio Grossi.

12 *See*, Ernesto Rey Cantor, *Control de la Convencionalidad de Leyes y Derechos Humanos* (Porrúa, 2008); Susana Albanese (Ed.) *El control de convencionalidad* (Ediar, 2008); Oswaldo Ruiz-Chiriboga, *The Conventionality Control: Examples of (Un)successful Experiences in Latin America*, 3(1–2) Inter-American and European Human Rights Journal (2010); Ariel E. Dulitzky, *An Inter-American Constitutional Court? The Invention of conventionality control by the Inter-American Court of Human Rights*, 50 Tex. Int'l L. J. (2015); Laurence Burgorgue-Larsen, *Chronicle of a Fashionable Theory in Latin America. Decoding the Doctrinal Discourse on Conventionality Control, supra* n. 9; Jorge Contesse, *The final word? Constitutional dialogue and the Inter-American Court of Human Rights*, 15(2) International Journal of Constitutional Law 414–435 (2017).

Sergio García Ramírez,[13] Eduardo Ferrer Mac-Gregor Poisot[14] and Nestor Pedro Sagües;[15] in the use of this doctrine by the supreme courts of justice of some States parties to the American Convention, particularly by Argentina[16] and Mexico;[17] and in the several academic and professional forums organized by governments and professional institutions to inform legal practitioners and judges about conventionality control.[18]

The relevance and popularity of conventionality control may be connected with its singularity, since this doctrine has no parallel in any other system of human rights protection, either universal or regional.[19] It constitutes an innovative doctrine in the Inter-American System that seeks to empower domestic authorities to ensure that the creation, interpretation and enforcement of domestic law serve to protect (not to violate) human rights. But the same

---

13 *See*, Sergio García Ramírez, *The Conventional Internal Control Court*, V(28) IUS Revista del Instituto de Ciencias Jurídicas de Puebla (2011); Sergio García Ramírez, *The Relationship Between Inter-American Jurisdiction and States (National Systems): Some Pertinent Questions*, *supra* n. 2.

14 *See*, Eduardo Ferrer Mac-Gregor Poisot, *Interpretación conforme y control difuso de convencionalidad. El nuevo paradigma del juez mexicano*, in MIGUEL CARBONELL AND PEDRO SALAZAR (EDS.), *LA REFORMA CONSTITUCIONAL DE DERECHOS HUMANOS. UN NUEVO PARADIGMA* (Porrúa, 2012); EDUARDO FERRER MAC-GREGOR POISOT, *PANORÁMICA DEL DERECHO PROCESAL CONSTITUCIONAL Y CONVENCIONAL* (Marcial Pons, 2013).

15 *See*, Nestor Pedro Sagües, *El "control de convencionalidad", en particular sobre las constituciones nacionales, La Ley*, Year LXXIII, No. 35 (2009); Nestor Pedro Sagües, *International obligations and "conventionality control"*, 8(1) Estudios Constitucionales (2010).

16 *See*, Supreme Court of Justice of Argentina, M. 2333. XLII (Mazzeo, Julio Lilo *et al.*, Appeal for annulment and constitutional motion), July 13, 2007, §20.

17 *See*, Supreme Court of Justice of the Nation (Mexico), File 489/2010 (*expediente varios*), Aug. 31, 2010; Supreme Court of Justice of the Nation (Mexico), P./J. 21/2014 (*tesis aislada*), April 25, 2014.

18 *"Congreso Internacional de Derecho Procesal Constitucional Transnacional. Interacción entre el Derecho Nacional y el Derecho Internacional". IX Encuentro Iberoamericano y VI Congreso Mexicano de Derecho Procesal Constitucional* (Hermosillo, Sonora, Mexico, Dec. 3, 4 and 5, 2014); *"Curso de capacitación en la aplicación de la Convención Americana de Derechos Humanos". Centro de Estudios de Justicia de las Américas (CEJA)* (San Salvador, El Salvador, Aug. 20, 21 and 22, 2014).

19 It is possible to find other doctrines that are similar to conventionality control in the context of the European Union, but none exist in an international system of human rights protection. Examples are the doctrine of direct effect and supremacy of EU law, created by the European Court of Justice (*see*, Case 26/62, *Van Gens & Loos v. Nederlandse* [1963] E.C.R. 1; Case 106/77; *Italian Finance Administration v. Simmenthal* [1978] E.C.R. 269; Francisco Fernandez-Segado, *El juez nacional como juez comunitario europeo de derecho común. Las transformaciones constitucionales dimanantes de ello*, 13 Revista Mexicana de Derecho Constitucional (2005)); or the efforts of the European Commission to give more vigorous enforcement to competition laws in the EU (*see*, Case C-234/89, *Delimitis v. Henninger Bräu AG* [1991] E.C.R. I-935; Case T-24/90, *Automec Srl. v. E.C. Commission* [1992] 5 C.M.L.R. 431; Roger P. Alford, *Subsidiarity and competition: decentralized enforcement of EU competition laws*, Cornell International Law Journal (1994));. Jorge Contesse, *The International Authority of the Inter-American Court of Human Rights: A Critique of the Conventionality Control Doctrine*, 22 International Journal of Human Rights 17–18 (2018).

characteristics that make conventionality control so attractive – the idea that all domestic authorities have an international obligation to enforce the different sources of law in the Inter-American System, notwithstanding the existence of domestic law to the contrary – is also the source of criticism about its legality and convenience as a legal institution governed by international law. The strongest critiques have pointed out that conventionality control has no normative basis in the American Convention or in general international law, and that in fact this doctrine constitutes a bold and arbitrary act of judicial legislation that violates the principle of subsidiarity, hinders legal pluralism and endangers the political stability of the Inter-American System by trying to impose a radical monist view of the normative force of the American Convention and the jurisprudence of the Inter-American Court.[20]

The critiques of conventionality control could be right: this doctrine might presuppose a vertical understanding of the relationship between the law and institutions of the Inter-American System, and the law and institutions of the States parties to the American Convention.[21] But, while possible, this conclusion does not *necessarily* follow from the jurisprudence of the Inter-American Court on conventionality control, and certainly it is inconsistent with some of the most relevant structural and normative aspects of the Inter-American System.[22] So unless the Inter-American Court really aims to "transform" (through the force of its judgments) the subsidiary nature of the Inter-American System into some kind of unitary legal system for America with little or no room for

---

20 *See generally*, Cristina Binder, *The Prohibition of Amnesties by the Inter-American Court of Human Rights*, 12 German Law Journal 1216 (2011); Ezequiel Malarino, *Acerca de la Pretendida Obligatoriedad de la Jurisprudencia de los Órganos Interamericanos de Protección de Derechos Humanos para los Tribunales Judiciales Nacionales*, in SISTEMA INTERAMERICANO DE PROTECCIÓN DE LOS DERECHOS HUMANOS Y DERECHO PENAL INTERNACIONAL (Konrad-Adenauer-Stiftung, 2010); Ezequiel Malarino, *Judicial Activism, Punitivism, and Supranationalisation: Illiberal Tendencies of the Inter-American Court of Human Rights*, 12 International Criminal Law Review 665–695 (2012); Luigi Crema, 'Are Amnesties Still an Option? A Non-Policy Based Critique of the Inter-American Approach', Center for Civil and Human Rights, University of Notre Dame, Working Paper Series # 6, pp. 50–51 (2013); Jorge Contesse, *The International Authority of the Inter-American Court of Human Rights: A Critique of the Conventionality Control Doctrine*, *supra* n. 19, pp. 1–24.

21 *See*, Ariel E. Dulitzky, *An Inter-American Constitutional Court? The Invention of conventionality control by the Inter-American Court of Human Rights*, *supra* n. 12, p. 54 (on the notion that Inter-American Court developed the "principle of integration", which conceives human rights treaties of the Inter-American System and the jurisprudence of the Inter-American Court as "an integral part of domestic legal systems at the highest possible level".)

22 *See generally*, Eduardo Jiménez de Aréchaga, *La Convención Americana de Derechos Humanos como derecho interno*, Boletín da Sociedade Brasileira de Direito Internacional, 35–55 (1987–1989); THOMAS BUERGENTHAL, SELF-EXECUTING AND NON-SELF EXECUTING TREATIES IN NATIONAL AND INTERNATIONAL LAW, p. 320 (Martinus Nijhoff Publishers, 1992); DINAH SHELTON AND PAOLO G. CAROZZA, REGIONAL PROTECTION OF HUMAN RIGHTS, p. 113 (Oxford University Press, 2013).

legal pluralism, it is not obvious that the normative components and theoretical foundations of conventionality control necessarily imply the supremacy of the American Convention and the interpretations of the Inter-American Court over any consideration of domestic law. On the contrary, it is much more reasonable to treat conventionality control as a flexible juridical instrument that grants States ample spaces of freedom, so they are capable of deciding the best manner of "controlling" the "conventionality" of their domestic laws on the basis of the *Corpus Juris*.[23]

2. STRUCTURE

In light of these considerations, this book presents a descriptive, analytical, critical and normative study of the doctrine of conventionality control. *Descriptively*, it explains the precedents, creation, legal foundations and normative development of conventionality control as elaborated by the Inter-American Court in its jurisprudence, and conceptualized by some of its most prominent supporters. *Analytically*, it studies in detail the international obligations that derive from the existence of conventionality control, by exploring the different levels of connection among these obligations and several rules and principles of international and domestic law. *Critically*, it elaborates the strongest objections that could be raised against conventionality control as a legal institution specific to the Inter-American System, but governed by general international law. *Normatively*, it reconstructs conventionality control on the basis of the principle of subsidiarity, presenting a flexible version of this doctrine that it is legally sound and that could strengthen the dialogue between the Inter-American Court and judicial and political institutions at the domestic level. Accordingly, the analysis hereby presented is divided into four chapters.

Chapter 1 studies the development of the doctrine of conventionality control in the jurisprudence of the Inter-American Court. It begins by explaining how the creation of this doctrine is the result of progressive and innovative interpretations of Article 2 of the American Convention, a process that started years before *Almonacid* was decided.[24] It further argues that these interpretations changed the understanding of Article 2 from a norm with a programmatic nature, which was a position implicitly sustained in the *OC-14/94* (1994), to a

23 *See generally*, Paolo G. Carozza, *The Anglo-Latin Divide and the Future of the Inter-American System of Human Rights*, 5(1) Notre Dame Journal of International and Comparative Law 156 (2015); Paolo G. Carozza and Pablo González-Domínguez, *The final word? Constitutional dialogue and the Inter-American Court of Human Rights: A reply to Jorge Contesse*, 15(2) International Journal of Constitutional Law 436–442 (April 2017).

24 *See*, Laurence Burgorgue-Larsen and Amaya Úbeda de Torres, *The Inter-American Court on Human Rights. Case Law and Commentary*, *supra* n. 2, pp. 243–269.

norm that allowed the Inter-American Court to evaluate – even *in abstracto* – the compatibility between domestic law and the American Convention.[25] This theoretical position, which was adopted explicitly for the first time in the case of *Suárez Rosero v. Ecuador* (1997), and which acquired its strongest meaning in *Barrios Altos* and subsequent cases connected with transitional justice, justified higher intervention from the Inter-American Court in domestic legal systems, a condition that ultimately lead to the practice of ordering States to amend or repeal anti-conventional laws, and to adopt practices like conventionality control, in order to prevent future human rights violations.[26]

The creation of the doctrine of conventionality control is the highest step in the approach taken by the Inter-American Court since *Suárez Rosero*. Yet, the study of conventionality control, as an autonomous legal institution that is the source of international obligations for all the authorities of the State parties to the American Convention, is independent of the cases that preceded its creation. The complete understanding of conventionality control must take into account the cases specifically connected with the original conceptualization of this doctrine, and with all other cases that added new elements in later stages of the Inter-American Court's jurisprudence. Hence, Chapter 1 studies the decisions of *Almonacid, Dismissed Congressional Employees (Aguado-Alfaro) v. Peru* (2006), *La Cantuta v. Peru* (2007), and *Heliodoro Portugal v. Panama* (2008), which may be referred as the "foundational cases" on conventionality control. It also studies the further development of conventionality control until the decision in the *OC-24/17* (2017), focusing its attention on the judgments of *Radilla Pacheco v. Mexico* (2009), *Cabrera Garcia and Montiel Flores v. Mexico* (2010), *Gelman v. Uruguay* (2011), *Santo Domingo Massacre v. Colombia* (2012), the *Resolution of Compliance with Gelman v. Uruguay Case* (2013), the *OC-21/14* (2014), the *OC-22/16* (2016), *Andrade Salmón v. Bolivia* (2016) and the *OC-24/17* (2017).

Chapter 2 presents a legal analysis of the doctrine of conventionality control. This analysis is based on an evaluation of all the cases that are part of the "line of jurisprudence" (*línea jurisprudencial*) on conventionality control (studied in Chapter 1), but this time presented in a systematic manner. Specifically, Chapter 2 discusses five topics: (1) the *definition* and *legal foundations* of conventionality control: the latter based on Articles 1.1, 2 and 29 of the American Convention,

---

25 *See, International Responsibility for the Promulgation and Enforcement of Laws in Violation of the Convention (Arts. 1 and 2 American Convention on Human Rights).* Advisory Opinion OC-14, Inter-Am. Ct. H.R. (Ser. A) No. 14 (Dec. 9, 1994), §49; *El Amparo v. Venezuela Case.* Reparations (Art. 63(1) American Convention on Human Rights) Judgment, Inter-Am. Ct. H.R. (Ser. C) No. 28, (Sep. 14, 1996). Dissenting Opinion of A.A. Cançado Trindade, §3.

26 *See, Suárez Rosero v. Ecuador Case.* Judgment, Inter-Am. Ct. H.R. (Ser. C) No. 35 (Nov. 12, 1997) §98; *"The Last Temptation of Christ" v. Chile Case (Olmedo Bustos et al.).* Judgment, Inter-Am. Ct. H.R. (Ser. C) No. 73 (Feb. 5, 2001) §63–73, Operative para. 4.

and in Articles 26 and 27 of the Vienna Convention on the Law of Treaties; (2) the *subjects* of the obligation: the State authorities that shall exercise conventionality control; (3) the *object* of the obligation: the type of actions required by conventionality control; (4) the *paradox* of conventionality control: that it must be exercised *ex officio* by domestic authorities, but that they must act in the context of their respecting competences and respecting the corresponding procedural regulations as defined by domestic law (this is called the "*Aguado-Alfaro* clause"); (5) and the *parameters* of conventionality control: the type of domestic norms that must be subject to conventionality control, and the sources of international law that serve as a basis for that control.

Yet, conventionality control cannot be accurately evaluated, descriptively and normatively speaking, in isolation from rules and principles of domestic law, notwithstanding its nature as an international legal institution. From a descriptive perspective, conventionality control is connected with domestic law because its design and creation mirrors the recent transformation of Latin American constitutionalism, which opened the door for the incorporation of International Human Rights Law (IHRL) into domestic legal systems.[27] From a normative perspective, conventionality control is connected with domestic law in two crucial aspects: first, the obligation of domestic authorities to exercise conventionality control must be done in accordance with the "*Aguado-Alfaro* clause"; and secondly, domestic authorities, while exercising conventionality control, arguably shall consider the place that the different elements of the *Corpus Juris* occupy in constitutional law. Chapter 2 argues that the intrinsic relationship between conventionality control and domestic law "relativizes" the normative content of the doctrine in each State party to the American Convention, creating different "intensities" or "grades" of conventionality control in different legal systems.[28] Hence, Chapter 2 studies the most important aspects of domestic law that define this relationship, as well as their normative implications.

Chapter 3 questions the legal validity of the doctrine of conventionality control as an international legal institution. It takes a different direction than the two previous chapters, evaluating this doctrine if it is seen as a legal institution governed by general international law. Chapter 3 assumes that the Inter-American System is not a "self-contained" regime, which means that it

---

[27] *See*, Sergio García Ramírez (2015), *The Relationship Between Inter-American Jurisdiction and States (National Systems): Some Pertinent Questions*, *supra* n. 2, p. 133.

[28] *See*, *Cabrera Garcia and Montiel Flores v. Mexico*, *supra* n. 11. Reasoned Concurrent Opinion of Judge Eduardo Ferrer Mac-Gregor Poisot, §35; *Gender Identity, and equality and non-discrimination with regard to same-sex couples. State obligations in relation to change of name, gender identity, and rights from a relationship between same-sex couples (interpretation and scope of Articles 1(1), 3, 7, 11(2), 13, 17, 18 and 24, in relation to Article 1, of the American Convention on Human Rights*, *supra* n. 11. Dissenting Opinion of Judge Eduardo Vio Grossi, §120.

is structurally connected with general international law.[29] On that basis, three objections are formulated against conventionality control: (1) the obligation of conventionality control cannot be grounded in Article 2 of the American Convention, since this article was expressly created leaving complete freedom for States to define how to give effect to the *Corpus Juris*;[30] (2) Articles 26 and 27 of the Vienna Convention do not support the existence of conventionality control, since the obligations of those provisions neither affect the legal validity of domestic laws, nor do they impose direct obligations on State authorities;[31] (iii) the doctrine of conventionality control cannot be based on the jurisprudence of the Inter-American Court, since the doctrine of precedent does not exist in international law.[32]

These critiques are based on two structural assumptions that have defined the theory and practice of international law since its inception: that the consent of States as sovereigns is the most important factor for identifying the origin and extent of international rights and obligations as reflected in the text of a treaty;[33] and that there is a strict separation between how norms of international law confer rights and impose obligations on States as subjects of international law, and how the same norms are binding for specific authorities at the domestic level.[34] Chapter 3 shows the disconnection between these structural elements and the approach taken by the Inter-American Court in cases such as *Suárez Rosero*, *Barrios Altos*, and *Almonacid*. But without ignoring the normative reality of international law, Chapter 3 also explains some of the insufficiencies of legal positivism in areas of law connected with the protection of human dignity, arguing that the specific characteristics of these areas allow the existence of legal instruments, such as conventionality control, that reduce the theoretical and practical gap that exists between international law and domestic law.[35]

---

29 *See*, Report of the Study Group of the ILC on Fragmentation of International Law: difficulties arising from the diversification and expansion of International Law, Doc. No. A/CN4/L.682 (April 13, 2006).

30 *See*, Sixth Report on State Responsibility by Mr. Roberto Argo, Special Rapporteur – the internationally wrongful act of the State, source of international responsibility (continued), Ybk ILC, 1977, Vol. II (1) A/CN.4/302 and Add.1, 2 & 3.

31 *See*, Jean Salmon, *Article 26*, in *Olivier Corten and Pierre Klein* (Eds.), *The Vienna Conventions on the Law of Treaties. A Commentary*. Vol. I (Oxford University Press, 2011).

32 *See*, Ezequiel Malarino, *Acerca de la Pretendida Obligatoriedad de la Jurisprudencia de los Órganos Interamericanos de Protección de Derechos Humanos para los Tribunales Judiciales Nacionales*, *supra* n. 20, pp. 439–440.

33 *See*, *Military and Paramilitary Activities in and Against Nicaragua (Nicar. v. U.S.)*. Merits, 1986 I.C.J. 14 (Jun. 27) §269; Antony Clark Arendt, Legal Rules and International Society, p. 61 (Oxford University Press, 1999).

34 *See*, Ian Brownlie, *Principles of Public International Law*, pp. 31–38 (Oxford University Press, 7th ed., 2008).

35 *See generally*, Paolo G. Carozza, *Subsidiarity as a Structure Principle of International Law*, 97 Am. J. Int'l L., 63 (2003); Armin Von Bogdandy, *Pluralism, direct effect, and the ultimate say: On the relationship between international and domestic constitutional law*, 6 Int'l J. Const. L., 397–401 (2008).

Chapter 4 reconstructs the doctrine of conventionality control in the light of the principle of subsidiarity. It presents a new understanding of the legal and theoretical foundations of conventionality control – one that it is not based on idealist notions that hold the supremacy of international law and institutions over domestic law and institutions, but one that also responds to the critiques and challenges presented by legal positivism. Chapter 4 proves that Article 2 of the American Convention is a norm that recognizes a high but not absolute freedom for States to implement the Inter-American *Corpus Juris*, a condition that justifies the practice of the Inter-American Court to intervene and order States to repair structural causes of human rights violations, especially when States have proven themselves incapable or unwilling to modify the causes of those violations. Consequently, the creation of the doctrine of conventionality control in *Almonacid* is justified because it constitutes a legitimate *subsidium* created to combat a particularly serious problem in some Latin American States: the impunity for serious human rights violations produced by the existence and enforcement of amnesty laws that are manifestly anti-conventional and that are null *ab initio*.

Yet, the broader dimensions that conventionality control acquired in the cases that followed *Almonacid* opens the door for another type of discussion. Because there is a marked difference between creating a juridical instrument to assist States to fight against serious structural problems in concrete cases, and creating a doctrine that in its most extreme version reflects a radical monist approach that runs contrary to legal pluralism in the Inter-American System. Chapter 4 argues that in order to sustain the legal validity of the doctrine of conventionality control, it is necessary to distinguish its normative force (1) in cases where it constitutes a "guarantee of non-repetition" to avoid the future enforcement of laws and the continuation of practices that have been found anti-conventional by the Inter-American Court, and (2) where it is referred to as a doctrine with general applicability for all the authorities of the States parties to the American Convention. This distinction, and its accompanying normative consequences, allows the dual view that conventionality control is both a legal institution that must be enforced exactly as mandated by the Inter-American Court in specific cases, as well as a flexible mechanism that allows accommodation in different legal systems.

3. METHODOLOGY

This book takes an inductive approach, since it moves from the observation of a phenomenon in the jurisprudence of the Inter-American Court, to broader generalizations and theories. This approach was adopted because conventionality control was created – and has evolved – out of the challenges faced by the Inter-American Court in concrete cases. Hence, one may properly systematize and theorize about this doctrine only in the context of the efforts taken by the Inter-American Court to prevent future human rights violations caused by the existence and enforcement of anti-conventional laws or by anti-conventional interpretations of these laws, and to increase the effectiveness of the Inter-American *Corpus Juris* in the region. For this reason, the description and the analytical evaluation of conventionality control presented in Chapters 1 and 2 rely heavily on the evolution of the case law of the Inter-American Court from 1997 to 2018, and in the ideas of some of its most influential judges during the same period of time, particularly those of A.A. Cançado Trindade, García Ramírez and Ferrer Mac-Gregor Poisot.

But a comprehensive analysis of the doctrine of conventionality control could not be made only by looking at the case law of the Inter-American Court, since that would require accepting the premise that the Inter-American System is a self-contained regime that cannot be evaluated based on rules different than those established in the American Convention and the interpretations of the Inter-American Court. So, Chapter 3 rejects the idea that the Inter-American System is a self-contained regime, and assumes that the institutions and norms in the Inter-American System are or should be structurally connected with other norms and principles of general international law. This approach – which is that of an international lawyer, perhaps more than that of a constitutional lawyer or of a human rights activist – was motivated by a sincere desire to understand why this doctrine is so controversial to some serious legal scholars. This is why Chapter 3 presents an analysis of the text and the preparatory works of the American Convention, of the first interpretations made by the Inter-American Court of Article 2, of the Vienna Convention on the Law of Treaties, and of the classic theories that explain the structural aspects of public international law.

The evaluation of conventionality control from the perspective of the relevant rules and principles of public international law lead to two important conclusions: first, that this doctrine is indeed extremely innovative, since it challenges the original understanding of Article 2 of the American Convention, and of Articles 26 and 27 of the Vienna Convention; and second, that legal positivism cannot serve as a solid basis for sound criticism of conventionality control, since its rigid postulates fail to explain the legal reality of the twenty-first century, especially in areas connected with the protection of human dignity. It was thus necessary to find a conceptual basis (if there was any) that could explain and justify the existence of conventionality control, as an international legal institution that was created by an international court, but that has its effects fully at the domestic level. Still, this conceptual basis had also to be consistent with the normative content of the American Convention, with the political and structural realities in the Inter-American System, and with the pluralistic nature of the human rights project.

Radical monist views like those proposed by Cançado Trindade are attractive for their highly idealistic thesis, but they are not sound. They lack connection with the normative and political realities of the Inter-American System, and reflect a view whose ultimate consequences call for an absolutist understanding of the human rights project that also allocates an unlimited degree of authority to international institutions. But the principle of subsidiarity proved to be a reasonable framework to theorize about the doctrine of conventionality control. This principle helps to make sense of the practice of the Inter-American Court to tackle structural problems at the State level through its jurisprudence, by ordering States to exercise conventionality control in order to prevent future human rights violations; but this approach does not assume or tries to impose the supremacy of the *Corpus Juris* over any other consideration of domestic law, and it does not understand the relationship between the Inter-American Court and State institutions in hierarchical terms.

Interpreting the American Convention and the powers of the Inter-American Court in light of the principle of subsidiarity allows a distinction to be drawn between two faces of conventionality control: one that requires State authorities to follow the jurisprudence of the Inter-American Court, without any possibility of deviation, when a domestic norm – or the way this norm is interpreted – has been found anti-conventional in a contentious case; and a second face that gives States ample freedom to decide how their authorities shall exercise conventionality control in cases where they have not been parties to a controversy, or where an interpretation is made by the Court in the exercise of its advisory jurisdiction, in this manner respecting and promoting legal pluralism and judicial dialogue, and strengthening the political stability of the Inter-American System. From this distinction followed the possibility of identifying the factors that should reasonably "regulate" the "intensity" of conventionality control in different States parties to the American Convention, and the theoretical key for further studies on how conventionality control shall "couple" in the domestic legal systems of Argentina, Mexico, Colombia, for example.

This methodology deliberately excludes other valid points of departure for analyzing conventionality control, although it is not contrary to an analysis from the perspective of other areas of law, such as constitutional law, procedural law or procedural constitutional law. In fact, the understanding of how conventionality control should operate in concrete domestic legal systems requires an analysis from the perspective of these areas of law. So the theory and practice in constitutional law would define how conventionality control couples with the rules that determine the incorporation of rules and principles of IHRL in domestic legal systems; procedural law would define how conventionality control couples with classic procedural notions such as "*res judicata*", or "*erga omnes* effects of international judgments"; and procedural constitutional law would define how conventionality control is connected with the notions of "constitutional control" and of "constitutional block".

This book, however, seeks to contribute to the understanding of conventionality control mainly from the perspective of fundamental rules and principles of public international law and of IHRL.

CHAPTER 1

JURISPRUDENTIAL DEVELOPMENT OF THE DOCTRINE OF CONVENTIONALITY CONTROL

From the moment that violations of protected human rights are found, the evaluation of the incompatibility of legal provisions between domestic law and the American Convention on Human Rights becomes ... no longer an abstract question. A law can per se be incompatible with the Convention to the extent that, for instance, inhibits the exercise of protected rights, even in the absence of a measure of application.
A.A. Cançado Trindade
Dissenting Opinion in the case of *El Amparo v. Venezuela* (1995)

1. INTRODUCTION

The study of the doctrine of conventionality control must start with a clarification: there is no article in the American Convention on Human Rights that expressly recognizes an international obligation for every public authority to perform an interpretation of domestic law in accordance with the Inter-American *Corpus Juris*, or to refrain from the enforcement of that law if no valid interpretation is possible. The creation of the doctrine of conventionality control – and therefore of each one of its technical components – is the result of a progressive and innovative interpretation performed by the Inter-American Court of Human Rights of the "general obligations" established in Articles 1.1 and 2 of the American Convention and of Articles 26 and 27 of the Vienna Convention on the Law of Treaties (hereinafter the Vienna Convention). The progressiveness of some of these interpretations (which served as the precedents for conventionality control) started years before the case of *Almonacid Arellano and others v. Chile* (2006) was decided.

The judgments that constitute the precedents for conventionality control developed the content of the obligation to ensure (Article 1.1), and progressively strengthened the normative force of Article 2.[1] These judgments modified the

---

1 *See*, Laurence Burgorgue-Larsen and Amaya Úbeda de Torres, *The Inter-American Court on Human Rights. Case Law and Commentary*, pp. 243–269 (Oxford University

understanding of Article 2 from being a norm with some sort of a programmatic nature – a position that supported the view that States have freedom to decide the means to ensure the rights protected by the Convention, and therefore that the Inter-American Court had little say in the specification of these means – to a norm that prescribed international obligations in the strongest sense of the word. This theoretical position opened the door for the Inter-American Court to evaluate the conventionality of the legislative and other measures taken by the States to ensure their compliance with the American Convention. The same theoretical position ultimately resulted in the formulation of the doctrine of conventionality control as an "other measure" created by the Inter-American Court, so the States could give effect at the domestic level to the rights and freedoms recognized by the Inter-American *Corpus Juris*.

This chapter starts by showing how the understanding of the strong normative force of Article 2 initiated with the decision in *Suárez Rosero v. Ecuador* (1997). In this case, for the first time in its – then short – history, the Inter-American Court evaluated *in abstracto*, and in the exercise of its contentious jurisdiction, the compatibility between a domestic law and the American Convention. The Court did not establish any legal consequence as result of this evaluation, but it constituted a departure from its previous position on the question of whether or not the Court could, in the exercise of its contentious jurisdiction, evaluate the laws of the States parties to the American Convention, opening the door for further developments. This understanding reached new heights when the Court declared the nullity *ab initio* of certain types of amnesty laws in *Barrios Altos v. Peru* (2001), and when it started the practice of ordering States to amend or annul norms (including norms of constitutional hierarchy) that were found "anti-conventional",[2] as happened in the *"The Last Temptation of Christ" (Olmedo Bustos) v. Chile* (2001). The creation of the doctrine of conventionality control in *Almonacid* followed this path, since the Inter-American Court, on the basis of Articles 1.1 and 2, proposed this doctrine as an "other measure" for the States to comply with its international obligations to "ensure" the rights protected by the Convention.

Almonacid is the leading case on conventionality control. It allows an understanding of the context where this doctrine was created and its first technical formulation. For that reason, the second section of this chapter analyzes the arguments, norms and principles where the doctrine of conventionality control was originally grounded. It pays special attention to how the strong

Press, 2011) (for an explanation of the content and evolution of the meaning of Art. 2 in the jurisprudence of the Inter-American Court).

2 The term "anti-conventional" is used to express "not in accordance with the American Convention". The term is a direct translation of the word "*inconvencional*", which is a term inspired by analogy with the word "*inconstitucional*" (unconstitutional) and that is commonly used by the Court and by domestic authorities in Spanish-speaking countries.

normative force of Article 2 (and Article 1.1) is at the core of the Inter-American Court's position. This section also shows the elements that refined the foundations and technical components of the doctrine of conventionality control in the cases of the *Dismissed Congressional Employees (Aguado-Alfaro) v. Peru* (2007), *La Cantuta v. Peru* (2006) and *Heliodoro Portugal v. Panama* (2008).[3] In these cases, which may be deemed as "foundational cases", the Court made a clearer assessment of the connections between the obligations of States under Article 2 (and other provisions of the Convention), and the existence of the obligation of domestic judges to exercise conventionality control.

As a corollary of the first two sections of this chapter, the third section is an analysis of the further development that the doctrine of conventionality control has had in other cases until the decision of the *OC-24/17* (2016). The analysis is only focused on those cases that advanced the doctrine of conventionality control, either by clarifying its components, or by adding new elements not contemplated in the above-mentioned "foundational cases". Thus, this section starts with an analysis of *Boyce and others v. Barbados* (2007), where it was implied that all domestic norms (including constitutional norms) must be subjected to conventionality control. Then it analyzes *Radilla Pacheco v. Mexico* (2009), where the Court mentioned that the exercise of conventionality control included the obligation of interpreting domestic law in accordance with the Inter-American *Corpus Juris*. Then it succinctly analyzes *Cabrera García and Montiel Flores v. Mexico* (2010), where it was defined that all domestic authorities, and not just judges, were obligated to exercise conventionality control. Furthermore, the section analyses the *Resolution of Monitoring Compliance with Gelman v. Uruguay* (2013), the *OC-21/14* (2014), the *OC-22/16* (2016), and the *OC-24/17* (2017) where the Court discussed the binding nature of its jurisprudence in the context of conventionality control. Finally, the section refers to the decisions of *Santo Domingo Massacre v. Colombia* (2012) and *Andrade Salmón* (2016), where the idea of conventionality control was connected with the complementary or subsidiary nature of the Inter-American System.

It is important to clarify that this chapter has a descriptive nature. It does not pretend to make normative assertions of the doctrine of conventionality control. That evaluation will be made in the following chapters of the book. The purpose of this chapter is to present the elements in the Court's jurisprudence – as well as the ideas of some of its most prominent and influential judges – that explain how the doctrine of conventionality control came to life, the arguments and basic ideas that support it as reflected in *Almonacid* and other relevant cases, and the most relevant components that were added after *Heliodoro*. In short, this chapter allows the reader to understand the cases that preceded the creation of

---

3 These cases, taken altogether, are considered in this chapter as the "foundational cases" of the doctrine of conventionality control.

the doctrine of conventionality control, its origins and normative foundations, and the further development of the line of jurisprudence of conventionality control until the year 2018.

Before starting the analysis of this chapter, it is relevant to cite Articles 1.1 and 2 of the American Convention, since these two Articles are at the core of the architecture of conventionality control:

> **Article 1. Obligation to Respect Rights**
>
> The States Parties to this Convention undertake to respect the rights and freedoms recognized herein and to ensure to all persons subject to their jurisdiction the free and full exercise of those rights and freedoms, without any discrimination for reasons of race, color, sex, language, religion, political or other opinion, national or social origin, economic status, birth, or any other social condition.
>
> **Article 2. Domestic Legal Effects**
>
> Where the exercise of any of the rights or freedoms referred to in Article 1 is not already ensured by legislative or other provisions, the States Parties undertake to adopt, in accordance with their constitutional processes and the provisions of this Convention, such legislative or other measures as may be necessary to give effect to those rights or freedoms.[4]

2. PRECEDENTS OF THE DOCTRINE OF CONVENTIONALITY CONTROL

Articles 1.1 and 2 are the two key provisions to understand the origins and foundations of the doctrine of conventionality control.[5] The Inter-American Court conceptualized conventionality control as an "other measure" (in reference to the language of Article 2) that State authorities must take in order to "ensure" (in reference to the language of Article 1.1) the protection of the rights and freedoms recognized by the Inter-American *Corpus Juris*. Owing to the existence of conventionality control, domestic authorities have an obligation to take the "measure" of "controlling" that no domestic norm is enforced in a manner that produces a human rights violation, either by interpreting that norm in accordance with the Inter-American *Corpus Juris*, or by ceasing in its enforcement. Conventionality control constitutes – in the Court's theory – part

---

4 Organization of American States, American Convention on Human Rights, Nov. 22, 1969, O.A.S.T.S. No. 36, 1144, U.N.T.S. 123, Arts. 1.1 and 2.

5 *See*, Claudio Nash Rojas, *Control de Convencionalidad. Cuadernillo de la Corte Interamericana de Derechos Humanos No. 7*, p. 4 (Inter-American Court of Human Rights & Ministerio de Relaciones Exteriores de Dinamarca, 2015).

of the general obligations of the State under the Convention, because it is an effective mechanism for domestic authorities to ensure the protection of human rights at the domestic level, especially the right to have access to an effective judicial remedy.

However, this was not always the case. The text of Article 2 does not directly lead to an identification of any specific measure that States must take to comply with Article 1.1. Consistent with this view, the original understanding that the Inter-American Court had of its own powers and attributions did not include the capacity to evaluate the kind of legislative and other measures that States must take to comply with Article 2. The capacity to determine these measures was understood as an exclusive competence of the States parties to the Convention, which meant that the Court had to stay within the boundaries of *how* States had to incorporate and comply with the American Convention at the domestic level. But this understanding changed during the late nineties, when the Court started to evaluate the compatibility between certain domestic laws and the Convention, opening the door for a major involvement of the Court in determining the "legislative or other measures" that States must take to comply with their obligations under Article 2.

The change in the Court's practice was the cause and consequence of another important change: Article 2 was no longer understood as a norm of a programmatic nature, but as a norm with a strong prescriptive nature. States could now be declared internationally responsible for the type of legislative and other measures that they adopted at the domestic level, and the Court considered itself as the institution in charge of determining at the international level weather the State complied with its obligations under Article 2. This conception normalized the practice of the Court to evaluate the compatibility (the "conventionality") between domestic laws adopted by the State and the American Convention.[6] Following the same logic, the Court started to determine – in some cases with a high degree of specificity – the "other measures" that States must take to comply with the obligation of Article 1.1, which eventually included the requirement for State authorities to exercise conventionality control.

The following sections show the normative evolution of Articles 1.1 and 2 in the Court's jurisprudence, and show why this evolution constitutes the precedent of the creation of the doctrine of conventionality control.

6 *See generally*, Pablo González-Domínguez and Christian González Chacón, *Dos visiones de la fuerza normativa del artículo 2 de la Convención Americana sobre Derechos Humanos*, 23 Revista Iberoamericana de Derecho Procesal Constitucional, 2015 (for a study of the different positions that the Inter-American Court has taken regarding its own powers and attributions to review the conventionality of domestic laws and practices, and to order States to modify them).

2.1. THE ORIGINAL MEANING OF ARTICLES 1.1 AND 2

2.1.1. Article 1.1: Obligation to Respect Rights

Article 1.1 established the obligation to "respect" the rights and freedoms recognized by the Convention, and to "ensure" the free and full exercise of these rights without discrimination. The Court has consistently interpreted this article in the sense that the Convention is immediately enforceable at the international level, so States have a *legal* obligation to "respect" and to "ensure" the rights protected by the Convention in relation to all persons subject to their jurisdiction.[7] The consequence of the failure to comply with these duties is the international responsibility of the State and the duty to repair. Thus, Article 1.1 is intimately connected with Article 63.1 of the Convention, which confers contentious jurisdiction on the Inter-American Court in the following terms:

> 1. If the Court finds that there has been a violation of a right or freedom protected by this Convention, the Court shall rule that the injured party be ensured the enjoyment of his right or freedom that was violated. It shall also rule, if appropriate, that the consequences of the measure or situation that constituted the breach of such right or freedom be remedied and that fair compensation be paid to the injured party.[8]

The content of the obligations established by Article 1.1 has developed since the decision in the leading case of *Velásquez Rodríguez v. Honduras* (1988), which was the first case decided by the Court in the exercise of its contentious jurisdiction.[9] In *Velásquez Rodríguez*, the Court explained that Article 1.1 is fundamental to determining if a violation of the Convention could be attributed to the State. Specifically, the Court reasoned that if a violation of the Convention can be attributed to a public authority in accordance with the rules of international law, this fact could potentially result in the determination of the international responsibility of the State and the duty to repair.[10] The Court also defined that the obligation to "respect" means that the exercise of public authority finds its limits in the Convention, a condition that ultimately derives "from the fact that human rights are inherent attributes of human dignity and are, therefore,

7 *See, Velásquez Rodríguez v. Honduras*. Merits, Inter-Am. Ct. H.R. (Ser. C) No. 4 (July 29, 1988) §164; *see also* Cecilia Medina Quiroga, *La Convención Americana: Teoría y Jurisprudencia. Vida, Integridad Personal, Libertad Personal, Debido Proceso y Recurso Judicial*, p. 16 (Universidad de Chile & Facultad de Derecho & Centro de Derechos Humanos, 2003).

8 American Convention on Human Rights, *supra* n. 4, Art. 63.1.

9 *Velásquez Rodríguez v. Honduras, supra* n. 7, §164.

10 *Ibid.*

superior to the power of the State".[11] It is in this sense that State agents have a legal – not just a moral – obligation to abstain from violating human rights.[12]

The obligation to "ensure", on the other hand, is not limited to negative conducts (i.e. the duty of abstaining from violating rights), but rather requires States to take steps and: "organize the governmental apparatus and, in general, all the structures through which public power is exercised, so that they are capable of juridically ensuring the free and full enjoyment of human rights."[13] In cases of human rights violations – like the forced disappearance of Mr. Velásquez Rodríguez – the obligation to ensure means that States have the duty to "prevent, investigate and punish any violation of the rights recognized by the Convention and, moreover, if possible, attempt to restore the right violated and provide compensation as warranted for damages resulting from the violation".[14]

In the same venue, since *Velásquez Rodríguez*, it has been considered that the duty to ensure entails the obligation for the government to effectively behave in a manner consistent with the Convention, a condition that even "requires States to take positive actions that include not just the removal of domestic legal barriers to achieve these ends, but also to conduct its actions so as to effectively ensure the free and full exercise of human rights."[15] Consequently, States must "prevent human rights violations and use the means at its disposal to carry out a serious investigation of violations committed within its jurisdiction, to identify those responsible, to impose the appropriate punishment and to ensure the victim adequate compensation".[16]

Furthermore:

> 175. This duty to prevent includes all those means of a legal, political, administrative and cultural nature that promote the protection of human rights and ensure that any violations are considered and treated as illegal acts, which, as such, may lead to the

---

11 *Id.* §165; *see also The Word "Laws" in Article 30 of the American Convention on Human Rights.* Advisory Opinion OC-6, Inter-Am. Ct. H.R. (Ser. A) No. 6 (May 9, 1986) §21.

12 *See*, Cecilia Medina Quiroga, *La Convención Americana: Teoría y Jurisprudencia. Vida, Integridad Personal, Libertad Personal, Debido Proceso y Recurso Judicial*, *supra* n. 7, p. 16.

13 *Velásquez Rodríguez v. Honduras, supra* n. 7, §166.

14 *Ibid. See also, Id.* §167.

15 *See*, Cecilia Medina Quiroga, *La Convención Americana: Teoría y Jurisprudencia. Vida, Integridad Personal, Libertad Personal, Debido Proceso y Recurso Judicial*, *supra* n. 7, p. 21; for a detailed study of Art. 1.1, *see*, Eduardo Ferrer Mac-Gregor Poisot and Carlos Pelayo Möller, *Obligación de respetar los derechos*, in Christian Steiner and Patricia Uribe (Eds.), *Convención Americana sobre Derechos Humanos comentada*, pp. 45–71 (Suprema Corte de Justicia & Konrad Adenauer Stiftung, 2014).

16 *Velásquez Rodríguez v. Honduras, supra* n. 7, §174.

> punishment of those responsible and the obligation to indemnify the victims for damages. It is not possible to make a detailed list of all such measures, since they vary with the law and the conditions of each State Party. Of course, while the State is obligated to prevent human rights abuses, the existence of a particular violation does not, in itself, prove the failure to take preventive measures ...[17]

The interpretation adopted by the Court in *Velásquez Rodríguez* was one of the cornerstones of the Inter-American System. It set the tone for the development of a jurisprudence that responded to the vices of domestic legal systems in Latin America, where on many occasions the protections provided by the law and institutions were (and are) a "death letter" due to political and cultural constraints. The case of Honduras was a good example for this type of simulation of the law and institutions since, as Claudio Grossman – one of the litigants of *Velásquez Rodríguez* – narrates, the legal remedies provided by domestic law were ineffective in cases of disappearances because: "the imprisonment occurred in secret, the formal procedural requirements precluded effective relief, and officials ignored the petitions."[18] The Court also found that the judiciary was materially incapable of providing remedies owing to the threats and intimidation faced by judicial officials.[19]

The Court has conferred wide legal consequences to Article 1.1 since its first contentious case. The obligation to ensure was conceived as a duty that required domestic authorities not only to behave in a manner consistent with the substantive rights protected by the Convention, but also to positively act in order to produce structural changes in the laws, institutions and culture, so the State is capable of effectively protecting individuals against violations committed by State or non-State actors. In this logic, Article 1.1 imposed a due diligence standard, requiring States to affirmatively investigate, identify and punish the perpetrators of human rights violations.[20] The compliance of the due diligence duty required political, administrative, and cultural measures, including the

---

17 *Id.* §175.

18 Claudio Grossman, *The Velásquez Rodríguez Case: The Development of the Inter-American Human Rights System*, in John E. Noyes, Laura A. Dickinson and Mark W. Janis (Eds.), International Law Stories, p. 89 (Foundation Press, 2007); *Velásquez Rodríguez v. Honduras*, *supra* n. 7, §64.

19 *Velásquez Rodríguez v. Honduras*, *supra* n. 7, §74.

20 *Id.* §107; Claudio Grossman, *The Velásquez Rodríguez Case: The Development of the Inter-American Human Rights System*, in John E. Noyes, Laura A. Dickinson and Mark W. Janis (Eds.), *International Law Stories*, *supra* n. 18, at 93; Douglass Cassel, *Lessons from the Americas: Guidelines for International Responses to Amnesties for Atrocities*, 59 Law & Contemp. Probs. 210 (1996) (the author asks a question that is of particular relevance for this topic: what if a State enacts an amnesty that does not allow investigating and punishing those state agents responsible for human rights violations? That is the question that the Court would answer in *Barrios Altos* and in *Almonacid*, where the doctrine of conventionality control was created).

"removal of domestic legal barriers". Yet, the particularities of those measures depended entirely on "the law and the conditions of each State Party".[21]

The developments in *Velásquez Rodríguez* regarding the content of Article 1.1 inspired the Court's jurisprudence in further cases. The language used in this case left States free to decide the specific means on how to comply with their duty to ensure, but it also opened the door for the Court to specify – either in the body of its decisions or by ordering reparations – how this duty must be fulfilled by States.[22] This point is relevant since, as section 2.2 of this chapter proves, the understanding of the arguments that lead to the creation of the doctrine of conventionality control is partly based on the notion that the duty to ensure requires positive actions by domestic authorities. It served as one of the arguments to sustain that a domestic judge must not enforce norms that manifestly violate the Convention.

2.1.2. Article 2: Domestic Legal Effects

Article 2 requires States: "to adopt, in accordance with their constitutional processes and the provisions of the Convention, such legislative or other measures as may be necessary to give effect to the rights or freedoms." This provision reflects in the Convention the classical norm of "the rights of the person", by which a State that ratifies a treaty protecting human rights agrees to bring its domestic law and its practices in line with the terms of the treaty.[23] This norm was inspired by Article 2.2 of the International Covenant on Civil and Political Rights (ICCPR), with the aim of reinforcing the duty of States to adapt their domestic legal system in a manner consistent with their obligations to respect and ensure in terms of Article 1.1, but it was not considered to have

21 *Velásquez Rodríguez v. Honduras*, *supra* n. 7, §175.

22 *See*, Eduardo Ferrer Mac-Gregor Poisot and Carlos Pelayo Möller, *Obligación de respetar los derechos*, in Christian Steiner and Patricia Uribe (Eds.), *Convención Americana sobre Derechos Humanos comentada*, *supra* n 15, p. 49; *see generally, Barrios Family v. Venezuela*. Merits, Reparations and Costs Judgment, Inter-Am. Ct. H.R. (Ser. C) No. 237 (Nov. 20, 2011) §124; *see also González et al. ("Cotton Field") v. Mexico*. Preliminary Objection, Merits, Reparations and Costs Judgment, Inter-Am. Ct. H.R. (Ser. C) No. 205 (Nov. 16, 2009) §287.

23 American Convention on Human Rights, *supra* n. 4, Art. 2; for an analysis of the normative components of Art. 2, *see*, Laurence Burgorgue-Larsen and Amaya Úbeda de Torres, *The Inter-American Court on Human Rights. Case Law and Commentary*, *supra* n. 1, p. 250; *see also* Cecilia Medina Quiroga, *Las Obligaciones de los Estados bajo la Convención Americana sobre Derechos Humanos*, in *La Corte Interamericana de Derechos Humanos. Un Cuarto de Siglo: 1979–2004*, pp. 251–254 (OEA-ICtHR, 2005); *see also* Eduardo Ferrer Mac-Gregor Poisot and Carlos Pelayo Möller, *Obligación de respetar los derechos*, in Christian Steiner and Patricia Uribe (Eds.), *Convención Americana sobre Derechos Humanos comentada*, *supra* n. 15, pp. 72–98.

"full legal force".[24] In Chapter 3 the reasons for the adoption of Article 2 and its connection with the ICCPR are explained in detail. For now, it is relevant to mention that two reasons explain the existence and content of this article.

The first reason is that the drafters of the Convention understood that the effectiveness of the Treaty depended also on the existence of domestic laws that allowed its appropriate enforcement by domestic authorities, notwithstanding the existence of legal obligations for the State derived from Article 1.1 and from general international law. Article 2 is a reinforcement of the obligations derived from Article 1.1. The second reason is substantive. Article 2 was a norm that required States to give specificity to the provisions of the Convention, since some of them were drafted as general dispositions. In the negotiation process the Chilean State cited Article 16(5) of the draft (Article 17.5) and Article 17(2) as examples of rights that required specification through domestic law, and in that manner defended the inclusion of Article 2.[25] Héctor Gros Espiell explained the reasons for the inclusion of Article 2 in his concurrent opinion in the *Advisory Opinion on the Enforceability of the Right to Reply or Correction (Arts. 14 (1), 1(1) and 2 of the American Convention on Human Rights)*:

> 6. [W]hen its inclusion [of Article 2] was proposed, it was clarified that its only purpose was to clarify and specify, making more decisive, immediate and direct the enforcement of such an obligation [of Article 1], but without thereby alter or ignore the essential obligation derived from Article 1. Without this logical interpretation of why Article 2 in the Convention was included, [its inclusion] would be meaningless. Moreover, it would lead to the irrational and absurd result that Article 1 would be inapplicable if the measures that Article 2 refers are not dictated.[26]

The normative force of Article 2 was not originally conceived as strong as that of Article 1.1, which imposes a *legal* obligation to respect and to ensure the rights protected by the Convention. In *Velásquez Rodríguez*, the Court interpreted that the obligation imposed by Article 1.1 is "much more direct than that contained in Article 2".[27] It seems that Article 2 was originally devised as a norm that may be called "programmatic in nature", in the sense that it imposed obligations for the State to take "legislative or other measures" to remedy the absence of direct

---

24 *See, Inter-American Specialized Conference on Human Rights*, San José, Costa Rica, Nov. 7–22, 1969, Proceedings and Documents, OEA.Ser.K/XVI/1.2, 1978, Doc. 5.

25 *See Id.*; *see also* Cecilia Medina Quiroga, *Las Obligaciones de los Estados bajo la Convención Americana sobre Derechos Humanos*, in *La Corte Interamericana de Derechos Humanos. Un Cuarto de Siglo: 1979–2004*, *supra* n. 23, p. 33.

26 *Enforceability of the Right to Reply or Correction (Arts. 14(1), 1(1) and 2 American Convention on Human Rights)*. Advisory Opinion OC-7, Inter-Am. Ct. H.R. (Ser. A) No. 7 (Aug. 29, 1986) §6.

27 *Velásquez Rodríguez v. Honduras*, *supra* n. 7, §168.

and immediate enforceability of the rights contained in the Convention. But Article 2 does not specify the content of those measures, since it leaves freedom for the States to decide the content of those measures "in accordance with their constitutional processes and the provisions of this Convention".[28] As explained by Cecilia Medina Quiroga:

> The first obligation of the State is to ensure that international norms operate within its jurisdiction, corresponding to the State, and not to international law, to decide the most appropriate manner to comply with the Convention, which may be the incorporation of these rules directly or enacting norms that reproduce international law. In any case once that an international norm is ratified by the State, it must bring all its domestic law in conformity with the Convention.
>
> 17. The fact that individuals can exercise and enjoy their human rights is a primary responsibility of States, which are those who are better placed to assure that this can happen in a daily and immediate manner; international supervision is always late and usually *ex post*.[29]

It is arguably in this spirit that – in its first decisions – the Court interpreted Article 2 to create general guidelines on how the duty of States to adapt their domestic law to the Convention shall be fulfilled, but it did not interpret it as an article with enough specification and normative value to impose enforceable legal obligations on the State at the international level.[30] Accordingly, in the *Advisory Opinion on the International Responsibility for the Promulgation and Enforcement of Laws in Violation of the Convention (Arts. 1 and 2 of the American Convention on Human Rights)*, the Court decided that the obligation to adopt all necessary measures to give effect to the rights and freedoms guaranteed by the Convention: "includes the commitment not to adopt those that would result

---

28 For an analysis of the original meaning of Art. 2, *see* LAURENCE BURGORGUE-LARSEN AND AMAYA ÚBEDA DE TORRES, *THE INTER-AMERICAN COURT ON HUMAN RIGHTS. CASE LAW AND COMMENTARY*, *supra* n. 1, p. 254; *see also* Cecilia Medina Quiroga, *Las Obligaciones de los Estados bajo la Convención Americana sobre Derechos Humanos*, in LA CORTE INTERAMERICANA DE DERECHOS HUMANOS. UN CUARTO DE SIGLO: *1979–2004*, *supra* n. 23, pp. 22–24; *see generally*, Rodolfo Vigo, *Constitucionalización y Neoconstitucionalismo: algunos riesgos y algunas prevenciones*, in MARCOS DEL ROSARIO (ED.), *SUPREMACÍA CONSTITUCIONAL*, p. 222 (Porrúa, 2011). (This section uses the term "programmatic" in the sense explained by Vigo, as norms that are not binding as a matter of law, until another constituted power establishes their binding character. The author does not talk about Art. 2 of the Convention, but only provides a general definition.)

29 CECILIA MEDINA QUIROGA, *LA CONVENCIÓN AMERICANA: TEORÍA Y JURISPRUDENCIA. VIDA, INTEGRIDAD PERSONAL, LIBERTAD PERSONAL, DEBIDO PROCESO Y RECURSO JUDICIAL*, *supra* n. 7, pp. 16 and 17.

30 *See*, *International Responsibility for the Promulgation and Enforcement of Laws in Violation of the Convention (Arts. 1 and 2 American Convention on Human Rights)*. Advisory Opinion OC-14, Inter-Am. Ct. H.R. (Ser. A) No. 14 (Dec. 9, 1994) §49; *see also El Amparo v. Venezuela*. Judgment, Inter-Am. Ct. H.R. (Ser. C) No. 19 (Jan. 18, 1995) §60.

in the violation of those very rights and freedoms."[31] But in the same Advisory Opinion the Court did not consider that the international responsibility of the State could be declared for the enactment of domestic laws that were contrary to the Convention, since:

> 49. The contentious jurisdiction of the Court is intended to protect the rights and freedoms of specific individuals, not to resolve abstract questions. There is no provision in the Convention authorizing the Court, under its contentious jurisdiction, to determine whether a law that has not yet affected the guaranteed rights and freedoms of specific individuals is in violation of the Convention. As has already been noted, the Commission has that power and, in exercising it, would fulfill its main function of promoting respect for and defense of human rights. The Court also could do so in the exercise of its advisory jurisdiction, pursuant to Article 64(2).[32]

The Court considered that its competence was limited to addressing violations of specific rights that resulted from the commission of an act attributable to public authorities (this is the same as saying when Article 1.1 was violated). Only in those circumstances shall the Court be able to declare the international responsibility of the State and the duty to repair, in accordance with the limits imposed by Article 63.1 of the Convention.[33] Similarly, it might happen that a self-executing domestic law (*ley autoaplicativa*) produces a human rights violation for its mere existence. In this hypothesis the Court could address the case because a violation of a human right would occur by reason of the mere existence of the domestic law. But it would be the violation of a substantive right that would open the door for the Court to exercise its contentious jurisdiction, and not the autonomous violation of Article 2.

The centrality of Article 1.1 – as the source of *legal* obligations for the States parties to the Convention – leads to the conclusion that even in cases where a violation of a right protected by the Convention was the result of the existence or enforcement of a domestic law *per se* incompatible with the provisions of the Convention, the international responsibility of the State would be the result of the

---

31 *International Responsibility for the Promulgation and Enforcement of Laws in Violation of the Convention (Arts. 1 and 2 American Convention on Human Rights).* Advisory Opinion OC-14, *supra* n. 30, §36; *see, Cesti Hurtado v. Peru Case.* Judgment, Inter-Am. Ct. H.R. (Ser. C) No. 56 (Sep. 29, 1999) §166; *Cesti Hurtado v. Peru Case.* Preliminary Objections. Judgment, Inter-Am. Ct. H.R. (Ser. C) No. 49 (Jan. 26, 1999) §166; *Certain Attributes of the Inter-American Commission on Human Rights (Arts. 41, 42, 44, 46, 47, 50 and 51 of the American Convention on Human Rights).* Advisory Opinion OC-13, Inter-Am. Ct. H.R. (Ser. A) No. 13 (Jul. 16, 1993) §26; *Velásquez Rodríguez v. Honduras, supra* n. 7, §164.

32 *International Responsibility for the Promulgation and Enforcement of Laws in Violation of the Convention (Arts. 1 and 2 American Convention on Human Rights).* Advisory Opinion OC-14, *supra* n. 30, §49.

33 American Convention on Human Rights, *supra* n. 4, Art. 63.1.

failure to "respect" and/or "ensure" a specific right or freedom once the domestic law produced its effects, and not due to the mere existence of that domestic law.[34] Implied in this view was the notion that the definition and implementation of the specific measures (legislative or of other nature) that States shall take to guarantee the compliance with the Convention was a competence reserved for the States, not for the Court.

In this stage of its jurisprudence, the Court considered the Inter-American Commission of Human Rights to be the institution of the Inter-American System that was competent to find if a domestic law was in violation of the Convention, and to recommend States to adopt domestic measures to guarantee a better protection of human rights in terms of Article 2.[35] The competence of the Commission came from Article 41(b), which establishes that one of the main functions of the Commission is making recommendations to the member States when it considers such action advisable "for the adoption of progressive measures in favor of human rights within the framework of their domestic law and constitutional provisions as well as appropriate measures to further the observance of those rights". In this sense the Court established in the *OC 14/94* that:

> 39. As a result of the foregoing, the Commission may recommend to a State the derogation or amendment of a conflicting norm that has come to its attention by any means whatsoever, whether or not that norm has been applied to a concrete case. That determination and recommendation may be addressed by the Commission directly to the State [Art. 41(b)] or be included in the reports referred to in Articles 49 and 50 of the Convention.[36]

2.2. THE STRENGTHENING OF THE NORMATIVE FORCE OF ARTICLE 2

The understanding of the programmatic nature of Article 2 changed when the Court started the practice of reviewing domestic laws *in abstracto*, and when it started to order States to amend specific laws and adopt specific practices in order to fulfill their obligations to adopt "such legislative or other measures

---

34 *International Responsibility for the Promulgation and Enforcement of Laws in Violation of the Convention (Arts. 1 and 2 American Convention on Human Rights)*. Advisory Opinion OC-14, *supra* n. 30, §49.

35 *Certain Attributes of the Inter-American Commission on Human Rights (Arts. 41, 42, 44, 46, 47, 50 and 51 of the American Convention on Human Rights)*. Advisory Opinion OC-13/93, *supra* n. 31, §26.

36 *See, International Responsibility for the Promulgation and Enforcement of Laws in Violation of the Convention (Arts. 1 and 2 American Convention on Human Rights)*. Advisory Opinion OC-14, *supra* n. 30, §39.

as may be necessary to give effect to those rights or freedoms" (Article 2). As explained by Laurence Burgorgue-Larsen, this shift of its previous jurisprudence opened the door for the Court to progressively address – at the international level – questions regarding the compatibility between domestic laws and the Convention. In the view of the French scholar, this new approach happened in good part thanks to the judicial strategy of the Inter-American Commission, which alleged together the violation of Articles 1.1 and 2 before the Court,[37] and by the action of some judges who argued the indissolubility of the two provisions.[38] The following paragraphs explain how this development occurred in the jurisprudence of the Inter-American Court from *Suárez Rosero* (1997) to *Almonacid* (2006).

2.2.1. *The Power of the Inter-American Court to Review Domestic Laws*

The first time that the Court reviewed a domestic law *in abstracto*, and in the exercise of its contentious jurisdiction, was in *Suárez Rosero* (1997). The Court evaluated the compatibility between Article 114 *bis* of the Ecuadorian Criminal Code (ECC) and the American Convention.[39] The article of the Ecuadorian law allowed detained persons to be released when certain conditions existed, but did not include persons charged with offenses punishable under the Law on Narcotic Drugs and Psychotropic Substances (LNDPS). This rule was applied against Mr. Suárez Rosero. The Court evaluated the article in the light of Article 2. It concluded that the distinction made by the LNDPS between persons charged with offenses under the LNDPS, and persons charged with other offenses under the ECC, was contrary to the rights protected by the Convention. The reason was that the LNDPS deprived "part of the prison population of a fundamental right, on the bases of a crime of which it is accused and, hence, intrinsically injures everyone in that category".[40]

---

37 *See, Suárez Rosero v. Ecuador Case.* Judgment, Inter-Am. Ct. H.R. (Ser. C) No. 35 (Nov. 12, 1997) §93.

38 *See, Caballero Delgado and Santana v. Colombia.* Reparations and Costs (Art. 63(1) American Convention on Human Rights). Judgment, Inter-Am. Ct. H.R. (Ser. C) No. 31 (Jan. 29, 1997). Dissenting Opinion of A.A. Cançado Trindade, §6–9; *see also El Amparo v. Venezuela Case.* Reparations (Art. 63(1) American Convention on Human Rights) Judgment, Inter-Am. Ct. H.R. (Ser. C) No. 28, (Sep. 14, 1996). Dissenting Opinion of A.A. Cançado Trindade §3; *see generally*, A.A. Cançado Trindade, *The Operation of the Inter-American Court of Human Rights*, in David J. Harris and Stephen Livingston (Eds.), *The Inter-American System of Human Rights*, pp. 140–141 (Oxford University Press, 1998); *see*, Laurence Burgorgue-Larsen and Amaya Úbeda de Torres, *The Inter-American Court on Human Rights. Case Law and Commentary*, *supra* n. 1, p. 254.

39 *Suárez Rosero v. Ecuador Case*, *supra* n. 37, §95.

40 *Id.* §98.

For this chapter, the importance of this case comes from paragraph 98 of the judgment, where the Inter-American Court stated that: "this law violates *per se* Article 2 of the Convention, *whether or not it was enforced in the instant case*."[41] The Inter-American Court used Article 2 for the first time as a norm that served to evaluate the compatibility between a domestic law and the Convention in a contentious case, asserting that it was not necessary for there to be a link between the enforcement of the domestic norm and the violation to the Convention. The reasons why the Court adopted this approach were not explained in *Suárez Rosero*, but from there on the Court functioned – at least in one part of its jurisprudence – under the assumption that the existence of a domestic law that *per se* is contrary to the Convention constitutes a breach of the Treaty. It also asserted its authority to determine specific orders for the State to adapt their domestic legal system in a manner consistent with the Convention.[42]

The dissenting opinion of A.A. Cançado Trindade (who was the President of the Court in 1997) in *El Amparo v. Venezuela* (1996) throws light on the reasons that motivated the shift in the Court's jurisprudence. In *El Amparo* the Court abstained "from making in the abstract on the compatibility of Venezuela's Code of Military Justice" and concluded that it "does not deem appropriate to order the Venezuelan State to undertake the reforms sought by the Commission".[43] Cançado Trindade disagreed. He considered that the Court had competence to decide on the conventionality of the Venezuelan Code since that law constituted a "real threat" to those persons that face a situation where the law was applicable. Therefore "[i]f it were necessary to wait for the effective application of a law causing a damage, the duty of prevention could hardly be sustained".[44] In this view the Court was bound by the duty to prevent future human rights violations, and for that reason it was authorized to order Venezuela to take specific measures to modify those elements that represented a threat for individuals. In his words:

> Precision has been given to the wide scope of [the duty to prevent], which comprises all the measures, legislative and administrative and others, which promote the safeguard of human rights and ensure that the violations of these are effectively treated as unlawful acts, bringing about sanctions on those responsible for them. Reparation, as a generic concept, encompasses also these elements, besides the indemnities due to the victims. Full reparation, which in the present context appears as the reaction of the juridical order of protection to the facts in breach of the guaranteed rights, has a wide scope. It includes,

41 *Ibid*; *see also* Laurence Burgorgue-Larsen and Amaya Úbeda de Torres, *The Inter-American Court on Human Rights. Case Law and Commentary*, *supra* n. 1, p. 258.

42 *See generally*, Manuel Fernando Quinche-Ramirez, *El Control de Convencionalidad y el Sistema Colombiano*, 12 Revista Iberoamericana de Derecho Procesal Constitucional 165 (2009).

43 *El Amparo v. Venezuela*. Judgment, Inter-Am. Ct. H.R. (Ser. C) No. 19, (Jan. 18, 1995), §60.

44 *Id.* Dissenting Opinion of Judge A.A. Cançado Trindade, §3.

> besides the *restitutio in integrum* (restoration of the previous situation of the victim, whenever possible) and the indemnities (in the light of the general principle of the *neminem laedere*), the rehabilitation, the satisfaction and – significantly – the guarantee of non-repetition of the acts in violation of human rights (the duty of prevention).

Those guarantees of non-repetition that the Brazilian judge mentioned included, *inter alia*, the modification of anti-conventional laws. Two years later, in *Castillo Petruzzi v. Peru* (1999), the Court found that Peru violated Article 2 of the American Convention by adopting emergency laws No. 25.475 and 25.259, which were enacted in order to combat terrorism.[45] It is not necessary to go into the details of the case. What is relevant is that several provisions of these two laws allowed the victims of the case to be sentenced to life imprisonment by a faceless military tribunal for the crime of treason, which in the Court's view constituted a violation of several rights of the Convention.[46] The Court declared invalid the procedures conducted against the victims for constituting violations of several rights of the Convention, including Articles 8 (Right to a Fair Trial) and 25 (Right to Judicial Protection), and it also ordered the State to amend the laws that were found and declared anti-conventional.[47] The Court continued, strengthening the strong normative force of Article 2 by establishing that:

> The general duty under Article 2 of the Convention implies the adoption of measures of two kinds: on the one hand, the elimination of any norms and practices that in any way violate the guarantees provided under the Convention; on the other hand, the promulgation of norms and the development of practices conducive to the effective observance of those guarantees.[48]

This approach regarding the implications of Article 2 was followed in subsequent cases where the Court evaluated the compatibility between domestic laws and the Convention,[49] reaching an important moment in the famous case of

---

45 *See, Castillo Petruzzi et al. v. Peru*. Judgment, Inter-Am. Ct. H.R. (Ser. C) No. 52 (May 30, 1999) §207.

46 *Id.* Operative paras. 2 to 11 (the Court found violations of Arts. 1(1), 2, 5, 7(5) and 7(6), 8(1) 8(2)(b) (c) (d) (f) and (h), 8(5), 9 and 25).

47 *Id.* Operative para. 14 (the Court ordered the State to "adopt the appropriate measures to amend those laws that this judgment has declared to be in violation of the American Convention on Human Rights and to ensure the enjoyment and exercise of the rights recognized in the American Conventin on Human Rights to all persons subject to its jurisdiction, without exception").

48 *Id.* §207.

49 *See generally, Hilaire, Constantine and Benjamin et al. v. Trinidad and Tobago*, Merits, Reparations, and Costs Judgment, Inter-Am. Ct. H.R. (Ser. C) No. 94 (Jun. 21, 2002) §113; *Juvenile Reeducation Institute v. Paraguay*. Judgment, Inter-Am. Ct. H.R. (Ser. C) No. 112 (Sep. 2, 2004) §206; *Lori Berenson Mejía v. Peru*. Judgment, Inter-Am. Ct. H.R. (Ser. C) No. 119 (Nov. 25, 2004) §219; *Caesar v. Trinidad and Tobago*. Judgment, Inter-Am. Ct. H.R. (Ser. C) No. 123 (Mar. 11, 2005) §91.

"The last temptation of Christ" (2001). This case involved the violation of the right to freedom of thought and expression, as the result of the judicial censorship that impeded the cinematographic exhibition of the film *The Last Temptation of Christ*. The censorship was based on the enforcement of a constitutional provision (Article 19(12) of the Chilean Constitution) and a Statutory Law (Decree Law 679).[50] In this case the Court decided that

> 90. … by maintaining cinematographic censorship in the Chilean legal system, the State failed to comply with the obligations to adapt its domestic law to the Convention in order to make effective the rights embodied in it, as established in Articles 2 and 1(1) of the Convention.[51]

The Court ordered Chile to amend its domestic law in order to eliminate prior censorship, so the obligations under Article 1.1, related to Article 13 of the Convention, could be effectively fulfilled.[52]

2.2.2. The Nullity Ab Initio *of Domestic Laws*

"The last temptation of Christ" shows how far the Court considered the normative force of Article 2 of the Convention, which allowed the evaluation of a law of constitutional hierarchy.[53] Yet, the highest point in this type of evaluation came in the context of what might be called processes of "transitional justice", specifically in the decision of *Barrios Altos* (2001). In this case, the Court decided that the amnesty laws 26479 and 26492 – enacted by the State of Peru during the government of Alberto Fujimori – were incompatible with the Convention. These laws exonerated members of the army, police force and civilians who had violated human rights from 1980 to 1995, including those responsible for the killing of 15 persons in a party in the district of Lima called "Barrios Altos".[54] Consequently, these laws prevented the investigation of violations of what the

---

50 *See, "The Last Temptation of Christ" v. Chile Case (Olmedo Bustos et al.).* Judgment, Inter-Am. Ct. H.R. (Ser. C) No. 73 (Feb. 5, 2001), §63–73.

51 *Id.* §90.

52 *Id.* Operative para. 4 in relationship with §88 (the Court, unanimously declared that: "4. Finds that the State must amend its domestic law, within a reasonable period, in order to eliminate prior censorship to allow exhibition of the film 'The Last Temptation of Christ', and must provide a report on the measures taken in that respect to the Inter-American Court of Human Rights, with six months of the notification of the judgment.").

53 *"The Last Temptation of Christ" (Olmedo-Bustos et al.) v. Chile.* Monitoring Compliance with Judgment. Order of the Inter-American Court of Human Rights (Nov. 28, 2003) §2 (the Chilean State amended its Constitution, eliminating the existence of cinematographic censorship).

54 *See, Barrios Altos v. Peru Case.* Judgment, Inter-Am. Ct. H.R. (Ser. C) No. 75 (Mar. 14, 2001) §2 i.

Court referred to as non-derogable rights (right to access to justice, truth and reparation) derived from the commission of serious human rights violations.[55]

The Court concluded that Peru had failed to comply with its duties under Articles 1.1 and 2 because the State adopted the two amnesty laws that precluded the identification of the individuals who were responsible for serious human rights violations, obstructed the investigation and access to justice, and prevented the victims and their next of kin from knowing the truth and receiving the corresponding reparation.[56] The Court finished the section dedicated to the evaluation of the amnesty law by stating the following:

> 44. Owing to the manifest incompatibility of self-amnesty laws and the American Convention on Human Rights, the said laws lack legal effect and may not continue to obstruct the investigation of the grounds on which this case is based or the identification and punishment of those responsible, nor can they have the same or a similar impact with regard to other cases that have occurred in Peru, where the rights established in the American Convention have been violated.[57]

It was the first time that the Inter-American Court had acted as some sort of constitutional court. It not only asserted that the law was incompatible with the American Convention (as in *Suárez Rosero*), or declared the international responsibility of the State for the existence of an anti-conventional law (as in *The Last Temptation of Christ*); the position of the Court was stronger than ever before, because it nullified the domestic law under the bases of a treaty and general international law.[58] However, this case was also different from previous cases that involved the existence of anti-conventional laws, because the nullity of amnesty laws 26479 and 26492 was not only the result of their mere incompatibility with Article 2. These laws were also null *ab initio* because they prevented the investigation of violations of what the Court qualified as non-derogable rights,[59] in cases of serious human rights violations.[60] This is a relevant consideration because it seems that the interpretation of Article 2 in

---

55 *Id.* §41.

56 *Id.* §43.

57 *Id.* §44.

58 *See*, Cristina Binder, *The Prohibition of Amnesties by the Inter-American Court of Human Rights*, 12 German Law Journal 1212 (2011) (Binder cited Antonio Cassese, who referred to this decision in the following terms: "it's the first time that an international court determined that national laws are devoid of legal effects within the state system where they have been adopted and consequently obliges the state to act as if these laws have never been enacted.").

59 These rights are access to justice, truth and reparation. The right to the truth was defined by the Inter-American Court as "the right of the victim or his next of kin to obtain clarification of the events that violated human rights and the corresponding responsibilities for the competent organs of the state, through the investigation and prosecution that are established in Articles 8 and 25 of the Convention". *See, Barrios Altos v. Peru Case. Judgment, supra* n. 54, §48.

60 *Id.* §41.

Barrios Altos does not imply the view that the mere inconsistency of a domestic law with the Convention derives in the nullity *ab initio* of that law.

The most logical reading of this decision is that the nature of the rights that were violated (access to justice, truth and reparation), and the gravity of the offenses that caused these violations (a massacre perpetrated by the police), ultimately were crucial to the adoption of such a strong monist position about the force of the Convention – as two judges suggested in their concurrent opinions of that case. Cançado Trindade suggested that the nullity of self-amnesty laws is the result of the violation of international human rights norms that belong to the domain of *jus cogens*.[61] In the same sense – but under a different basis – Sergio García Ramírez reflected that the duty of the State to respect the fundamental rights of all persons subject to its jurisdiction, and the duty to provide the necessary means to this end (Article 1(1) and 2), combined with the most recent developments of international criminal law, require that "the impunity of conduct that most gravely violates the essential legal rights protected by both forms of international law is inadmissible".[62]

3. CREATION OF THE DOCTRINE OF CONVENTIONALITY CONTROL

The approach taken by the Court in *Barrios Altos* appears to be based on the notion that there are legal consequences derived from the incompatibility between a domestic law and the Convention, that the degree of those consequences follows the gravity of the incompatibility of the domestic law and the Convention and other provisions of general international law, and that the Court has the capacity to determine the consequences of that incompatibility and determine the measures to avoid future violations – in this case to determine the nullity *ab initio* of the law so justice was made for the victims and their relatives. These assumptions are certainly detached from the position of the *OC-14/94* and *El Amparo*, where the Court expressly decided to keep itself within "the boundaries of international law", refused to evaluate the compatibility of domestic laws and the Convention, and with more reason avoided "intruding" in matters that have been traditionally understood as exclusive competences of the State.

The *rationale* of *Barrios Altos* prevailed in this particular period of time of the Inter-American Court's jurisprudence. It was maintained in the next cases connected with amnesty laws, including *Almonacid* and *La Cantuta v. Peru* (2006).[63] Both cases involved the existence and enforcement of amnesty laws

---

61 *Id.* Concurring Opinion of A.A. Cançado Trindade, §11.

62 *Id.* Concurring Opinion of Sergio García Ramírez, §12–14.

63 *See generally*, Eduardo Ferrer Mac-Gregor Poisot and Pablo González-Domínguez, *Death Penalty, Amnesty Laws and Forced Disappearances: Three Topics of the Inter-American*

that were considered by the Court null *ab initio*. The Court repeated its previous position that the nullity of amnesty laws is the result of the failure of States to adapt their domestic law to the Convention – in terms of Article 2 – and a subsequent failure to guarantee the realization of justice for the victims of serious human rights violations and crimes against humanity.[64] In *Almonacid*, however, the Court went one step further than in *Suárez Rosero*, *"The Last Temptation of Christ"* and *Barrios Altos* concerning the implications of Articles 1.1 and 2 (in connection with Articles 8.1 and 25). It decided that domestic judges are prohibited from enforcing laws that are contrary to the object and purpose of the Treaty and that are null *ab initio*, because the judiciary must perform a sort of "conventionality control" in order to guarantee the effectiveness of non-derogable rights protected by the Convention.

Starting with *Almonacid* the Court developed the notion that domestic judges have an obligation to ensure that the Convention is not adversely affected by the enforcement of domestic laws that are contrary to the Convention and that are null *ab initio*.[65] For this reason, judges must remove, through the exercise of conventionality control, the legal obstacles that impede the full force and effect of the Convention, which is an obligation based on the Convention and on general international law. Specifically, in the Court's view, conventionality control is based on Articles 1.1 and 2, and in Articles 26 and 27 of the Vienna Convention.[66] This reasoning constitutes the legal grounds and the core of the doctrine of conventionality control. It was progressively developed in three cases: *Almonacid, Aguado-Alfaro* and *Heliodoro*.

The first two parts of this section explain these decisions in detail, with an emphasis on *Almonacid*. The third part of the section explores a theoretical aspect that explains the existence of the doctrine: the idea that the American Convention

---

Corpus Juris in Criminal Law, 5(1) Notre Dame Journal of International and Comparative Law Article 4 (2015) (this article presents a detail analysis of the evolution of the Court's jurisprudence on amnesty law).

64 *See, Almonacid Arellano et al. v. Chile*. Preliminary Objections, Merits, Reparations and Costs Judgment, Inter-Am. Ct. H.R. (Ser. C) No. 154, (Sep. 26, 2006) §112, Operative para 3; *see La Cantuta v. Peru*. Merits, Reparations and Costs, Judgment, Inter-Am. Ct. H.R. (Ser. C) No. 162, (Nov. 29, 2006) §167, Operative para 7.

65 *See*, Laurence Burgorgue-Larsen and Amaya Úbeda de Torres, *The Inter-American Court on Human Rights. Case Law and Commentary*, *supra* n. 1, p. 260 (The authors referred to the criterion that establishes the doctrine of conventionality control as: "the highest point of the position taken by the Court in matters of amnesty laws. Not only did they confirm the earlier judgments in *Suárez Rosero* and *Barrios Altos* but they also opened new avenues where the domestic courts would have a major role to play".); *see generally, La Cantuta v. Peru*. Merits, Reparations and Costs, Judgment, Inter-Am. Ct. H.R. (Ser. C) No. 162, (Nov. 29, 2006), Concurrent Opinion of A.A. Cançado Trindade (Cançado Trindade also frames the criteria set forth in *Almonacid* as a "step in the evolution" in the fight against impunity. This fight is directed to guarantee that amnesty laws are not an obstacle for the investigation and punishment of those responsible for human rights violations".)

66 *See*, Claudio Nash Rojas, *Control de Convencionalidad. Cuadernillo de la Corte Interamericana de Derechos Humanos No. 7*, *supra* n. 5, p. 4.

has direct effect on State authorities by virtue of Article 1.1. This theoretical aspect is referred to as the "hidden pillar of the doctrine of conventionality control" because – although it is a crucial aspect in the Court's construction in *Almonacid* – it is not explicitly discussed in the Court's jurisprudence. This pillar can be traced back to the ideas of Cançado Trindade, who occupied a bench in the Court from 1997 (when the Court departed from its criterion of the *Advisory Opinion 14/94*) until 2008 (when *Heliodoro* was decided), as well as on the position of other judges that have more recently reflected on this topic, especially of García Ramírez and Eduardo Ferrer Mac-Gregor Poisot.

3.1. ANALYTICAL EVALUATION OF *ALMONACID*

3.1.1. The Facts of the Case and the Reasoning of the Inter-American Court

The human rights violations that led to the decision in *Almonacid* took place in the context of the first years of the military regime headed by General Augusto Pinochet after the *coup d'état* of 1973, where the Chilean authorities implemented a policy of widespread repression against the alleged political opponents of the regime.[67] This policy was particularly violent during the first months after the *coup*, where State officials systematically perpetrated massive, arbitrary and summary executions.[68] Notwithstanding this context, the Chilean government issued the Decree Law No. 2.191 of 1978, granting amnesty for all crimes committed between September 11, 1973, and March 10, 1978.[69] Law No. 2.191 aimed at strengthening the relations of Chile as one nation and to strengthen national unity,[70] but ignored the costs of the human rights violations that followed the *coup* and impeded the investigation and punishment of those State agents responsible for the extra-judicial execution of Luis Alfredo Almonacid, which took place on September 16, 1973.[71]

The Court analyzed if Chile had complied with the negative obligation of the State of not committing extra-judicial executions, and with the positive obligation to investigate, identify and punish the perpetrators of the crime. At this point *Almonacid* followed the jurisprudence regarding the positive and negative obligations for States parties to the Convention regarding serious human rights violations, which was inaugurated in *Velásquez Rodríguez*.[72]

67 *See, Almonacid Arellano et al. v. Chile, supra* n. 64, §82.4.
68 *Id.* §82.4.
69 *Id.* §82.10.
70 *Id.* §82.10.
71 *Id.* §82.9.
72 *See,* Douglass Cassel, *El fallo Almonacid de la CIDH, y las obligaciones que de allí emanan para el Estado de Chile*, in Paulina Veloso (Ed.), *Justicia, Derechos Humanos y el Decreto Ley de Amnistía*, p. 81 (PNUD, 2010).

The Court also evaluated whether Chile had complied with the general obligations established in Article 2 by keeping in force and applying Decree Law No. 2.191, even after Chile ratified the American Convention in 1990. Finally, the Court evaluated if the enforcement of Decree Law No. 2.191 constituted a violation of Articles 8.1 and 25 in connection with Article 1.1.[73]

For that purpose the Court followed a four-step analysis: first, it evaluated whether the extra-judicial execution of Mr. Almonacid constituted a crime against humanity; second, in the case that it was a crime against humanity, whether that crime may be susceptible to amnesty; third, in the case that such crime may not be susceptible to amnesty, whether the State had violated the Convention by keeping in force Decree Law No. 2.191; finally, the Court analyzed whether the enforcement of such Decree Law by the judicial authorities constituted a violation of Articles 8.1 and 25 of the Convention.[74] On this basis the Court decided the following:

1. Extra-judicial executions committed in the context of general and systematic attacks against civilians constitute crimes against humanity, and a violation of the *jus cogens* norm that prohibits the commission of such crimes.[75] The Court found evidence that the extra-judicial execution of Mr. Almonacid was committed following a systematic and generalized pattern of violence against civilian population, and thus it was considered a crime against humanity.[76]
2. International Law prohibits the enactment of amnesty laws that include crimes against humanity, since these types of crimes are serious human rights violations that affect mankind as a whole,[77] and therefore they must be punished.[78] The obligation to investigate these types of crimes arises from general international law and from Article 1.1, which includes the duty to punish serious human rights violations.[79] Consequently, Chile could not have neglected its duty to investigate, identify and punish those responsible for an extra-judicial execution – that constituted a crime against humanity – by enforcing amnesty laws or other similar provisions.[80]
3. Amnesty laws that include crimes against humanity are overtly incompatible with the wording and with the spirit of the American

---

73 *See, Almonacid Arellano et al. v. Chile, supra* n. 64, §90.
74 *Ibid.*
75 *Id.* §93–103.
76 *Id.* §104.
77 *Id.* §105.
78 *Id.* §106.
79 *Id.* §110.
80 *Id.* §114.

Convention in such a manner that its existence generates its nullity *ab initio*, and the international responsibility of the State for violations of Article 2.[81] Consequently – given its nature – the Court found that Decree Law 2.191 "does not have any legal effects and cannot remain as an obstacle for the investigation of the facts inherent to the instant case".[82]

4. The enforcement of amnesty laws that are in violation of the Convention and that do not have any legal effects, constitutes a violation of Articles 8.1 and 25 in relation to Article 1.1. The relatives of Mr. Almonacid were prevented from exercising their right to a hearing by a competent, independent and impartial court, and were prevented from recourse to an effective and adequate remedy owing to the enforcement by the judiciary of Decree Law 2.191.[83] Therefore, the State had violated the right to access to justice, truth and reparation of Mr. Almonacid's next of kin.

3.1.2. The Creation of the Doctrine of Conventionality Control

The Court declared the incompatibility between Decree Law 2.191 and the Convention, but did not require Chile to repeal that law. It limited its orders to ask the State that "Decree Law 2.191 does not continue to hinder the investigation, prosecution, and, if applicable, punishment for similar violations in Chile".[84] However, it is undeniable that this Decree Law was valid at the time where the violations to the Convention took place, and that continued to be valid after *Almonacid* was decided – at least if seen exclusively from the perspective of domestic constitutional law. Why did the Court decide not to ask Chile to remove the Decree Law from its books? One option would be that it was not necessary because it had already declared its nullity *ab initio*. Another option was because it did not want to touch such a sensitive question of Chilean politics. A third option is one like that sustained by Douglass Cassel, who qualified the flexibility of the Court as recognition of the complexities of the politics in Chile regarding existence of Decree Law 2.191.[85]

The position of the American scholar seems logical. It explains that *Almonacid* introduced a criterion that can be qualified as a "middle ground" between adopting a radical monist approach, and recognizing absolute freedom for Chile to decide how to expel Decree Law 2.191 from its legal system. So, the Court

---

81 *Id.* §115–122.

82 *Id.* §119.

83 *Id.* §123–128.

84 *Id.* §172.6.

85 *See*, Douglass Cassel, *El fallo Almonacid de la CIDH, y las obligaciones que de allí emanan para el Estado de Chile*, in Paulina Veloso (Ed.), *Justicia, Derechos Humanos y el Decreto Ley de Amnistía*, *supra* n. 72, p. 87.

apparently intervened in a manner that ensures that the Decree Law did not produce more human rights violations but without declaring or ordering the annulment of the law: judges must act as "guardians" of the Convention in case that any law impedes the access of the victims of human rights violations to justice. So the Court established that, when the legislative fails to comply with Article 2, the judiciary is still bound to honor the obligation to comply with its duty of "respect" and "ensure" in terms of Article 1.1.[86] For this reason, Chilean judges must exercise "conventionality control" in order to avoid the enforcement of Law 2.191, remedying in this manner the failure of the legislative in terms of Article 2 and to guarantee compliance with Articles 1.1, 8 and 25. On this basis, the Inter-American Court established the following:

> 124. The Court is aware that domestic judges and courts are bound to respect the rule of law, and therefore, they are bound to apply the provisions in force within the legal system. But when a State has ratified an international treaty such as the American Convention, its judges, as part of the State, are also bound by such Convention. This forces them to see that all the effects of the provisions embodied in the Convention are not adversely affected by the enforcement of laws which are contrary to its purpose and that have not had any legal effects since their inception. *In other words, the Judiciary must exercise a sort of "conventionality control" between the domestic legal provisions that are applied to specific cases and the American Convention on Human Rights.* To perform this task, the Judiciary has to take into account not only the treaty, but also the interpretation thereof made by the Inter-American Court, which is the ultimate interpreter of the American Convention.
>
> 125. By the same token, the Court has established that "according to international law, the obligations that it imposes must be honored in good faith and domestic laws cannot be invoked to justify their violation." This provision is embodied in Article 27 of the Vienna Convention on the Law of Treaties.[87]

3.1.3. The Theory Behind Conventionality Control

The theory behind these paragraphs seems to be that the obligations to respect and ensure the rights of the Convention have direct effect on the judiciary, and that the Court has the authority to decide the "necessary measures" (in terms of Article 2) by which judges should comply with this duty. This position certainly challenges the well-settled notion that international obligations do not bind specific authorities unless otherwise established by the treaty or by domestic law, and that States have the absolute freedom to decide the manner by which those

86 *Almonacid Arellano et al. v. Chile, supra* n. 64, §123.
87 *Id.* §124–125 (emphasis added).

obligations are fulfilled at the domestic level.[88] But the line of reasoning followed in *Almonacid* shows that the Court reads Articles 1.1 and 2 as provisions with the necessary substance (the normative strength) to guide the conduct of domestic judges, so they are capable of ensuring the rights protected by the Convention once the legislative power fails its duties under Article 2. The Court in this form transcended – or ignored – the dualistic understanding that international law must be "implemented" at the domestic level in order to be invoked in a court of law as a standard to evaluate the constitutionality of domestic law. In the words of García Ramírez in *La Cantuta*:

> 8. ... the Court has also made it clear that the obligations undertaken by a State upon becoming a party to the international convention on human rights are binding upon that State as a whole. This extends to executive, legislative and judicial bodies, as well as self-governed bodies outside of the domain of the three traditional branches, which are a part of the State itself. Therefore, it is inadmissible for one of such bodies to refrain from complying with an obligation that binds the State of which it is a part, or to directly acts in violation thereof, on the grounds that another body has failed to fulfill its own duties in the general system for the adoption of and compliance with international obligations (...)[89]

Beyond political and practical considerations that may have surrounded the decision of the Court, and the collaborative attitude of the Chilean and the Peruvian governments that defended *Almonacid* and *La Cantuta*, it is reasonable to argue that the special circumstances that surrounded these cases gave legitimacy to the Court to create the doctrine of conventionality control. It does not seem to be a coincidence that this doctrine emerged in a case that involved the creation and enforcement of a law that flagrantly violated Articles 1.1 and 2, that hindered the access to justice for the victims and their relatives (in violation to Articles 8.1 and 25), that obstructed the investigation of a crime against humanity committed in the context of a military dictatorship, and that prevented the administration of justice and the granting of reparations. It is for the multiple and grave violations that were involved in the creation and enforcement of Law No. 2.191 – considered altogether – that judges shall not enforce that law in the future:

> 145. As explained in paragraph 119 of this Judgment, the Court finds that, inasmuch as it seeks to grant amnesty to persons responsible for crimes against humanity,

---

88 *See generally*, Ariel E. Dulitzky, *An Inter-American Constitutional Court? The Invention of conventionality control by the Inter-American Court of Human Rights*, 50 Tex. Int'l L. J. 57 (2015); Cristina Binder, *The Prohibition of Amnesties by the Inter-American Court of Human Rights*, *supra* n. 58, p. 1216; Luigi Crema, "Are Amnesties Still an Option? A Non-Policy Based Critique of the Inter-American Approach", Center for Civil and Human Rights, University of Notre Dame, Working Paper Series # 6 (2013), p. 50–51.

89 *La Cantuta v. Peru*, *supra* n. 65, Concurrent Opinion of Sergio García Ramírez, §8.

> Decree Law No. 2.191 is inconsistent with the American Convention and, therefore, has no legal effects; consequently, the State must: i) ensure that it does not continue to hinder the investigation of Mr. Almonacid-Arellano's extra-legal execution and the identification and, as appropriate, punishment of those responsible, and ii) ensure that Decree Law No. 2.191 does not continue to hinder the investigation, prosecution and, as appropriate, punishment of those responsible for similar violations perpetrated in Chile.[90]

The language used by the Inter-American Court in paragraph 124 of *Almonacid* must be read in the context of the above-mentioned considerations. This allows an understanding of the full meaning of the obligations created by the doctrine of conventionality control, which aims to guarantee that the effects of the provisions embodied in the American Convention are not adversely affected by laws that: (1) "are contrary to its object and purpose", and that (2) *"have not had any legal effect since their inception"*.[91] This means that judges have an obligation under Article 1.1 and 2 to exercise conventionality control of domestic laws that are contrary to: (1) "the protection of the basic rights of individual human beings, irrespective of their nationality",[92] and that (2) violate the rights of access to justice, truth and reparation, by preventing the investigation for the most serious human rights violations, such as torture, extra-judicial, summary or arbitrary executions, and crimes against humanity.[93] In other words – at least in its original meaning – it is possible to say that the obligation of judges to exercise conventionality control is *essentially* connected both with the nature of the rights violated (which were considered as "non-derogable" rights), and with the gravity of the crimes committed by State agents (an extrajudicial execution qualified as a crime against humanity). This is what determined in the first place the nullity *ab initio* of amnesty laws, and also opened the door for the creation of the doctrine of conventionality control.[94]

---

90 *Almonacid Arellano et al. v. Chile, supra* n. 64, §145.

91 *Id.* §124 (emphasis added).

92 *See, The Effect of Reservations on the Entry into Force of the American Convention on Human Rights (Arts. 74 and 75).* Advisory Opinion OC-2, Inter-Am. Ct. H.R. (Ser. A) No. 2 (Sep. 24, 1982) §29; *Restrictions to the Death Penalty (Arts. 4(2) and 4(4) American Convention on Human Rights).* Advisory Opinion OC-3, Inter-Am. Ct. H.R. (Ser. A) No. 3 (Sep. 8, 1983) §65; *see also* American Convention on Human Rights, *supra* n. 4, Preamble (the Inter-American Court established, since its early interpretations, that "the object and purpose of the American Convention involves the protection of the basic rights of individual human beings, irrespectively of their nationality, both against the state of their nationality and all other contracting states)."

93 *See, Almonacid Arellano et al. v. Chile, supra* n. 64, §119; *see also Barrios Altos v. Peru Case.* Judgment, *supra* n. 55, §41.

94 *See, La Cantuta v. Peru, supra* n. 65, §157; *see generally*, A.A. Cançado Trindade, *La búsqueda de la realización de la justicia en la era de los Tribunales Internacionales*, in Eduardo Ferrer Mac-Gregor Poisot and Alfonso Herrera Garcia (Ed.), *Diálogo Jurisprudencial en Derechos Humanos. Entre Tribunales Constitucionales y Cortes Internacionales*, p. 1361 (Tirant Lo Blanch, 2013).

The Court also linked the foundations of the doctrine of conventionality control to the general obligations under Articles 26 and 27 of the Vienna Convention. These articles make positive law the obligation to perform treaties in good faith, and establish the prohibition to invoke domestic law as a justification for the failure to perform a treaty.[95] Since the *OC-14/94*, the Inter-American Court has connected the obligation to adopt the necessary measures to make effective the rights and liberties recognized in the American Convention with the general principles established in the above-mentioned articles of the Vienna Convention, although certainly with a different connotation than in *Almonacid*.[96] Following the notion that Article 1.1 has direct effect on the judiciary, Articles 26 and 27 of the Vienna Convention support the argument that domestic judges cannot abstain to fulfill their obligations to respect and ensure the rights recognized in the Convention, despite the existence of domestic laws to the contrary.[97]

The doctrine of conventionality control evolved in subsequent cases, which introduced new elements to strengthen its foundations and clarify its effects. These cases also opened new avenues for the use of this doctrine in different circumstances than those specifically referred to the enforcement of domestic laws that impeded the investigation of serious human rights violations and that were null *ab initio*, as it happened in *Almonacid* and *La Cantuta*.

3.2. THE STRENGTHENING OF THE DOCTRINE OF CONVENTIONALITY CONTROL

3.2.1. Aguado-Alfaro*: Conventionality Control and the Duty of Domestic Judges to Ensure the Effectiveness of the American Convention*

The first of these cases was *Aguado-Alfaro*.[98] This case involved the dismissal of a group of 257 employees from the National Congress of the Republic of

95 *See, Almonacid Arellano et al. v. Chile*, *supra* n. 64, §125.

96 *International Responsibility for the Promulgation and Enforcement of Laws in Violation of the Convention (Arts. 1 and 2 American Convention on Human Rights)*. Advisory Opinion OC-14, *supra* n. 30, §35.

97 *See generally*, *Cabrera Garcia and Montiel Flores v. Mexico*, Preliminary Objections, Merits, Reparations and Costs Judgment, Inter-Am. Ct. H.R. (Ser. C) No. 220 (Nov. 26, 2010). Reasoned Concurrent Opinion of Judge Eduardo Ferrer Mac-Gregor Poisot, §59; *see generally*, Ernesto Rey Cantor, *Control de la Convencionalidad de Leyes y Derechos Humanos* p. LIX (Porrúa, 2008); *see also* Cristina Binder, *The Prohibition of Amnesties by the Inter-American Court of Human Rights*, *supra* n. 58, p. 1217.

98 It is important to notice that *Aguado-Alfaro* was decided two months after *Almonacid*, which means that the Court did not hesitate to use the precedent generated in *Almonacid* in a different situation than the concrete context where it was originally created.

Peru by resolutions adopted by Congress.[99] The decision was part of the process to rationalize the personnel of the Congress of the Republic on the basis of Decree Law No. 25640.[100] This Decree Law also prohibited challenging through *amparo* action the effects that its provisions may have on those affected by its enforcement.[101] The existence of this law, and in general the political environment of the lack of independence of the judiciary, contributed to the declaration of inadmissibility of the judicial remedies at the domestic level exercised by those affected by the process of rationalization of personnel.[102] Only years after the dismissal of the employees did one civil court declare the complaint admissible and ordered that the plaintiffs be reinstalled in the position they had occupied when their rights were affected.[103] However, the Lima Supreme Court of Justice (LSCJ) later revoked this judgment under procedural or admissibility considerations.[104] The Constitutional Court of Peru (CCP) upheld the decision of the LSCJ.[105]

The Inter-American Court found that the mere existence of the limitations imposed by Decree Law No. 25640 to the exercise of judicial remedies was contrary to the right to a genuine and effective access to justice, in violation of Articles 25 and 8.1 of the American Convention.[106] It also found that the existing domestic remedies were not effective because they were not truly appropriate for establishing whether there had been human rights violations and for providing whatever was necessary to repair those violations.[107] For this reason the Inter-American Court considered that the LSCJ or the CCP should have evaluated the merits of the claims presented by the dismissed employees, even when *amparo* actions may have expired under procedural considerations.[108] Accordingly,

99 *Dismissed Congressional Employees (Aguado-Alfaro et al.) v. Peru.* Preliminary Objections, Merits, Reparations and Costs Judgment, Inter-Am. Ct. H.R. (Ser. C) No. 158, (Nov. 24, 2006) §89.13.

100 *Id.* §89 (9).

101 *See*, Decree Law No. 25640 of July 21, 1992, published on July 24, 1992, authorizing the Commission to Administer the Patrimony of Congress to carry out the process of streamlining the personnel of the Congress of the Republic. Cited in *Id.* §89 (9).

102 *Id.* §89 (15).

103 *Id.* §89 (22).

104 *Id.* §89 (24).

105 *Id.* §89 (28).

106 *Id.* §119. (The Court found that, in a democratic society, a norm containing a prohibition against contesting the possible effects of its application or interpretation, cannot be considered a valid limitation of those affected by the decree to a genuine and effective access to justice, which is a human right that cannot be arbitrarily restricted, reduced or annulled.)

107 *Id.* §124. (It is important to mention that the LSCJ declared the *amparo* inadmissible because the appellants had not filed this recourse within the legally established time period.)

108 *Id.* §126. (The Court recognized that not always, and in every case, do the domestic organs and courts have to decide on the merits of a case. There are instances where cases might be dismissed because of procedural considerations. But procedural rules that leave ineffective judicial recourse in violation of the American Convention, cannot be considered as valid reasons to dismiss petitions of victims of human rights violations.)

for the Inter-American Court, domestic judges should have used their authority to exercise judicial review and block the enforcement of procedural norms that served as the basis for the dismissal of the employees' petitions in order to guarantee their right to access to justice.[109] In this context the Court made reference to the doctrine of conventionality control in the following terms:

> 128. When a State has ratified an international treaty such as the American Convention, the judges are also subject to it; this obliges them to ensure that the *effet utile* of the Convention is not reduced or annulled by the application of laws contrary to its provisions, object and purpose. In other words, the organs of the Judiciary should exercise not only a control of constitutionality, but also of "conventionality" *ex officio* between domestic norms and the American Convention, evidently in the context of their respective spheres of competence and the corresponding procedural regulations. This function should not be limited exclusively to the statements or actions of the plaintiffs in each specific case, although neither does it imply that this control must always be exercised, without considering other procedural and substantive criteria regarding the admissibility and legitimacy of these types of action.[110]

The Inter-American Court followed the same structure and a similar language as that used in *Almonacid*. However, five important changes can be noted: first, the obligation to exercise conventionality control was explicitly linked to the duty of judges to ensure the effectiveness of the American Convention. Second, the Court established that conventionality control shall be exercised *ex officio*, regardless of whether the parties involved in the particular controversy requested it. Third, the Court decided that conventionality control shall be exercised by domestic judges in accordance with the procedural regulations applicable to a particular case, except when the enforcement of a procedural rule violates a right protected by the American Convention. Fourth, the Court clarified that the doctrine of conventionality control does not confer powers on domestic judges to act outside of their attributions under domestic law; they must do it "in the context of their respective sphere of competence". Fifth, the Court changed the language in a manner that the exercise of conventionality control was not essentially linked to the nullity *ab initio* of a law.[111]

For the purpose of this section, the most important of the above-mentioned changes is the notion that judges have an obligation to ensure that the effectiveness of the American Convention is not affected or annulled by the enforcement of laws that are contrary to its provisions, object and purpose. In the Court's jurisprudence, the principle of effectiveness provides that States

---

109 *Id.* §127.

110 *Id.* §128.

111 Contrary to the case of the self-amnesty law that produced a violation of Art. 2 in *Almonacid*, the laws involved in *Aguado-Alfaro* were not null *ab initio*.

must guarantee compliance with the provisions of the Convention and its proper effects in a "truly practical and effective manner given the special nature of human rights treaties".[112] The principle derives from the general obligation to adopt legislative and other measures as may be necessary to ensure that the provisions of the Convention have full force and effect within the domestic legal system.[113] This means that – based on the criterion created in *Almonacid* – the Court considers that judges shall exercise conventionality control because they have a *direct obligation to guarantee the full force and give maximum effect to the rights protected in the American Convention.*[114] Consequently, in *Aguado-Alfaro*, the obligation to exercise conventionality control was expressly connected with the obligations of the judiciary in accordance with Article 2.

In the case of *La Cantuta* the Court integrated the criteria settled in the cases of *Almonacid* and *Aguado-Alfaro* regarding the connection between the doctrine of conventionality control and the general obligations of Articles 1.1 and 2.[115] The Court decided that the Peruvian judiciary was prohibited from enforcing Law No. 26.479 (an amnesty law) because it was null *ab initio*, as it was established in *Barrios Altos*. Consequently, judges, as part of the State, had a duty not to enforce Law No. 26.479 in order to investigate, identify and punish those responsible for serious human rights violations (Article 1.1). By failing to comply with the duty to exercise conventionality control, the State also failed to take adequate measures to comply with its obligations to guarantee the effectiveness of the rights protected by the American Convention (as required by Article 2).[116]

3.2.2. Heliodoro: *Complete Explanation of the Foundational Elements of the Doctrine of Conventionality Control*

The theory that underlines the Court's use of conventionality control in the cases of *Aguado-Alfaro* and *La Cantuta* was clarified in *Heliodoro*. This case involved violations of the Convention committed by the State of Panama for the forced

---

112 *Ivcher Bronstein v. Peru.* Merits, Competence Judgment, Inter-Am. Ct. H.R. (Ser. C) No. 54, (Sep. 24, 1999) §37; *see generally, "The Last Temptation of Christ" (Olmedo Bustos et al.) v. Chile, supra* n. 53, §87.

113 *Garrido and Baigorria v. Argentina Case.* Reparations (Art. 63(1) American Convention on Human Rights) Judgment, Inter-Am. Ct. H.R. (Ser. C) No. 39, (Aug. 27, 1998) §68–70.

114 *See, Case of Dismissed Congressional Employees (Aguado-Alfaro et al.) v. Peru.* Request for Interpretation of the Judgment on Preliminary Objection, Merits, Reparations and Costs Judgment of Nov. 30, 2007. (Ser. C) No. 174. Dissenting Opinion of A.A. Cançado Trindade §9; *see also* Jo M. Pasqualucci, *The Practice and Procedure of the Inter-American Court of Human Rights*, p. 301 (Cambridge University Press, 2nd ed., 2013).

115 *La Cantuta v. Peru, supra* n. 65, §80 (58).

116 *Id.* §167–174; *See also Id.* Concurrent Opinion of Sergio García Ramírez, §3.

disappearance and extra-judicial execution of Mr. Heliodoro Portugal, and the failure to investigate and punish those agents responsible for the crimes.[117] The State failed to conduct an effective criminal procedure owing to the lack of legislation defining the forced disappearance of persons as an autonomous criminal offense,[118] which violated Article III of the Inter-American Convention on Forced Disappearance of Persons (ICFDP), the general obligation of the State to adapt its domestic law to the Convention, and the obligation of the judiciary to exercise conventionality control.[119]

The Court observed that, considering the particularly grave nature of the forced disappearance of persons, the protection offered by the Panamanian law on crimes such as abduction, kidnapping, torture and homicide was insufficient.[120] For this reason, faced with the imperative of avoiding impunity, the Court considered the existence of a duty of the State to use all penal resources available to protect the fundamental rights that are affected in cases of forced disappearances.[121] This meant that domestic judges should have exercised conventionality control to fill the legal lacunae of the criminal code in order to guarantee the prosecution and punishment of perpetrators of forced disappearances, in accordance with the standard established by Article III of the ICFDP, even when that crime had not been defined as an autonomous offense by domestic law.[122] In the words of the Court:

> 180. The Court has found that this principle [the principle of *effet utile*] requires the adoption of two types of measure: (i) the repeal of laws and practices of any kind that entail a violation of the guarantees established in the Convention, or that disregard the rights recognized therein or impede their exercise, and (ii) the enactment of laws and the development of practices conducive to respect for those guarantees. More precisely, regarding the adoption of those measures, it is important to notice that the defense of or respect for human rights, arising from international commitments concerning the work of the Judiciary, must be achieved through the so-called "conventionality control." According to this principle, every judge must ensure the *effet utile* of international instruments so that they are not reduced or annulled by the application of domestic laws and practices contrary to the object and purpose of the international instrument or standard for the protection of human rights.[123]

---

117 *See, Heliodoro Portugal v. Panama.* Preliminary Objections, Merits, Reparations and Costs Judgment, Inter-Am. Ct. H.R. (Ser. C) No. 186, (Aug. 12, 2008), Operative paras. 4 to 8.

118 *Id.* §176–179, and 183.

119 *See, Id.* §179–180.

120 *See, Id.* §181.

121 *See, Id.* §182.

122 *See*, María Carmelina Londoño Lázaro, *The Legality Principle and the Conventionality Control: Confluences and Developments in the Inter-American Court of Human Rights*, 128 Boletin Mexicano de Derecho Comparado 808 (2010).

123 *Heliodoro Portugal v. Panama, supra* n. 117, §180.

Heliodoro defined the most complete account regarding the foundations of the doctrine of conventionality control. It made clear that, in the Court's view, the judiciary must carry out conventionality control as a "necessary measure" (Article 2), in order to remove legal obstacles that impede the full force and effect of the Convention within the domestic legal system (principle of effectiveness). Using the metaphorical language of García Ramírez, while the obligation to ensure (Article 1.1) is the "shield and sword" (*escudo y espada*) of the obligation to respect, the obligations derived from Article 2 become the "face" (*el rostro*) of that obligation. This "face" includes the juridical and structural order of the State, its attributions and practices, as well as the measures that modify the social structures that permit those violations.[124] The doctrine of conventionality control is one of the "faces", the "means", by which the judiciary must comply with its duty to respect and ensure human rights at the domestic level.[125] It is a "face" created by the Court to increase the effectiveness of the Convention at the domestic level, especially in cases that involve the existence of anti-conventional laws that are null *ab initio*.

3.3. THE HIDDEN PILLAR OF CONVENTIONALITY CONTROL: THE DIRECT EFFECT OF THE AMERICAN CONVENTION

The legal basis of the doctrine of conventionality control is found in the construction made by the Court of the interaction between Articles 1.1 and 2 of the American Convention, and Articles 26 and 27 of the Vienna Convention.[126] This construction is controversial for several reasons that will be explored and discussed in subsequent chapters. This sub-section is limited to exploring a theoretical aspect that underlines the interpretations made by the Court before and after the decision of *Almonacid*. This is what could be called the "hidden pillar" of conventionality control: the notion that the American Convention (and in general all the *Corpus Juris*) has a direct effect on State authorities, specifically on the judiciary. This theoretical assumption is what allows arguing that domestic judges are obligated to guarantee the effectiveness of the Convention in terms of Articles 1.1 and 2, and that Article 26 and Article 27 of the Vienna Convention support the existence of an obligation to exercise conventionality control. Without accepting this theoretical position, the doctrine of conventionality control would be in theoretical problems due

124 *See*, Sergio García Ramírez, *The Conventional Internal Control Court*, Year V, 28 IUS Revista del Instituto de Ciencias Jurídicas de Puebla 146 (2011).

125 *See generally*, Ernesto Rey Cantor, *Control de Convencionalidad de las Leyes y Derechos Humanos*, *supra* n. 97 at 195.

126 *See*, Claudio Nash Rojas, *Control de Convencionalidad. Cuadernillo de la Corte Interamericana de Derechos Humanos No. 7*, *supra* n. 5, p. 4.

to the generally accepted understanding that the obligations of international law are directed at States as subjects of international law, and not to specific authorities such as judges, unless otherwise expressly established in the treaty or by domestic law.

In *Almonacid*, the Inter-American Court did not explain why the judiciary – not the State – was obligated to comply with Article 1.1 by setting aside domestic law to the contrary, which is the basis to argue that judges have an obligation to exercise conventionality control. The Court simply mentioned,

> 123. ... when the Legislative Power fails to set aside and / or adopts laws which are contrary to the American Convention, *the Judiciary is bound to honor the obligation to respect rights as stated in Article 1(1) of the said Convention*, and consequently, it must refrain from enforcing any laws contrary to such Convention.[127]

So once the doctrine was created, the Court never had to look back to the discussion of whether or not the Convention had direct effect, because the criteria had already been settled in its jurisprudence. Consequently, in subsequent cases, the reason why the judiciary was "bound to honor the obligation to respect rights" was because that was already established in the Court's jurisprudence (specifically in paragraph 124 of *Almonacid*).

Yet – although the Court never explained this point – it is indeed possible to know how this notion came to life by observing the theoretical positions of García Ramírez and Cançado Trindade in some concurrent opinions. By studying the views of these two judges one can explain how the Court jumped so easily – in paragraph 124 of *Almonacid* – to the conclusion that the American Convention had some kind of direct effect on State authorities, and therefore that they were obligated to exercise conventionality control without the existence of a secondary rule of domestic origin that created such obligation. The next paragraphs reflect briefly on the ideas of the Mexican and the Brazilian former judges of the Inter-American Court.

3.3.1. *The State as a Unity: The Theoretical Proposition of García Ramírez in* Myrna Mack Chang v. Guatemala *(2003)*

The idea that the American Convention has direct effect on State authorities started being developed in the same document where the language of "conventionality control" was used first. García Ramírez – in his reasoned concurrent opinion in the case of *Myrna Mack-Chang v. Guatemala* (2003)[128] – argued that the

127 *Almonacid Arellano et al. v. Chile, supra* n. 64, §123 (emphasis added).

128 *See, Myrna Mack Chang v. Guatemala Case*. Judgment, Inter-Am. Ct. H.R. (Ser. C) No. 101 (Nov. 25, 2003). Concurrent Opinion of Sergio García Ramírez, §26–32.

agents that represent the State in its international relations, and whose acts may give rise to legal consequences at the international level, for instance when they accept the international responsibility of the State or the commission of certain acts, cannot condition the compliance with the obligations derived from that acceptance of responsibility to what other domestic bodies decide under domestic legislation.[129] If that were a legitimate claim, the former Mexican judge argued, it would mean that the actions of the judiciary at the domestic level are outside of the scope of the "conventionality control": outside of the Court's competence to evaluate the acts and laws of the States parties to the Convention, and to determine the legal consequences for those acts.[130]

This reflection was motivated by the contradiction that sometimes exists between certain declarations of State representatives at the international stage (i.e. before the Commission or the Court), and the possible position that other organs within the State may take regarding the same question. So García Ramírez drew a distinction between the legitimacy that these discrepancies may have under domestic law (for example based on the principle of the separation of powers), and their inadequacy in the light of international law. Particularly, he clarified that once an international tribunal decides on the international responsibility of the State, the consequences that derive from that judgment must be complied with by the State, notwithstanding any potential discrepancy between the content of the decision and the rules of the domestic legal system.[131] Consequently:

> 27. For the effects of the American Convention and of the exercise of the contentious jurisdiction of the Inter-American Court, *the State is considered integrally, as a whole. Accordingly, responsibility is global; it concerns the State as a whole and cannot be subject to the division of authority established in domestic law.* At the international level, it is not possible to divide the State, to bind before the Court only one or some of its organs, to grant them representation of the State in the proceeding – without this representation affecting the whole State – and excluding other organs from this treaty regime of responsibility, leaving their actions outside the "treaty control" (*control de convencionalidad*) that involves the jurisdiction of the international court.[132]

The language used by García Ramírez could be very well considered simply as a different way of naming and specifying what is already clear in the Convention and general international law: the duty of States parties to a controversy to "comply with the judgments of the Court in any case to which they are parties"

129 *Id.* §65–72.
130 American Convention on Human Rights, *supra* n 4, Arts. 63, 67 and 68.
131 *See, Myrna Mack Chang v. Guatemala Case, supra* n. 128. Reasoned Concurrent Opinion of Sergio García Ramírez, §26.
132 *Id.* §27 (emphasis added).

(Article 68 of the Convention), and the prohibition against invoking the provisions of internal law as justification for the failure to perform a treaty (Article 27 of the Vienna Convention). So, certainly, the most logical reading of the opinion in *Myrna*, is that it was motivated precisely to remind the States about their duty to comply with the judgments of the Court in cases where they are party to a controversy, and where they have accepted the international responsibility for the commission of certain acts before the Commission or Court. Consequently, the term of "conventionality control" used in *Myrna* referred to a very different concept than the one used in *Almonacid.*

Yet, this criterion has been interpreted – by García Ramírez himself – in the sense that the State appears before the Court as a "unity", "as a whole", which means that it cannot "condition" the compliance with the judgments of the Court due to provisions of the domestic legal system. Domestic authorities cannot avoid the fulfillment of the obligations derived from the American Convention for reasons based on domestic law. This means that the existence of different branches of government, the existence of different levels of government, the existence of a fixed hierarchy of international rules at the domestic level, or any other consideration of domestic law, is irrelevant as an excuse for complying with the decisions of the Inter-American Court.[133] This position can be expressly observed in his opinion in *La Cantuta* (mentioned above) where he established that:

> 8. ... the Court has also made it clear that the obligations undertaken by a State upon becoming a party to the international convention on human rights are binding upon that State as a whole. This extends to executive, legislative and judicial bodies, as well as self-governed bodies outside of the domain of the three traditional branches, which are a part of the State itself. Therefore, it is inadmissible for one of such bodies to refrain from complying with an obligation that binds the State of which it is a part, or to directly acts in violation thereof, on the grounds that another body has failed to fulfill its own duties in the general system for the adoption of and compliance with international obligations ...[134]

García Ramírez's proposition in his concurrent opinion in *Myrna* opened the door for arguing the direct effect of the Convention on State authorities, although it is not clear at all that in that opinion he was asserting a different conclusion from what was already clear in Article 68 of the Convention and 27 of the Vienna Convention. The former Mexican judge never makes an argument in any other concurrent opinion connecting the decision in paragraphs 123 and 124 of *Almonacid* and his criterion of the State obligated as a "whole". But in an

133 *See*, Sergio García Ramírez, *The Conventional Internal Control Court*, *supra* n. 124, p. 140.
134 *La Cantuta v. Peru*, *supra* n. 65, Concurrent Opinion of Sergio García Ramírez, §8.

academic paper he argued – before the decision in *Myrna* – that if the duty of the State to comply with the Convention does not admit divisions between federal and State authorities (Article 28 of the American Convention), even more so it is not possible to argue the division of powers between different branches of government to avoid the fulfillment of the obligations derived from human rights treaties.[135]

The problem that apparently concerned García Ramírez is that the lack of effects of the *Corpus Juris* based on domestic law creates what he calls a "strange immunity" in favor of some sectors of the State to enforce the Convention. For this reason – he considered – it is necessary that States take measures so all domestic authorities comply with Articles 1.1 and 2 of the Convention. In the case of the judiciary these measures would require the existence of a procedure that allows the enforcement both of the Convention and the judgments of the Court, just as he suggested in his concurrent opinion in *Tibi v. Ecuador* (2004).[136] In this last opinion, the notion that some domestic authorities are "immune" to the obligations derived from the Convention appears to be unacceptable, since that condition opens the door for human rights violations and the ineffectiveness of the decisions of the Inter-American Court.

This reasoning sheds light on why the Court assumed, in *Almonacid*, that the Chilean judiciary could not resist the enforcement of the Convention and the jurisprudence of the Court under considerations based on domestic law (specifically, Law 2.191). It is in this sense that the notion of the obligations of international law as binding on the State as a "unity" (using the language of the opinion in *Myrna*), and the requirement to guarantee the efficacy of the Convention in order to avoid the "strange immunity" generated by the division of powers, are two powerful ideas that perhaps influenced the Court's position in paragraphs 123 and 124 of *Almonacid*, opening the door for the creation of the doctrine of conventionality control. Under a similar approach, the Court has extended the duty to exercise conventionality control to all State authorities, as it was stated in *Gelman v. Uruguay* (2011). Eduardo Ferrer Mac-Gregor Poisot explained the position in *Gelman* in his reasoned concurrent opinion in the Monitoring Compliance of the Judgment in the same case (2013).

---

135 *See*, Sergio García Ramírez, *El Futuro del Sistema Interamericano de Protección de los Derechos Humanos*, in Eduardo Ferrer Mac-Gregor Poisot (Ed.), *Derecho Procesal Constitucional*, Vol. II 1595–1598 (Porrua, 4th ed., 2003).

136 *Id.*, pp. 1595–1598; *see also Tibi v. Ecuador*. Preliminary Objections, Merits, Reparations and Costs Judgment, Inter-Am. Ct. H.R. (Ser. C) No. 114 (Sep. 7, 2004). Concurrent Opinion of Sergio García Ramírez, §5; *see generally*, Walter Carnota, *The Inter-American Court of Human Rights and Conventionality Control* (July, 2012), p. 16, at https://ssrn.com/abstract=2116599 or http://dx.doi.org/10.2139/ssrn.2116599 (last accessed Feb. 10, 2018).

3.3.2. *The Moral Imperative to Fight Against Impunity: The Theoretical Construction of the Right to Access to Justice in the View of Cançado Trindade*

The majority of scholars have focused their attention on the influence that García Ramírez's concurrent opinions had in the creation of the doctrine of conventionality control. And they are right to do so. But it is also important to consider the influence that the views of Cançado Trindade might have had on the existence of conventionality control. Particularly, it is pertinent to reflect on the notion sustained by the Brazilian judge that the judiciaries are directly obligated to enforce the American Convention, and therefore that they shall not enforce domestic laws that violate the provisions of the Convention.[137] This position seems to be the result of the theoretical presupposition that international human rights law is superior to domestic law, and that the sovereignty of State must not to limit the protection of human rights.[138]

Cançado Trindade's view finds their concrete expression in the development of the existence of the "right to access to justice (right to effective jurisdictional protection, the *right to Law*) as a *jus cogens* imperative",[139] which was conceptually constructed by the Brazilian judge and at some point was even accepted by the Court.[140] It is true that the idea of the right to access to justice *lato sensu* has not been followed with the same strength since the Brazilian judge left the bench and the Court favored the more "technical" approach promoted by other judges,[141] particularly by Cecilia Medina Quiroga, but it is also true that this view was at its highest point at the moment that *Almonacid* was decided in 2006. As mentioned earlier, the foundations of conventionality control were no longer relevant after the doctrine was created, because it was the precedent itself that was relevant, not the reasoning and ideas that were behind its creation.

In a nutshell, the right to access to justice is the result of the hermeneutical combination of the right to an effective remedy (right to access to justice *stricto sensu*, Article 25), the right to due process (Article 8), the obligation to respect rights (Article 1.1) and the obligation to adopt the necessary measures

137 *See*, A.A. Cançado Trindade, *Os Tribunais Internacionais e a Realizacao da Justica*, p. 54 (RENOVAR, 2015).

138 *Id.*, p. 49. (The author argues that the position of an international tribunal can be based just on principles of justice and not based on the will of the States: *"Deste prisma, a postura básica de um tribunal internacional sópode ser principista, sem fazer concessoes indevidas ao voluntarismo estatal."*)

139 *See*, *Almonacid Arellano et al. v. Chile*, *supra* n. 64, Reasoned Concurrent Opinion of A.A. Cançado Trindade, §24.

140 *See*, *Goiburú et al. v. Paraguay Case.* Merits, Reparations and Costs Judgment, Inter-Am. Ct. H.R. (Ser. C) No. 153 (Sep. 22, 2006) §131.

141 *See*, Laurence Burgorgue-Larsen and Amaya Úbeda de Torres, *The Inter-American Court on Human Rights. Case Law and Commentary*, *supra* n. 1, pp. 684–685.

to give effect to the Convention (Article 2). In Cançado Trindade's view, the indivisibility of all human rights and the moral imperative to guarantee their effective protection allows the above-mentioned articles to be taken "all together" and the formulation of the existence of the right "to the direct access to a competent tribunal, by means of an effective and expedite remedy, and the right to promptly be heard by such independent and impartial tribunal, at both national and international levels (Articles 8 and 25)".[142] The combination of Articles 8 and 25 is also preceded by the notion that Article 25 is closely linked with the general obligation of Article 1.1 in conferring functions of protection upon the domestic law of States parties to the Convention, and that Articles 1.1 and 2 are also "ineluctably intertwined" since both are obligations incumbent upon States by the application of general law itself – of the principle of *pacta sunt servanda.*[143]

At the heart of this view is the goal of achieving the effectiveness of judicial remedies, since the right to an effective remedy constitutes "one of the basic pillars not just of the American Convention but of the rule of law itself in a democratic society in the sense of the Convention".[144] The importance of this right is such for the *ordre public* that transcends the individual interest of States parties to the Convention, and it has the status of a *jus cogens* norm. Consequently, in this view, the protection of the right of access to justice cannot depend on the domestic status of international human rights norms or the attributions of domestic authorities, and must be applied in all circumstances as an obligation of results.[145] Arguably, it is for this reason too that internal organs of the State are called upon to apply international norms directly; so domestic authorities "cannot revoke conventional norms which bind the State, above all in the domain of human rights protection".[146] In the words of Cançado Trindade:

> 21. Articles 25 and 1(1) of the Convention are mutually reinforcing, in the sense of securing the compliance with one and the other in the ambit of domestic law. *Articles 25 and 1(1) require, jointly, the direct application of the American Convention in the domestic law of the States Parties.* In the hypothesis of alleged obstacles of domestic law, Article 2 of the Convention comes into operation, requiring the harmonization

---

142 *Pueblo Bello Massacre v. Colombia.* Judgment, Inter-Am. Ct. H.R. (Ser. C) No. 140 (Jan. 31, 2006). Reasoned Concurrent Opinion of Judge A.A. Cançado Trindade, §61–62.

143 *See*, A.A. Cançado Trindade, *The Access of Individuals to International Justice*, p. 52 (Oxford University Press, 2011); *see also Caballero Delgado and Santana v. Colombia.* Reparations and Costs (Art. 63(1) American Convention on Human Rights), *supra* n. 38, Dissenting Opinion of A.A. Cançado Trindade, §6–9.

144 *Castillo Páez v. Peru Case.* Judgment Inter-Am. Ct. H.R. (Ser. C) No. 34 (Nov. 3, 1997) §82.

145 *Pueblo Bello Massacre v. Colombia.* Judgment, Inter-Am. Ct. H.R. (Ser. C) No. 140 (Jan. 31, 2006). Reasoned Concurrent Opinion of Judge Cançado Trindade, §64 (emphasis added).

146 *See*, A.A. Cançado Trindade, *The Access of Individuals to International Justice*, *supra* n. 143, p. 84.

> with the Convention of the domestic law of the States Parties. These latter are obliged, by Articles 25 and 1(1) of the Convention, to establish a system of simple and prompt local remedies, and to give them effective application. If de facto they do not do so, due to alleged lacunae or insufficiencies of domestic law, they incur into a violation of Articles 25, 1(1) and 2 of the Convention.[147]

The ideas mentioned above are particularly directed to the duty of the judiciary to directly enforce the Convention, because judges are the primary State's agents in charge of protecting the right of access to justice (which, as mentioned above, in this view is a *jus cogens* norm), and since they have a relevant role in safeguarding internationally recognized human rights.[148] Accordingly, in Cançado Trindade's construction, domestic judges have an international obligation to ensure that the right to an effective remedy (*lato sensu*) is not violated, and for that reason they must guarantee that justice is served for the victims of human rights violations. It is logical to suggest that the Brazilian judge supported – and perhaps contributed – to the view proposed by paragraphs 123 and 124 of *Almonacid*. If domestic judges are directly obligated by the Convention, he should have also supported the existence of the doctrine of conventionality control as a mechanism to achieve the effectiveness of the right of access to justice. This position can be inferred from his concurrent opinion in *Aguado-Alfaro*, where he mentions that:

> 2. As I have been maintaining for many years, effective recourses under domestic law, to which specific provisions of human rights treaties refer expressly, are part of the international protection of human rights. In this regard, it should not be forgotten, as the Court indicates in this judgment, that:
>
> "When a State has ratified an international treaty such as the American Convention, the judges are also subject to it; this obliges them to ensure that the *effet util* of the Convention is not reduced or annulled by the application of laws contrary to its provisions, object and purpose. In other words, the organs of the Judiciary should exercise not only a control of constitutionality, but also of 'conventionality' ex officio between domestic norms and the American Convention; evidently within the framework of their respective jurisdictions and the corresponding procedural regulations ..."
>
> 3. In other words, the organs of the Judiciary of each State Party to the American Convention should have an in-depth knowledge of and duly apply not only constitutional law but also international human rights law; should exercise ex officio the conventionality control with the constitution (constitutionality) and with international treaties (conventionality), considered together, since the international

[147] *Genie Lacayo v. Nicaragua Case*, Interpretation of the Judgment, Inter-Am. Ct. H.R. (Ser. C) No. 45 (Jan. 29, 1997). Dissenting Opinion of Judge A.A. Cançado Trindade, §21.

[148] *See*, A.A. Cançado Trindade, *The Access of Individuals to International Justice*, *supra* n. 143, p. 210.

> and national legal systems are in constant interaction in the domain of the protection of the individual.[149]

Some reminiscences of this type of approach can be seen in the position of Ferrer Mac-Gregor Poisot. In his concurrent opinion in *Liakat Ali Alibux v. Suriname* (2014), the Mexican judge argued that the right to an effective remedy (Article 25.1) requires the existence of judicial remedies that not only protect the principle of legality, but also the rights protected by the Constitution and the Convention. The existence of this right is referred to as the "right to the guarantee of fundamental rights", and it integrates the protection established in Articles 25.1, 1.1, 2, and 29(b). In this view, the existence of the right to the guarantee of fundamental rights creates an obligation for the States to take the appropriate legislative measures to ensure that "remedies" at the domestic level are adequate to protect fundamental rights, which includes that judicial authorities exercise conventionality control.[150] In this sense the Mexican judge argues that:

> 91. Even when the conventionality control has as a basic characteristic that it may be exercised by authorities and courts in various degrees of intensity (depending on their competencies and legal powers), Article 25 of the American Convention clearly establishes the right of all persons to have access to an effective judicial remedy so that a competent authority, with jurisdiction to issue a binding decision, may determine whether or not there has been a violation of a fundamental right claimed by the person filing the action, and that the remedy is useful to restitute to the interested party the enjoyment of his right and to repair it, if it finds there has been a violation. As was previously mentioned, the existence of these guarantees, and by extension, of a model of the conventionality control "constitutes one of the basic pillars, not only of the American Convention, but also of the rule of law in a democratic society as per the Convention".[151]

4. FURTHER DEVELOPMENT OF THE DOCTRINE OF CONVENTIONALITY CONTROL

The cases of *Almonacid, Aguado-Alfaro, La Cantuta* and *Heliodoro* defined the essential components of the doctrine of conventionality control. Besides these "foundational cases" the Court has referred to conventionality control in more than 25 other judgments in the exercise of its contentious jurisdiction,

149 *Dismissed Congressional Employees (Aguado-Alfaro et al.) v. Peru, supra* n. 114, Reasoned Concurrent Opinion of A.A. Cançado Trindade, §2 and 3.

150 *See, Liakat Ali Alibux v. Suriname.* Preliminary Objections, Merits, Reparations and Costs Judgment, Inter-Am. Ct. H.R. (Ser. C) No. 276 (Jan. 30, 2014). Reasoned Concurrent Opinion of Judge Eduardo Ferrer Mac-Gregor Poisot, §71 to 90.

151 *Id.* §91.

and in three Advisory Opinions.[152] The core of the obligations derived from conventionality control has been kept intact notwithstanding its constant reiteration, although some of these decisions have expanded some of its specific elements in important ways: the type of domestic norms that are subject to conventionality control (*Boyce*, 2007); the duty to interpret all domestic legal

[152] *Boyce et al. v. Barbados.* Preliminary Objection, Merits, Reparations and Costs Judgment, Inter-Am. Ct. H.R. (Ser. C) No. 158 (Nov. 20, 2007) §78, 79; *Radilla Pacheco v. Mexico.* Preliminary Objections, Merits, Reparations and Costs Judgment, Inter-Am. Ct. H.R. (Ser. C) No. 209 (Nov. 29, 2009) §339–340; *Manuel Cepeda Vargas v. Colombia.* Preliminary Objections, Merits, Reparations and Costs Judgment, Inter-Am. Ct. H.R. (Ser. C) No. 213 (May 26, 2010) §207, 208; *Xákmok Kásek Indigenous Community. v. Paraguay.* Merits, Reparations and Costs Judgment, Inter-Am. Ct. H.R. (Ser. C) No. 214 (Aug. 24, 2010) §311, 312; *Fernández Ortega et al. v. Mexico.* Preliminary Objection, Merits, Reparations and Costs Judgment, Inter-Am. Ct. H.R. (Ser. C) No. 215 (Aug. 30, 2010) §236, 237; *Rosendo-Cantú and other v. Mexico.* Preliminary Objection, Merits, Reparations and Costs Judgment, Inter-Am. Ct. H.R. (Ser. C) No. 216 (Aug. 31, 2010) §219, 220; *Ibsen Cárdenas and Ibsen Peña v. Bolivia.* Merits, Reparation and Costs Judgment, Inter-Am. Ct. H.R. (Ser. C) No. (Sep. 1, 2010) §202; *Vélez Loor v. Panama.* Preliminary Objections, Merits, Reparations and Costs Judgment, Inter-Am. Ct. H.R. (Ser. C) No. 218 (Nov. 23, 2010) §288; *Gomes Lund et al. ("Guerrilha do Araguaia") v. Brazil.* Preliminary Objections, Merits, Reparations and Costs Judgment, Inter-Am. Ct. H.R. (Ser. C) No. 219, 106 (Nov. 24, 2010) §176, 177; *Cabrera Garcia and Montiel Flores v. Mexico*, Preliminary Objections, Merits, Reparations and Costs Judgment, Inter-Am. Ct. H.R. (Ser. C) No. 220 (Nov. 26, 2010) §225, 226 and 233; *Gelman v. Uruguay.* Preliminary Objections, Merits, Reparations and Costs Judgment, Inter-Am. Ct. H.R. (Ser. C) No. 221 (Feb. 24, 2011) §193, 239; *Chocron, Chocron v. Venezuela.* Preliminary Objections, Merits, Reparations and Costs Judgment, Inter-Am. Ct. H.R. (Ser. C) No. 227 (Jul. 1, 2011), §164, 165 and 172; *Lopez Mendoza v. Venezuela.* Merits, Reparations and Costs Judgment, Inter-Am. Ct. H.R. (Ser. C) No. 233 (Nov. 29, 2011) §226; *Fontevecchia y D'Amico v. Argentina.* Merits, Reparations and Costs Judgment, Inter-Am. Ct. H.R. (Ser. C) No. 238 (Nov. 29, 2011) §93; *Atala Riffo and daughters v. Chile.* Merits, Reparations and Costs Judgment, Inter-Am. Ct. H.R. (Ser. C) No. 239 (Feb. 24, 2012) §281–284; *Furlan and Family v. Argentina.* Preliminary Objections, Merits, Reparations and Costs Judgment, Inter-Am. Ct. H.R. (Ser. C) No. 246, (Aug. 31, 2012) §303–305; *Rio Negro Massacres v. Guatemala.* Preliminary Objections, Merits, Reparations and Costs Judgment, Inter-Am. Ct. H.R. (Ser. C) No. 250 (Sep. 4, 2012) §303–305; *Gudiel Alvarez et al. ("Diario Militar") v. Guatemala.* Merits, Reparations and Costs Judgment, Inter-Am. Ct. H.R. (Ser. C) No. 253 (May 25, 2010) §330; *Santo Domingo Massacre v. Colombia.* Preliminary Objections, Merits and Reparations Judgment, Inter-Am. Ct. H.R. (Ser. C) No. 259 (Nov. 30, 2012) §142; *J. v. Peru.* Preliminary Objections, Merits, Reparations and Costs Judgment, Inter-Am. Ct. H.R. (Ser. C) No. 275, (Nov. 27, 2013) §407; *Liakat Ali Alibux v. Suriname*, Preliminary Objections, Merits, Reparations and Costs Judgment, Inter-Am. Ct. H.R. (Ser. C) No. 276 (Jan. 30, 2014) §151; *Norín Catrimán et al. (Leaders, members and activist of the Mapuche Indigenous People) v. Chile.* Merits, Reparations and Costs Judgment, Inter-Am. Ct. H.R. (Ser. C) No. 279 (May 29, 2014) §436; *Expelled Dominicans and Haitians v. Dominican Republic.* Preliminary Objections, Merits, Reparations and Costs Judgment, Inter-Am. Ct. H.R. (Ser. C) No. 282 (Aug. 28, 2014) §311; *Rights and guarantees of children in the context of migration and/or in need of international protection.* Advisory Opinion OC-21, Inter-Am. Ct. H.R. (Ser. A) No. 21 (Aug. 19, 2014) §31; *Rochac Hernández et al. v. El Salvador.* Merits, Reparations and Costs Judgment, Inter-Am. Ct. H.R. (Ser. C) No. 285 (Oct. 14, 2014) §244; *García Ibarra et al. v. Ecuador.* Preliminary Objections, Merits, Reparations and Costs Judgment, Inter-Am. Ct. H.R. (Ser. C) No. 306 (Nov. 17, 2015) §103; *Chinchilla Sandoval v. Guatemala.* Preliminary Objection, Merits, Reparations and Costs Judgment, Inter-Am. Ct. H.R.

norms in accordance with the *Corpus Juris* (*Radilla*, 2009); the duty of all State authorities to exercise conventionality control (*Cabrera*, 2010); the duty of States to comply with the judgments of the Inter-American Court through conventionality control (*Gelman*, 2013); the parameters of conventionality control (*OC-22/16*); and the relationship between conventionality control and the principle of subsidiarity or complementarity (*Santo Domingo Massacre*, 2012, and *Andrade*, 2016).[153] In this section these developments are succinctly explained.

4.1. CONVENTIONALITY CONTROL MUST BE EXERCISED ON ALL NORMS OF A DOMESTIC LEGAL SYSTEM

In *Boyce* (2007), the Court referred to the duty of domestic judges to exercise conventionality control even on constitutional norms. This case involved the international responsibility of the State of Barbados for the violation of Article 2 in connection with Articles 1.1, 4.1, 4.2 and 25, caused by the mandatory nature of the death penalty imposed on Lennox Ricardo Boyce and three other individuals. The four victims in the case were sentenced to the death penalty in accordance with the provisions of Article 2 of the Offences Against the Person Act 1868 (OAPA), which provides that: "[a]ny person convicted of murder shall be sentenced to and suffer death."[154] Furthermore, Article 26 of the Constitution of Barbados established a "saving clause" that prevented courts from declaring the unconstitutionality of existing laws that had been enacted before the Constitution entered into force in 1966. On the basis of Article 26 of

---

(Ser. C) No. 312 (Feb. 29, 2016) §242; *Entitlement of legal entities to hold rights under the Inter-American human rights system (Interpretation and scope of Art. 1(2), in relation to Arts. 1(2), 8, 11(2), 13, 16, 21, 24, 25, 29, 30, 44, 46 and 62(3) of the American Convention on Human Rights, as well as of Article 8(1)(A) and (B) of the Protocol of San Salvador).* Advisory Opinion OC-22/16, Inter-Am. Ct. H.R. (Ser. A) No. 22 (Feb. 26, 2016) §26; *Tenorio Roca et al. v. Peru.* Preliminary Objections, Merits, Reparations and Costs Judgment, Inter-Am. Ct. H.R. (Ser. C) No. 314 (Jun. 22, 2016) §231; *Andrade Salmón v. Bolivia.* Merits, Reparations and Costs Judgment, Inter-Am. Ct. H.R. (Ser. C) No. 330 (Dec. 1, 2016) §93; and *Gender Identity, and equality and non-discrimination with regard to same-sex couples. State obligations in relation to change of name, gender identity, and rights from a relationship between same-sex couples (interpretation and scope of Articles 1(1), 3, 7, 11(2), 13, 17, 18 and 24, in relation to Article 1, of the American Convention on Human Rights.* Advisory Opinion OC-24, Inter-Am. Ct. H.R. (Ser. A) No. 14 (Nov. 24, 2017).

153 *See*, Silvia Serrano Guzmán, *El control de convencionalidad en la jurisprudencia de la Corte Interamericana de Derechos Humanos* (Comisión Nacional de los Derechos Humanos, 2013) (for an analysis of the jurisprudence of the Inter-American Court on conventionality control); *see generally*, Claudio Nash Rojas, *Control de Convencionalidad. Cuadernillo de la Corte Interamericana de Derechos Humanos No. 7*, *supra* n. 5, p. 4; (this is the most recent official publication of the Inter-American Court on conventionality control until fall 2017).

154 *Boyce et al. v. Barbados*, *supra* n. 152, §75.

the Constitution, the highest Court of appeal in Barbados, the Judicial Committee of the Privy Council (JCPC), held that the existing remedies could not review the constitutionality of Article 2 of the OAPA (adopted in 1868).[155] However, the JCPC held in 2004 that if it were not for the saving clause, it would have declared that the mandatory death penalty goes against the constitutional right of everyone to be free from cruel, inhuman and degrading punishment.[156]

The Inter-American Court asserted that, in accordance with its previous jurisprudence on the death penalty, Article 2 of the OAPA was a norm that affected the right not to be arbitrarily deprived of life and was *per se* incompatible with the American Convention, the State being obligated to remove that norm from its legal system as mandated by Article 2 of the Convention.[157] The Court noted that the conclusion arrived by the JCPC in regard to the impossibility to review the constitutionality of Article 2 of OAPA went through a purely constitutional analysis. This analysis did not take into account the State's obligations under the American Convention and the Vienna Convention.[158] Consequently, the Inter-American Court concluded that, as a matter of international law, the analysis of the JCPC should not have been limited to assessing whether OAPA was unconstitutional, but should have also considered whether the law was conventional in order to determine whether the OAPA restricted or violated the rights recognized by the Convention.[159] In other words, the JCPC should have conducted a conventionality control, and not only a constitutional control of domestic legislation.

Through conventionality control, the JCPC should have prevented the application of Article 26 of the Constitution, since this provision denied the citizens of Barbados in general, and the alleged victims in particular, of the right to judicial protection against violations of the right to life.[160] Consequently, since *Boyce*, it is possible to say that the Court decided that judges must exercise conventionality control on all the norms of the domestic legal system (including its constitutional norms) to ensure the realization of the rights recognized by the Convention in accordance with Articles 1.1 and 2. This approach conceptually distinguished between constitutional control and conventionality control, because judges must not only control the constitutionality of domestic laws, but also their conventionality.[161] One reading of this view is that domestic

---

155 *Id.* §75.

156 *Id.* §76.

157 *Id.* §72.

158 *Id.* §77.

159 *Id.* §77.

160 *Id.* §78.

161 *See*, Silvia Serrano Guzmán, *El control de convencionalidad en la jurisprudencia de la Corte Interamericana de Derechos Humanos*, *supra* n. 153, at 28; *see generally*, Claudio Nash Rojas, *Control de Convencionalidad. Cuadernillo de la Corte Interamericana de Derechos Humanos No. 7*, *supra* n. 5, at 7.

authorities should interpret or set aside constitutional rules that are contrary to the *Corpus Juris*.[162]

4.2. CONVENTIONALITY CONTROL AS A DUTY TO INTERPRET DOMESTIC NORMS IN A MANNER CONSISTENT WITH THE INTER-AMERICAN *CORPUS JURIS*

Radilla (2009) is particularly relevant in the normative development of the doctrine of conventionality control. In this case the Court emphasized, for the first time, that the obligation of judges to exercise conventionality control includes not only the duty not to enforce laws that are contrary to the provisions of the *Corpus Juris* (which was the focus in *Almonacid* and *Aguado-Alfaro*), but also the duty to interpret domestic laws in accordance with the Convention and the Court's jurisprudence.[163] This approach signified an important addition to the doctrine in regard to what was originally established in the foundational cases. The Court noted that sometimes human rights violations are produced due to the way domestic legislation is interpreted and enforced, and not necessarily by the manifest anti-conventionality of domestic law. For this reason, domestic authorities should ensure that the interpretation of domestic law does not violate human rights, and conventionality control is the means to achieve this goal.

Radilla is the first in a series of cases against Mexico involving violations to Articles 8 and 25 in regard to Articles 1.1 and 2. These violations were connected with the enforcement of Article 57 of the Code of Military Justice and Article 13 of the Political Constitution of Mexico. These articles served as a basis for denying civil judges jurisdiction on cases that involved crimes committed by members of the army, that were not connected with military discipline, and where the victims

162 It is relevant to point out that the approach taken in *Boyce* has only been used in this case. In other cases (i.e. *Radilla*) the Court did not order Mexican domestic judges to cease in the enforcement of a constitutional rule, but to interpret that norm in accordance with the *Corpus Juris*. The decision of the Inter-American Court in *Boyce*, however, could very well be read as an assertion not only of the direct effect of the *Corpus Juris*, but also of its supremacy. For a position that reads the position of the Court regarding the conventionality control as an affirmation of the supremacy of the *Corpus Juris*, *see* Ariel E. Dulitzky, *An Inter-American Constitutional Court? The Invention of conventionality control by the Inter-American Court of Human Rights*, *supra* n. 88, p. 54 (on the notion that the Court created a "principle of integration" along with the doctrine of conventionality control).

163 *See, Radilla Pacheco v. Mexico*, *supra* n. 156, §340; *see also Atala Riffo and daughters v Chile.* Merits, Reparations and Costs Judgment, Inter-Am. Ct. H.R. (Ser. C) No. 239 (Feb. 24, 2012) §284, and *Andrade Salmón v. Bolivia. Merits*, Reparations and Costs Judgment, *supra* n. 152, §93.

of those violations were civilians.[164] The jurisprudence of the Inter-American Court had restricted the exercise of military criminal jurisdiction since *Castillo Petruzzi*.[165] Following this precedent, the Court reasoned in *Radilla* that Article 57 of the Mexican Code of Military Justice was partially incompatible with the Convention, and that it had to be modified in accordance with Article 2 of the Convention. But the Court also reasoned that Article 13 of the Constitution was not *per se* incompatible with the Convention and that the problem was the way it was interpreted by federal judges.

Consequently, the Court ruled that judges shall conduct conventionality control, so it was:

> 340. ... necessary that the application of the regulations or their interpretation, as jurisdictional practices and a manifestation of the State's public order, be adjusted to the same purpose sought by Article 2 of the Convention. In practical terms, the interpretation of Article 13 of the Political Constitution of Mexico shall be coherent with the conventional and constitutional principles of the due process of law and the right to a fair trial, included in Article 8(1) of the American Convention and the relevant regulations of the Mexican Constitution.[166]
>
> Therefore, it is necessary that the constitutional and legislative interpretations regarding the material and personal competence criteria of military jurisdiction in Mexico be adjusted to the principles established in the jurisprudence of this Tribunal, which have been reiterated in the present case (*supra* paras. 272 through 277).[167]

Since the decision in *Radilla* it has been considered that the doctrine of conventionality control requires that authorities make a "consistent interpretation" (*interpretación conforme*) of all the norms of the domestic legal system and the *Corpus Juris*, regardless of whether or not the law is *per se* incompatible with the Convention. This means a complement to what was established since *Almonacid*, since now domestic authorities shall cease in the application of an anti-conventional norm, always acting within their respective competences and the corresponding procedural regulations, *only* if it is not possible to perform a consistent interpretation. This case is also relevant because it was the first time the Court used the doctrine of conventionality control as a way to prevent future human rights violations by establishing it as a "guarantee of non-repetition" in the section of reparations of the judgment.

---

164 *Id.* §280 and 282; *see generally, Fernández Ortega et al. v. Mexico, supra* n. 152; *Rosendo-Cantú and other v. Mexico, supra* n. 152; *Cabrera Garcia and Montiel Flores v. Mexico, supra* n. 152.

165 *See, Castillo Petruzzi et al. v. Peru, supra* n. 45, §128; *Lori Berenson Mejía v. Peru*. Judgment, Inter-Am. Ct. H.R. (Ser. C) No. 119 (Nov. 25, 2004) §142.

166 *Radilla Pacheco v. Mexico, supra* n. 152, §338.

167 *Id.* §340.

4.3. ALL STATE AUTHORITIES MUST EXERCISE CONVENTIONALITY CONTROL

In *Cabrera* (2010), the Court extended the range of the authorities that are obligated to perform conventionality control by stating that: "all [State] institutions, including its judges" are subject to the Convention and are obliged to ensure its effectiveness.[168] This change in language was adopted in order to ensure that every domestic authority materially exercising jurisdictional functions would exercise conventionality control, including "Courts or Chambers or Constitutional Tribunals, as well as the Supreme Courts of justice and other high courts".[169] This case is also important for the concurring opinion of Ferrer Mac-Gregor Poisot (*ad hoc* judge in that case), where he explained in detail the developments and challenges of the doctrine until 2010.[170] This concurring opinion is an important reference point for understanding the scope and characteristics of conventionality control, although it is important to keep in mind that the doctrine has evolved – and continues to evolve – in subsequent cases.

Following the same vein, in *Gelman* the Court reaffirmed the position of *Cabrera* by stating that all State authorities – including democratic instances – must exercise conventionality control, so: "when a State is party to an international treaty such as the American Convention, *all its organs*, including its judges and other bodies linked to the administration of justice at all levels" should exercise an *ex officio* conventionality control.[171] This approach apparently follows the logic of *Velásquez Rodríguez* and the concurrent opinion of Judge García Ramírez in *Myrna Mack*, in the sense that the duty to fulfill the general obligations established in Articles 1.1 and 2 requires that the entire State apparatus be directed to respect and ensure the rights and freedoms protected by the Convention. With the approach taken in *Gelman*, the Court took an aggressive step to allow conventionality control to serve as a mechanism for all State authorities – not only those that exercise jurisdictional functions – to ensure the effectiveness of the Convention. In the words of the Court:

> 239. The democratic legitimacy of specific facts in a society is limited by the norms of protection of human rights recognized in international treaties, such as the

---

168 *See, Cabrera Garcia and Montiel Flores v. Mexico*, *supra* n. 152, §225.

169 *Id.* Reasoned Concurrent Opinion of Judge Eduardo Ferrer Mac-Gregor Poisot, §20.

170 *See, Gelman v. Uruguay.* Monitoring Compliance with the Judgment. Order of the Inter-American Court of Human Rights. Reasoned Concurrent Opinion of Eduardo Ferrer Mac-Gregor Poisot; and *Liakat Ali Alibux v. Suriname*, *supra* n. 152, Reasoned Concurrent Opinion of Eduardo Ferrer Mac-Gregor Poisot.

171 *Gelman v. Uruguay*, *supra* n. 156, §193 (emphasis added); *see Expelled Dominicans and Haitians v. Dominican Republic*, *supra* n. 152, §311; *see Rochac Hernández et al. v. El Salvador*, *supra* n. 152, §244.

American Convention, in such a form that the existence of one true democratic regime is determined by both its formal and substantial characteristics, and therefore, particularly in cases of serious violations of nonrevocable norms of International Law, the protection of human rights constitutes a impassable limit to the rule of the majority, that is, to the forum of the "possible to be decided" by the majorities in the democratic instance, those who should also prioritize "control of conformity with the Convention" (*supra* para. 193), which is a function and task of any public authority and not only the Judicial Branch.[172]

4.4. CONVENTIONALITY CONTROL AND THE PRINCIPLE OF SUBSIDIARITY OR COMPLEMENTARITY

In the *Resolution of Monitoring Compliance with Gelman*, the Court also established that there are two different "manifestations" of States' obligations to exercise conventionality control on the basis of the Court's jurisprudence, depending on whether or not the State has been party to a controversy.[173] The first manifestation is that conventionality control has an important role in the compliance with the judgments of the Court, specifically by domestic authorities that belong to a State that has been condemned in an international procedure.[174] Through conventionality control domestic authorities must comply with the orders of the Court notwithstanding domestic regulations, interpretations and contrary practices. As explained by Ferrer Mac-Gregor Poisot, the judgments of the Court acquire the authority of *res judicata* effective *inter partes*, which means that all State authorities have the obligation to comply with all the provisions of a judgment in a prompt, full and effective manner. In this type of case the State is totally bound to the criterion developed by the Court on the basis of Articles 67 and 68.1 of the Convention.[175]

The second manifestation is that the jurisprudence of the Court binds States that are not parties to a particular controversy by the "mere fact of being parties to the American Convention" and because they have a duty to exercise conventionality control.[176] Here the Court stated that conventionality control has been "conceived as an institution that it is used to enforce International Law, in this case International Human Rights Law, and specifically the American Convention and its sources, including the Court's jurisprudence".[177]

172 *Gelman v. Uruguay*, *supra* n. 152, §239.
173 *See, Gelman v. Uruguay.* Monitoring Compliance with the Judgment, *supra* n. 170, §67.
174 *Id.* §73.
175 *Id.* §73.
176 *Id.* §70.
177 *Id.* §65.

With the same logic, in the *OC-21/14*, the *OC-22/16* and the *OC-24/17*, the Court reasoned that "the duty of prevention" requires not only that the interpretations of the Court in the exercise of its contentious jurisdiction are relevant for the exercise of conventionality control. State authorities must also take into consideration the Court's interpretations in the exercise of its advisory jurisdiction, since "the main purpose of the advisory jurisdiction is to obtain a judicial interpretation on one or various articles of the Convention or other treaties concerning the protection of human rights in the States of the Americas".[178]

Notwithstanding the approach taken by the Court since *Almonacid* – that calls for greater implementation of International Law at the state level, and particularly of its own interpretations – since the case of *Santo Domingo Massacre*, it has also emphasized the existence of an intimate connection between the principle of subsidiarity or complementarity and the doctrine of conventionality control.[179] This is a topic of great importance, since it has the potential to open the door for a more harmonious understanding of conventionality control in the context of the relationships between the Court and State institutions (the last chapter of this book deals precisely with this question). In this sense, in *Andrade* (2016), the Court reasoned that the complementary nature of the international jurisdiction means that the Inter-American System does not substitute domestic jurisdictions, but rather that it serves as a complement to them. So States shall solve by their own means the human right violations that occur in their jurisdictions before being obligated to respond before the institutions of the Inter-American System. It is in this context that conventionality control is intimately connected with the principle of subsidiarity or complementarity, since it constitutes an obligation for State authorities so "the interpretation and

---

178 *Rights and guarantees of children in the context of migration and/or in need of international protection.* Advisory Opinion OC-21, *supra* n. 152, §31; *Entitlement of legal entities to hold rights under the Inter-American human rights system (Interpretation and scope of Article 1(2), in relation to Articles 1(2), 8, 11(2), 13, 16, 21, 24, 25, 29, 30, 44, 46 and 62(3) of the American Convention on Human Rights, as well as of Article 8(1)(A) and (B) of the Protocol of San Salvador).* Advisory Opinion OC-22–16, *supra* n. 152, §26; and *Gender Identity, and equality and non-discrimination with regard to same-sex couples. State obligations in relation to change of name, gender identity, and rights from a relationship between same-sex couples (interpretation and scope of Articles 1(1), 3, 7, 11(2), 13, 17, 18 and 24, in relation to Article 1, of the American Convention on Human Rights*, *supra* n. 152, §26.

179 *See*, *Santo Domingo Massacre v. Colombia.* Preliminary Objections, Merits and Reparations Judgment, *supra* n. 152, §142; *Gelman v. Uruguay.* Monitoring Compliance with the Judgment, *supra* n. 170, §70; *García Ibarra et al. v. Ecuador.* Preliminary Objections, Merits, Reparations and Costs Judgment, *supra* n. 152, §103; and *Andrade Salmón v. Bolivia.* Merits, Reparations and Costs Judgment, *supra* n. 152, §93; *see also* Laurence Burgorgue-Larsen, *Chronicle of a Fashionable Theory in Latin America. Decoding the Doctrinal Discourse of Conventionality Control*, in Yves Haeck, Oswaldo Ruiz-Chiriboga and Clara Burbano-Herrera (Eds.), *The Inter-American Court of Human Rights: Theory and Practice, Present and Future*, pp. 658–659 (Intersentia, 2015).

enforcement of domestic law is consistent with the international human rights obligations of the state".[180] Furthermore, the Court stated that:

> 94. From the foregoing follows that, in the Inter-American System, there is a dynamic and complementary control of the obligations of the states of respecting and guaranteeing human rights, jointly between domestic authorities (primarily obligated) and international instances (in complementary manner), so the criteria for decision, and the mechanisms for protection, both national and international, can be complemented to each other. Thus, the jurisprudence of the Court shows cases where the Court considers decisions of domestic courts to support and conceptualize violations to the American Convention in specific cases; in other cases it has been recognized that, in accordance with the international obligations of the state, domestic courts have taken appropriate measures to remedy the situation that gave rise to a case; have already resolved the alleged violation; have arranged reasonable reparations, or have exercised an adequate control of conventionality. In this sense, the Court has pointed out that State responsibility under the Convention can only be demanded at the international level after the State has had the opportunity to recognize, where appropriate, a violation of a right, and to make reparations by its own means of the damage caused.[181]

5. CONCLUSION

The doctrine of conventionality control is intimately connected with the progressive strengthening of the normative force of Article 2 in the Court's jurisprudence. The theoretical position assumed by the Court in *Suárez Rosero* understood that Article 2 had the nature of a prescriptive provision (not a norm with a programmatic nature), which opened the door for the Court to evaluate the specific content of the "legislative" and "other measures" that States must take to comply with their duties under Articles 1.1 and 2. The progressive development of this idea derived in the creation of the doctrine of conventionality control, as a specification made by the Court of the "other measures" that all the authorities of the States parties to the Convention must take in order to guarantee the effectiveness of the Convention notwithstanding the existence of domestic law to the contrary.

The legal grounds of the doctrine of conventionality control are the general obligations of the State (Articles 1.1 and 2), the principle of *pacta sunt servanda* (Article 26 of the Vienna Convention) and the prohibition of the State to use domestic law as a justification for the failure to perform a treaty (Article 27 of the Vienna Convention). There is also a "hidden" foundational element that sustains

---

180 *Andrade Salmón v. Bolivia.* Merits, Reparations and Costs Judgment, *supra* n. 152, §93.

181 *Andrade Salmón v. Bolivia.* Merits, Reparations and Costs Judgment, *supra* n. 152, §94 (free translation).

conventionality control: the notion that the Convention has a direct effect on State authorities as a matter of international law, which includes the view that the domestic judiciary must guarantee the effectiveness of the Convention. This "pillar" is revolutionary because it clashes against the orthodox understanding of the principles of indifference, as will be explained in Chapter 3 of this book. Nonetheless, conventionality control has been well settled in the Court's jurisprudence.

Conventionality control has continued its normative development in the Court's jurisprudence after the foundational cases, although its core elements have remained intact. It is true that the methodology followed by the Court in creating and developing conventionality control is questionable for several reasons, which are explored in depth in subsequent chapters. But the Court itself – and a great number of scholars – has understood that its jurisprudence has the legitimacy and legal force to advance the legal standards in the Inter-American System, both at the international and the domestic level. For that reason, the study of the origins, foundations and jurisprudential development, as explained in this chapter, has heavily relied on the line of jurisprudence of conventionality control from *Alomacid* until the decision of the *OC-24/17* (2016).

CHAPTER 2
LEGAL ANALYSIS OF THE DOCTRINE OF CONVENTIONALITY CONTROL

Various modern constitutions have confronted this question [the connection between the domestic system and the international system] and provided solutions that "build a bridge" between the two legal orders that ultimately benefit that who must be favored: the human being … If there is such clear and unequivocal connection – or at least one that is sufficient and intelligible, and that it is not lost in uncertainties or a diversity of interpretations – and international instruments are immediately applicable in the domestic sphere, domestic courts shall carry out their own "conventionality control".

Sergio García Ramírez

Reasoned Concurrent Opinion in the *Aguado-Alfaro Case* (2006)

1. INTRODUCTION

The Inter-American Court of Human Rights has progressively defined the normative aspects of the doctrine of conventionality control in its jurisprudence. The foundational cases of *Almonacid Arellano et al. v. Chile*, *Dismissed Congressional Employees (Aguado-Alfaro) v. Peru*, and *Heliodoro Portugal v. Panama* were complemented in important aspects by the decisions of *Boyce et al. v. Barbados*, *Radilla Pacheco v. Mexico*, *Cabrera Garcia and Montiel Flores v. Mexico*, *Gelman v. Uruguay*, *Santo Domingo Massacre v. Colombia*, and more recently in *Andrade Salmón v. Bolivia*.

The progressive development of conventionality control in the Court's jurisprudence makes it possible to say that the evolution of this doctrine has had an empirical nature. It has responded to the particular challenges that the Court identified in concrete cases, especially when it found that the existence, interpretation and/or enforcement of domestic laws were the causes of human rights violations at the State level. For this reason, the specific characteristics of conventionality control cannot be understood or evaluated either in the abstract – as a "finished" doctrine created in *Almonacid* – or by just looking at the foundational cases, or by just looking at the last decision where the doctrine was mentioned. It is necessary to analyze all the different elements of the "line of jurisprudence" on conventionality control, in order to achieve a proper understanding of the specific obligations derived from its existence.[1]

The approach followed by the Court to develop conventionality control might produce uncertainty about what is the exact content of this doctrine. This condition has been a legitimate source of concern and confusion among scholars and judges. Several questions might be formulated in this sense: Is it possible to define conventionality control? Who is obligated to exercise conventionality control: judges, legislators, teachers in public schools? What are the types of acts required by conventionality control: the nullification and non-enforcement of anti-conventional laws, or the consistent interpretation of domestic law? What type of State acts must be "controlled": statutory laws and judgments, or also the conduct of police officers? What are the norms that must be used as parameters for the control: treaties, customary rules, or also the decisions enacted solely by the President of the Inter-American Court when interpreting the Convention? Chapter 2 studies in detail the characteristics of conventionality control in a systematic manner, in order to answer some of these questions.

The analysis of this chapter is mainly based on the Court's jurisprudence and the opinions of the most important scholars that have reflected on these topics. It is divided into two general sections. The first section presents and discusses (1) the most accurate definition that has been developed on conventionality control, as well as the legal basis for the existence of this doctrine; (2) the "subjects" of the obligation: the authorities that have an obligation to exercise conventionality control; (3) the "object" of the obligation: the type of actions required by conventionality control; (4) the "paradox" provoked by the fact that conventionality control must be exercised *ex officio* by domestic authorities, but that they must act in the context of their competences and respecting the corresponding procedural regulations; and (5) the "parameters" of conventionality control: the types of domestic laws that must be subject to conventionality control, and the sources of international law that serve as a basis for that control. The analysis presented in each one of these sections seeks to clarify and systematize the normative elements of conventionality control.

One of the central questions that underlines some of the discussions presented in this chapter is how conventionality control must operate in different domestic legal systems, because some – if not all – of the specific elements of this doctrine challenge the absolute freedom that States have historically had under

---

1 *See generally*, Claudio Nash Rojas, *Control de Convencionalidad. Cuadernillo de la Corte Interamericana de Derechos Humanos No. 7* (Inter-American Court of Human Rights & Ministerio de Relaciones Exteriores de Dinamarca, 2015) (this handbook presents the most recent analysis of the jurisprudence of the Inter-American Court on conventionality control); *see also* Silvia Serrano Guzmán, *El control de convencionalidad en la jurisprudencia de la Corte Interamericana de Derechos Humanos* (Comisión Nacional de los Derechos Humanos, 2013).

international law to decide the best manner to implement their international obligations at the domestic level. The chapter will not discuss the abstract theoretical challenges that conventionality control poses to the manner by which the relationship of international law and domestic legal systems is understood in the Inter-American System. That discussion takes place in Chapters 3 and 4. Chapter 2, section 3 however, discusses and exemplifies the different levels of the relationship between conventionality control and the constitutional rules of the domestic legal systems of the States parties to the American Convention, with particular emphasis on the paradigmatic example of Mexico.

2. ELEMENTS OF THE DOCTRINE OF CONVENTIONALITY CONTROL

2.1. DEFINITION AND LEGAL FOUNDATIONS

2.1.1. Definition

The Court established the core elements of conventionality control in the foundational cases of *Almonacid*, *Aguado-Alfaro* and *Heliodoro*. These cases consolidated a formula that could qualify as the Court's definition of conventionality control, whose core is the following:

> 128. ... when a State has ratified an international treaty such as the American Convention, the judges are also subject to it; this obliges them to ensure that the *effet utile* of the Convention is not reduced or annulled by the application of laws contrary to its provisions, object and purpose.[2]

In the *Resolution of Compliance with Gelman*, the Court also added that the concept of conventionality control has been conceived as "an institution that is used to apply International Law, in this case the International Human Rights Law, and specifically the American Convention and its sources, including the jurisprudence [of the IACtHR]".[3] Finally, in *Andrade*, the Court mentioned that conventionality control requires that "the interpretation and enforcement of domestic law is consistent with the international human rights obligations of the State".[4]

2 *Dismissed Congressional Employees (Aguado-Alfaro et al.) v. Peru.* Preliminary Objections, Merits, Reparations and Costs Judgment, Inter-Am. Ct. H.R. (Ser. C) No. 158 (Nov. 24, 2006) §128.

3 *Gelman v. Uruguay.* Monitoring Compliance with the Judgment. Order of the Inter-American Court of Human Rights of March 20, 2013, §65.

4 *Andrade Salmón v. Bolivia.* Merits, Reparations and Costs Judgment, Inter-Am. Ct. H.R. (Ser. C) No. 330 (Dec. 1, 2016) §93.

The last translated judgment where conventionality control was mentioned is in *Expelled Dominicans and Haitians v. Dominican Republic* (2014), where the Court stated that:

> 311. … when a State is a party to an international treaty such as the American Convention, all its organs, including its judges, are also subject to that treaty, which obliges them to ensure that the effects of the provisions of the Convention are not impaired by the application of norms that are contrary to its object and purpose. The judges and organs involved in the administration of justice at all levels are obliged to exercise *ex officio* a "control of conventionality" between domestic laws and the American Convention; evidently within the framework of their respective jurisdictions and the corresponding procedural regulations. In this task, they must take into account not only the treaty, but also its interpretation by the Inter-American Court, ultimate interpreter of the American Convention.[5]

This language has been almost the same since *Aguado-Alfaro*.[6] Yet it is important to mention that usually the Court indistinctly cites *Almonacid* and some other cases as the authority to sustain the use of conventionality control, and then explains the specific consequences that the existence of the doctrine has for the concrete case.[7] For instance, in *Rosendo-Cantú v. Mexico* (2010) the Court referred to conventionality control in paragraph 219 of the judgment (which is part of the section on "Reparations"), and then in paragraph 220 explained that in the context of the case it was necessary "to ensure that the constitutional and legislative interpretation of criteria for the personal and material jurisdiction of the military jurisdiction in Mexico are adapted to the principles established in the Court's case law".[8] The methodology followed by the Court – of maintaining

---

5 *Expelled Dominicans and Haitians v. Dominican Republic.* Preliminary Objections, Merits, Reparations and Costs Judgment, Inter-Am. Ct. H.R. (Ser. C) No. 282 (Aug. 28, 2014) §311 (information updated until September 2, 2017).

6 *See*, List of Cases and Opinions.

7 *See, La Cantuta v. Peru.* Merits, Reparations and Costs Judgment, Inter-Am. Ct. H.R. (Ser. C) No. 162 (Nov. 29, 2006) §173 (the Court cited *Almonacid*); *Boyce et al. v. Barbados.* Preliminary Objection, Merits, Reparations and Costs Judgment, Inter-Am. Ct. H.R. (Ser. C) No. 158 (Nov. 20, 2007) §78–79 (the Court cited *Almonacid* and *La Cantuta*); *Heliodoro Portugal v. Panama.* Preliminary Objections, Merits, Reparations and Costs Judgment, Inter-Am. Ct. H.R. (Ser. C) No. 186 (Aug. 12, 2008) §180 (the Court cited *Almonacid* and *Boyce*); *Xákmok Kásek Indigenous Community. v. Paraguay.* Merits, Reparations and Costs Judgment. Inter-Am. Ct. H.R. (Ser. C) No. 214 (Aug. 24, 2010) §311–312 (the Court cited *Almonacid, La Cantuta*, and *Radilla*); and *Fernández Ortega et al. v. Mexico.* Preliminary Objection, Merits, Reparations, and Costs Judgment, Inter-Am. Ct. H.R. (Ser. C) No. 215 (Aug. 30, 2010) §236–237 (the Court cited *Almonacid, La Cantuta*, and *Radilla*).

8 *Rosendo Cantú and other v. Mexico.* Preliminary Objection, Merits, Reparations, and Costs Judgment, Inter-Am. Ct. H.R. (Ser. C) No. 216 (Aug. 31, 2010) §220 (the Court continued: "This implies that, regardless of any legal reforms that the State must adopt (*infra* para. 222), it is incumbent upon the judicial authorities, based on control of conventionality, to order immediately and *ex officio* that the case be heard by the ordinary criminal justice system.").

almost unaltered the language of the doctrine in one paragraph, and then to refer to the specific consequences of the existence of the doctrine – might create the impression that the normative content of conventionality control has remained almost unaltered throughout the Court's jurisprudence, or that in fact there are different versions of conventionality control. Yet this is an inaccurate approach.

Conventionality control has evolved in its normative elements after *Almonacid*, but this evolution cannot be observed simply by looking at the specific paragraph where the doctrine is mentioned in the Court's jurisprudence. It must be observed both in relation to the paragraphs where it is mentioned (i.e. paragraph 219 of *Rosendo* and paragraph 128 of *Aguado-Alfaro*), and in relation to the consequences that conventionality control has for particular cases (i.e. in paragraph 220 of *Rosendo* and paragraph 127 of *Aguado-Alfaro*). It is true that the language used by the Court usually only reproduces the changes of its previous jurisprudence in regard to the general formulation of the doctrine, and omits mentioning the specifications to concrete cases (which are also relevant for the understanding of the obligations that emerge from the existence of conventionality control). For that reason, it becomes difficult to assert an accurate definition of conventionality control just by looking at one decision of the Court – even if it is the last decision where conventionality control was mentioned – being necessary to also consider how it was applied in concrete cases.

Thus, an accurate definition of conventionality control requires an analytical evaluation of all the decisions where the Court has used this doctrine. Following that approach, Eduardo Ferrer Mac-Gregor Poisot recently developed a definition of conventionality control that in my view is the most accurate to this day:

> *(Domestic) Conventionality Control.* International obligation in charge of all State authorities of the States Parties to the San José Pact to interpret any domestic legal norm (constitution, statutory law, decree law, regulation, etc.) in accordance with the American Convention and, in general, with the *Inter-American Corpus Juris*, which is integrated by the American Convention on Human Rights, the jurisprudence of the Court, and other binding human rights instruments; if there is clear incompatibility between the domestic legal standard and the *Corpus Juris*, State authorities should refrain from enforcing domestic legal standards to prevent violations of internationally protected human rights. State authorities must exercise conventionality control *ex officio*, but always acting within their respective competences and the corresponding procedural regulations.[9]

---

9 Eduardo Ferrer Mac-Gregor Poisot, *Control de Convencionalidad (sede interna)*, in Eduardo Ferrer Mac-Gregor Poisot, Fabiola Martínez Ramírez, and Giovanni Figeroa Mejía (Eds.), *Diccionario de Derecho Procesal Constitucional y Convencional*, Vol. I, p. 233 (Poder Judicial de la Federación, Consejo de la Judicatura Federal, Universidad Nacional Autónoma de México & Instituto de Investigaciones Jurídicas, 2014).

This definition reflects the most recent developments in the jurisprudence of the Inter-American Court on this subject, and for that reason it shall be considered authoritative. It distinguishes (1) the international nature of the obligation to exercise conventionality control (as it has been implicit since *Almonacid*); (2) that conventionality control creates an obligation for "all state authorities of the States parties to the San José Pact" and not only its judges (following *Cabrera* and *Gelman*); (3) the two most relevant facets of the doctrine: that there is a duty to "interpret" domestic norms in accordance with the Inter-American *Corpus Juris* (following *Radilla* and *Andrade*), and a duty to "refrain" from the enforcement of any domestic law contrary to the *Corpus Juris*; (4) that State authorities must exercise conventionality control "*ex officio*", but "always acting within their respective competences and the corresponding procedural regulations" (as mentioned since *Aguado-Alfaro*); (5) that conventionality control must be exercised on all domestic norms (as it has been implicit since *Boyce*); and (6) that the parameter for conventionality control is the Inter-American *Corpus Juris* (as it was mentioned since the *Resolution of Compliance with Gelman*).

Each one of the components of the definition requires further elaboration, which is the object of the following sections. But before entering in that analysis, it is relevant to reflect briefly on some aspects of the legal basis of conventionality control.

2.1.2. Legal Foundations

It is important to keep in mind that there is no article in the American Convention or any other treaty of the Inter-American System that expressly recognizes an international obligation for every State authority to interpret domestic law in accordance with the *Corpus Juris*, or to refrain from the enforcement of that law if no valid interpretation is possible. The creation of conventionality control – and therefore of its legal basis and technical components – is the result of a progressive and innovative interpretation of Articles 1.1 and 2 of the American Convention and of Articles 26 and 27 of the Vienna Convention on the Law of Treaties. The existence of conventionality control thus represents an assertive specification made by the Court of the type of "other measures" that all State authorities must take to ensure that

> 124. ... all the effects of the provisions embodied in the Convention are not adversely affected by the enforcement of laws which are contrary to its purpose and [in the case of certain types of amnesty laws] that have not had any legal effects since their inception.[10]

---

[10] *Almonacid Arellano et al. v. Chile.* Preliminary Objections, Merits, Reparations and Costs Judgment, Inter-Am. Ct. H.R. (Ser. C) No. 154 (Sep. 26, 2006) §124; *see*, Paolo G. Carozza and

State authorities must exercise conventionality control because they are bound by their duty to "ensure" the rights protected by the Convention (Article 1.1) in cases where the legislature fails to set aside laws contrary to its provisions.[11] In principle, this notion follows what the Court has mentioned for decades: that the Convention must be complied with by all State authorities. Since *Velásquez*, the Court has mentioned that the duty to "ensure" requires States to organize the governmental apparatus and all the structures through which the exercise of public power is manifested, so that the State is able to legally ensure the full enjoyment of human rights, and it is able to comply with the obligation to prevent, investigate and punish any violation of human rights and repair the damage produced to the victims and their relatives.[12] The Court has also established that the obligation to ensure requires not just the existence of a legal system designed to comply with the Convention, but that the government shall "conduct itself so as to effectively ensure the free and full exercise of human rights".[13]

Yet the theory behind paragraphs 123–125 goes one step further. It states that the obligations to respect and ensure the rights and freedoms recognized in the Convention (in terms of Article 1.1) have direct effect on the judiciary, and that the Court has the authority to decide the necessary measures (in terms of Article 2) by which judges should comply with this duty. This position certainly challenges the traditional notion that international obligations do not bind specific authorities unless otherwise established by the treaty or by domestic law, and that States have the absolute freedom to decide the manner by which those obligations are fulfilled at the domestic level.[14] But the line of reasoning followed in *Almonacid* and subsequent cases shows that the Court interprets Articles 1.1 and 2 as provisions that must guide the conduct of domestic authorities (not the conduct of the State, as an abstraction), in a manner that they are "able to ensure the *effet utile* of the international instruments so that they are not reduced or annulled by the application of domestic laws and practices contrary to the object

---

Pablo González-Domínguez, *The final word? Constitutional dialogue and the Inter-American Court of Human Rights: A reply to Jorge Contesse*, 15(2) International Journal of Constitutional Law 437 (April 2017); *see generally*, Cecilia Medina Quiroga, *The American Convention on Human Rights. Crucial Rights and their Theory and Practice*, p. 32 (Intersentia, 2016).

11 *See, Almonacid Arellano et al. v. Chile, supra*, n. 10, §124.

12 *See, Velásquez Rodríguez v. Honduras*. Merits, Inter-Am. Ct. H.R. (Ser. C) No. 4 (July 29, 1988) §166.

13 *Id.* §167.

14 *See generally*, Ariel E. Dulitzky, *An Inter-American Constitutional Court? The Invention of conventionality control by the Inter-American Court of Human Rights*, 50 Tex. Int'l L. J. 57 (2015); Cristina Binder, *The Prohibition of Amnesties by the Inter-American Court of Human Rights* 12 German Law Journal 1216 (2011); Luigi Crema, "Are Amnesties Still an Option? A Non-Policy Based Critique of the Inter-American Approach", Center for Civil and Human Rights, University of Notre Dame, Working Paper Series # 6 (2013), pp. 50–51.

and purpose of the [American Convention]" in the event that the legislative power fails to comply with its duties under Article 2.[15]

Scholars have recently developed a subsidiary legal basis for the existence of conventionality control, arguing that conventionality control finds support in Article 29(b) of the Convention.[16] This article imposes the duty not to "restrict the enjoyment or exercise of any right or freedom recognized by virtue of the laws of any State Party or by virtue of another convention to which one of the said States is a party".[17] The Court has interpreted this article to establish that "if in the same situation both the American Convention and another international treaty are applicable, the rule most favorable to the individual must prevail" (*pro personae* principle),[18] and that human rights limitations

> 67. ... must be subjected to an interpretation that is strictly limited to the "just demands" of a "democratic society", which takes account of the need to balance the competing interests involved and the need to preserve the object and purpose of the Convention.[19]

Taking these elements into consideration Ferrer Mac-Gregor Poisot argued in his concurrent opinion in *Cabrera* that since all the powers of the State have an obligation to comply with the Convention (which includes an obligation to comply with Article 29), domestic judges, through their interpretations, must "allow the broadest enjoyment and exercise of the rights and freedoms protected by the Convention and its additional protocols. This, in turn, implies making restrictive interpretations whenever these treaties are being limited".[20] It follows from this reasoning that conventionality control finds support on the duty of the State authorities to always prefer the enforcement of the norm (whether

---

15 *See, Heliodoro Portugal v. Panama*. Preliminary Objections, Merits, Reparations and Costs Judgment, Inter-Am. Ct. H.R. (Ser. C) No. 186 (Aug. 12, 2008) §180; *see generally, Dismissed Congressional Employees (Aguado-Alfaro et al.)*. Preliminary Objections, Merits, Reparations and Costs Judgment, Inter-Am. Ct. H.R. (Ser. C) No. 158 (Nov. 24, 2006) §128; Paolo G. Carozza and Pablo González-Domínguez, *The final word? Constitutional dialogue and the Inter-American Court of Human Rights: A reply to Jorge Contesse*, *supra* n. 10, p. 437.

16 *See, Cabrera Garcia and Montiel Flores v. Mexico*. Preliminary Objections, Merits, Reparations and Costs Judgment, Inter-Am. Ct. H.R. (Ser. C) No. 220 (Nov. 26, 2010). Reasoned Concurrent Opinion of Eduardo Ferrer Mac-Gregor Poisot, §62; *see generally*, Susana Albanese, *La internacionalización del derecho constitucional y constitucionalización del derecho internacional*, in Susana Albanese (Ed.) *El control de convencionalidad*, p. 18 (Ediar, 2008); *see also* Claudio Nash Rojas, *Control de Convencionalidad. Cuadernillo de la Corte Interamericana de Derechos Humanos No. 7*, *supra* n. 1, p. 5.

17 Organization of American States, American Convention on Human Rights, Nov. 22, 1969, O.A.S.T.S. No. 36, 1144, U.N.T.S. 123, Art. 29(b).

18 *Compulsory Membership in an Association Prescribed by Law for the Practice of Journalism (Arts. 13 and 29 American Convention on Human Rights)*. Advisory Opinion OC-5, Inter-Am. Ct. H.R. (Ser. A) No. 5 (Nov. 13, 1985) §52.

19 *Id.* §67.

20 *See, Cabrera Garcia and Montiel Flores v. Mexico*, *supra* n. 16. Reasoned Concurrent Opinion of Eduardo Ferrer Mac-Gregor Poisot, §62.

international or domestic) or a jurisprudential standard (whether created by the Inter-American Court (ICtHR) or by a supreme court) that guarantees a better protection of human rights, and on the duty to always interpret domestic norms in a manner consistent with the legal standards (whether international or domestic) that provides a greater protection for human rights.

The legal basis of conventionality control is indeed controversial. An external observer of the Inter-American System could raise several objections based on traditional understandings of the rules and principles of public international law, particularly on the classic topic of the relationship between international law and domestic legal systems. Perhaps the strongest objection would be based on the observation that Article 2 of the American Convention must be understood in light of the ordinary meaning given to its terms and in the light of its object and purpose, which would show that that article had a programmatic nature and that no specific "necessary measure" (like conventionality control) could be potentially derived from its content. This and other potential objections to the legal basis of conventionality control require a detailed elaboration and discussion, and for that reason they are not treated in this chapter. That elaboration and discussion is the sole objective of Chapter 3 of this book.

For now it is enough to say that the *legal* basis for conventionality control – as understood by the Court until 2018 – is to be found in Articles 1.1 and 2 of the American Convention, and in Articles 26 and 27 of the Vienna Convention on the Law of Treaties. Scholars have also argued that Article 29(b) constitutes a foundation for conventionality control.

2.2. SUBJECTS OF THE OBLIGATION

2.2.1. The Judiciary, on All Its Levels

The obligation to exercise conventionality control is primarily directed to State judges, which must exercise conventionality control in order to honor – in good faith – the obligation to ensure the free and full exercise of the rights protected by the Convention, and the obligation to adopt the necessary measures to give effect to those rights and freedoms.[21] The jurisprudence of the Court, and the consensus of the most influential scholars, confirm that the language used since *Almonacid* means that the obligation to exercise conventionality control is directed at all judges that act as State authorities, regardless of their grade (i.e. first or second instance judges),[22] area of expertise (i.e. civil and criminal),[23] quantity (special

21 *See*, *Almonacid Arellano et al. v. Chile*, *supra* n. 10, §123–124.

22 *See*, *Rosendo-Cantú and other v. Mexico*, *supra* n. 8, §165 in relation to §219.

23 *See*, *Heliodoro Portugal v. Panama*, *supra* n. 15, §180 in relation to §192; *see*, *Atala Riffo and daughters v. Chile*. Merits, Reparations and Costs Judgment, Inter-Am. Ct. H.R. (Ser. C) No. 239 (Feb. 24, 2012) §182 in relation to §284.

judges that hear cases of special importance), or if they act materially as judges even if they are not formally part of the judiciary (constitutional judges, military judges, or public prosecutors).[24] It also means that it is irrelevant if the judge is part of the federal or the provincial government, which would be a consequence derived from the operation of Article 28 of the American Convention (federal clause)[25] and Article 29 of the VCLT (territorial scope of treaties).[26] Domestic judges shall guarantee the effectiveness of the Inter-American *Corpus Juris* just as the Inter-American Court exercises the same function at the international level.[27]

In *Cabrera*, the Court established that the obligation to exercise conventionality control includes not just "the Judiciary" but also "the Judiciary, at all its levels".[28] This change of language (which is better appreciated in the Spanish version of the judgment)[29] has been adopted to make clear that conventionality control

> 20. … must be carried out by *any and all judges or courts that materially perform judicial functions*, including, of course, the Courts, Chambers or Constitutional Courts, and the Supreme Courts of Justice and other high judicial bodies of the twenty-four countries have signed and ratified or acceded to the American Convention on Human Rights.[30]

---

24 *See, Rio Negro Massacres v. Guatemala.* Preliminary Objections, Merits, Reparations and Costs Judgment, Inter-Am. Ct. H.R. (Ser. C) No. 250 (Sep. 4, 2012) §262.

25 American Convention on Human Rights, *supra* n. 17, Art. 28 ("Where a State Party is constituted as a federal state, the national government of such State Party shall implement all the provisions of the Convention over whose subject matter it exercises legislative and judicial jurisdiction.").

26 *See*, United Nations, Vienna Convention on the Law of Treaties, 23 May 1969, United Nations, Treaty Series, Vol. 1155, p. 331, Art. 29 ("Unless a different intention appears from the treaty or is otherwise established, a treaty is binding upon each party in respect of its entire territory"); *see*, Sergio García Ramírez, *The Conventional Internal Control Court*, V 28 IUS Revista del Instituto de Ciencias Jurídicas de Puebla 141 (2011) (the author recalls Art. 29 of the Vienna Convention to explain that the judicial organs, as part of the State, are obligated by IHRL. For the Mexican scholar this conclusion is extended to the jurisdiction of the federal state and the provincial judges).

27 *See*, Sergio García Ramírez, *The Relationship Between Inter-American Jurisdiction and States (National Systems): Some Pertinent Questions*, 1(1) Notre Dame Journal of International and Comparative Law 123 (2015) (in the words of the author: "the Inter-American Court understood that the emerging doctrine of conventionality control would be exercised by national adjudicators, in the manner in which the Inter-American Court, by its very nature the controller of conventionality, exercised this function in the international sphere.").

28 *Cabrera Garcia and Montiel Flores v. Mexico, supra* n. 16, §225; *Gelman v. Uruguay.* Preliminary Objections, Merits, Reparations and Costs Judgment, Inter-Am. Ct. H.R. (Ser. C) No. 221 (Feb. 24, 2011) §193.

29 *Cabrera Garcia and Montiel Flores v. Mexico, supra* n. 16, §225. (The Spanish version of the case reads as follows: "*Los jueces y órganos vincunlados a la administración de justicia en todos los niveles* … ").

30 *See, Cabrera Garcia and Montiel Flores v. Mexico, supra* n. 16. Reasoned Concurrent Opinion of Eduardo Ferrer Mac-Gregor Poisot, §20.

The change of language appeared to be in anticipation of the argument that constitutional courts have no obligation to perform conventionality control because they are outside of the judicial power. Yet the Court prevented the formulation of such an argument, clarifying that every State authority materially acting as a judge has an obligation to perform conventionality control.[31]

2.2.2. All State Authorities

Since *Cabrera*, but even more expressly since *Gelman*, the Court has considered that the obligation to exercise conventionality control is not only directed at the judiciary, but that "when a State is party to an international treaty such as the American Convention, *all its organs*, including its judges and other bodies linked to the administration of justice at all levels" should exercise an *ex officio* conventionality control.[32] This was indeed an approach that constituted a radical departure from the previous criteria regarding the subjects of the obligation to exercise conventionality control. By "radical", it means that the new approach affected one of the core elements of the original understanding of the doctrine. As explained in Chapter 1, in *Almonacid* conventionality control was created primarily with the aim of specifying a duty *for the judiciary* so they would comply with their obligations under Article 1.1 by "controlling" the existence and enforcement of anti-conventional laws, and specifically those that do not allow appropriate access to justice (in terms of Article 8.1 and 25) for the victims of serious human rights violations. The doctrine was thus directed at judges because they are the authority in charge of exercising judicial review.

The language introduced by the Court since *Cabrera* and *Gelman* expands the obligation to other State authorities different than judges, a condition that creates uncertainty on how a doctrine that naturally fits in the day-to-day work of judges (especially those that have the authority to exercise judicial review), would fit in the work of the executive or the legislative. By expanding the scope of the subjects of conventionality control in such a manner, the Court logically also expanded the obligations derived from the doctrine to a totality of public officials that includes the president of a State and the legislators in a federal congress, but that in theory also includes a police officer in a small town and

31 *See*, Laurence Burgorgue-Larsen, *La Erradicación de la Impunidad: Claves para Desifrar la Política Jurisprudencial de la Corte Interamericana de Derechos Humanos*, in Eduardo Ferrer Mac-Gregor Poisot (Ed.), *El Control Difuso de la Convencionalidad. Diálogo entre la Corte Interamericana y los Jueces Nacionales*, p. 40 (Funda, 2012).

32 *Gelman v. Uruguay*, *supra* n. 28, §193 (emphasis added); *see Expelled Dominicans and Haitians v. Dominican Republic*, *supra* n. 5, §311; *see*, *Rochac Hernández et al. v. El Salvador*. Merits, Reparations and Costs Judgment, Inter-Am. Ct. H.R. (Ser. C) No. 285 (Oct. 14, 2014) §244.

a teacher in a public school. The problem with this approach is that it could weaken the distinctiveness of conventionality control, as a doctrine whose original aim was increasing the effectiveness of the *Corpus Juris* through the judicial remedies that judges could provide.

The new approach presents practical and theoretical problems because, as García Ramírez points out, it is now necessary to draw new specific lines and "to develop elaborate interpretations or candid and barely pertinent clarifications and rectifications".[33] In this point Diego García Sayán has called for "caution" in the manner that conventionality control is constructed in the Court's jurisprudence, so it is not forgotten that this doctrine is primarily directed at the judiciary.[34] This concern is legitimate because there is a danger that conventionality control is fused (or confused) with the general obligations imposed by Article 1.1, which might compromise the strength and internal logic of conventionality control as a "necessary measure" to ensure the right of access to justice.

Yet it is also possible to argue that the expansion of the "subjects" of conventionality control that has occurred since *Cabrera* and *Gelman* can be explained in light of the particular stage in the line of jurisprudence of conventionality control, and therefore that it should not be considered as controversial as it appears from the outset. In the foundational cases, conventionality control primarily required domestic judges to avoid the enforcement of domestic laws that were manifestly incompatible with the *Corpus Juris* – in order to guarantee the right of access to justice. But after the decision in *Radilla* the Court introduced the principle of consistent interpretation as part of the obligations derived from conventionality control, which is an obligation that can be fulfilled by authorities different than judges.

Thus, the most logical understanding on how domestic authorities – that do not belong to the judiciary and do not have the power to exercise judicial review – must exercise conventionality control is precisely by following the principle of consistent interpretation. It is in this *restricted sense* that a police officer in, let's say, the municipality of Aguascalientes, Mexico, must exercise conventionality control when he or she enforces an article of the municipal code of traffic regulations. The police officer would be required to "ensure" the rights and freedoms protected by the Convention, by taking the "necessary measure" (exercising conventionality control) of not enforcing a regulation in a *manner*

33 Sergio García Ramírez, *The Relationship Between Inter-American Jurisdiction and States (National Systems): Some Pertinent Questions*, *supra* n. 27, p. 144.

34 *See, Discurso pronunciado por el Juez Diego García Sayán en la inauguración del 48 periodo de sesiones de la Corte Interamericana de Derechos Humanos* (held in Mexico City, October 7–11, 2013).

that would produce a violation to the *Corpus Juris*. But only in the case that the police officer is authorized by domestic law not to enforce that regulation, would his or her obligations under conventionality control be limited to performing a consistent interpretation of the law in accordance with the *Corpus Juris*. Any domestic authority that belongs to the executive or the legislative power can do this type of interpretation without – in principle – violating the principle of the rule of law or the separation of powers.

The expansion of the subjects of conventionality control takes to its ultimate consequences the logic that the general obligations of Articles 1.1 and 2 have a direct effect on the State as a "whole" (using García Ramírez's language in *Myrna*). Because if all State authorities have the obligation to respect and ensure the rights protected by the American Convention (Article 1.1); and this obligation requires domestic authorities to take the "necessary measures" to achieve the effectiveness of Article 1.1 (Article 2); and conventionality control is a necessary measure that requires a consistent interpretation of domestic law with the American Convention; then all State authorities shall exercise conventionality control and therefore interpret domestic law in accordance with the American Convention. It is in this sense understandable that the Court reasoned that all State authorities must exercise at least a certain degree of conventionality control in their respective spheres of competences.

Yet García Ramírez could be right in pointing out that the expansion of the subjects of conventionality control requires the drawing of specific lines to define the specific obligations for different types of domestic authorities. The danger of the Court – or States – of not doing so is that it could create the impression that all State authorities must act as some kind of domestic judge, which is absurd and contrary to fundamental precepts of public law. This means that it might be good that States regulate through legislation, the manner that conventionality control shall be exercised in their jurisdiction. But, considering the above-mentioned, it is also possible to suggest that the Court's position since *Cabrera* and *Gelman* does not necessarily endanger the logic and legitimacy of conventionality control. Since *Aguado-Alfaro* conventionality control includes the notion that State authorities must always act in accordance with their competences as defined by domestic law, which means that a police officer would have to do as much as she can in order to accommodate her conduct as a police officer, but nothing more. The same can be said about judges or any other State authority.

Consequently, there is no reason to believe that the existence of an obligation for all State authorities to interpret domestic law in accordance with the *Corpus Juris* would alter the distribution of powers at the domestic level, or would damage the specificity of conventionality control as a legal institution whose main purpose is to increase the effectives of the *Corpus Juris* and the strengthening of the role of the judiciary for the protection of human rights in the States parties to the Convention.

2.3. OBJECT OF THE OBLIGATION

2.3.1. Distinguishing the "Core" and the "Periphery" of Conventionality Control

The proper understanding of the legal effects of conventionality control requires an analysis of the specific actions (acts and omissions) that domestic authorities shall execute owing to the existence of this doctrine.[35] This analysis leads to a first distinction: what we may call the "core" of the obligation, and what we may call its "peripheral" aspects. The "core" is constituted by the two conducts involved in the most common formulation of conventionality control: (1) the execution of a consistent interpretation between domestic laws and the standards contained in the *Corpus Juris*; and (2) the avoidance of the enforcement of domestic laws that cannot be interpreted in accordance with the *Corpus Juris*. The "peripheral" aspects would require other actions that include domestic authorities acting in a positive manner to fill the legal lacunae of domestic legal systems (as mentioned in *Heliodoro*); or that the legislative power controls the political choices of the majority in order to avoid the enactment of laws contrary to the *Corpus Juris* (as mentioned in *Gelman*); among others that have been – and will be – defined by the Court in its jurisprudence.

2.3.2. The "Core" of Conventionality Control

2.3.2.1. Obligation to Exercise a Consistent Interpretation of Domestic Law

The first conduct required by conventionality control is that domestic authorities perform a consistent interpretation between domestic law and the *Corpus Juris*. This means that, in case that a clause of a constitution or a statutory norm allows two or three interpretations, domestic authorities shall prefer the one that is in accordance with and not against the *Corpus Juris*.[36] The principle of consistent interpretation has been recognized in constitutional law as a way of protecting the balance between the internationalization of domestic legal systems and the compliance with domestic law.[37] For instance, the Constitutional Court of Germany adopted in *Görgülü* the principle that domestic statutory rules should

---

[35] *See generally*, Enciclopedia Jurídica, at : http://www.enciclopedia-juridica.biz14.com/d/obligaci%C3%B3n/obligaci%C3%B3n.htm (last accessed Jan. 11, 2018).

[36] *See*, Nestor Pedro Sagües, *International obligations and "conventionality control"*, 8(1) *Estudios Constitucionales*, 130 (2010); *see Cabrera Garcia and Montiel Flores v. Mexico*, *supra* n. 16. Reasoned Concurrent Opinion of Eduardo Ferrer Mac-Gregor Poisot, §41.

[37] *See generally*, Donald P. Kommers and Russell A. Miller, *The Constitutional Jurisprudence of the Federal Republic of Germany*, pp. 302–304 (Duke, 3rd ed., 2012) (on how the Constitutional Court of Germany has interpreted the Basic Law striking a balance between openness and national sovereignty: "Openness to international law, the Court has insisted, is not a suicide pact.").

be, in principle, interpreted in conformity with rules of international law, so courts would have to give compelling reasons in the case that they depart from a rule or principle of international law.[38] In a similar fashion, the Supreme Court of Justice of the United States decided, in the leading case of *Schooner Charming Betsy*, that an act of Congress ought never to be construed to violate the law of nations if any other possible construction remains.[39]

In the context of conventionality control, the duty of State authorities to exercise a consistent interpretation is independent of the compatibility between domestic law and the *Corpus Juris*. In *Radilla*, the Inter-American Court expressly established that it did not consider pertinent the modification of Article 13 of the Mexican Constitution, but only that the interpretation of that article was made in accordance with the elements of the *Corpus Juris* regarding the material and personal criteria of military jurisdiction in Mexico, specifically in accordance with the conventional and constitutional principles of due process of law and the right to a fair trial.[40] The Court explained that Article 2 of the Convention required not just the suppression or adoption of new legislation, but also the existence of State practices that lead to the effective observance of the Convention.[41] This meant that the existence of domestic legislation is not enough to comply with Article 2, it being also necessary "that the application of the regulations or their interpretation, as jurisdictional practices and a manifestation of the State's public order, be adjusted to the same purpose sought by Article 2 of the Convention".[42]

This criterion is even clearer since *Atala Riffo and daughters v. Chile* (2011), where the Court decided that judges shall interpret statutory laws in a manner consistent with the American Convention and the interpretations of the Inter-American Court, even when those laws were not *per se* incompatible with the *Corpus Juris*.[43] In *Atala*, the Court refrained from analyzing the compatibility of a particular piece of legislation and the American Convention, because it was not pertinent for the case, and because the representatives did not provide sufficient arguments that would have suggested that the violation was the result of the law *per se*.[44] The problem in that case was the *way* that domestic law was enforced by Chilean judges, which lead to the reasoning that conventionality control requires that "legal and administrative interpretations and proper judicial

38 *See*, Constitutional Court of Germany, 111 BVerfGE 307 (Görgülü), February 26, 2004; *see Id.* pp. 319–325.

39 *Murray v. The Charming Betsey*, 6 U.S. 64 (U.S. 1804).

40 *See, Radilla Pacheco v. Mexico*. Preliminary Objections, Merits, Reparations and Costs Judgment, Inter-Am. Ct. H.R. (Ser. C) No. 209 (Nov. 29, 2009) §340 and 341.

41 *Id.* §338.

42 *Ibid.*

43 *See, Atala Riffo and daughters v. Chile, supra* n. 23, §280–284.

44 *Id.* §f.

guarantees should be applied in accordance with the principles established in the jurisprudence of the Court in the present case".[45] Just like in *Radilla*, the Court focused its reasoning on how conventionality control should serve as a technique that affects the interpretation of the law, and not on the more rigid understanding that implies the non-enforcement of an anti-conventional piece of legislation.[46] Following this logic, in the *OC-24/17* the Court stated that by virtue of conventionality control, Article 54 of the Costa Rican Civil Code shall be interpreted in accordance with the standards regarding gender identity, as defined by the Court in the body of the Opinion.[47]

Scholars have classified in different ways this facet of the object of conventionality control. Nestor Pedro Sagües considers that, since *Radilla*, conventionality control has a "positive" (*positiva*) or "constructive" (*constructivo*) effect, and not just a "negative" (*negativo*) or "destructive" (*destructivo*) effect.[48] Owing to this "positive effect" local judges shall harmonize domestic law in accordance with the rules of the American Convention and the Court's jurisprudence, not being necessary to cease in the enforcement of domestic law.[49] In a similar fashion, Pablo Contreras has considered this facet as a "weak" version of conventionality control, in opposition to a "strong" version that requires not enforcing a law that is found anti-conventional.[50] Contreras also suggests that the weak version of conventionality control includes the notion of directives (*directriz*) for all State authorities, in the sense that it defines openly how political authorities (and not just judges) shall behave on a daily basis.[51] This approach is relevant to understanding the manner by which all State authorities are obligated to exercise conventionality control after the decisions of *Cabrera* and *Gelman*, particularly regarding the obligation of all State authorities to "construct" (not just control, in the strong sense of the word) the content of the

---

45 *Ibid.*

46 *Id.* §284; *see also Norín Catrimán et al. (Leaders, members and activist of the Mapuche Indigenous People) v. Chile.* Merits, Reparations and Costs Judgment, Inter-Am. Ct. H.R. (Ser. C) No. 279 (May 29, 2014) §464.

47 *See, Gender Identity, and equality and non-discrimination with regard to same-sex couples. State obligations in relation to change of name, gender identity, and rights from a relationship between same-sex couples (interpretation and scope of Articles 1(1), 3, 7, 11(2), 13, 17, 18 and 24, in relation to Article 1, of the American Convention on Human Rights.* Advisory Opinion OC-24, Inter-Am. Ct. H.R. (Ser. A) No. 14 (Nov. 24, 2017), §171; *see generally Andrade Salmón v. Bolivia.* Merits, Reparations and Costs Judgment, Inter-Am. Ct. H.R. (Ser. C) No. 330 (Dec. 1, 2016) §93.

48 *See*, Nestor Pedro Sagües, International Obligations and "Conventionality Control", *supra* n. 36, p. 130.

49 *Ibid.*

50 *See*, Pablo Contreras, *Conventionality Control, International Deference, and National Discretion in the Inter-American Court of Human Rights Case Law*, 2 Revista Ius et Praxis 254 (2014).

51 *Id.* §256.

law and judicial decisions in accordance with the norms and principles of the Inter-American *Corpus Juris*.[52]

2.3.2.2. Obligation to Avoid the Enforcement of Anti-Conventional Laws

The second conduct required by the core of the conventionality control is what has been called by Sagües the "negative" (*negativa*) or the "destructive" (*destructiva*) facet of conventionality control.[53] This facet requires State authorities not to enforce domestic laws that are manifestly incompatible with the *Corpus Juris*, of course when the State authority has the power to do so in accordance with domestic law (*see* section 2.4 of this chapter).[54] State authorities have the mission of "purging" (using García Ramírez's language) anti-conventional laws that would not allow the observance of the obligations to respect and ensure the rights protected by the *Corpus Juris*.[55] In the words of the Court:

> 123. ... when the Legislative Power fails to set aside and / or adopts laws which are contrary to the American Convention, the Judiciary is bound to honor the obligation to respect rights as stated in Article 1(1) of the said Convention, and consequently, it must *refrain from enforcing laws contrary to such Convention*.[56]

Refraining from enforcing laws contrary to the object and purpose of the Convention was indeed the first obligation defined by the Court when the doctrine of conventionality control was elaborated.[57] In *Almonacid*, the Court reasoned that the enforcement of Decree Law No. 2.191 – a self-amnesty law with "no legal effects" – was the cause for the violation of the right of Mr. Almonacid's next of kin of access to justice, truth and reparation (all of them considered as non-derogable rights in the Court's jurisprudence).[58] Following the analysis in *Barrios Altos* regarding the nullity *ab initio* of self-amnesty laws, the Court reasoned that the obligation to ensure the rights protected by the Convention (Article 1.1) required domestic judges to exercise conventionality control, which meant not to enforce Decree Law 2.191 in order to protect the rights of the victims.[59]

---

52 *Ibid.*

53 Nestor Pedro Sagües, *International Obligations and "Conventionality Control"*, *supra* n. 36, pp. 128–129.

54 *Ibid.*

55 *See generally*, Sergio García Ramírez, *The Relationship Between Inter-American Jurisdiction and States (National Systems): Some Pertinent Questions*, *supra* n. 27, p. 141.

56 *Almonacid Arellano et al. v. Chile*, *supra* n. 10, §123 (emphasis added).

57 *Id.* §123.

58 *Id.* §126.

59 *Id.* §128.

A similar approach was taken in other cases that involved the enforcement of amnesty laws that had no legal effects since their inception.[60] In *Gomez Lund et al. ("Guerrilha do Araguaia") v. Brazil* (2010), the Court asserted the lack of legal effects of those provisions of a Brazilian amnesty law that impeded the investigation and punishment of serious human rights violations.[61] The Court reasoned that the State violated the Convention by enacting the amnesty law and by failing to exercise conventionality control over that law, which ultimately produced a violation of Articles 8 and 25 in connection with Articles 1.1 and 2 of the Convention.[62] A similar approach was adopted in *Gelman*, where the Court reaffirmed the domestic authorities' obligation to exercise conventionality control "particularly dealing with cases of serious human rights violations [where] the principle of the investigation of the facts and the determination of the punishment of those responsible must prevail".[63]

The cases of transitional justice clearly show how conventionality control was conceived as a mechanism to guarantee the effectiveness of the Convention in cases where a domestic law lacks legal effects as a matter of international law. Yet this does not mean that the "negative" facet of the obligation to exercise conventionality control depends on the nullity of a specific piece of legislation. Since the decision in *Aguado-Alfaro* (decided two months after *Almonacid*) the Court has defined that domestic authorities shall exercise conventionality control over those laws that are *only* contrary to the Convention (this means that they are not null *ab initio* as a matter of international law, like certain types of amnesty laws are). Thus, it is implicit in this view that even when a specific domestic law is valid in the domestic legal system, domestic authorities shall guarantee that: "the *effet utile* of the Convention is not reduced or annulled by the application of laws contrary to its provisions, object and purpose".[64]

Therefore, since *Aguado-Alfaro*, the obligation of domestic authorities to exercise conventionality control has been considered a vehicle to "purge" domestic laws that, although anti-conventional, are still valid as a matter of constitutional and international law. This facet of the obligation to exercise conventionality control can be observed in the majority of the cases where the Court has found that a domestic norm is anti-conventional but that it does not lack legal effects. For instance, in *Boyce*, the Court found that Article 26 of the Constitution of Barbados was anti-conventional because it denied the victims

---

60 *See, Gomes Lund et al. ("Guerrilha do Araguaia") v. Brazil.* Preliminary Objections, Merits, Reparations and Costs Judgment, Inter-Am. Ct. H.R. (Ser. C) No. 219, §106 (Nov. 24, 2010) §174; *see also Gelman v. Uruguay, supra* n. 28, §232.

61 *Id.* §174.

62 *Id.* §177.

63 *Gelman v. Uruguay, supra* n. 28, §193–194.

64 *Dismissed Congressional Employees (Aguado-Alfaro et al.) v. Peru, supra* n. 2, §128; *see also Xákmok Kásek Indigenous Community. v. Paraguay, supra* n. 7, §311–312.

of the case the right to "seek judicial protection against violations of their right to life".[65] The Court found that the Judicial Committee of the Privy Council should have avoided the enforcement of Article 26 by exercising conventionality control, in order to comply with its obligations under Article 2 and 1.1 of the Convention, and specifically their obligation to ensure the right to a judicial remedy.[66]

2.3.3. *The "Periphery" of Conventionality Control*

The Court's jurisprudence shows that the obligation of domestic authorities to exercise conventionality control also requires other type of conduct. We may call these conducts the "peripheral" aspects of the object of the obligation to exercise conventionality control, since they have been defined by the Court responding to a specific set of circumstances in concrete cases. In these cases, the Court has considered that the obligation of domestic authorities to exercise conventionality control includes other "measures" to guarantee the effectiveness of the *Corpus Juris*, but these measures appear to be contingent – and therefore not essential to the requirements of conventionality control as a general doctrine. Three types of conduct can be included in this list: (1) the obligation to fill legal lacunae; (2) the obligation of the legislative power to control the creation of domestic norms; and (3) the obligation to guarantee the effectiveness of the Court's judgments.

2.3.3.1. Obligation to Fill Legal Lacunae

The first peripheral conduct is that domestic authorities must act positively and fill legal lacunae in domestic criminal law, in order to prosecute those responsible for the crime of forced disappearance of persons.[67] This facet of conventionality control has only been mentioned in the narrow context of cases where the State failed to comply with its obligations to define, in its domestic legislation, the forced disappearance of persons as an autonomous criminal offense, which is an obligation derived from Article III of the Inter-American Convention on Forced Disappearance of Persons (IACFDP). In these cases, States failed to develop effective criminal norms that encompass the constituent elements of the forced disappearance of persons as defined since *Velásquez*, where the Court acknowledges the gravity, complexity and necessity to confront

---

65 *Boyce et al. v. Barbados*, *supra* n. 7, §79.

66 *Id.* §78–80.

67 *See*, María Carmelina Londoño Lázaro, *The Legality Principle and the Conventionality Control: Confluences and Developments in the Inter-American Court of Human Rights*, 128 Boletin Mexicano de Derecho Comparado 809 (2010).

this crime in an integral fashion.[68] Article III of the IACFDP establishes the following:

> The States Parties undertake to adopt, in accordance with their constitutional procedures, the legislative measures that may be needed to define the forced disappearance of persons as an offense and to impose an appropriate punishment commensurate with its extreme gravity. This offense shall be deemed continuous or permanent as long as the fate or whereabouts of the victim has not been determined.[69]

The cases where the Court took this approach are *Heliodoro* and *Ibsen Cárdenas and Ibsen Peña v. Bolivia*.[70] On both occasions domestic courts failed to appropriately prosecute those responsible for forced disappearances owing to a lack of legislation, which in itself constituted a violation of Article III of the IACFDP, as well as a violation of the rights of the victims and their relatives. Hence, the Court considered that judges must act positively to remedy the failure of the legislative power in order to comply with its obligations under the IACFDP, and thus:

> 183. ... [f]aced with the imperative of avoiding impunity in cases of forced disappearance, when this has not been defined as an autonomous offense, the State must use all the penal resources available to it that relate to protecting the fundamental rights that may be affected in such cases.[71]

2.3.3.2. Obligation to Control the Democratic Process

The second peripheral conduct is that the legislative power must exercise conventionality control in order to avoid the enactment of anti-conventional laws. In *Gelman*, the Court determined that the existence of democratic regimes does not guarantee *per se* the fulfillment of the State's international obligations under Article 2, even when they create laws that reflect the desires and convictions of the majority as represented in congress or by referendum. The Court reasoned that democratic legitimacy in a society is limited by the framework of the protection for human rights recognized by the American Convention.[72] So truly democratic regimes find in international law a formal

---

68 *See, Velásquez Rodríguez v. Honduras, supra* n. 12, §181.

69 Organization of American States (OAS), Inter-American Convention on Forced Disappearance of Persons, 9 June 1994, Adopted at Belém do Pará, on 9 June 1994, at the twenty-fourth regular session of the General Assembly of the OAS.

70 *See, Heliodoro Portugal v. Panama, supra* n. 7, §180; *see also Ibsen Cárdenas and Ibsen Peña v. Bolivia*. Merits, Reparation and Costs Judgment, Inter-Am. Ct. H.R. (Ser. C) No. 217 (Sep. 1, 2010) §198–202.

71 *See, Heliodoro Portugal v. Panama, supra* n. 7, §183.

72 *Gelman v. Uruguay, supra* n. 28, §239.

and a substantive limit on what can be decided by majorities in a democratic instance (such as the legislative power).[73]

On this theoretical basis, the Court stated that the adoption of amnesty laws that allow impunity for serious human rights violations are outside the limits of democratic deliberation, and in this sense the legislative power (and not just the judiciary) should exercise conventionality control and avoid the adoption of laws that would be anti-conventional.[74] This approach seeks to make the *Corpus Juris* a directive (*directriz*) for domestic authorities in the creation of new laws, just as a constitutional text serves as a basis – and a limit – for congresses on their decisions. In the words of the Court in *Gelman*:

> 238. The fact that the Expiry Law of the State has been approved in a democratic regime and yet ratified or supported by the public, on two occasions, namely, through the exercise of direct democracy, does not automatically or by itself grant legitimacy under International Law.[75]

2.3.3.3. Obligation to Guarantee the Effectiveness of the Inter-American Court's Judgments

The third peripheral conduct is connected with the obligation of domestic authorities to ensure the effectiveness of the Court's judgments in any case where the State is a party to a controversy. This facet of the obligation has been mentioned in the *Resolution of Compliance with Gelman*, where the Court established that the obligation of domestic authorities to exercise conventionality control "has a relevant role in the compliance or implementation of a judgment of the Inter-American Court, especially when that compliance is in charge of domestic judges".[76] The Court reasoned that all State authorities have an obligation to comply with the judgment of the Court in terms of Article 68.1 of the Convention.[77] This means that they are obligated to guarantee that the effectiveness of the decisions of the Court are not affected by the enforcement of norms contrary to the object and purpose of the treaty.[78] Therefore,

> 68. … precisely because conventionality control is an institution that serves as an instrument for implementing international law, in this case where there is *res judicata* it merely requires using it to comply in full and in good faith with the order in the judgment of the Court in the case, so it would be incongruous to use that tool as justification

---

73 *Ibid.*
74 *Ibid.*
75 *Id.* §238.
76 *Gelman v. Uruguay*. Monitoring Compliance with the Judgment, *supra* n. 3, §73.
77 *Id.* §68.
78 *Ibid.*

> for failure to comply [with the Convention], in accordance with was stated above (*supra* 60–65).[79]

This facet of conventionality control presupposes the direct effect of Article 68.1 of the Convention. This approach is another manifestation of the view that States are obligated by the Convention as "a whole", which means that it is not the State as a legal entity that shall comply with the international obligations of the State in terms of Article 68.1, but it is each domestic authority that is obligated to guarantee the effectiveness of the Court's judgments when they have the character of *res judicata*. So the criterion of the *Resolution of Compliance with Gelman* seems to suggest that the obligation of domestic authorities to exercise conventionality control is even stronger when there is a judgment against a particular State, because in this circumstance domestic authorities are obligated to "control" domestic norms not just because they have obligations on the basis of Articles 1.1 and 2, but also by virtue of Article 68.1 of the Convention.[80]

2.4. SPECIAL FEATURES OF THE OBLIGATION TO EXERCISE CONVENTIONALITY CONTROL: THE "*AGUADO-ALFARO* CLAUSE"

2.4.1. Conventionality Control Shall Be Exercised Ex Officio

One of the most relevant and controversial characteristics of the doctrine of conventionality control is that it requires domestic authorities to exercise conventionality control *ex officio*.[81] This characteristic has been considered as an aspect of the principle of *iura novit curia* (the judge knows the law and jurisprudence of the Convention), meaning that all judges should be aware of the content of the relevant rules and principles of the *Corpus Juris*, and that they must enforce these rules and principles every time they are able to do so in order to guarantee the effectiveness of the Convention "regardless of whether the parties invoked it".[82] Hence, domestic authorities are expected to take a strong *pro victim* approach and avoid excessive formalisms that leave victims of human rights violations without judicial protection.[83] They must exercise a consistent

---

79 *Ibid.*

80 *See, Cabrera Garcia and Montiel Flores v. Mexico, supra* n. 16. Reasoned Concurrent Opinion of Eduardo Ferrer Mac-Gregor Poisot, §63; *see generally*, Oswaldo Ruiz-Chiriboga, *The Conventionality Control: Examples of (Un)successful Experiences in Latin America*, 3(1–2) Inter-American and European Human Rights Journal 204 (2010).

81 *See, Dismissed Congressional Employees (Aguado-Alfaro et al.) v. Peru. supra* n. 2, §128.

82 *Cabrera Garcia and Montiel Flores v. Mexico, supra* n. 16. Reasoned Concurrent Opinion of Eduardo Ferrer Mac-Gregor Poisot, §42.

83 However, it is reasonable to expect that domestic judges should act *ex officio* under the rules that the Inter-American Court has previously established regarding the operation of

interpretation of domestic law with the Inter-American *Corpus Juris*, and – if possible – cease in the enforcement of those domestic laws that are manifestly incompatible with the obligations of the State in terms of Articles 1.1 and 2.

In *Aguado Alfaro* (for a description of this case *see* section 3.2.1), the Court evaluated a limitation imposed by a domestic piece of Peruvian legislation that prohibited challenging the effects that the law had on those affected by its existence. The Court considered that this law constituted a violation of the right to a genuine and effective access to justice, and therefore that it was incompatible with Articles 8.1, 25, 1.1 and 2.[84] Therefore, in the Court's view, the Lima Supreme Court of Justice (LSCJ), and the Constitutional Court of Peru (CCP), should have evaluated the merits of the claims presented by the victims of the case, even when the *amparo* actions may have expired on procedural considerations.[85] The LSCL and the CCP had the authority not to enforce that law, so they should have taken a *pro victim* approach and blocked the enforcement of procedural norms that served as a basis for the dismissal of the employees' petitions in violation of the rights of the victims.[86]

2.4.2. The "Aguado-Alfaro *Clause*"

It is true that this aspect of conventionality control potentially enters in conflict with those domestic legal systems that – for instance – do not recognize the *iura novit curia* principle, or those that give privilege to the principle that a court cannot award a party more than a person has claimed, and that a court can base its decisions only on the allegations made by the parties.[87] Yet the tensions derived from the operation of this principle are partly reconciled when analyzed in conjunction with another fundamental element of the doctrine of conventionality control: domestic authorities must exercise conventionality control "in the context of their respective competences and the corresponding procedural regulations".[88] This phrase is what this chapter calls the "*Aguado-Alfaro* clause". This clause does not attempt to question the existence of the obligation of domestic authorities to exercise conventionality control *ex officio*,

---

the principle of *iura novit curia. See generally, Fermín Ramírez v. Guatemala.* Judgment, Inter-Am. Ct. H.R. (Ser. C) No. 126 (Jun. 20, 2005) §74.

84 *See, Dismissed Congressional Employees (Aguado-Alfaro et al.) v. Peru, supra* n. 2, §119.

85 *Id.* §126.

86 *Id.* §128.

87 *See generally*, Paolo G. Carozza, *The Anglo-Latin Divide and the Future of the Inter-American System of Human Rights*, 5(1) Notre Dame Journal of International and Comparative Law 161 (2015) (on how common law countries have a much more restricted view of the *iura novit curia* principle than countries with a civil law tradition).

88 *Dismissed Congressional Employees (Aguado-Alfaro et al.) v. Peru, supra* n. 2, §128.

but it seeks to "calibrate" its "intensity" in a manner that the operation of the *Corpus Juris* can be harmonized with domestic law.[89]

In other terms, the "*Aguado-Alfaro* clause" is the solution that the Court found to determine a limit to the obligation of domestic authorities to exercise conventionality control *ex officio*. So even when domestic authorities must take a strong *pro victim* approach, they cannot act beyond the powers conferred on them by domestic law, or disregard the procedural regulations that shape the judicial process.[90] And indeed this element could not be absent from the design of the doctrine, since the Court has no authority to confer powers and attributions on domestic authorities, and since the formalities of judicial procedures are not just consistent with the obligations of States under the American Convention. They are also necessary to protect other important values like the existence of legal certainty, the proper and functional administration of justice, and the effective judicial protection of human rights.[91]

For this reason, it is possible to say that the doctrine of conventionality control – in principle – leaves untouched the competence for States to decide how they organize the powers and attributions of domestic authorities (for instance if there is a diffuse or concentrated system of judicial review), and on the type of formalities for the admissibility and substantiation of legal remedies (which are usually determined by procedural codes, or more generally by procedural constitutional law).[92] The design of conventionality control on this point allows its adaptation to different legal systems, both in terms of *who* shall exercise conventionality control (particularly in its "negative" facet) and on *how* it must be exercised.[93] In other words, the *Aguado-Alfaro* clause leaves a margin of appreciation for States to decide the "intensity" of the obligation

89 *See*, *Cabrera Garcia and Montiel Flores v. Mexico*, *supra* n. 16. Reasoned Concurrent Opinion of Eduardo Ferrer Mac-Gregor Poisot, §35; *see*, Sergio García Ramírez, *The Conventional Internal Control Court*, *supra* n. 26, at 152.

90 For this reason, it is inaccurate to argue that the doctrine of conventionality control is intended to confer "attributions" on judges, or to automatically modify the rules of the procedure, as some authors have argued. *See generally*, Ernesto Rey Cantor, *Control de la Convencionalidad de Leyes y Derechos Humanos*, p. 46 (Porrúa, 2008); Ernesto Jiniesta, *Control de Convencionalidad Ejercido por los Tribunales y Salas Constitucionales*, in *El Control Difuso de la Convencionalidad. Diálogo entre la Corte Interamericana y los Jueces Nacionales* pp. 277–278 (Funda, 2012); Jorge Contesse, *The Final Word? Constitutional Dialogue and the Inter-American Court of Human Rights*, 15(2) International Journal of Constitutional Law 415 (2017).

91 *Dismissed Congressional Employees (Aguado-Alfaro et al.) v. Peru*, *supra* n. 2, §126; *see*, Sergio García Ramírez, *The Conventional Internal Control Court*, *supra* n. 26, pp. 141 and 142.

92 *See*, María Carmelina Londoño Lázaro, *The Legality Principle and the Conventionality Control: Confluences and Developments in the Inter-American Court of Human Rights*, *supra* n. 67, p. 806.

93 Sergio García Ramírez, *The Conventional Internal Control Court*, *supra* n. 26, p. 151.

to exercise conventionality control.[94] Connected with this point, the Court recently established in *Liakat Ali Alibux v. Suriname* (2014) that:

> 124. Finally, in relation to the arguments of the representative and the Commission (*supra* paras. 112 and 113) on the violation of the right to judicial protection due to the absence of a Constitutional Court, although the Court recognizes the importance of such bodies as protectors of constitutional mandates and fundamental rights, the American Convention does not impose a specific model for the regulation of issues of constitutionality and control for conformity (sic) with the Convention. In this sense, the Court recalls that the obligation to monitor the compliance between domestic legislation and the American Convention is delegated to all bodies of the State, including its judges and other mechanisms related to the administration of justice at all levels.[95]

Consequently, in domestic legal systems where State authorities (especially judges) have more attributions and powers to exercise judicial review, and where there is more freedom to operate under the principle of *iura novit curia*, the obligation to exercise conventionality control is more "intense" (using Ferrer Mac-Gregor Poisot's language) than in systems where domestic judges have less attributions and/or where procedural regulations are stricter.[96] So the most reasonable reading of conventionality control is that it does not require a particular system of judicial review (for instance, diffuse or concentrated), although there might be some controversy regarding what States *should* do to make the doctrine (and in general human rights) more effective at the domestic level.[97] Some might argue that the States should adopt a system of diffuse judicial review, and others might consider that States have complete freedom to decide what system of judicial review is better for their particular circumstances. What is relevant here is that the doctrine of conventionality control – as it was originally designed, and remains today – does not seek to impose a particular view on how the attributions of domestic authorities should be distributed.

The "*Aguado-Alfaro* clause" is a fundamental element for the proper understanding of the nature of conventionality control (that recognizes important spaces of freedom for States to decide the "intensity" of the obligation), and therefore not paying proper attention to this element creates the risk of misunderstanding the original design of the doctrine of conventionality control. For instance, Ariel E. Dulitzky qualifies the formula introduced by the Court

---

94 *See, Cabrera Garcia and Montiel Flores v. Mexico, supra* n. 16. Reasoned Concurrent Opinion of Eduardo Ferrer Mac-Gregor Poisot, §34–40.

95 *Liakat Ali Alibux v. Suriname*, Preliminary Objections, Merits, Reparations and Costs Judgment, Inter-Am. Ct. H.R. (Ser. C) No. 276 (Jan. 30, 2014) §124.

96 *See, Cabrera Garcia and Montiel Flores v. Mexico, supra* n. 16. Reasoned Concurrent Opinion of Eduardo Ferrer Mac-Gregor Poisot, §36–37; *see*, Nestor Pedro Sagües, *International Obligations and "Conventionality Control", supra* n. 36, p. 121; *see*, Sergio García Ramírez, *The Conventional Internal Control Court, supra* n. 26, pp. 151–152.

97 *See*, Sergio García Ramírez, *The Conventional Internal Control Court, supra* n. 26, p. 152.

since *Aguado-Alfaro* as a "simplistic" solution to the operation of conventionality control in countries where tribunals are not authorized to perform judicial review or conventionality control, or where there is a system of concentrated constitutional control, or where judges are forbidden to resolve more than what was requested by the parties.[98] For the Argentinean scholar, conventionality control fails to consider these relevant questions with its design, which calls for the supremacy of international law, the direct implementation of the *Corpus Juris* and the existence of a system of diffuse constitutionality and conventionality control by domestic judges.

Yet, these are precisely some of the questions that the "*Aguado-Alfaro* clause" tries to solve: so yes, judges must take a *pro victim* approach (they shall do as much as they can to protect human rights), and cease in the enforcement of domestic laws that are anti-conventional; but they must also act within the circle of authority that domestic law recognizes, and they must respect the procedural regulations that shape the judicial process. Therefore, it is possible to say that if a domestic tribunal is not authorized to exercise judicial review by domestic law (in its negative face, following Sagües' categories), then it cannot refrain from enforcing another domestic law even if that law happens to be anti-conventional; or if a State has a system of concentrated conventionality control, then conventionality control (in its negative face) must be exercised only by those courts that have the power to exercise judicial review.

In connection with this discussion, García Ramírez explained, since his concurrent opinion in *Aguado-Alfaro*, that conventionality control (in its negative face) could have a diffuse nature, which means that it could be in the hands of all the courts when they have to decide cases in which the provisions of international human rights treaties are applicable.[99] But the Mexican jurist has always interpreted his own words – and those of the Court – in the sense that the doctrine of conventionality control does not seek to impose a uniform system of judicial review for all the States parties of the Convention, but that:

> It is perfectly possible, in my view, that the legal order recognizes specific powers (that might be conceptualized in "degrees" of competence) for the performance of the control [of conventionality] and the force of the domestic judicial decisions in that sense.[100]

98 *See*, Ariel E. Dulitzky, *An Inter-American Constitutional Court? The Invention of conventionality control by the Inter-American Court of Human Rights*, *supra* n. 14, pp. 60–61.

99 *See*, *Dismissed Congressional Employees (Aguado-Alfaro et al.) v. Peru*, *supra* n. 2, Reasoned Concurrent Opinion of Sergio García Ramírez, §12.

100 Sergio García Ramírez, *The Conventional Internal Control Court*, *supra* n. 26, p. 151; *see*, Paolo G. Carozza and Pablo González-Domínguez; *The final word? Constitutional dialogue and the Inter-American Court of Human Rights: A reply to Jorge Contesse, International Journal of Constitutional Law*, *supra* n. 10, p. 438.

2.5. PARAMETERS OF CONVENTIONALITY CONTROL

2.5.1. Domestic Laws Subject to Conventionality Control

The doctrine of conventionality control requires domestic authorities to ensure that the American Convention is not adversely affected by the enforcement of "laws" that are contrary to its object and purpose.[101] The writings of scholars that have reflected on this particular point show that the notion of "laws" includes every juridical norm of general character, which means that conventionality control must be exercised on all kinds of norms that are part of the domestic legal system, such as statutory laws, constitutional norms, decrees, rules of procedure etc.[102] In this sense, the Court has decided that domestic authorities must exercise conventionality control over constitutional norms in *Boyce* and *Radilla*;[103] over Decree-Laws in *Almonacid*[104] and *Aguado-Alfaro*;[105] and over statutory norms in *Gelman*;[106] just to mention some examples. It is logical to expect that these criteria would also be extended to other types of domestic norms contrary to the *Corpus Juris*, no matter if their origin is the legislative, executive or even if it comes from the judiciary – for instance in the case of the judgments of high courts that are binding as general norms, as the Court suggested in the case of *Expelled Dominicans and Haitians v. Dominican Republic* (2014).[107]

Of course, this type of approach is not free from controversy. Asking domestic authorities to "control" the "conventionality" of every juridical norm (including constitutional norms and the jurisprudence of supreme courts) could be contrary to the principle of constitutional supremacy and the rule of law, which are structural principles in domestic legal systems of the States parties to the Convention. So the tension about this point is obvious, since it ignores the theories and norms that regulate the relationship between international and domestic law. Perhaps for this reason some scholars – and the IACtHR itself, for instance in *Boyce* – have suggested that the obligation to perform

101 *See, Almonacid Arellano et al. v. Chile, supra* n. 10, §124 (the ICtHR stated that "the Judiciary is bound to honor the obligation to respect rights as stated in Article 1(1) of the said Convention, and consequently, it must refrain from enforcing any laws contrary to such Convention".)

102 *See*, Nestor Pedro Sagües, *International Obligations and Conventionality Control, supra* n. 36, p. 124.

103 *See, Radilla Pacheco v. Mexico, supra* n. 40, §340; *Boyce et al. v. Barbados, supra* n. 7, §77.

104 *See, Almonacid Arellano et al. v. Chile, supra* n. 10, §126.

105 *See, Dismissed Congressional Employees (Aguado-Alfaro et al.) v. Peru, supra* n. 2, §127.

106 *See, Gelman v. Uruguay, supra* n. 28, §239.

107 *See, Expelled Dominicans and Haitians v. Dominican Republic, supra* n. 5, §325; *see generally*, Juan Carlos Hitters, *Constitutional Control and Conventionality Control. Comparison (Criteria Established by the Inter-American Court of Human Rights)*, 7(2) Constitutional Studies 120 (2009).

conventionality control over constitutional norms is justified because the American Convention has some sort of supremacy over rules of domestic origin.[108] If this is true, then there is no contradiction between the doctrine of conventionality control and the principle of constitutional supremacy: it actually constitutes a denial of the principle of constitutional supremacy and an assertion of the supremacy of the *Corpus Juris* – in a pure and extreme form of monism.

Nevertheless, as it is discussed later in this chapter (*see* section 3), and in the next chapters (*see* Chapters 3 and 4), assuming the supremacy of the *Corpus Juris* does not find support in the most common understanding of the normative force of international law, not even in the context of the constitutional law of the States parties to the American Convention.[109] There are reasons and evidence to argue that the relationship between international law and domestic legal systems does not work in a monist manner, and that it is still the case that international law and domestic law are both supreme in their respective spheres of application.[110] If this is true then domestic authorities shall exercise conventionality control following the hierarchy that constitutional law confers on the different elements of the *Corpus Juris*, always applying the principle of consistent interpretation in order to avoid – as much as possible – that domestic laws overrule treaty obligations. This point requires further elaboration (which is done later in this book),[111] so here it is enough to say that conventionality

---

108 *See*, Ernesto Jiniesta, *Control de Convencionalidad Ejercido por los Tribunales y Salas Constitucionales*, in *El Control Difuso de la Convencionalidad. Diálogo entre la Corte Interamericana y los Jueces Nacionales*, *supra* n. 90, p. 281.

109 e.g. the decision of the Supreme Court of Justice of Argentina in the decision CSJ 368/1998 (34-M)/CS1 (2017), and the decision of the Supreme Court of Justice of Uruguay in the Judgment No. 20 (2013), shows that even when there is wide openness to the enforcement of international law at the domestic level, some States still consider that they are not bound to follow the decisions of the Inter-American Court when this would constitute a violation of their constitutions. *See*, Supreme Court of Justice of Argentina, Judgment CSJ 368/1998 (34-M)/CS1 (*Ministerio de Relaciones Exteriores y Cultos/ informe sentencia dictada en el caso Fontevecchia y D'Amico v. Argentina por la Corte Interamericana de Derechos Humanos*), Feb 14, 2017; Supreme Court of Justice of Uruguay, Judgment No. 20 (*Excepción de Inconstitucionalidad Arts. 1, 2 y 3 de la Ley No. 18.831, IUE 2-109971/2011*), Feb 22, 2013; *see*, Dissenting Opinion of Judge Carlos Fayt in Supreme Court of Justice of Argentina, M. 2333. XLII (Mazzeo, Julio Lilo *et al.*, Appeal for annulment and constitutional motion), Jul. 13, 2007, §16, 18, 30, 31 (in the view of minister Fayt in *Mazzeo*, the reopening of criminal investigations would derive in a violation of the principle of double jeopardy and the principle of legality, both highly protected by the Constitution of Argentina).

110 *See*, Dinah Shelton, *International Law and Domestic Legal Systems*, p. 3 (Oxford University Press, 2011) (the author explains that although there is a debate as to whether international law is supreme over domestic legal systems, the starting point is that it is for the State to organize its legal system and determine the process for giving its consent to be bound by norms of international law).

111 *See*, chapter 4, section 4.3.2

control must be exercised on each domestic law of the States parties to the American Convention in accordance with their constitutional systems of law (*see*, section 3.2).

2.5.2. Sources of Law that Serve as a Basis for Conventionality Control

The doctrine of conventionality control aims to increase the use of international human rights law at the domestic level, particularly the American Convention and the interpretations of the Inter-American Court.[112] It provides State authorities with a juridical instrument to use their powers and attributions in order to avoid that the enforcement of anti-conventional laws is the cause of human rights violations. But one may ask: What are the specific sources of international law that domestic authorities shall use to "control" the "conventionality" of domestic laws, either in its positive or its negative facet (following Sagües' categories)? This is a particularly relevant question because there is some obscurity as to what the rules and principles are exactly that State authorities shall follow as parameters for conventionality control, and because there has not been too much academic discussion on how the different degrees of obligatoriness of the treaties and the Court's interpretations - considered as sources of international law - could affect the use of these sources of law. The following paragraphs contribute to answer some aspects of these questions.

2.5.2.1. Treaty Law

Since *Almonacid* it has been clear that the first parameter for conventionality control is the American Convention. The Court established in paragraph 124 of this judgment that:

> 124. ... when a State has ratified an international treaty such as the American Convention, its judges, as part of the State, are also bound by such Convention. This forces them to see that all the effects of the *provisions embodied in the Convention* are not adversely affected by the enforcement of laws which are contrary to its purposes and that have not had any legal effects since their inception.[113]

Therefore, as explained in Chapter 1, section 3.3, in the Court's view, the American Convention has some kind of direct effect on State authorities. This means that conventionality control shall be exercised considering the rights recognized in the text of the treaty, and - presumably - as much as these rights

112 *See*, *Gelman v. Uruguay*. Monitoring Compliance with the Judgment, *supra* n. 3, §65.
113 *Almonacid Arellano et al. v. Chile*, *supra* n. 10, §124 (emphasis added).

are binding as a matter of international law (considering, for instance, if there are reservations or declarations made by States).

But the American Convention is not the only source of treaty law that serves as a parameter for conventionality control. After *Aguado-Alfaro*, García Ramírez reasoned that conventionality control must be exercised on the basis of other treaties with the same nature as the American Convention, meaning that judges should exercise conventionality control taking into account the rights recognized in other human rights treaties and protocols of the Inter-American System.[114] The list of these instruments include the Additional Protocol to the American Convention on Human Rights in the Area of Economic, Social and Cultural Rights "Protocol of San Salvador", the Inter-American Convention on the Prevention, Punishment and Eradication of Violence against Women "Convention of Belem do Para" and the Inter-American Convention on the Elimination of All Forms of Discrimination against Persons, among others.[115]

The practice of the Court also supports this proposition. For instance, in *Heliodoro* and *Ibsen*, the Court referred to the obligation of domestic judges to exercise conventionality control to comply with the State obligations derived from Article III of the Inter-American Convention on Forced Disappearance of Persons. In this view the State had to use all the penal resources available in order to prosecute and punish those responsible for the crime of the forced disappearance of persons.[116] A similar approach was followed in *Rio Negro Massacre*, and in *Gudiel Alvarez et al. ("Diario Militar") v. Guatemala* (2012), where the Court stated the following:

> 261. [T]his Court has established in its case law that when a State is a party to international treaties such as the American Convention on Human Rights, the Inter-American Convention on Forced Disappearances, the Inter-American Convention to Prevent and Punish Torture, and the Convention Belém do Pará, these treaties are binding on all its organs, including the Judiciary, whose members must ensure that the effects of the provisions of the said treaties are not impaired by the application of laws or interpretations contrary to their object and purpose.[117]

---

114 *See, Dismissed Congressional Employees (Aguado-Alfaro et al.) v. Peru, supra* n. 2, Reasoned Concurrent Opinion of Sergio García Ramírez, §2; *see also Cabrera Garcia and Montiel Flores v. Mexico, supra* n. 16. Reasoned Concurrent Opinion of Eduardo Ferrer Mac-Gregor Poisot, §45; *see generally*, Juan Carlos Hitters, *Constitutional Control and Conventionality Control. Comparison (Criteria Established by the Inter-American Court of Human Rights), supra* n. 107, p. 120; *see*, Nestor Pedro Sagües, *International Obligations and "Conventionality Control", supra* n. 36, p. 126.

115 To see a full list of the instruments of the Inter-American System, *see*, http://www.corteidh.or.cr/index.php/en/about-us/instrumentos.

116 *See, Heliodoro Portugal v. Panama, supra* n. 7, §183.

117 *Gudiel Alvarez et al. ("Diario Militar") v. Guatemala.* Merits, Reparations and Costs Judgment, Inter-Am. Ct. H.R. (Ser. C) No. 253 (May 25, 2010) §330; *see, Rio Negro Massacres v. Guatemala, supra* n. 24, §261.

2.5.2.2. The Jurisprudence of the Inter-American Court

There is less clarity – perhaps because there is much more controversy – regarding what the Court meant when it established that "[t]o perform this task [conventionality control], the Judiciary *has to take into account not only the treaty, but also the interpretation thereof made by the Inter-American Court*, which is the ultimate interpreter of the American Convention".[118]

The controversy surrounding the language used by the Court in paragraph 124 of *Almonacid* starts from considerations about the existence of an obligation for States – and even more, an obligation for domestic authorities of those States – to enforce the judgments of the Court in cases where they are not parties to a controversy.[119]

The problem with this view comes from the traditional understanding that the judgments of international courts are subsidiary means for the determination of rules of law, which means that only norms contained in treaties, custom and general principles of law, are (strictly speaking) sources of rights and obligations at the international level. Yet the doctrine of conventionality control seems to assume that the judgments of the Inter-American Court are autonomous sources of law, since they develop the meaning and scope of the rights protected by the American Convention and other treaties of a similar nature. So, in this view, once the Court interprets a treaty, domestic authorities must exercise conventionality control on the basis of treaty law and taking into account those interpretations made by the Court.

García Ramírez explained the basis of this approach since his concurrent opinion in *Aguado-Alfaro*. The Mexican jurist argued that, since States gave authority to the Court to interpret and enforce the American Convention, this means that "the Court possesses the capacity to define the meaning and scope of the corresponding norms, not only for purposes of a concrete case, but also for all hypotheses arising from the case".[120] So "once the 'interpretation and application criteria' has been established [by the Court], the States will include them in their legal system, through policies, laws and judgments that give transcendence, universality and effectiveness to the rulings of the Court".[121]

---

118 *See, Almonacid Arellano et al. v. Chile, supra* n. 10, §124 (emphasis added).

119 The American Convention does not recognize a system of precedents, and it is generally accepted that the decisions or international courts are binding just for the parties of a concrete dispute. *See*, American Convention on Human Rights, *supra* n. 17, Art. 68.

120 Sergio García Ramírez, *The Relationship Between Inter-American Jurisdiction and States (National Systems): Some Pertinent Questions, supra* n. 27, p.136; *see, Dismissed Congressional Employees (Aguado-Alfaro et al.) v. Peru, supra* n. 2, Reasoned Concurrent Opinion of Sergio García Ramírez, §7; *see generally, Cabrera Garcia and Montiel Flores v. Mexico, supra* n. 16. Reasoned Concurrent Opinion of Eduardo Ferrer Mac-Gregor Poisot, §59.

121 *See, Dismissed Congressional Employees (Aguado-Alfaro et al.) v. Peru*, Reasoned Concurrent Opinion of Sergio García Ramírez, *supra* n. 2, §8.

The reason that justifies the obligation of States to incorporate the decisions of the Inter-American Court may be called a practical solution to the fact that the decisions of the Court are subject to the principle of relativity (borrowing the language of *amparo* trials), so:

> 8. In keeping with the jurisdictional logic that underpins the Court's establishment and operation, it could not be considered that it would need to hear hundreds or thousands of cases on a single treaty-based issue – which would involve an enormous neglect of the individual – in other words, all the litigations that are ever filed in all the countries, resolving one by one the facts that violate rights, and guaranteeing, also one by one, the specific rights and freedoms.[122]

The legal basis to affirm the binding character of the judgments of the Inter-American Court beyond concrete cases might come from an interpretation of Articles 62.3 and 67 of the American Convention. These articles recognize that

> [t]he jurisdiction of the Court shall comprise all cases concerning the interpretation and application of the provisions of this Convention that are submitted to it, provided that the States Parties to the case recognize or have recognized such jurisdiction, whether by special declaration pursuant to the preceding paragraphs, or by special agreement (Article 62.3),

and that

> [t]he judgment of the Court shall be final and no subject to appeal (Article 67).

One possible reading of these articles is that the fact that the Court has the jurisdiction to interpret the Convention in "last instance", means that its decisions are highly authoritative beyond any particular cases, which means that its decisions must be implemented by State authorities.

It is true that the understanding of the Court's jurisprudence with normative value beyond the case where the decision was taken responds more to the practical need to increase the effectiveness of human rights at the domestic level and prevent future human rights violations,[123] than on a criterion based on a well-settled rule of international law. Yet this understanding is consistent with the practice of litigation at the international level, in the sense that the previous judgments of the Court are usually considered highly authoritative sources

---

122 *Id.* §8.

123 *Ibid*; *see*, *Gelman v. Uruguay.* Monitoring Compliance with the Judgment, *supra* n. 3, Reasoned Concurrent Opinion Eduardo Ferrer Mac-Gregor Poisot, §31–33.

of law in the procedures decided by the institutions of the Inter-American System.[124] The doctrine of conventionality control expands this practice to the domestic level. It follows the notion that domestic courts are directly bound by the American Convention, and therefore that they should avoid the international responsibility of the State being compromised owing to the enforcement of anti-conventional laws, especially those that have been already declared as such by the Court.

That being said – and acknowledging that the discussion on this point is far from being over – it is necessary to explain *which* interpretations must be taken into account by domestic authorities when exercising conventionality control and to what degree. The opinion of judges and scholars on this point is that the normative criterions that are relevant for the exercise of conventionality control include those that arise from every interpretation that the ICtHR makes of any treaty of the Inter-American System.[125] This means that the interpretations reflected on judgments, provisional measures, interpretation of the judgments, monitoring compliance with judgments, and advisory opinions are directly binding on State authorities, and therefore that they are parameters for conventionality control.

In the *Resolution of Compliance with Gelman*, the Court emphasized that its jurisprudence is binding at two levels: to the State party to the controversy, and to the States that are parties to the Convention but that were not parties to the controversy.[126] The Court mentioned that:

> 69. In situations where the State has not been a party to the international process in which the jurisprudence was established, by the mere fact of being party to the American Convention, all of its public authorities and bodies, including democratic bodies involved in the administration of justice on all levels, are obligated by the treaty.[127]

Ferrer Mac-Gregor Poisot also mentioned in his concurrent opinion of that decision that the binding authority of the Court's judgments acquires two dimensions: "a) in a subjective and direct manner against all State parties to the American Convention; and b) in an objective and indirect manner against all State parties to the American Convention."[128]

---

124 *See generally*, Marc Jacob, *La Función Sistémica del Precedente: Perspectivas del Derecho Internacional*, in ARMIN VON BOGDANDY, EDUARDO FERRER MAC-GREGOR POISOT, AND MARIELA MORALES ANTONIAZZI, *LA JUSTICIA CONSTITUCIONAL Y SU INTERNACIONALIZACIÓN: ¿HACIA UN IUS CONSTITUTIONALE COMMUNE EN AMÉRICA LATINA?* Vol. II, p. 684 (Instituto de Investigaciones Juridicas & Instituto Iberoamericano de Derecho Constitucional & Max Institut Fur Auslandishes Offentliches Rechts und Volkerrecht, 2010).

125 *See*, Sergio García Ramírez, *The Conventional Internal Control Court*, *supra* n. 26, at 138.

126 *See*, *Gelman v. Uruguay.* Monitoring Compliance with the Judgment, *supra* n. 3, §67.

127 *Id.* §69; *see*, Sergio García Ramírez, *The Relationship Between Inter-American Jurisdiction and States (National Systems): Some Pertinent Questions*, *supra* n. 27, p. 136.

128 *Gelman v. Uruguay.* Monitoring Compliance with the Judgment, *supra* n. 3, Reasoned Concurrent Opinion of Eduardo Ferrer Mac-Gregor Poisot, §31–33.

By considering the human rights treaties of the Inter-American System and all the decisions of the Inter-American Court as directly enforceable, the above-mentioned Mexican jurist has also talked about the existence of a "conventionality block" as a parameter for the exercise of conventionality control.[129] In his view, domestic authorities have an international legal obligation to enforce the standards of the Inter-American System against any domestic law to the contrary (unless the domestic norm confers a greater protection of rights), in order to ensure the effectiveness of an IHRL at the domestic level. Hence domestic authorities (especially judges) must be aware of the rules, principles and interpretations that come from a treaty law and the decisions of the Inter-American Court, in order to ensure the free and full exercise of the rights and freedoms protected by the Convention. In a similar logic, the Court reasoned in the *OC-21/14* that:

> 31. ... the Court considers that the different organs of the State must carry out the corresponding control of conformity with the Convention, based also on the considerations of the Court in exercise of its non-contentious or advisory jurisdiction, which undeniably shares with its contentious jurisdiction the goal of the inter-American human rights system, which is "the protection of the fundamental rights of the human being."[130]

In the same sense, in the *OC-22/16* the Court states that:

> The Court recalls, as it has done on other occasions, that the interpretative function to be carried out in the exercise of its advisory jurisdiction differs from its contentious jurisdiction in that there are no "parties" involved in the advisory procedure and there is also no dispute over to solve. The central purpose of the advisory jurisdiction is to obtain a judicial interpretation of one or more provisions of the Convention or of other treaties concerning the protection of human rights in the American States. In this vein, the Advisory Opinions fulfill, to some extent, the proper function of a preventive conventionality control.[131]

---

129 *See, Cabrera Garcia and Montiel Flores v. Mexico, supra* n. 16. Reasoned Concurrent Opinion of Eduardo Ferrer Mac-Gregor Poisot, §50.

130 *Rights and guarantees of children in the context of migration and/or in need of international protection.* Advisory Opinion OC-21, Inter-Am. Ct. H.R. (Ser. A) No. 21 (Aug. 19, 2014) §31.

131 *Entitlement of legal entities to hold rights under the Inter-American human rights system (Interpretation and scope of Article 1(2), in relation to Articles 1(2), 8, 11(2), 13, 16, 21, 24, 25, 29, 30, 44, 46 and 62(3) of the American Convention on Human Rights, as well as of Article 8(1)(A) and (B) of the Protocol of San Salvador).* Advisory Opinion OC-22/16, Inter-Am. Ct. H.R. (Ser. A) No. 22 (Feb. 26, 2016) §26; *see also, Gender Identity, and equality and non-discrimination with regard to same-sex couples. State obligations in relation to change of name, gender identity, and rights from a relationship between same-sex couples (interpretation and scope of Articles 1(1), 3, 7, 11(2), 13, 17, 18 and 24, in relation to Article 1, of the American Convention on Human Rights.* Advisory Opinion OC-24, *supra* n. 47, §26.

2.5.2.3. The Existence of an Inter-American *Corpus Juris*

It is in this context that the language of "Inter-American *Corpus Juris*" has been used by scholars – not by the Court – as a manner to identify the sources of law that serve as parameters for conventionality control.[132] The language of *Corpus Juris*, which has been referred to throughout this book, is a Latin term that refers to "the sum or collection of laws".[133] It has been used by other courts to describe the sources or law applicable at the international level, for instance by the ICJ in the Advisory Opinion on the *Legal Consequences for States of the Continued Presence of South Africa in Namibia (South West Africa), notwithstanding Security Council Resolution 276 (1970)*.[134] The Inter-American Court also used the language of the *Corpus Juris* in the Advisory Opinion OC-16/99 to identify "a set of instruments of international human rights law of varied content and juridical effects (treaties, conventions, resolutions and declarations)."[135]

The Inter-American *Corpus Juris* could be defined as the set of binding legal instruments in the Inter-American System, which serve as parameters for evaluating a State's conduct at the international level (it is the parameter for what some have called the "concentrated conventionality control"), and for the exercise of the ("diffuse") conventionality control at the domestic level. Consequently, the *Corpus Juris* includes the American Convention, treaties of a similar nature,[136] the interpretation of treaties made by the Court in the exercise of its contentious, advisory, preventive, and monitoring jurisdiction, and other instruments of soft law such as the American Declaration of the Rights and Duties of Man, or the decisions of the Inter-American Commission on Human Rights, to name some.[137] In short, the Inter-American *Corpus Juris* is another way to call what has been referred to in this Chapter as the "sources of law that serve as the basis for conventionality control".

---

132 *See*, Sergio García Ramírez, *The Conventional Internal Control Court*, *supra* n. 26, p. 127; *see also Cabrera Garcia and Montiel Flores v. Mexico*, *supra* n. 16. Reasoned Concurrent Opinion of Eduardo Ferrer Mac-Gregor Poisot, §45.

133 Black's Law Dictionary, p. 369 (West Publishing Company, 8th ed, 2004).

134 *See generally*, *Legal Consequences for States of the Continued Presence of South Africa in Namibia (South West Africa), notwithstanding Security Council Resolution 276 (1970)*, Advisory Opinion, 1971 I.C.J. (June 21), p. 19 (the ICJ reflected how the *Corpus Juris* on self-determination has been enriched with the developments that have occurred since 1919); *see also* Jorge Rivero Evia, *Corpus Iuris Internacional*, in Eduardo Ferrer Mac-Gregor Poisot, Fabiola Martínez Ramírez and Giovanni Figeroa Mejía (Eds.), *Diccionario de Derecho Procesal Constitucional y Convencional*, Vol. I, *supra* n. 9, p. 258.

135 *The Right to Information on Consular Assistance in the Framework of the Guarantees of the due Process of Law*. Advisory Opinion OC-16, Inter-Am. Ct. H.R. (Ser. A) No. 16 (Oct. 1, 1999) §115.

136 *See*, *Dismissed Congressional Employees (Aguado-Alfaro et al.) v. Peru*, *supra* n. 2, Reasoned Concurrent Opinion of Sergio García Ramírez, §2.

137 *See*, Sergio García Ramírez, *The Conventional Internal Control Court*, *supra* n. 26, p. 135.

There has not been too much elaboration on how the different binding nature of the different sources of international law that are part of the *Corpus Juris* affects the obligation of domestic authorities to exercise conventionality control. This is because the Inter-American *Corpus Juris* is constituted by norms derived from treaties, but also from norms that might be qualified as soft law (i.e. the decisions of the Inter-American Commission). Notwithstanding the silence of the Court and of scholars on this point, it is logical to assume that these differences do matter at a normative level. So a norm contained in the text of the American Convention (or in any other treaty of the Inter-American System) presumably has more normative weight than – let's say – a resolution adopted by the General Assembly of the Organization of American States (OAS). Perhaps the answer to this question is that, in principle, domestic authorities must enforce the normative elements that are part of the Inter-American *Corpus Juris* depending on how binding these elements are for States as a matter of international law.[138]

If this is correct – and the binding nature of the sources of law that constitute the *Corpus Juris* depends on the binding nature of those sources of law from the perspective of international law – then treaty law must be considered the first element of this *Corpus Juris*.[139] This means that, if a State has an obligation under the American Convention or a treaty of a similar nature (this means if the human rights treaty of the Inter-American System has been signed, ratified and has entered into force), then the norms contained in that treaty must serve as the first parameter for the exercise of conventionality control. This approach would also mean that the existence of reservations and declarations affect these parameters, the same as they affect the obligations derived from treaty law for States at the international level. Because reservations and declarations truly modify the obligations for specific States in multilateral treaties, as the Vienna Convention on the Law of Treaties establishes in Article 2(1) regarding reservations:

> "reservation" means a unilateral statement, however phrased or named, made by a State, when signing, ratifying, accepting, approving or acceding to a treaty, whereby it purports to exclude or to modify the legal effect of certain provisions of the treaty in their application to that State; (e) "negotiating State" means a State which took part in the drawing up and adoption of the text of the treaty.[140]

---

138 The problem with this position is that the Court itself does not always follows the rules of international law that define the normative value of instruments of international law.

139 For an analysis of the different aspects that affect the binding nature of treaties, *see generally*, ANTHONY AUST, MODERN TREATY LAW AND PRACTICE, pp. 16–31 and 125–177 (Cambridge University Press, 2007).

140 Vienna Convention on the Law of Treaties, *supra* n. 26, Art. 2(1); *see*, ANTHONY AUST, *MODERN TREATY LAW AND PRACTICE*, *supra* n. 139, p. 131.

If this approach is also applicable for other sources of law that are part of the *Corpus Juris*, then the jurisprudence of the Inter-American Court should be considered with a relevant but secondary role (in relation to treaty law) as part of the *Corpus Juris*. In international law judicial decisions are not strictly speaking a formal source of law, as established in Article 38 of the ICJ Statute – which labels them as "subsidiary means".[141] Yet, as Ian Brownlie points out, the fact that judicial decisions are "subsidiary means" should not be exaggerated, since a coherent body of jurisprudence has naturally important consequences for the law.[142] So even when it might not be possible to label the jurisprudence of the Inter-American Court as a precedent (as is understood in constitutional law), this source of law should certainly be considered an integral part of the *Corpus Juris* that requires it to be "taken into consideration" (using the language of *Almonacid*), both by the institutions of the Inter-American System, and by State authorities in the exercise of diffuse conventionality control.[143]

In the same vein, the sources of soft law on human rights must be considered part of the *Corpus Juris* – although with a different binding nature than other sources of "hard law". It is true that only treaties and the decisions of the Court are the main parameters for the exercise of conventionality control (as mentioned in *Almonacid*), but there are also other legal instruments that are still relevant for the determination of the rules of law on human rights, even when they do not constitute "hard law".[144] The practice of the Inter-American Court has showed the benefits of using soft law instruments in order to interpret the American Convention, finding in other specialized organs the precise language that allows strengthening the position of the Court in questions that are not clearly covered in the text of treaty law.[145] This practice has been present since *Velásquez*,[146] and there is no reason to consider that domestic authorities should not use the developments that occur in international law to make better interpretations of human rights treaties.[147]

---

141 United Nations, Statute of the International Court of Justice, 18 April 1946, Art. 38(1)(d).

142 Ian Brownlie, *Principles of Public International Law*, p. 19 (Oxford University Press, 7th ed., 2008).

143 *Id.* p. 21 (on the notion that the ICJ, although strictly speaking it does not observe a doctrine of precedent, strives nevertheless to maintain judicial consistency).

144 *See*, Jeffrey L. Dunoff, Steven R. Ratner, and David Wippman, *International Law. Norms, Actors, Process*, p. 89 (Aspen, 2010) (on the nature and binding character of soft law).

145 Dinah Shelton, *The Promise of Regional Human Rights Systems*, in Burns H. Weston and Stephen P. Marks, (Eds.), *The Future of International Human Rights*, p. 372 (Transnational Publishers, 1999).

146 *Velásquez Rodríguez v. Honduras*, *supra* n. 12, §151–153.

147 *See generally*, Gerald L. Neuman, *Import, Export, and Regional Consent in the Inter-American Court of Human Rights*, 19(1) European Journal of International Law 114 (2008) (on the notion that the use of sources of "soft law" should not bypass the consensual elements of treaty law. The author criticizes the approach of the Inter-American Court, which appears to treat all the processes that generate norms (whether of soft or hard law) as valid forms

In this sense it is relevant to recall what the Court mentioned in *Pacheco Tineo v. Bolivia* (2013).[148] In this case the Court took into account the principles and regulations of refuge law – including the directives and other criteria of the Office of the United Nations High Commissioner for Refugees – in order to determine the rights of a person as an asylum seeker.[149] In the words of the Court:

> 143. Thus, when determining the compatibility of the acts and omissions of the State, or of its norms, with the Convention or other treaties over which it has competence, the Court may interpret the obligations and rights contained in them in light of other pertinent treaties and norms. Thus, by using the sources, principles and criteria of international refugee law as a special normative applicable to situations concerning the determination of the refugee status of a person and their corresponding rights in a way that is complementary to the provisions of the Convention, the Court is not assuming a ranking between norms.[150]

Yet, one may ask: why not simply follow the criterion that gives a greater protection for human rights, no matter its normative force in accordance with international law? In the view of the author, there are three reasons why the understanding the *Corpus Juris* (as a parameter for conventionality control, both at the international and the domestic level) should be connected with Article 38 of the Statute of the ICJ.

First, because the norms of the American Convention and the jurisprudence of the Inter-American Court are sources of international law, which makes it logical to suppose that the *Corpus Juris* should be understood as a "collection" of norms of international law (not of norms of constitutional law). The American Convention is a treaty governed by international law, and the Inter-American Court is an international tribunal whose attributions and jurisdiction are that of an international tribunal (not that of a constitutional court), which also means that the normative value of its jurisprudence is also governed by rules of international law. The same can be said about the other legal instruments that are

---

of "evolution" of a State's obligations. This criticism would also be applicable for domestic authorities if they treat the sources of law that constitute the *Corpus Juris* in a similar manner as the Inter-American Court does it).

148 *See also Entitlement of legal entities to hold rights under the Inter-American human rights system (Interpretation and scope of Article 1(2), in relation to Articles 1(2), 8, 11(2), 13, 16, 21, 24, 25, 29, 30, 44, 46 and 62(3) of the American Convention on Human Rights, as well as of Article 8(1)(A) and (B) of the Protocol of San Salvador).* Advisory Opinion OC-22/16, Inter-Am. Ct. H.R. (Ser. A) No. 22 (Feb. 26, 2016) §34–70.

149 *See generally, Pacheco Tineo Family v. Plurinational State of Bolivia*, Preliminary Objections, Merits, Reparations and Costs Judgment, Inter-Am. Ct. H.R. (Ser. C) No. 272 (Nov. 25, 2013) §38 to 63; *see also* American Convention on Human Rights, *supra* n. 17, Art. 22.

150 *Pacheco Tineo Family v. Plurinational State of Bolivia, supra* n. 149, §143.

part of the *Corpus Juris* (like the decisions of the Inter-American Commission or the resolutions of the General Assembly of the OAS): they are created by international institutions, and governed by international law.

Second, because the rules and principles that define the relevant normative aspects of the sources of international law (i.e. when they come into force, their hierarchy, and how they interact among them) already exist in international law. This means that the Court already has a recognized body of solid standards to conceptualize the components and interactions among the sources of law that constitute the *Corpus Juris*. Following these rules and principles would give legitimacy and legal certainty on how State authorities should use treaty law, the interpretations of the Inter-American Court, and the rules and principles of soft law, as parameters for conventionality control. On the contrary, not following these rules and principles of international law could lead to the perception that the Inter-American Court is being arbitrary on defining how and why domestic judges should exercise conventionality control on this or that basis.

Third, because by referring to a well-settled body of legal standards (like those of the Vienna Convention and the ICJ Statute), domestic courts would avoid abusing the analogical use of categories of constitutional law when interpreting the American Convention. It is true that the language of constitutional law might serve to have a better understanding of certain aspects of IHRL, but the meaning of both branches of law (constitutional law and IHRL) cannot simply be mixed without the danger of creating tensions in the use of the *Corpus Juris*, and in the relationship between the Court and the Commission and the institutions of the States parties to the American Convention. It is a much safer vehicle that the conceptualization and the use of the *Corpus Juris* – and in general of human rights norms – is based on existent and well-settled notions of public international law.

3. THE RELATIONSHIP BETWEEN THE DOCTRINE OF CONVENTIONALITY CONTROL AND DOMESTIC LEGAL SYSTEMS

This chapter has considered conventionality control as the source of international legal obligations. But a complete analysis of this doctrine cannot be made exclusively from the perspective of international law. Conventionality control is intimately connected, both from a descriptive and a normative perspective, with the constitutional law of the States parties to the American Convention. From a descriptive perspective, the connection exists because the creation and design of this doctrine mirrors the phenomenon of the "national acceptance of international human rights law" that has occurred in Latin America during the last three decades, which has allowed "conventional standards to acquire constitutional status".[151] From a normative perspective, the connection exists because conventionality control is regulated by domestic law in accordance with the "*Aguado-Alfaro* clause", and – arguably – by other procedural and substantive norms of constitutional law.

This section explores some aspects of this relationship. It starts by explaining the trends in Latin American constitutionalism that influenced the creation of conventionality control (they are part of what García Ramírez has called the "American Voyage").[152] The section then *argues* that the "graduation" of the "intensity" of conventionality control depends not only on the "*Aguado-Alfaro* clause", but also on the same trends that inspire the creation of this doctrine: the rules that define the level of incorporation of the Inter-American *Corpus Juris* at the domestic level, and the existence of procedural mechanisms at the State level for the judicial protection of human rights. Finally, the section briefly discusses the Mexican example in order to show how the operation of conventionality control is intimately connected with the "openness" of specific domestic legal systems to the incorporation of international law at the domestic level.

3.1. THE "LATIN AMERICAN VOYAGE"

The creation and design of the doctrine of conventionality control is connected with several transformations of constitutional law that have occurred in Latin America during the last three decades.[153] García Ramírez has metaphorically explained that:

> the nations of the Americas have made and are making their own voyage into the wind, from a certain point of departure, towards the common destiny sought by humanity: the arrival port that implies the definitive reign of human rights.[154]

The creation of conventionality control is one of the last steps (chronologically speaking) of the "Latin American voyage" to increase the effectiveness of international human rights law at the domestic level, which means that this

---

151 *Cabrera Garcia and Montiel Flores v. Mexico, supra* n. 16. Reasoned Concurrent Opinion of Eduardo Ferrer Mac-Gregor Poisot, §25; *see*, Sergio García Ramírez, *The Relationship Between Inter-American Jurisdiction and States (National Systems): Some Pertinent Questions, supra* n. 27, p. 20; *see generally*, Héctor Fix-Zamudio, *El derecho internacional de los derechos humanos en las Constituciones latinoamericanas y en la Corte Interamericana de Derechos Humanos*, XXV (75) Boletin Mexicano de Derecho Comparadom (1992).

152 Sergio García Ramírez, *The Relationship Between Inter-American Jurisdiction and States (National Systems): Some Pertinent Questions, supra* n. 27, p. 4.

153 *See generally*, Rodrigo Uprimny, *The Recent Transformation of Constitutional Law in Latin America: Trends and Challenges* 89 Tex. L. Rev., 1587 (2010–2011).

154 Sergio García Ramírez, *The Relationship Between Inter-American Jurisdiction and States (National Systems): Some Pertinent Questions, supra* n. 27, p. 4.

doctrine – just as many other aspects in the Court's jurisprudence – was created in the context of the "up's and down's, vicissitudes, advances and setbacks of the American voyage, and in the complex of relations between the international organs (especially the Court) and the national systems"[155]

One of the crucial elements of the "Latin American voyage" has been the construction of "bridges" to mitigate the conflict between the "rule of the national legal order and the domain of the international legal order".[156] These bridges have allowed a more harmonious understanding of the relationship between the law and the institutions of the Inter-American System, and the law and institutions of the States parties to the Convention. These bridges have operated at three levels: normative, political and practical.[157] The first formal bridge is materialized in the "openness" of those States that have constitutionalized human rights norms contained in treaties, allowing the primacy of human rights norms (constitutional or international) in relation with other norms of domestic legal systems.[158] Examples of this type of approach can be found – for instance – in the constitutional texts of Argentina,[159] Bolivia,[160] Brazil,[161] Colombia,[162] Guatemala,[163] Mexico,[164] Panama,[165] Peru,[166] Uruguay[167] and Venezuela.[168]

The second formal bridge is "jurisdictional", because it has been "constructed" by the decisions of the Supreme and Constitutional courts of several States parties to the Convention.[169] Some domestic courts have interpreted their

155 *Id.* p. 6.

156 *Id.* p. 9.

157 *Id.* p. 10.

158 *Id.* p. 12; *see also* Rodrigo Uprimny, *The Recent Transformation of Constitutional Law in Latin America: Trends and Challenges*, *supra* n. 153, p. 1591; *see generally*, Gongora Mena, Eduardo, *Inter-American Judicial Constitutionalism: On the Constitutional Rank of Human Rights Treaties in Latin America through National and Inter-American Adjudication*, p. 243 (IIDH, 2011).

159 *See generally*, Constitution of Argentina, May 1, 1853 (Argentina), Art. 75.22.

160 *See generally*, Political Constitution of the Plurinational State of Bolivia, Feb. 7, 2009 (Bolivia), Arts. 13.II, 13.IV and 256.

161 *See generally*, Political Constitution of the Federative Republic of Brazil, Oct. 5, 1988 (Brazil), Art. 5.LXXVI.2.

162 *See generally*, Political Constitution of Colombia, Jul. 1991 (Colombia), Art. 93.

163 *See generally*, Political Constitution of the Republic of Guatemala, May 31, 1985 (Guatemala), Art. 46.

164 *See generally*, Political Constitution of the United Mexican States, Feb. 5, 1917 (Mexico), Art. 1.

165 *See generally*, Political Constitution of the Republic of Panama, Oct. 11, 1972 (Panama), Art. 17.

166 *See generally*, Political Constitution of Peru, Dec. 29, 1993 (Peru), Fourth Final and Transitory Provision.

167 *See generally*, Constitution of the Oriental Republic of Uruguay, 1967 (Uruguay), Art. 72.

168 *See generally*, Constitution of the Bolivarian Republic of Venezuela, Dec. 30, 1999 (Venezuela), Art. 23.

169 *See*, Sergio García Ramírez, *The Relationship Between Inter-American Jurisdiction and States (National Systems): Some Pertinent Questions*, *supra* n. 27, p. 16; *see generally*,

constitutions making possible the incorporation of the jurisprudence of the Inter-American System to decide human rights cases at the domestic level.[170] The Inter-American Court noticed this trend in *Cabrera*, referring to the decisions of the Constitutional Chamber of the Supreme Court of Costa Rica,[171] the Constitutional Court of Bolivia,[172] the Constitutional Court of the Dominican Republic,[173] the Constitutional Court of Peru,[174] the Supreme Court of Justice of Argentina,[175] and the Constitutional Court of Colombia.[176] These courts "progressively favored dynamic interpretations that promote and enable the acceptance of human rights established in international treaties",[177] strengthening the "openness" of constitutional law towards IHRL and increasing the reception of the jurisprudence of the Inter-American Court as a valid source of law at the domestic level.[178]

In the Court's rhetoric – since *Cabrera* – conventionality control was created noticing that the maximum expression of State sovereignty in constitutional democracies (materialized in rules of constitutional law) had changed through the political decisions of the legislative power (which amended the constitutional texts in order to make the domestic legal system more "open" to the incorporation of IHRL) and/or the judiciary (which started using the American Convention or the jurisprudence of the Inter-American Court to decide cases that involved violations of fundamental rights). This phenomenon led to a higher incorporation of IHRL by the judiciary in several Latin American States. So it is reasonable to sustain that the Inter-American Court created conventionality control as a new "bridge" (in the language of García Ramírez) or as a "necessary measure" (in the language of the Convention) departing from a double premise: "judges are

---

Diego García Sayán, *The Inter-American Court and Constitutionalism in Latin-America*, 89 Tex. L. Rev., 1838 (2010–2011).

170 *See, Cabrera Garcia and Montiel Flores v. Mexico, supra* n. 16, §226–232.

171 *See generally*, Constitutional Chamber of the Supreme Court of Justice of Costa Rica, Opinion 2313-95 (Case File 0421-S-90), May 9, 1995, §VII.

172 *See generally*, Constitutional Court of Bolivia, Case File N° 2006-13381-27-RAC, May 10, 2010.

173 *See generally*, Supreme Court of Justice of the Dominican Republic, Resolution N° 1920-2003, Nov. 13, 2003.

174 *See generally*, Constitutional Tribunal of Peru, Case File N° 2730-2006-PA/TC, July 21, 2006, §12; Constitutional Tribunal of Peru, Judgment 00007-2007-PI/TC (*Colegio de Abogados del Callao v. Congreso de la República*), June 19, 2007, §26.

175 *See generally*, Supreme Court of Justice of the Republic of Argentina, Case file 224.XXXIX (Esposito, Miguel Angel s/ motion of statute of limitation of the criminal proceeding brought by his defense), Dec. 23, 2004, Considering §6; Supreme Court of Justice of Argentina, Mazzeo, Julio Lilo *et al.*, Appeal for annulment and constitutional motion. M. 2333. XLII, July 13, 2007, §20.

176 *See*, Constitutional Court of Colombia, Judgment C-010/00, Jan. 19, 2000, §6.

177 *See, Cabrera Garcia and Montiel Flores v. Mexico, supra* n. 16. Reasoned Concurrent Opinion of Eduardo Ferrer Mac-Gregor Poisot, §26.

178 *See*, Sergio García Ramírez, *The Relationship Between Inter-American Jurisdiction and States (National Systems): Some Pertinent Questions, supra* n. 27, p. 16.

the primordial guarantors of human rights, and States are fully committed to observing human rights and to complying with the obligations resulting from their neglect or violation."[179] In the words of Ferrer Mac-Gregor Poisot:

> 29. Clearly, the Inter-American Court created the doctrine of "diffuse conventionality control" noting the trend toward the "constitutionalization" or "nationalization" of "international human rights law" and particularly the acceptance of conventional jurisprudence as a "hermeneutic" element and for the "control" of domestic regulations by the domestic courts themselves. In other words, the Inter-American Court received the influx of jurisprudential practice by the national judges in order to create the new doctrine of "diffuse conventionality control".[180]

3.2. NORMATIVE ASPECTS THAT SHAPE THE OPERATION OF CONVENTIONALITY CONTROL IN DOMESTIC LEGAL SYSTEMS: A FIRST APPROACH

From a normative perspective, at least two elements of domestic law affect the operation of conventionality control in the States parties to the Convention. The first are the "respective competences and the corresponding procedural regulations", as was defined by the "*Aguado-Alfaro* clause".[181] As mentioned in a previous section [*see* section 2.4.2 for a full analysis on this topic], this clause "calibrates" the "intensity" of conventionality control by establishing that domestic authorities – while exercising conventionality control – cannot act beyond the powers conferred on them by domestic law, or disregard the procedural regulations that shape the judicial process. So States have the freedom to decide how they organize the powers and the attributions of domestic authorities (for instance which judges have the authority to avoid the enforcement of anti-conventional laws), and on the type of formalities for the admissibility and substantiation of legal remedies (which are usually determined by codes of procedure).

In this chapter's hypothesis, the second element that affects the operation of conventionality control at the domestic level comes from the norms of constitutional law that determine the level of incorporation of the Inter-American *Corpus Juris* in specific domestic legal systems. Because unless the doctrine of conventionality control implies the supremacy of the *Corpus Juris*

179 *See*, Sergio García Ramírez, *The Relationship Between Inter-American Jurisdiction and States (National Systems): Some Pertinent Questions*, *supra* n. 27, p. 17; *see generally*, Diego García Sayán, *The Inter-American Court and Constitutionalism in Latin-America*, *supra* n. 169, p. 1838.

180 *Cabrera Garcia and Montiel Flores v. Mexico*, *supra* note 16. Reasoned Concurrent Opinion of Eduardo Ferrer Mac-Gregor Poisot, §29.

181 *See*, *Dismissed Congressional Employees (Aguado-Alfaro et al.) v. Peru*, *supra* n. 2, §128.

(a position that is highly debatable, both from the perspective of international law and of constitutional law) the norms that determine the hierarchy of IHRL as domestic law are relevant to assert the intensity of conventionality control in one of its crucial aspects: the sources of international law that serve as parameters for conventionality control. Hence, the intensity of the obligation for domestic authorities to apply the *Corpus Juris* should be evaluated depending on how domestic law incorporates these sources of international law in a particular State. This position is not incompatible with the notion that the *Corpus Juris* has a direct effect because – although to different degrees – all States parties to the Convention recognize international law as domestic law.

In this manner, in States that recognize the constitutional hierarchy of norms derived from human rights treaties, the intensity of the obligation for judges to enforce the American Convention while exercising conventionality control should be considered "higher" than in those States that recognize the "supra-legality" of those norms. So, for instance, a State like Guatemala, which recognizes the principle that "in the field of human rights treaties and agreements approved and ratified by Guatemala have precedence over municipal law",[182] the intensity of this aspect of conventionality control should be different from in a State like El Salvador, which recognizes the "supra-legality" of treaties, and that prohibits the ratification of treaties that conflict with constitutional provisions.[183] Something similar could be said about States that give a special status to specific human rights instruments, such as the case of the Constitution of Argentina. This Constitution includes a list of human rights instruments with constitutional hierarchy that includes human rights declarations (which are not binding as a matter of international law).[184]

It follows that the level of recognition that the jurisprudence of the Inter-American Court has as domestic law also affects the operation of conventionality control at the domestic level. So, for instance, States that recognize the jurisprudence of the Inter-American Court as part of their "constitutional block", the intensity of the obligation for domestic authorities to "take into consideration" (using the language of *Almonacid*) that aspect of the *Corpus Juris* should be higher than in those States that only recognize treaties as sources of constitutional rights. Consequently, one State can legitimately decide that, as a matter of domestic law, the jurisprudence of the Inter-American Court – including the standards developed in Advisory Opinions – has the same normative value as

182 Political Constitution of the Republic of Guatemala, *supra* n. 163, Art. 46; Constitutional Chamber of the Republic of Guatemala, Oct. 19, 1990, File No. 280-90, §VIII).

183 *See*, Constitution of the Republic of El Salvador, Dec. 15, 1983 (El Salvador), Arts. 144, 145 and 149; Constitutional Chamber of the Supreme Court of Justice of El Salvador, Jun. 6, 2008, Judgment 31-2004AC (*Caso de Inconstitucionalidad de la Ley del Sistema de Ahorro para Pensiones*).

184 Constitution of Argentina, *supra* n. 159, Art. 75.22.

the American Convention (as is the case of Costa Rica).[185] But other States could decide that it is a relevant – not a decisive – standard of interpretation to define the extent of protection of fundamental rights (as is the case of Colombia).[186] There are several examples in Latin American constitutionalism that show the pluralism that exists in the recognition of the value that the jurisprudence of the Inter-American Court has as a domestic source of law.

The Supreme Court of Justice of the Dominican Republic (SCJDR) decided in Resolution No. 1920 of 2003 that the Dominican Republic has a "constitutional block" to which all legislation is subject to formal and material validity.[187] The constitutional block is integrated by two normative sources of law of equal rank: (1) the national, formed by the Constitution and the domestic constitutional jurisprudence; and (2) the international, formed by the international pacts and conventions, advisory opinions and the decisions of the Inter-American Court.[188] For the SCJDR, the fact that the Dominican Republic is party to the American Convention, and that it has accepted the jurisdiction of the Inter-American Court, leads to the conclusion that the provisions of the American Convention and the interpretations made by the Inter-American Court are binding for the judiciary. Consequently, "judges are obligated to apply the provisions of the constitutional block as the primary source of their decision, making, even *ex officio*, the determination of the constitutional validity of the acts and rules under consideration".[189]

The Constitutional Tribunal of Peru (CTP) has followed a similar path, recognizing international treaties and the jurisprudence of the Inter-American Court as sources of law incorporated to the Constitution of Peru. The Constitution of Peru establishes in Article 55 that "[t]reaties concluded by the State and in force are part of national law".[190] So in case No. 2730-2006-PA/TC (2006) the CTP interpreted Article 55 and concluded that "international human rights treaties are not only part of national law", but also that public authorities are obligated to incorporate the content of those treaties to the constitutional rights through an "hermeneutical exercise".[191] For the CTP there is a "substantial core identity" (*identidad nuclear sustancial*) between constitutionalism and the international system of human rights protection.[192] This identity is based on "the legal conviction of the value of the dignity of the human person, for whose

185 *See*, Opinion 2313-95 (Case File 0421-S-90), May 9, 1995, *supra* n. 171, §VII.
186 *See*, Judgment C-010/00, January 19, 2000, *supra* n. 176, §6.
187 *See*, Resolution N° 1920-2003, Nov. 13, 2003, *supra* n. 173.
188 *Id.*
189 *Id.*
190 Political Constitution of Peru, *supra* n. 166, Art. 55.
191 Case File N° 2730-2006-PA/TC, July 21, 2006, *supra* n. 174, §9 (the language used by the Peruvian Court, in Spanish, reads as follows: *"ejercicio hermenéutico incorporen en el contenido protegido de los derechos constitucionales los ámbitos normativos de los derechos humanos reconocidos en los referidos tratados."*).
192 *Ibid.*

protection and service is leaded, in last and definitive instance, the exercise of any power".[193] The CTP also established that the obligation concerning the interpretation of constitutional rights not only extends to the content of the Convention, but also to the interpretation thereof made by the Inter-American Court.[194] The binding nature of the jurisprudence of the Inter-American Court is not only referred to in its operative part, but also in the *ratio decidendi* and even in cases where the Peruvian State has not been a party to the controversy.[195]

It is possible to find similar approaches to those of the Dominican Republic and Peru in Costa Rica, Colombia, Argentina, and Mexico.

The Political Constitution of Costa Rica in Article 7 provides that "public treaties, the international agreements and the concordats, duly approved by the Legislative Assembly, will have from their promulgation or from the day designated by them, authority superior to that of the laws;"[196] Article 48 provides that " ... the recourse of amparo to maintain or reestablish the enjoyment of the other rights consecrated in this Constitution, as well as those of a fundamental character established in the international instruments concerning human rights, applicable in the Republic."[197] Considering these provisions the Constitutional Court of Costa Rica reasoned in case 0421-S-90 (1995) that since international treaties have a constitutional status in accordance with the Constitution of Costa Rica, and that the interpretations of the Inter-American Court – either in the exercise of its contentious or advisory jurisdiction – have the same normative value as the American Convention, it follows that domestic authorities have the same obligation to uphold these interpretations as is required to enforce the Convention.[198]

The Political Constitution of Colombia provides in Article 93 that "[i]nternational treaties and agreements ratified by the Congress that recognize human rights and that prohibit their limitation in states of emergency have priority domestically"; it also provides that "[t]he rights and duties mentioned in this Charter will be interpreted in accordance with international treaties on human rights ratified by Colombia".[199] On interpreting Article 93 of the Constitution, the Constitutional Court of Colombia established in case C-010/00 that since

> there is no doubt that the jurisprudence of international institutions in charge of interpreting treaties constitutes a relevant hermeneutical criterion for establishing the meaning of the constitutional provisions on fundamental rights.[200]

---

193 *Ibid.*
194 *Id.* §11.
195 *Id.* §12.
196 Political Constitution of the Republic of Costa Rica, Nov. 7, 1949 (Costa Rica), Art. 7.
197 *Id.* Art. 48.
198 Opinion 2313-95 (Case File 0421-S-90), May 9, 1995, *supra* n. 171, §VII.
199 Political Constitution of Colombia, *supra* n. 162 Art. 93.
200 Judgment C-010/00, January 19, 2000, *supra* n. 176, §7.

But the jurisprudence of the Inter-American Court does not constitute an autonomous formal source of constitutional law within the Colombian legal system, which means that – although authoritative – its binding nature depends on its incorporation in a decision of the Constitutional Court or any other domestic institution authorized to create law.[201]

The Constitution of the Argentine Nation recognizes in Article 75.22 a list of human rights treaties – including the American Convention – that have constitutional hierarchy, and that are complementary to the rights and guarantees recognized in the first part of the Constitution. Thereby, the rights established in the Constitution and in treaties constitute a "federal constitutionality block".[202] The case of Argentina in relation to the constitutional openness to international human rights – widely studied by scholars – was reflected in the jurisprudence of the Supreme Court of Justice of the Argentine Nation (SCJAN), which since the case *Ekmekdjan c/Sofovic* (1992) has stated that "the interpretation of the Pact [of San Jose] must be guided by the jurisprudence of the Inter-American Court of Human Rights – one of whose objectives is the interpretation of the Pact of San José".[203] The same openness can be seen in *Mazzeo, Lulio Lilo and others* (2007), where the SCJAN expressly referred to the doctrine of conventionality control (as was established by the Inter-American Court in *Almonacid*) to determine the nullity of a pardon awarded by the President of Argentina on behalf of the alleged perpetrators of acts of torture.[204]

If the hypothesis of this section is correct, and as judges Humberto Sierra Porto and Eduardo Vio Grossi have recently suggested,[205] then the operation of conventionality control must be different in Panama than in Argentina,

---

201 *See*, Political Constitution of Colombia, *supra* n. 162, Art. 93. *See*, Luis Andres Fajardo, *Implementación del Sistema Interamericano de Derechos Humanos en Colombia a través del bloque de constitucionalidad*. Serie Documentos de Investigación en Derecho No. 11, p. 129 (Diké, 2010); *see also* Rodrigo Uprimny Yepes, *Bloque de Constitucionalidad, Derechos Humanos y Proceso Penal*, p. 94 (Consejo Superior de la Judicatura Sala Administrativa & Escuela Judicial "Rodrigo Lara Bonilla" & Universidad Nacional de Colombia, 2008).

202 Constitution of Argentina, *supra* n. 159, Art. 75.22; *see*, Andrés Gil Domínguez, *El bloque de la constitucionalidad federal y los informes de la Comisión Interamericana de Derechos Humanos*, II, 58 Revista Argentina de Derecho Constitucional 58 (2001).

203 Supreme Court of Justice of the Republic of Argentina, *Case of Ekmekdjan c/Sofovic*, Dec. 23, 2004, §21.

204 *See*, M. 2333. XLII (Mazzeo, Julio Lilo *et al.*, Appeal for annulment and constitutional motion), July 13, 2007, *supra* n. 175, §20.

205 *See*, *Dismissed Employees of Petroperú et al. v. Peru*. Preliminary Objections, Merits, Reparations and Costs Judgment, Inter-Am. Ct. H.R. (Ser. C) No. 334 (Nov. 23, 2017). Dissenting Opinion of Judge Humberto Sierra Porto, §24; *Gender Identity, and equality and non-discrimination with regard to same-sex couples. State obligations in relation to change of name, gender identity, and rights from a relationship between same-sex couples (interpretation and scope of Articles 1(1), 3, 7, 11(2), 13, 17, 18 and 24, in relation to Article 1, of the American Convention on Human Rights*. Advisory Opinion OC-24, Inter-Am. Ct. H.R. (Ser. A) No. 14 (Nov. 24, 2017). Dissenting Opinion of Judge Eduardo Vio Grossi, §120.

since both States have different systems of judicial review and different rules for the incorporation of IHRL. Panama has no system of diffuse judicial review and treaty norms, in general, do not have constitutional hierarchy. Whereas Argentina has a system of diffuse judicial review, the Constitution recognizes the constitutional hierarchy of the American Convention (among other human rights instruments), and the SCJAN considers the jurisprudence of the Inter-American Court as a relevant guide to interpret the American Convention.[206] In the view of this section these differences *do matter* at a normative level, since there is no rule of the American Convention – or in general international law – that requires homogeneity regarding any of the above-mentioned aspects. This means that the understanding of the intensity of conventionality control depends on the level of incorporation that the *Corpus Juris* has in specific States.

3.3. THE CASE OF MEXICO

The recent transformations of the Mexican legal system provide an excellent example of how the intensity of conventionality control is deeply connected with the existence of norms and judicial decisions of domestic origin. Mexico's recent amendment to its Constitution in 2011,[207] the adoption of a new law of *amparo*,[208] and some decisions of the Supreme Court of Justice of the Nation (SCJN),[209] have opened the door for the ample incorporation of the *Corpus Juris* at the domestic level, and for the express acceptance of conventionality control as an obligation for all domestic authorities. But the openness of Mexico's legal system and the incorporation of conventionality control did not happen automatically, or just because the Inter-American Court decided *Radilla*, or thanks to the personal or ideological convictions of the Ministers of the SCJN. It is logical to suggest that the acceptance of conventionality control in Mexico

---

206 *See*, Political Constitution of the Republic of Panama, *supra* n. 165, Arts. 165 and 203; *see also* Allan R. Brewer-Carías, *El Sistema Panameño de control concentrado de la constitucionalidad en el derecho comparado* paper presented in the *Segundas Jornadas de Derecho Procesal Jorge* p. 5 (1995); Elena I. Highton, *Sistema concentrado y difuso de control de constitucionalidad*, in Armin von Bogdandy, Eduardo Ferrer Mac-Gregor Poisot, and Mariela Morales Antoniazzi, *La Justicia Constitucional y su Internacionalización: ¿Hacia un Ius Constitutionale Commune en América Latina?* Volume I (Instituto de Investigaciones Juridicas & Instituto Iberoamericano de Derecho Constitucional & Max Institut Fur Auslandishes Offentliches Rechts und Volkerrecht, 2010), p. 152.

207 *See*, Political Constitution of the United Mexican States, *supra* n. 164, as amended in June 2011 (these amendments were referred as "constitutional amendments in *amparo* and human rights", published in June 2011. For an explanation of the content and importance of these amendments *see* http://www2.scjn.gob.mx/red/constitucion/inicio.html (last accessed Dec. 7, 2017)).

208 *See*, Ley de Amparo (Mx.) (published in April 2, 2013.)

209 *See*, Supreme Court of Justice of the Nation (Mexico), File 489/2010 (*expediente varios*), Aug. 31, 2010; File 293/2011 (*contradicción de tesis*), Sept. 3, 2013.

is connected with other factors that determine the openness of Mexico's legal system to the incorporation of the *Corpus Juris*.[210]

Without the intension of being exhaustive, three factors have been relevant in this sense. The first comes from the recognition of the constitutional hierarchy of human rights norms established in treaties, and the existence of principles that allow their effective application by national authorities.[211] These principles include: the principle of consistent interpretation; the pro persona principle; the recognition of the principles of universality, interdependence, indivisibility and progressiveness; and the recognition of the obligations of prevention, investigation, punishment and reparation for human rights violations.[212] The core of the ample opening to IHRL is reflected in Article 1 of the Political Constitution of the United Mexican States. This article reads as follows:

> Article 1. In the United Mexican States, all individuals shall be entitled to the human rights granted by this Constitution and the international treaties signed by the Mexican State, as well as to the guarantees for the protection of these rights. Such human rights shall not be restricted or suspended, except for the cases and under the conditions established by this Constitution itself.
>
> The provisions relating to human rights shall be interpreted according to this Constitution and the international treaties on the subject, working in favor of the protection of people at all times. All authorities, in their areas of competence, are obliged to promote, respect, protect and guarantee the human rights, in accordance with the principles of universality, interdependence, indivisibility and progressiveness. As a consequence, the State must prevent, investigate, penalize and redress violations to the human rights, according to the law.
>
> ...
>
> Any form of discrimination, based on ethnic or national origin, gender, age, disabilities, social status, medical conditions, religious, opinions, sexual orientation, marital status, or any other form, which violates the human dignity or seeks to annul or diminish the rights and freedoms of the people, is prohibited.[213]

The second comes from Article 103, Section I, of the Mexican Constitution. This article provides that the federal courts shall resolve all disputes concerning "laws or acts issued by the authority, or omissions committed by the authority, which infringe the fundamental rights recognized and protected by this Constitution and the international treaties signed by Mexico".[214] This means that after the

210 *See generally*, MIGUEL CARBONELL AND PEDRO SALAZAR (EDS.), *LA REFORMA CONSTITUCIONAL DE DERECHOS HUMANOS. UN NUEVO PARADIGMA* (UNAM, 2011).

211 *See*, POLITICAL CONSTITUTION OF THE UNITED MEXICAN STATES, *supra* n. 164, Art. 1.

212 *Ibid.*

213 *Ibid.*

214 POLITICAL CONSTITUTION OF THE UNITED MEXICAN STATES, *supra* n. 164, Art.103-I.

adoption of the new *Amparo* Statute (2013), this remedy shall protect the violations of human rights recognized in treaties where Mexico is a party.[215] The *amparo* remedy is the fundamental institution of the Mexican legal system for the judicial protection of human rights, and until recently it was understood that it was only valid against "laws or acts of authority that infringe *constitutional rights*". But the current text of the new *Amparo* Statute (based on Article 103 of the Constitution) has extended this protection so that there is a "ductile, large and effective enough space to enforce any possible violation of Human Rights" – including human rights from international sources.[216]

The third comes from a decision of the SCJN in the *Expediente Varios 912/10*, where the Ministers decided how to comply with the decision of the Inter-American Court in *Radilla*.[217] In this decision the SCJN took a position that has been fundamental to the operation of conventionality control in the Mexican legal system. The SCJN acknowledged the existence of an obligation for all Mexican judges to exercise conventionality control under the terms established by the Inter-American Court in its jurisprudence. This approach involved a new interpretation of Article 133 of the Mexican Constitution, opening the door for local judges to exercise a "diffuse control of constitutionality [and of conventionality]".[218] Furthermore, the SCJN also established that the exercise of conventionality control "at any time means the elimination or disregard of the presumption of constitutionality of statutory laws, but, precisely, starts from this assumption by allowing contrasting [constitutional and international law and statutory law] prior to its application".[219]

In this way the SCJN defined three "steps" that Mexican judges must follow when exercising conventionality control:

> [i] Consistent interpretation (*lato sensu*). This means that the country's judges, like all other authorities of the Mexican State, shall interpret the legal system in light of human rights as protected by the Constitution and in international treaties to which

215 *See*, Ley de Amparo (Mx.) (published on April 2, 2013).

216 Marcos Del Rosario and Raymundo Gil Rendón, *El juicio de amparo a la luz de la reforma constitucional de 2011*, in Biblioteca Jurídica Virtual del Instituto de Investigaciones Jurídicas de la UNAM, p. 67 http://historico.juridicas.unam.mx/publica/librev/rev/qdiuris/cont/15/cnt/cnt4.pdf (last accessed Jan. 11, 2018); *see generally*, Eduardo Ferrer Mac-Gregor Poisot and Rubén Eduardo Sánchez Gil, *El nuevo juicio de amparo. Guía de la reforma constitucional y la nueva ley de amparo*, p. 76 (Porrúa, 2013).

217 *See generally*, File 489/2010 (*expediente varios*), August 31, 2010, *supra* n. 209.

218 File 489/2010 (*expediente varios*), August 31, 2010, *supra* n. 209. *See generally*, Eduardo Ferrer Mac-Gregor Poisot, *Interpretación conforme y control difuso de convencionalidad. El nuevo paradigma del juez mexicano*, in Miguel Carbonell and Pedro Salazar (Eds.), *La Reforma Constitucional de Derechos Humanos. Un nuevo paradigma*, *supra* n. 210, p. 405.

219 File 489/2010 (*expediente varios*), August 31, 2010, *supra* n. 209.

> the Mexican State is a party, at all times favoring the broadest protection for the person.
>
> [ii] Consistent interpretation (*stricto sensu*). This means that when there are several valid interpretations, judges shall, based on the presumption of the constitutionality of laws, prefer the one that allows the law being in accordance with the human rights established in the Constitution and in the international treaties to which the Mexican State is a party, in order not to interfere or undermine the essential content of these rights.
>
> [iii] Avoid the enforcement of the law when the above-mentioned alternatives are not possible. This does not affect or break with the logic of the principle of the separation of powers and federalism, but strengthens the role of judges to be the last resort to ensure the primacy and effective application of the human rights established in the Constitution and international treaties to which Mexico is a party.[220]

In the same sense, the SCJN established in the *Contradicción de tesis 293/2011* that the jurisprudence of the Inter-American Court is binding on Mexican judges, whenever it provides a better protection for human rights.[221] This criterion applies even in cases where Mexico has not been a party to a controversy, which implies a constitutional recognition of the jurisprudence of the Inter-American Court as some kind of precedent for Mexican authorities. The only exception to this principle seems to be in those cases where there is express restriction to a right recognized in the Constitution.[222] The legal basis to sustain this criterion is Article 1 of the Constitution, since the SCJN considered that the pro persona principle obligates judges to always prefer the legal standard (whether it comes from a treaty or a judicial decision) that provides greater human rights protection, except when there is an express restriction to a right in the Constitution. On this basis it was established that judges shall adhere to the following criterion:

> [i] when the judgment was issued in a case in which the Mexican State has not been party, the applicability of the precedent should be determined based on the verification of the existence of the same reasons that led to the decision; [ii] in all cases where possible, the Inter-American jurisprudence shall be harmonized with the national jurisprudence; and [iii] if its harmonization is impossible, the most favorable standard for the protection of human rights should be applied.[223]

It is true that the intensity of the doctrine of conventionality control in Mexico's domestic legal system is directly related to the way the Ministers of the SCJN

---

220 *Id.* §33.

221 File 293/2011 (*contradicción de tesis*), *supra* n. 209.

222 *Id.*

223 *Id.*

decided to comply with the judgment of the Inter-American Court in *Radilla*. The Ministers could very well have taken a different approach when defining the scope of conventionality control in the Mexican legal system, for example by simply stating that in cases that involved military jurisdiction judges shall not enforce the anti-conventional laws of the Code of Military Justice (for an analysis of *Radilla see* Chapter 1, section 4.2). But it is also true that the decision of the Ministers to give general effect to conventionality control is much more consistent with the Mexican constitutional system after the reform of 2011 and the adoption of the new *Amparo* Statute. These new constitutional and statutory rules have opened the door to confer greater attributions to local judges, and to incorporate elements of the *Corpus Juris* as parameters for controlling the constitutionality and conventionality of laws in Mexico.

The Mexican example supports the view that conventionality control is part of a broader phenomenon of the incorporation of IHRL in the States parties to the American Convention. For this reason, the normative and operational aspects of this doctrine should not be understood as exclusively depending on international law or constitutional law. This example also supports the thesis that the obligatoriness of conventionality control is primarily based on the American Convention and the Court's jurisprudence, but that it is also influenced by different elements of constitutional and procedural law: the attributions of judges to exercise constitutionality control on the basis of IHRL, the place that the different elements of the *Corpus Juris* have in constitutional law, and the existence of constitutional principles or procedural mechanisms to guarantee the effective protection of human rights by domestic authorities.

4. CONCLUSION

The understanding of the different elements of the doctrine of conventionality control as an international legal institution requires an analytical evaluation of the Inter-American Court's jurisprudence from *Almonacid* to the *OC-24/17*. This analysis allows the conclusion that conventionality control is an international obligation that must be fulfilled by all the authorities of the States parties to the American Convention, whether they belong to the executive, legislative or judicial power. The obligation to exercise conventionality control consists – in its core – in a mandate to execute an interpretation of every domestic law in accordance with the Inter-American *Corpus Juris*, which is integrated by the American Convention, treaties of a similar nature (like the "Protocol of San Salvador" or the "Convention of Belem do Para"), the jurisprudence of the Inter-American Court (in its contentious or advisory jurisdiction), and other sources of soft law in the Inter-American System (like the decisions of the Inter-American Commission, or those of the General Assembly of the OAS); and in case no consistent interpretation is possible, domestic authorities must cease in the enforcement of anti-conventional laws.

It is important to keep in mind that conventionality control is intimately connected with norms of domestic origin, both from a descriptive and a normative perspective. From a descriptive perspective, conventionality control is connected with domestic law because its design and creation mirrors some of the recent transformation of Latin American constitutionalism. These transformations opened the door for the incorporation of IHRL to domestic legal systems, and for the recognition of judges as primordial guarantors of human rights at the domestic level. From a normative perspective, conventionality control is connected with domestic law in a crucial aspect: domestic authorities shall exercise conventionality control in accordance with their respective competences and the corresponding procedural regulations, which are entirely defined by domestic law. The chapter sustained the hypothesis that conventionality control is also intimately connected with the place the *Corpus Juris* occupies in domestic legal systems, since it is not possible to consider that – as a matter of international law – the *Corpus Juris* is supreme to domestic law.

The normative connections between conventionality control and rules of domestic law lead to a final conclusion: the operation of conventionality control should be considered to be legitimately different in each State party to the American Convention, since there is pluralism in the manner that States allocate competences to their authorities (especially to exercise judicial review), and because there are different levels of incorporation of the *Corpus Juris* in different States (some confer constitutional status to the American Convention and the jurisprudence of the Inter-American Court, but others do not). This should mean that the intensity of conventionality control lies in the "bridges" that increase (or decrease) the implementation of the *Corpus Juris* at the domestic level, and on the role that domestic authorities (especially judges) play in the protection of human rights at the domestic level, which are questions that must be solved by legislators and judges in each State party to the American Convention.

CHAPTER 3

QUESTIONING THE LEGAL VALIDITY OF THE DOCTRINE OF CONVENTIONALITY CONTROL

But just as the laws of each state have in view the advantage of that state, so by mutual consent it has become possible that certain laws should originate as between all states, or a great many states; and it is apparent that the laws thus originating had in view the advantage, not of particular states, but of the great society of states. And this is what is called the law of nations, whenever we distinguish that term from the law of nature.

Hugo Grotius
The Law of War and Peace, 1625

1. INTRODUCTION

There is no doubt that the doctrine of conventionality control constitutes one of the most relevant topics in the recent jurisprudence of the Inter-American Court of Human Rights. This relevance can be observed on the multiple occasions that the Court has made reference to conventionality control since 2006,[1] in the various concurrent opinions of several judges of the Court who have discussed the topic,[2] on the continuous publication of articles and books written by judges

---

1 *See generally, Almonacid Arellano et al v. Chile.* Preliminary Objections, Merits, Reparations and Costs Judgment, Inter-Am. Ct. H.R. (Ser. C) No. 154 (Sep. 26, 2006) §124 to *Rochac Hernández et al. v. El Salvador.* Merits, Reparations and Costs Judgment, Inter-Am. Ct. H.R. (Ser. C) No. 285 (Oct. 14, 2014) §244; *see generally,* Claudio Nash Rojas, *Control de Convencionalidad. Cuadernillo de la Corte Interamericana de Derechos Humanos No. 7* (Inter-American Court of Human Rights & Ministerio de Relaciones Exteriores de Dinamarca, 2015) and Silvia Serrano Guzmán, *El control de convencionalidad en la jurisprudencia de la Corte Interamericana de Derechos Humanos* (Comisión Nacional de los Derechos Humanos, 2013).

2 *See generally, Dismissed Congressional Employees (Aguado-Alfaro et al.) v. Peru.* Preliminary Objections, Merits, Reparations and Costs Judgment, Inter-Am. Ct. H.R. (Ser. C) No. 158 (Nov. 24, 2006) Reasoned Concurrent Opinions of Sergio García Ramírez and A.A. Cançado Trindade; *see also Cabrera Garcia and Montiel Flores v. Mexico.* Preliminary Objections, Merits, Reparations, and Costs Judgment, Inter-Am. Ct. H.R. (Ser. C) No. 220 (Nov. 26, 2010). Reasoned Concurrent Opinion of Judge Eduardo Ferrer Mac-Gregor Poisot.

and scholars in Latin America and other regions,[3] in the use of this doctrine by domestic courts – for instance – in Argentina[4] and Mexico,[5] and in the several academic and professional forums organized by governments and professional institutions to inform legal practitioners and judges about conventionality control.[6] The production of legal materials on this doctrine is such that it is possible to consider it as an autonomous international legal institution specific to the Inter-American System of Human Rights. However, notwithstanding the enormous volume of jurisprudential and academic commentary on the origins and different elements of the doctrine of conventionality control, little has been said about its controversial nature. With the exception of a few scholars who have developed short – although well-reasoned – critiques of conventionality control,[7] no attempt has been made to seriously evaluate the legal basis of conventionality control if seen as an international institution governed by public international law.

---

3 *See generally*, Nestor Pedro Sagües, *International obligations and "conventionality control"*, 8(1) Estudios Constitucionales, (2010); Juan Carlos Hitters, *Constitutional Control and Conventionality Control. Comparison (Criteria Established by the Inter-American Court of Human Rights)*, 7(2) Constitutional Studies (2009); Sergio García Ramírez, *The Relationship Between Inter-American Jurisdiction and States (National Systems): Some Pertinent Questions*, 1(1) Notre Dame Journal of International and Comparative Law (2015); Ernesto Rey Cantor, *Control de la Convencionalidad de Leyes y Derechos Humanos* (Porrúa, 2008).

4 *See*, Supreme Court of Justice of Argentina, M. 2333. XLII (Mazzeo, Julio Lilo *et al.*, Appeal for annulment and constitutional motion), July 13, 2007.

5 *See*, Supreme Court of Justice of the Nation (Mexico), File 489/2010 (*expediente varios*), August 31, 2010; Supreme Court of Justice of the Nation (Mexico), P./J. 21/2014 (*tesis aislada*), April 25, 2014.

6 *See*, *"Congreso Internacional de Derecho Procesal Constitucional Transnacional. Interacción entre el Derecho Nacional y el Derecho Internacional"* (IX Encuentro Iberoamericano y VI Congreso Mexicano de Derecho Procesal Constitucional, Hermosillo, Sonora, Mexico, Dec. 3, 4 and 5, 2014); *"Curso de capacitación en la aplicación de la Convención Americana de Derechos Humanos"* (Centro de Estudios de Justicia de las Américas (CEJA), San Salvador, El Salvador, Aug. 20, 21 and 22, 2014).

7 *See*, Jorge Contesse, *The International Authority of the Inter-American Court of Human Rights: A Critique of the Conventionality Control Doctrine*, 22 International Journal of Human Rights 17–18 (2018). Jorge Contesse, *The Final Word? Constitutional dialogue and the Inter-American Court of Human Rights*, 15(2) International Journal of Constitutional Law (2017); Ariel E. Dulitzky, *An Inter-American Constitutional Court? The Invention of conventionality control by the Inter-American Court of Human Rights*, 50 Tex. Int'l L. J. 57 (2015); Cristina Binder, *The Prohibition of Amnesties by the Inter-American Court of Human Rights*, 12 German Law Journal 1216 (2011); Luigi Crema, "Are Amnesties Still an Option? A Non-Policy Based Critique of the Inter-American Approach", Center for Civil and Human Rights, University of Notre Dame, Working Paper Series # 6 50–51 (2013); *see generally*, Guillermo Enrique Estrada Adán, *Una Visión del Control de Convencionalidad desde el Derecho Internacional*, in Maria Leoba Castaneda Rivas, *Homenaje al Maestro Edmundo Elías Musi* (Porrúa, 2013); Ezequiel Malarino, *Judicial Activism, Punitivism, and Supranationalisation: Illiberal Tendencies of the Inter-American Court of Human Rights*, 12 International Criminal Law Review 665–695 (2012).

One may ask: why do this analysis if conventionality control is a good idea and if the doctrine has been well received by some courts and scholars? Would it not be better simply to ignore those who do not agree with conventionality control, qualifying their arguments as invalid for being against the evolution of human rights and the strengthening of its mechanisms of protection? Not in my view. Serious academic inquiry requires taking a step back in controversial questions in order to understand why they are controversial in the first place, and what the reasons that generate sound and serious opposition are.[8] More important, the legitimacy of conventionality control (and of any development of legal standards, especially if it is promoted by courts and not by the States) is strengthened as much as judges and scholars are capable of responding, in legal terms, to the criticism that is formulated in legal terms. In keeping with this spirit, this chapter seeks to develop the objections and weak points of conventionality control seen from the perspective of public international law.

To achieve this purpose, the chapter assumes that the Inter-American System is governed by rules and principles of general international law, including those established in the Vienna Convention on the Law of Treaties (VCLT). Hence, the point of departure of this chapter is that the fact that the doctrine of conventionality control is consolidated in the jurisprudence of the Inter-American Court does not automatically mean that there is no legitimate controversy surrounding its legal grounds and normative components. This point of departure is – of course – not free of controversy. Some may argue that the Inter-American System of Human Rights has its own rules and principles of operation, and therefore that it is not bound by rules of general character, or that those rules acquire its meaning depending on the interpretations of the Court in the benefit of the protection of human rights. The chapter rejects that position. It considers that, although it is true that the norms and principles of the Inter-American System have specific characteristics, they are also structurally connected with other rules and principles of general international law.[9]

The three objections formulated against the doctrine of conventionality control could be summarized in the following manner: first, the obligation to exercise conventionality control cannot be grounded on Article 2 of the American Convention on Human Rights, since this article was created leaving

8 *See*, Alexei Julio Estrada, *Comentario al articulo "Control de convencionalidad interamericano: una mera aplicacion del derecho internacional", de Karlos Castilla*, Derecho del Estado no. 34, Universidad Externado de Colombia 51–53 (2015) (responding to these critiques is important even when the criticism is based on superficial or contradictory reasons).

9 *See*, Report of the Study Group of the ILC on Fragmentation of International Law: difficulties arising from the diversification and expansion of International Law, Doc. No. A/CN4/L.682 (April 13, 2006), conclusion 14 (the section assumes what the ILC concludes, in the sense that international law is a legal system, and therefore that its rules and principles act in relation to, and should be interpreted against, the background of other rules and principles).

absolute freedom for States to determine how to implement the American Convention at the domestic level. Second, a sound reading of Articles 26 and 27 of the VCLT would not support the conclusion that judges must exercise conventionality control, since the obligations of those provisions neither automatically affect the legal validity of domestic laws (even if they are manifestly incompatible with a rule of international law), nor do they impose direct obligations on State authorities. Third, the doctrine of conventionality control cannot be grounded merely on the Court's jurisprudence, since the doctrine of precedent is non-existent in international law.

Then, the chapter discusses two structural assumptions that underline the above-mentioned critiques. It takes a step back in order to explain why conventionality control enters in contradiction with two structural notions that have defined the theory and practice of international law since its inception: that the consent of States as sovereigns is the most important factor to identify the origin and extent of international rights and obligations; and that there is a strict separation between the manner that norms of international law confer rights and impose obligations on States as subjects of international law (as legal persons), and the manner by which the same norms bind specific authorities at the domestic level. The analysis shows the disparity between the positivistic understanding of these structural elements of general international law – and their normative consequences – and the approach taken by the Court in cases such as *Suárez Rosero v. Ecuador*, *Barrios Altos v. Peru* and *Almonacid Arellano et al. v. Chile*, and that has been maintained until the *OC-24/17* (2016).

It is fundamental to keep in mind that the objective of this chapter is not to plainly reject the doctrine of conventionality control as an international legal institution. It seeks to understand the weak points of its existence if seen from a positivistic understanding of relevant rules and principles of public international law that gives great priority to the principle of sovereignty. It also aims to explain in a better fashion where the "innovative" character of this doctrine lies, and thus reject the position of those that consider that the obligation to exercise conventionality control has always existed, or that there is nothing new or radical in its postulates.[10] The section also seeks to open the door for the analysis of the next chapter, where legal arguments in favor of conventionality control are developed, and where there is formulated a

---

[10] *See generally*, Cecilia Medina Quiroga, *The American Convention on Human Rights. Crucial Rights and their Theory and Practice* 32 (Intersentia, 2016) (the author states that "what is behind this control is not much more that what the Court has said throughout its many years of work. With the decision that States must exercise conventionality control, the Court simply enhances the fact that States Parties to a treaty are obligated to ensure that the Convention's provisions are complied with by any and all State agents, and it is therefore necessary for them to take these obligations into consideration in all their performances.").

proposal of the form that conventionality control should take in order to be a vehicle for the effective realization of human rights in the States parties to the American Convention.

2. OBJECTIONS TO THE DOCTRINE OF CONVENTIONALITY CONTROL BASED ON POSITIVE INTERNATIONAL LAW

2.1. FIRST OBJECTION: THE "ANTI-CONVENTIONALITY" OF THE DOCTRINE OF CONVENTIONALITY CONTROL

The first and obvious objection that can be formulated against the doctrine of conventionality control is that no article in the American Convention – or in any other treaty of the Inter-American System – creates an international obligation for domestic authorities to interpret domestic law in accordance with the *Corpus Juris*, or to refrain from the enforcement of that domestic law if no valid interpretation is possible. The creation of conventionality control – and therefore of each one of its technical components – is the result of a progressive and innovative interpretation of Articles 1.1 and 2, and Articles 26 and 27 of the VCLT. Therefore, its origins are the result of the agreement of judges – and not the agreement of States – to solve the problem that represents the enforcement of anti-conventional laws that produce human rights violations.

It is true that Article 2 imposes an obligation on States to take the "legislative and other measures" necessary to ensure that all persons subject to their jurisdiction are capable of exercising the rights and freedoms protected by the American Convention. But an orthodox reading of this article, based on the principle of sovereignty, would serve little as a justification for conventionality control. The reason for this is that the text of Article 2, the reasons for its adoption (that can be analyzed in the *Travaux Préparatoires* of the American Convention), and the original understanding of its content and effects (that can be observed in the first decisions of the Inter-American Court) would support the position that this article was originally understood as "programmatic", with no direct effect on State authorities, and not as the source of enforceable legal obligations.

If this position is correct, then the Court's interpretation since *Suárez Rosero* (where Article 2 was read as a provision with a high prescriptive force), and the decision in *Almonacid* (where it was implied that Articles 1.1 and 2 had a direct effect and that it was possible to derive specific obligations from these articles), constituted a departure from what was originally agreed upon by the States parties to the American Convention, and from the original position of the Inter-American Court on this particular question. This would also mean that conventionality control finds weak grounds in positive international law, as it is detached from the text of the American Convention, and therefore that it cannot be considered as a source of obligations for the States parties. This view – of course – gives a preponderant role to States' consent as the only source of international rights and obligations. The following sub-sections present the arguments that support these propositions.

2.1.1. The Protection to the Sovereignty of States as an Essential Component of Article 2

The above-mentioned could be verified by looking at the ordinary meaning of the text of Article 2, which in principle leaves absolute freedom for States regarding the "legislative and other measures" that must be adopted to ensure the effectiveness of the American Convention. One may argue that Article 2 lacks specificity about the kind of measures (legislative or other) that must be adopted by States in order to give effect to the rights and freedoms protected by the American Convention. The article simply establishes that States: "undertake to adopt … such legislative or other measures as may be necessary to give effect to those rights or freedoms", and that these measures should be taken by the State: "in accordance with the constitutional processes and the provisions of [the] American Convention." What measures? In this view, those that the State considers appropriate, whenever they are considered effective by State authorities for the protection of human rights.

The lack of specificity about the substantive measures that States must take to comply with Article 2, and the recognition that these measures must be taken in accordance with internal constitutional processes, suggests that it is in the State's exclusive sphere of competences to decide the best manner to give full force to the American Convention in terms of substance (the measure itself) and process (the procedure to adopt the measure). It also means that no *specific* measure (legislative or other) can be derived from Article 2, and that the American Convention is not self-executing.[11] Arguing the opposite certainly changes the original understanding of this provision.

True, by virtue of Article 2 States have an obligation to adopt "legislative and other measures" to comply with their obligation to respect and ensure. Yet, in this view, the dualistic understanding of the relationship between international law and domestic legal systems, which is based on the principle of sovereignty,

---

[11] *See*, Cristina Binder, *The Prohibition of Amnesties by the Inter-American Court of Human Rights*, *supra* n. 7, p. 1216 (the author explains that: "the need for an effective implementation of the American Convention at the national level does not necessarily give the Inter-American Court the competence to decide *how* this is to be done. Rather, it would be up to the respective State to decide how best to comply with its obligations under the ACHR in accordance with the specificities of its domestic legal system.").

would lead to the conclusion that the language of Article 2 is based in the understanding that the sovereign capacity of States includes the right to decide the best manner to comply with the American Convention. This right would include the exclusive capacity to determine if the American Convention is self-executing or not, the hierarchical level of a treaty in the domestic legal system, the organs and the manner of ensuring its effectiveness, and the laws and practices that States might take to guarantee that effectiveness.[12] Connected with this point the International Law Commission has established the following:

> The structure of the State and the functions of its organs are not, in general, governed by international law. It is a matter for each State to decide how its administration is to be structured and which functions are to be assumed by government. But while the State remains free to determine its internal structure and functions through its own law and practice, international law has a distinct role.[13]

2.1.2. The Distinction Between "Obligations of Specific Conduct" and "Obligations of Results" as Tools to Understand the Meaning of Article 2

The notion that States have a right to exclusively decide the best manner to comply with a treaty at the domestic level is supported by a longstanding tradition that identifies the obligations of international law not just by looking at the *content* of the norms (the literal language) that contain these obligations, but also by looking at the *manner* in which those norms impose their requirements upon a State.[14] This theoretical approach allows distinguishing between cases where the means (the "legislative or other measures", using the language of the American Convention) for fulfilling certain obligations imposed by international law are determined at the international level, and those cases where these means are determined at the domestic level.[15]

Roberto Argo developed the above-mentioned distinction, explaining that in the first case the obligations imposed by international law categorically call for

12 *See generally*, Thomas Buergenthal, *Self-Executing and Non-self Executing Treaties in National and International Law*, p. 320 (Martinus Nijhoff Publishers, 1992).

13 Responsibility of States for Internationally Wrongful Acts, Ybk ILC, 2001, Vol. II (Pt. II), 39; *see also* Dinah Shelton and Paolo G. Carozza, Regional Protection of Human Rights p. 113 (Oxford University Press, 2013).

14 *See*, Sixth Report on State Responsibility by Mr. Roberto Argo, Special Rapporteur – the internationally wrongful act of the State, source of international responsibility (continued), Ybk ILC 1977, Vol. II (1) A/CN.4/302 and Add.1, 2 & 3., §2.

15 *See*, Sixth Report on State Responsibility by Mr. Roberto Argo, Special Rapporteur – the internationally wrongful act of the State, source of international responsibility (continued), *supra* n. 14, §4.

the use of specific means to achieve a certain goal (called obligations of means or obligations of specific conduct), and in the second case the obligations imposed by international law leave the State free to choose among various means how to comply with that obligation (called obligations of result).[16] Accordingly, an obligation of international law to adopt specific means to obtain certain results exists *only* when the treaty imposes an "obligation of specific conduct" (i.e. the obligation to adopt a specific domestic law or policy to comply with the treaty).[17] In this sense, for example, as referred to by Argo, Article 10 of the State Treaty for the Re-establishment of an Independent and Democratic Austria of 15 May 1955, establishes the duty of States to legislate in the following manner:

> Austria undertakes to maintain and continue to implement the principles contained in the laws and legal measures adopted by the Austrian Government and parliament since 1st May, 1945, and approved by the Allied Commission for Austria, aimed at liquidation of the remnants of the Nazi regime and at the reestablishment of the democratic system, and to complete the legislative and administrative measures already taken or begun since 1st May, 1945, *to codify and give effect to the principles set out in Articles 6, 8 and 9 of the present Treaty, and insofar as she has not yet done so to repeal or amend all legislative and administrative measures adopted between 5th March, 1933, and 30th April, 1945, which conflict with the principles set forth in Articles 6, 8 and 9.*[18]

The same degree of specificity can be found in other human rights treaties, both at the Universal level and in the Inter-American System. For instance, Article 2 paragraph 1(c) of the 1965 International Convention on the Elimination on All forms of Racial Discrimination established that: "Each State Party shall take effective measures to … amend, rescind or nullify any laws and regulations which have the effect of creating or perpetuating racial discrimination wherever it exists." An even clearer example of a treaty that imposes obligations of a specific conduct is the provision of Article III of the Inter-American Convention on the Forced Disappearance of Persons, which establishes, in Article I, that the States parties to the Convention undertake: "To take legislative, administrative, judicial, and any other measure necessary to comply with the commitments undertaken", specifying in Article II the definition of the crime of forced disappearance, and in Article III ordering States parties to define the forced disappearance in its legal system by adopting:

> … in accordance with their constitutional procedures, the legislative measures that may be needed to define the forced disappearance of persons as an offense and to impose an

16 *Id.* §4.

17 *Id.* §11.

18 State Treaty for the Re-establishment of an Independent and Democratic Austria, 15 May 1955, Art. 10 (emphasis added).

> appropriate punishment commensurate with its extreme gravity. This offense shall be deemed continuous or permanent as long as the fate or whereabouts of the victim has not been determined.[19]

But in cases where international law stays "at the boundaries of the State machinery", and merely requires the State to ensure a particular situation (to obtain certain result), an orthodox reading of the treaty law would lead to the conclusion that there is absolute freedom for States to decide whatever means they choose to fulfill the obligation imposed by international law. If Argo is correct on this point, it follows that international responsibility cannot exist owing to the means chosen by the State to comply with its international obligations, whenever it indeed complies with the results required by the treaty. And in case it fails to achieve those results, the international responsibility of the State would be the result of the failure to achieve the results required by the treaty, and not by the means – or lack of them – chosen, or not chosen, by the State.[20]

According to this view, Article 2 of the International Covenant on Civil and Political Rights (ICCPR) is one of those norms where the lack of specificity of its content should be interpreted in the sense that the State is "left free to employ some other means if it sees fit, provided that such means equally enables it to achieve *in concreto* the full realization of the rights prescribed by the Covenants".[21] Notwithstanding that the legislative means is expressly indicated by Article 2 of the ICCPR as the most normal and most appropriate means to achieve the purposes of the Covenant, Argo understands that States can choose whatever means they deem convenient to comply with the treaty. Some influential international tribunals have reasoned in a similar fashion, noticing that those cases where a norm of international law imposes an obligation of results, the breach of that obligation occurs by the *enforcement* of a domestic law that is contrary to a treaty, and not by the *enactment* of that law or by its mere *existence.*[22]

---

19 Organization of American States (OAS), Inter-American Convention on Forced Disappearance of Persons, 9 June 1994, Adopted at Belém do Pará, on 9 June 1994, at the twenty-fourth regular session of the General Assembly of the OAS, Art. III.

20 *Id.* §15.

21 *See*, Sixth Report on State Responsibility by Mr. Roberto Argo, Special Rapporteur – the internationally wrongful act of the State, source of international responsibility (continued), *supra* n. 14, §18.

22 *See*, *Id.*, §36; *see also Certain German interests in Polish Upper Silesia*, 1926 P.C.I.J., Ser. A, No. 7 (Aug. 25), at 19 (the Permanent Court established that: "It might be asked whether a difficulty does not arise from the fact that the Court would have to deal with the Polish law of July 14th, 1920. This, however, does not appear to be the case … The Court is certainly not called upon to interpret the Polish law as such; but there is nothing to prevent the Court's giving judgment on the question whether or not, *in applying that law,* * Poland is acting in conformity with its obligations towards Germany under the Geneva Convention." (emphasis added); *see generally*, *De Becker v. Belgium*, Appl. No. 214/5, Eur. Ct. H.R. (1962).

This position follows the notion that a State's international obligations are limited to complying with the substantive elements of the treaty, so the competence of an international court or tribunal is limited to evaluating the failure of a State to achieve that concrete result required by international law. In other words, international courts and tribunals have no legal basis to evaluate the means chosen by the State to comply with a treaty provision, and with stronger reason they cannot order States to adopt specific means (legislative or other) unless it is expressly established by the treaty. This appeared to be the understanding that the Inter-American Court had before *Suárez Rosero*, and it was also the same understanding that the European Court of Human Rights had since its first decisions, as it is reflected in *De Becker v. Belgium* (1962).[23] In that case the European Court decided that it was not called to give a decision on an abstract problem regarding the compatibility of a domestic Act with the European Convention, but only: "on the specific case of the application of such an Act to the Applicant and to the extent to which the latter would, as a result, be prevented from exercising one of the rights guaranteed by the American Convention."[24]

2.1.3. Subsidiary Sources of Criticism

2.1.3.1. Preparatory Works of the American Convention

The preparatory works of the American Convention (the *Travaux Préparatoires*) suggest that Article 2 was created precisely on the understanding that the American Convention imposes obligations of results (using Argo's categories) and that the Treaty was not self-executing. The discussions in the Inter-American Specialized Conference on Human Rights show that the drafters of the American Convention conceived that it was within the States' exclusive sphere of competences to decide the "legislative or other measures" as may be necessary to give effect to the rights and freedoms protected by the American Convention.[25] Paradoxically for the analysis in this section, this conclusion is plausible precisely from the reasons put forth in the first place by the delegation of Chile to include Article 2 as part of the American Convention.[26]

---

23 *See, De Becker v. Belgium, supra* n. 22.

24 *Id.* §14.

25 *See generally*, Organization of American States (OAS), Charter of the Organisation of American States, Apr. 30, 1948, amended by the Protocol of Buenos Aires of Feb. 27, 1967; amended by the Protocol of Cartagena de Indias of Nov. 16, 1985 and amended by the Protocol of Managua of Oct. 6, 1993 which entered into force on Jan. 29, 1996, Preamble and Arts. 1, 2(b) and 3(b).

26 *See generally*, Inter-American Specialized Conference on Human Rights, San José, Costa Rica, Nov. 7–22, 1969, Proceedings and Documents, OEA.Ser.K/XVI/1.2, 1978, Doc. 5, at 38;

The Chilean delegation defended the inclusion of this article because some States would need to adopt domestic measures to make the rights recognized in the American Convention effective, notwithstanding the fact that some of these States automatically incorporate (*incorporan*) treaty provisions into domestic law once a treaty is ratified. The inclusion of Article 2 was thought to be relevant precisely because of the normative pluralism that existed in the States that participated in the Specialized Conference on how international law was incorporated into their domestic legal systems (from the perspective of domestic law, some States are dualists and some monists), and because there was an understanding about the freedom that existed for States to comply with the obligation to take the necessary steps to make human rights effective in their territories. There seems to be no doubt that the efficacy of the American Convention – not its normative value as a matter of international law – depended on its incorporation into domestic legal systems, in accordance with the political choices of State authorities.

Additionally, the drafters of the American Convention identified that the adoption of domestic legislation (as required by Article 2) was especially important to make effective those articles of the American Convention that expressly required protecting certain rights by statutory law. Following this logic, Article 2 would reinforce the obligation of States to actually enact those laws and comply with the treaty on its terms.[27] In this restricted sense, it might be possible to consider the existence of an "obligation of means" in those particular articles of the American Convention where States agreed that a right shall be protected "by law" (as happens with Article 4.1). Yet, in this view, even then Article 2 would not be sufficient to establish that this is an autonomous obligation to enact legislation for the protection of every right.[28] In any case, either if it is possible to argue the existence of an obligation of means regarding certain articles of the American Convention, or if it is not possible, the inclusion of Article 2 happened precisely because there was an understanding that the American Convention needed to be implemented at the domestic level in order to be applicable as domestic law.

The position of the delegations of Ecuador, Guatemala and the United States regarding the inclusion of Article 2 supports the view that it was adopted

---

see, Laurence Burgorgue-Larsen and Amaya Úbeda de Torres, *The Inter-American Court of Human Rights. Case Law and Commentary* 252–253 (Oxford University Press, 2011); *see also* Dunshee de Abranches, C.A. *Comparative Study of the United Nations Covenants on Civil and Political Rights and on Economic Social and Cultural Rights and of the Draft Inter-American Convention on Human Rights*, Inter-American Yearbook on Human Rights p. 193 (1968).

27 *See*, Inter-American Specialized Conference on Human Rights, *supra* n. 26, p. 40.

28 *See generally*, Eduardo Jimenez de Aréchaga, *International Responsibility, Manual of Public International Law*, p. 545 (Sorensen, 1968).

considering that the normative force of the American Convention within domestic legal systems was *necessarily* linked to secondary rules of domestic origin (i.e. norms that establish the constitutional hierarchy of treaties), and that States had the exclusive right to decide the manner of implementing the American Convention. Arriving at the opposite conclusion – that Article 2 implies the supremacy of the American Convention – would make the discussion that took place with the drafters in the Specialized Conference unintelligible.

The Ecuadorian delegation proposed to replace Article 1 of the project (which included the current Articles 1.1 and 2 of the American Convention) with analogous provisions to Article 2 and 3 of the ICCPR, in order to avoid any contradiction between the adoption of the American Convention and the principles of national sovereignty, self-determination of peoples and constitutional supremacy.[29] This way, Ecuador wanted to maintain as part of the American Convention an article that established a duty for the States to take legislative and other measures to give effect to the rights protected by the American Convention, but wanted to avoid the use of any language that represented a threat to the notion of constitutional supremacy in their domestic legal system.[30] The Ecuadorian proposal was ultimately rejected because leaving Article 2 as the only "general obligation" would potentially compromise the normative force of the American Convention as a treaty that is directly enforceable at the international level.

The Guatemalan delegation proposed the inclusion of an article with similar language to the Chilean proposal (similar to Article 2.2 of the ICCPR), but adding a phrase that made it clear that States were in charge of defining the measures (legislative or other) that had to be taken in order to guarantee the effectiveness of the American Convention at the domestic level. In the Guatemalan delegation's proposal Article 2 would have the same language as the current version of that article, but with the following addition: "the observation of human rights fundamentally rests on the conditions of each country, in the actions that the country promotes for that effect, and in the guarantees that the country confers."[31] Ultimately this proposal was rejected, but the proposal supports the view that Article 2 was adopted to reinforce the notion that States had the right to decide the domestic measures that would be adopted to comply with the obligation of Article 1.1.

The United States delegation supported the inclusion of the Chilean proposal but also issued a formal declaration. This declaration establishes that Article 2

29 Inter-American Specialized Conference on Human Rights, *supra* n. 26, p 104.
30 *Ibid.*
31 *Id.* p. 111.

existed to clarify the legal effects of the ratification of the domestic law, under the understanding that the article is flexible enough so each country could make the Convention operative in a manner consistent with its national practices.[32] The United States understood Article 2 as an authorization for domestic authorities to make the Treaty operational and effective through the enactment of domestic laws, but in any way considered the American Convention as a self-executing Treaty – or supreme to their constitution. The full text of the United States formal declaration is particularly illustrative to prove this point, and for that reason is copied integrally:

> The United States agrees that this Article should be included in the draft American Convention since it helps to clarify the legal effect of ratification on the domestic law of the respective parties. The Article is sufficiently flexible so that each country can best implement the treaty consistent with its domestic practice. Some countries may choose to make the Articles of the treaty directly effective as domestic law and this Article would permit them to do so. The comments made by Chile suggest that its own practice may vary depending on the text of each Article. Others may prefer to rely solely on domestic law to implement the Articles of the treaty. In the U.S. we would interpret this Article as authorizing us to follow the last course in the case of matters within Part I, the substantive portions, of the draft American Convention. That will permit us to refer, where appropriate, to our Constitution, to our domestic legislation already in existence, to our court decisions and to our administrative practice as carrying out the obligations of the American Convention. It will also mean that we will be able to draft any new legislation that is needed in terms that can be readily and clearly assimilated into our domestic codes. *In other words, it is not the intention of the U.S. to interpret the Articles of the treaty in Part I as being self-executing.*[33]

The above-mentioned conclusion is strengthened by the fact that Article 2 was inspired by Article 2.2 of the ICCPR, which is an article that recognizes a great degree of freedom for States to decide how to incorporate the substantive provisions of the ICCPR at the domestic level.[34] The decision of the Human Rights Committee in the *General Comment No. 3* (1994) shows that Article 2.2 of the ICCPR "generally leaves it to the States parties to choose their method

32 *Id.* p. 149.

33 *Id.* p.146 (emphasis added).

34 *Id.* p.145; *see also Enforceability of the Right to Reply or Correction (Arts. 14(1), 1(1) and 2 American Convention on Human Rights)*. Advisory Opinion OC-7, Inter-Am. Ct. H.R. (Ser. A) No. 7 (Aug. 29, 1986). Separate Opinion of Héctor Gros Espiell, §6 ("It must be remembered that the source of Article 2 is Article 2 (2) of the United Nations International Covenant on Civil and Political Rights, which, as much by its location in the instrument as by its text, constitutes an obvious complement to the essential obligation imposed by the first paragraph of said Article 2 (of the ICCPR).").

of implementation in their territories within their framework set on in that Article".[35] This means that

> the primary responsibility for ensuring the rights and freedoms of the individual rests with each State, and the international character of the rights is manifested mainly by the international obligation of the State to implement them through domestic measures.[36]

Consequently, if Article 2.2 of the ICCPR were relevant for the adoption of Article 2 of the American Convention, it would certainly support the conclusion that States have the freedom to decide the best way to implement both treaties (the American Convention and the ICCPR) at the domestic level.

2.1.3.2. The Understanding of the Programmatic Nature of Article 2 in the First Decisions of the Inter-American Court

The position sustained to this point is also consistent with the reasoning of the Inter-American Court in the *Advisory Opinion OC/14-94*. On that occasion, the Inter-American Court had to answer the question presented by the Inter-American Commission about "the legal effects of a law that manifestly violates the obligations the State assumed upon ratifying the American Convention", a question that implicitly required an interpretation of Articles 1 and 2 of the American Convention.[37]

The Court responded in consonance with its criterion in *Velásquez*. It reasoned that States have an obligation to adopt such legislative or other measures as may be necessary to give effect to the rights and freedoms recognized by the American Convention, which includes the obligation to refrain from adopting measures that conflict with the object and purpose of the Treaty.[38] But the Court clarified that the question presented by the Commission refers only to the legal effects of domestic law seen through the lenses of international law, because it was "not appropriate for the Court to rule on its domestic legal effect within the State concerned. That determination is within the exclusive jurisdiction of the national courts and should be decided in accordance with their laws".[39]

---

35 UN Human Rights Committee (HRC), CCPR General Comment No. 3: Article 2 (Implementation at the National Level), 29 July 1981, §1; *see also* UN Human Rights Committee (HRC), CCPR General Comment No. 4: Article 3 (Equal Right of Men and Women to the Enjoyment of All Civil and Political Rights), 30 July 1981 §4.

36 *See*, Vratislav Pechota, The Development of the Covenant on Civil and Political Rights, in Louis Henkin (Ed.), *The International Bill of Rights. The Covenant on Civil and Political Rights*, p. 46 (Columbia University Press, 1981).

37 *See, International Responsibility for the Promulgation and Enforcement of Laws in Violation of the Convention (Arts. 1 and 2 American Convention on Human Rights).* Advisory Opinion OC-14, Inter-Am. Ct. H.R. (Ser. A) No. 14 (Dec. 9, 1994) §31 and 32.

38 *Id.* §33.

39 *Id.* §34.

After arriving at this conclusion, the Court remembered that international obligations prohibit States from invoking their domestic laws as a justification for the non-fulfillment of those obligations,[40] but considered that its competence as an international tribunal was limited just to address "concrete violations of the human rights of a specific individual" because there is no article of the American Convention that authorizes the Court to review *in abstracto* the compatibility between the domestic laws and the American Convention.[41] On this approach – which was changed after *Suárez Rosero* (*see* Chapter 1, section 2.2.1) – the Court is limited only to deciding if the actions attributed to the State constituted a violation of the American Convention, regardless of whether or not such action is consistent with the State's domestic law.[42] As a consequence the Court stated that:

> 49. The contentious jurisdiction of the Court is intended to protect the rights and freedoms of specific individuals, not to resolve abstract questions. There is no provision in the American Convention authorizing the Court, under its contentious jurisdiction, to determine whether a law that has not yet affected the guaranteed rights and freedoms of specific individuals is in violation of the American Convention. As has already been noted, the Commission has that power and, in exercising it, would fulfill its main function of promoting respect for and defense of human rights. The Court also could do so in the exercise of its advisory jurisdiction, pursuant to Article 64(2).[43]

The criterion of the Inter-American Court reflects and confirms that Article 2 was not originally conceived as a source of any specific obligations that could lead to the declaration of the international responsibility of the State, which makes problematic arguing that specific obligations (like conventionality control) can be derived from this article. In sum, the first objection to the creation of the doctrine of conventionality control is that Article 2 does not have specific normative content, and it has the nature of programmatic norm. For this reason, it is not possible to derive any "legislative or other measure" that States shall take – as a matter of law, not political decision – in order to comply with Article 1.1, because that is an exclusive competence of the States parties to the American Convention. Thus, in this account, conventionality control cannot find its legal basis in Article 2, and could constitute a violation of the right of the States parties to the American Convention to decide the political and legal means to implement the American Convention.

---

40 *Id.* §35.

41 *Id.* §40–46.

42 *Id.* §48.

43 *Id.* §49.

2.2. SECOND OBJECTION: PROBLEMATIC INTERPRETATION OF THE VIENNA CONVENTION ON THE LAW OF TREATIES

The second source of criticism of the doctrine of conventionality control could be connected with the use that the Inter-American Court made of Articles 26 and 27 of the VCLT.[44] Since *Almonacid* the Court has supported the conclusion that domestic judges must exercise "conventionality control" because "according to international law, the obligations that (the American Convention) imposes must be honored in good faith and domestic laws cannot be invoked to justify their violation".[45] As mentioned in previous sections, the use of these articles suggests that the Court considers that domestic judges are obligated not to enforce domestic laws that violate the American Convention, partly because they must execute treaties in a manner that its purpose can be achieved (principle of good faith, in accordance with Article 26 of the VCLT), and because they are prohibited from "invok[ing] the provisions of its internal law as justification for its failure to perform a treaty" (Article 27 of the VCLT).

This type of interpretation is logical. Yet, an orthodox understanding of Articles 26 and 27 of the VCLT, which gives priority to the principle of sovereignty, does not necessarily support the position taken in *Almonacid*. Even when the approach followed by the Inter-American Court is consistent with the literal language of the above-mentioned articles, it faces similar problems than the conceptual construction on the effects of Articles 1.1 and 2 of the American Convention: it expands the normative scope of these articles in a manner that could be very well considered inconsistent with the content of the obligations derived from the VCLT. The following paragraphs explain how a reading that is attached to the positive content of Articles 26 and 27 of the VCLT would not only not support conventionality control, but actually might serve as a source of criticism for its existence. Before constructing this critique, first this section succinctly analyzes the basic normative components of Articles 26 and 27.[46]

---

44 In *Almonacid* (§125), the Court only referred to Art. 27 of the Vienna Convention to support its conclusion regarding the obligation of judges to exercise conventionality control. However, it is reasonable to suggest that the Court implicitly referred both to the obligations imposed by Art. 26 (*pacta sunt servanda*), and the obligation of Art. 27 (internal law and observance of treaties) by establishing that: "according to international law, the obligations that it imposes must be honored in good faith and domestic laws cannot be invoked to justify their violation. This provision is embodied in Article 27 of the Vienna Convention on the Law of Treaties." For this reason, in this section is considered that the Court is invoking both articles, even when it only referred expressly to Art. 27 of the Vienna Convention.

45 *Almonacid Arellano et al v. Chile*, *supra* n, 1, §125.

46 A complete analysis of the nature and scope of Arts. 26 and 27 can be found in Olivier Corten and Pierre Klein (Eds.), *The Vienna Conventions on the Law of Treaties. A Commentary*, Vol. I, pp. 659–701 (Oxford University Press, 2011); *see also* Oliver Dörr and Kirsten Schmalenbach (Eds.) *Vienna Convention on the Law of Treaties. A Commentary*, pp. 427–453 (Springer, 2012).

2.2.1. Nature and Scope of Articles 26 and 27 of the VCLT

Article 26 of the VCLT is generally conceived as the codification of a customary rule of international law,[47] which finds its origin in a principle of general international law or even of natural law.[48] The two distinct concepts embodied in this rule are the following: (1) every treaty possesses an obligatory character, which means that States have a legal – not a moral duty – to comply with their international commitments;[49] and (2) treaties must be performed in good faith, which means that the object of the treaty must be executed in a reasonable way and in such a manner that its purpose can be achieved.[50] The principle of good faith is in this form a substantive principle that clarifies the interpretation of the obligations that must be performed when States are parties to a treaty, which includes the notion that the parties must abstain from executing actions calculated to frustrate the object and purpose of the treaty.[51]

---

47 *See*, Declaration on the Rights and Duties of Nations, proposed at the Institute of International Law in October of 1921 by Albert de Lapradelle, Art. 2, §2 of the Draft, Institute of International Law, *Annuaire*, 1921, Vol. 28, p. 208; Art. 20 of the 1935 Harvard Draft, Harvard Law School, *Research in International Law*, Pt. III, Law of Treaties, American Journal of International Law, Supplement 1935, Vol. 29, p. 977; Art. 13 of the draft Declaration on Rights and Duties of States (1949), Report of the ILC on the works of its 1st session (1949), Official Records, General Assembly, 4th session (A/925), and the Declaration on Friendly Relations of 24 October 1970, A/RES/2625(XXV). *See also* Protocol of 17 January 1871 adopted at the London Conference, British and Foreign State papers, Vol. 61, pp. 1198–1199, the Preamble of the Covenant of the League of Nations; the Preamble to the Treaties of 16 October 1925; Art. 10 of the Havana Convention on Treaties, adopted on 20 February 1928 by the 6th International Conference of American States; the Preamble to the Charter of the United Nations; and Art. 14 of the Charter of the Organization of American States; and *see*, Malcolm N. Shaw, *International Law*, p. 811 (Cambridge University Press, 5th ed., 2003).

48 *See*, Jean Salmon, *Article 26*, in Olivier Corten and Pierre Klein (Eds.), *The Vienna Conventions on the Law of Treaties. A Commentary*, *supra* n. 46, pp. 662–663 (the author, referring to the explanation by Sir Gerald Fitzmaurice in the Fourth Report on the Law of Treaties (A/CN.4/120 of 17 March 1959, *YILC*, 1959, Vol. ii, p. 37), mentions that it is generally admitted that the rule of *pacta sunt servanda* is purely declaratory of the law, and that its basis is to be found prior to the Conventions that expresses it); *see also* Pufendorf, *De jure naturae and gentium*, bk. III, ch. III, iv, paras. 1 and 2, and Vattel, *Droit des gens*, bk. II, ch. XII, para. 163.

49 *See*, Jean Salmon, *Article 26*, in Olivier Corten and Pierre Klein (Eds.), *The Vienna Conventions on the Law of Treaties. A Commentary*, *supra* n. 46, p. 676 (the author explains that "the undisputed reception of the obligatory character of treaties to the parties results particularly from the fact that States normally honor their engagements.").

50 *Id.* pp. 677–678.

51 *See*, the Third Report to the ILC, Ybk ILC 1964, Vol. II, p. 7 (Sir Humphrey Waldock proposed the following language to govern the subject: "2. Good faith, inter alia, requires that a party to a treaty shall refrain from any acts calculated to prevent the due execution of the treaty or otherwise to frustrate its object." This provision was not included because it was considered as "implicit in the obligation to perform a treaty in good faith".).

The jurisprudence of the Permanent Court of International Justice (PCIJ) and the jurisprudence of the International Court of Justice are particularly rich concerning the application of good faith regarding treaties.[52] For instance, in *Gabcikovo-Nagymaros Project (Hungary/Slovakia)* the ICJ considered that the element of good faith is so important that it implies that the purpose of the treaty and the intentions of the parties in concluding the treaty should prevail over its literal application.[53] For the purposes of this section, it is particularly relevant to notice that one of the consequences of the operation of this rule is that a treaty must be performed notwithstanding any contrary provision in the internal law of the State. Consequently, if a treaty to which a State has consented is contrary to its domestic law, it is the obligation of that State to take any legislative measure necessary to perform its obligation, to modify its legislation if needed, or to take any necessary measures that must be observed by its citizens.[54] This is a truism that has been sustained even before the codification of the VCLT, as can be observed from the opinion of the PCIJ in its Advisory Opinion on the *Exchange of Greek and Turkish Population*, where it spoke of:

> [A] principle which is self-evident, according to which a State which has contracted valid international obligations is bound to make in its legislation such modifications as may be necessary to ensure the fulfillment of the obligations undertaken.[55]

Article 27 is also considered a customary rule of international law.[56] Its main purpose is to reassert the fundamental principle that international treaties must be performed in good faith. In this form this rule functions as a corollary of the principle of *pacta sunt servanda* by reinforcing the notion that the binding force of a treaty is determined solely by international law, which also entails that the execution of a treaty by the parties cannot depend on their respective

---

52 For decisions of the PCIJ, *see, Treatment of Polish Nationals and Other persons of Polish Origin or Speech in the Danzig Territory*. Advisory Opinion, 1932 P.C.I.J., Ser. A/B, No. 44 (Feb. 4), at 28; and *Minority Schools in Albania*. Advisory Opinion, 1935, Ser. A/B, No. 64 (Apr. 6), at 19 and 20; for decisions of the ICJ, *see, Conditions of Admission of a State to Memberships in the United Nations (Article 4 of the Charter)*. Advisory Opinion, 1948 I.C.J. (May 28), at 63; *Rights of Nationals of the United States of America in Morocco*. Judgment, 1952 I.C.J. (Aug. 27), at 212.

53 *See, Gabcikovo-Nagymaros Project (Hungary/Slovakia)*. Judgment, 1997 I.C.J. (Sep. 25), §142.

54 *See*, Jean Salmon, *Article 26*, in Olivier Corten and Pierre Klein (Eds.), *The Vienna Conventions on the Law of Treaties. A Commentary*, *supra* n. 46, p. 682.

55 *Exchange of Greek and Turkish Populations (Greece v. Turkey)*. Advisory Opinion, 1925 P.C.I.J. Ser. B, No. 10, (Feb. 25), at 20.

56 *See, Certain Questions of Mutual Assistance in Criminal Matters (Djibouti v. France)*, 2008 I.C.J. (Jun. 2008), §124; *see also* Annemie Schaus, *Article 27*, in Olivier Corten and Pierre Klein (Eds.), *The Vienna Conventions on the Law of Treaties. A Commentary*, *supra* n. 46, p. 691.

internal laws.[57] It also functions as a parallel principle to that of international responsibility, since the question of the breach of a treaty is essentially linked to the execution of the obligations established in the treaty and the justification for their non-performance. To this end, Article 27 excludes the defense of deviant internal law in international dispute settlement procedures, with the exception of those cases where the prerequisites of Article 46 of the Vienna Convention are met.[58]

This means that under Article 27 of the VCLT, a State cannot invoke the provisions of its internal law whether legislative, regulative, administrative, or jurisdictional to escape the binding force of a treaty.[59] In a similar fashion, a State cannot invoke gaps in its internal legislation, or the non-existence of domestic provisions, or modes of execution necessary for the implementation of an international obligation,[60] and it is also prohibited from claiming any internal provision concerning the procedure from the entry into force of the treaty to disregard international obligations.[61] As established by the PCIJ in the *Case of Treatment of Polish Nationals and Other Persons of Polish Origin or Speech in the Danzig Territory* (1932):

> [A]ccording to generally accepted principles, a State cannot rely, as against another State, on the provisions of the latter's Constitution, but only on international law and international obligations duly accepted ... Conversely, a State cannot adduce as against another State its own Constitution with a view to evading obligations incumbent upon it under international law or treaties in force.[62]

The above-mentioned paragraphs might be read in a manner that would lead to the conclusion that the VCLT clearly supports the position taken by the Inter-American Court in *Almonacid*, since the principles of good faith and *effet utile* are the international foundations for a State's duty to comply with treaties. Articles 1.1 and 2 of the American Convention reinforce and specify the obligation of States to take the necessary measures to make the rights and

---

57 Annemie Schaus, *Article 27*, in Olivier Corten and Pierre Klein (Eds.), *The Vienna Conventions on the Law of Treaties. A Commentary*, *supra* n. 46, p. 689.

58 *See*, Responsibility of States for Internationally Wrongful Acts, Ybk ILC, 2001, Vol. II (Pt. II), Art. 32 (this article reads as follows: "The responsible State may not rely on the provisions of its internal law as justification for failure to comply with its obligations under this part."); *see also* Kirsten Schmalenbach, *Article 27*, in Oliver Dörr and Kirsten Schmalenbach (Eds.), *Vienna Convention on the Law of Treaties. A Commentary*, *supra* n. 46, p. 453.

59 *Greco-Bulgarian Communities*, 1930, P.C.I.J., Ser. B, No. 17 (Jul. 31) p. 32; *see also S.S. Wimbledon*, 1923, P.C.I.J., Ser. A, No. 1 (Aug. 17) p. 29; *Certain German interests in Polish Upper Silesia*, 1926 P.C.I.J., Ser. A, No. 7 (Aug. 25) p. 19.

60 *See*, Annemie Schaus, *Article 27*, in Olivier Corten and Pierre Klein (Eds.), *The Vienna Conventions on the Law of Treaties. A Commentary*, *supra* n. 46, p. 693.

61 *Id.* p. 697.

62 *Treatment of Polish Nationals and Other persons of Polish Origin or Speech in the Danzig Territory*. Advisory Opinion, 1932 P.C.I.J., Ser. A/B, No. 44 (Feb. 4), 24.

freedoms of the American Convention effective, which means that the obligation to adopt "legislative and other measures" is based on the general principle of international law that obligations must be carried out in good faith and that domestic law must not be invoked as a reason for non-compliance. Yet, although this position is logical and consistent with the literal language of Articles 26 and 27 of the Vienna Convention, it is not obvious that these articles provide a foundation for the doctrine of conventionality control.

2.2.2. *The (In)compatibility Between the Doctrine of Conventionality Control and the VCLT*

The notion that Articles 26 and 27 of the VCLT could provide support to the doctrine of conventionality control could be put in doubt once all the relevant rules and principles of the VCLT that act in combination with these articles are properly considered. It is true that the *pacta sunt servanda* rule was created on the assumption that States will actually comply with their international commitments, and that they will take the necessary actions to achieve that purpose.[63] But it is equally true that the drafters of the VCLT took measures to strike a balance between the maintenance of the *status quo* in treaty obligations (that States must comply in good faith with treaty provisions notwithstanding any other consideration) and the protection of the sovereignty of States and other values such as justice and openness to change.[64]

In order to achieve the above-mentioned balance, the VCLT recognizes modalities and limitations to the rule of *pacta sunt servanda* that take the following forms: (1) the respect owed to freedom of contract and the establishment of an invalid regime for vices of consent;[65] (2) the clause of *rebus sic stantibus* in order to reconcile stability with progress;[66] (3) the *jus cogens*, contemplating the protection of the superior interests of the international community;[67] and (4) a close relation with the basic principles of the

---

63 *See*, Malcolm N. Shaw, *International Law*, *supra* n. 47, p. 812 (the author explains that the *pacta sunt servanda* rule "underlines every international agreement for, in the absence of a certain minimum believe that States will perform their treaty obligations in good faith, there is no reason for countries to enter into such obligations with each other").

64 *See*, Jean Salmon, *Article 26*, in Olivier Corten and Pierre Klein (Eds.), *The Vienna Conventions on the Law of Treaties. A Commentary*, *supra* n. 46, p. 660.

65 General Assembly, 22nd session, 6th committee, 974th meeting, Oct. 18, 1967, p. 98, §22–4 (Cuba); 980th meeting, Oct. 25, 1967, p. 129, §43 (United Arab Republic).

66 General Assembly, 21st session, 6th committee, 909th meeting, Oct. 13, 1966, p. 47, §32 (Bolivia); General Assembly, 22nd session, 6th committee, 974th meeting, Oct. 18, 1967, p. 98, §22–4 (Cuba); 976th meeting, Oct. 20, 1967, p. 108, §30 (China); 978th meeting, Oct. 23, 1967, p. 118, §6 (Hungary).

67 General Assembly, 22nd session, 6th committee, 975th meeting, Oct. 18, 1967, p. 104, §22–4 (Cuba); 976th session, Oct. 20, 1967, p. 107, §23 (Czechoslovakia).

Charter of the United Nations.[68] In this sense, the writings of the most prominent scholars show that the *pacta sunt servanda* rule is conceptually inseparable from other relevant rules of the VCLT, and from other principles like those established in Article 2 of the United Nations Charter. This article recognizes as foundational principles the sovereign equality of States (Article 2.1), and the prohibition against the intervention in matters that are "essentially within the domestic jurisdiction of any State" (Article 2.7).[69]

Article 26 of the VCLT by no means supports the conclusion that international law is "superior" to domestic law, as a literary and isolated reading of this article would suggest. The respect for the sovereignty of States is a requirement for the operation of this article, particularly regarding the normative effects that an international norm has for domestic authorities. Put in other terms, the obligation of States to comply in good faith with treaties is relativized by those normative aspects that derive from the rights of States as sovereigns. One of the manifestations of the sovereignty in international law is that States have the right to determine the specific manner by which domestic authorities have to enforce international law.

In a similar fashion, it is relevant to consider that although Article 27 strengthens the obligation of States to comply in good faith with their international obligations – by prohibiting that internal law be invoked to evade the binding force of a treaty – this rule works on the assumption that international law generally leaves States free to organize the implementation of their international obligations in the way most suitable to them, as long as those obligations are executed and the rights of third parties are safeguarded.[70] This is called the "principle of indifference" of the international legal order in regard to the mode of execution of international obligations in the internal legal order (hereinafter the principle of indifference).[71] It constitutes an essential element of Article 27.

---

68 General Assembly, 22nd session, 6th committee, 975th meeting, Oct. 19, 1967, p 104, para. 18 (Yugoslavia); 980th meeting, Oct. 25, 1967, p. 128, para. 29 (Bolivia); 981st meeting, Oct. 25, 1967, p. 138, §29 (Ecuador).

69 *See*, Jean Salmon, *Article 26*, in OLIVIER CORTEN AND PIERRE KLEIN (EDS.), *THE VIENNA CONVENTIONS ON THE LAW OF TREATIES. A COMMENTARY*, *supra* n. 46, pp. 660 and 685.

70 *See*, Annemie Schaus, *Article 27*, in OLIVIER CORTEN AND PIERRE KLEIN (EDS.), *THE VIENNA CONVENTIONS ON THE LAW OF TREATIES. A COMMENTARY*, *supra* n. 46, p. 689.

71 *See*, *Id.* p. 689. The principle of indifference has been sustained (although not necessarily with that name) by the most prestigious international tribunals, including the Inter-American Court. *See*, Cases 51-54/71 *International Fruit Company*, CJEC, 15 December 1971, ECR 1971, p. 1115; Cases 68-73/81 *Commission v. Belgium*, 2 Feb. 1982, ECR 1982, respectively at pp. 153, 163, 169, 175, 183, 189 (according to the Court of Justice of the European Communities: "When provisions of the Treaty of Regulations confer powers or impose obligations on Member States for the purpose of the implementation of Community law the question of how such powers are to be exercised and whether the States may entrust the implementation of such obligations to specific national authorities is solely a matter for the

This principle is so important in the understanding of how international obligations work, that even in cases where an international court or tribunal finds a State responsible for violations of a treaty provision due to the enforcement of domestic laws, it is generally accepted that that mere fact would neither affect the validity of the domestic laws that caused the violation to the treaty, nor would it impose new obligations on domestic authorities to act in a certain manner. It is understood that the domestic legal system and the international legal system have their own sphere of supremacy, so a State could be condemned time after time for the enforcement of certain domestic law and that fact would not affect the validity of that law.[72] For instance, the ICJ, when dealing with the question of how a State must comply with the judgment of the Court, recently decided in the *Request for Interpretation of the Judgment of 31 March in the Case concerning Avena and other Mexican Nationals (Mexico v. United States of America)* that:

> The obligation laid down in that paragraph (referring to paragraph 153 (9) of the Judgment) is indeed an obligation of result which clearly must be performed unconditionally; non performance of it constitutes internationally wrongful conduct. However, *the judgment leaves to the United States to choose the means of implementation, not excluding the introduction within a reasonable time of appropriate legislation, if deemed necessary under domestic constitutional law.* Nor moreover does the *Avena* Judgment prevent direct enforceability of the obligation in question, if such an effect is permitted by domestic law.[73]

The decision of the ICJ in *Avena* is an implicit operation of the principle of indifference – which might have been expressed in such a strong manner because one of the parties to the controversy was the United States. It also recalls Argo's distinction between obligations of means and obligations of result, in the sense that the obligations imposed by international law must be fulfilled as a matter of international law; yet, States are free to choose the means to do

---

constitutional system of each State."); *International Responsibility for the Promulgation and Enforcement of Laws in Violation of the Convention (Arts. 1 and 2 American Convention on Human Rights) supra* n. 37, §49 (As mentioned before, the Inter-American Court established that: "There is no provision in the American Convention authorizing the Court, under its contentious jurisdiction, to determine whether a law that has not yet affected the guaranteed rights and freedoms of specific individuals is in violation of the American Convention.").

72 *See*, Manuel Becerra, *La jerarquía de los tratados en el orden jurídico interno. Una vision desde la perspectiva del derecho internacional*, in Sergio García Ramírez and Mireya Castañeda (Eds.), *Recepción Nacional del Derecho Internacional de los Derechos Humanos y Admisión de la Competencia Contenciosa de la Corte Interamericana*, pp. 295 and 301 (UNAM & IIJ & Minister of Foreign Affairs & Inter-American Court of Human Rights, 2009).

73 *Request for Interpretation of the Judgment of 31 March in the Case concerning Avena and other Mexican Nationals (Mexico v. United States of America)*. Judgment, 2009 I.C.J. (Jan. 19), §44 (emphasis added).

so unless otherwise established by the treaty that creates the obligation. As has been explained in this and the previous section, if the idea that the Inter-American System is not a self-contained regime, this position could be accepted as a structural principle of international law that influences both the American Convention and the VCLT (as well as any other source of international law). It is indeed a position that gives a high degree of deference to the States, and which recognizes the principle of sovereignty as paramount. In the words of Aneme Schaus: "Article 27 of the Vienna Convention *merely* prescribes that in the international legal order, international law prevails over the internal law of the State."[74]

Consequently, in this view, it is possible to argue that the doctrine of conventionality control would only find normative support in the VCLT whenever it is not incompatible with the principles of the sovereign equality of States, the principle of non-intervention and the principle of indifference. So, a positivistic understanding of international law would not support any attempt to argue that the American Convention takes precedence over domestic law, and that international law has a direct effect on State authorities *because* Articles 26 and 27 impose those obligations on States parties to a treaty. The effects of the above-mentioned articles is not to assert the superiority of international law over domestic law in domestic legal systems, or to impose specific obligations on State authorities to give priority to international law over domestic law, which is a position wrongly sustained by some authors.[75] The determination of the hierarchical status of international law within domestic legal systems, and the authorities in charge of guaranteeing its effects, has been, in principle, and unless otherwise established by a rule of international law, an exclusive right of the States parties to a treaty.[76]

---

74 *See*, Annemie Schaus, *Article 27*, in Olivier Corten and Pierre Klein (Eds.), *The Vienna Conventions on the Law of Treaties. A Commentary*, *supra* n. 46, p. 701 (emphasis added).

75 *See*, Ernesto Rey Cantor, *Control de Convencionalidad de las Leyes y Derechos Humanos*, *supra* n. 3, pp. LXIV and LXXIII (the author provides the best example of a position that sustains that Art. 27 of the Vienna Convention – as well as the relevant jurisprudence of the PCIJ and the ICJ regarding that rule – supports the view that judges shall exercise conventionality control because it means that international law is supreme over domestic law. This position, however, appears to be based on a reading of international law that treats the Vienna Convention – and by extension the American Convention – as if it was a text of constitutional character).

76 *See*, Annemie Schaus, *Article 27*, in Olivier Corten and Pierre Klein (Eds.), *The Vienna Conventions on the Law of Treaties. A Commentary*, *supra* n. 46, p. 700 (the author explains that the primacy of international law over domestic law applies only with reference to the discharge by a State of its international obligations but that this does not mean that: "in case of conflict between an international obligation and a provision of international law, international law will necessary take over internal legal orders. It merely entails that, no matter what the content of the internal law of the State, it does not affect the international obligations of the State and the responsibility that the State might incur in case of non-compliance.").

2.3. THIRD OBJECTION: THE PROBLEM OF THE JURISPRUDENTIAL ORIGINS OF THE DOCTRINE OF CONVENTIONALITY CONTROL

The third source of criticism of the doctrine of conventionality control comes from its jurisprudential origins. Conventionality control was created in *Almonacid* in order to avoid the enforcement of an amnesty law, and then it was consolidated in the Court's jurisprudence in subsequent cases until the decision of the *OC-24/17* (2016). The constant reference to conventionality control has created the perception that its normative force increases as much as the Inter-American Court applies it to different cases, and as much as different high courts of different States of the region use the jurisprudence of the Inter-American Court as a binding and autonomous source of law. And this might be partially correct: the perception of the validity of conventionality control has been increasing in the last years precisely because of the constant use of the doctrine at the domestic and the international level.

However, from a formal perspective, the fact that conventionality control has been frequently mentioned in recent cases decided at the international and the national level does not necessarily mean that the normative force of the doctrine has increased – or even that this force exists at all – especially if what has been mentioned in the previous two sections are considered as valid reasons to assert the anti-conventionality of this doctrine. From this perspective, it is legally irrelevant that the Court has referred to conventionality control in more than 25 cases (from this perspective it could repeat it one hundred times and it would not have normative consequences), because there is no system of precedents in the Inter-American System. On this basis, the following paragraphs present three possible arguments against the attempt to ground the normative force of the obligation to exercise conventionality control in the normative force of the Inter-American Court's jurisprudence.

These objections can be summarized in the following manner: first, no article of the American Convention establishes a duty for States to follow the Court's jurisprudence in cases where they are not parties to the dispute; second, the obligatory character of conventionality control (which is a jurisprudential creation) cannot be inferred from the notion that the jurisprudence of the Court is binding (as the result of the doctrine of conventionality control), since that position implies a circular argument. Third, the legitimacy of conventionality control is diminished because *Almonacid* was decided in a specific context where the State of Chile did not attempt to make a strong defense of the amnesty laws enacted by Pinochet's regime in order to fight against impunity, even when this position implied a reduction of its freedom to deal with similar cases in the future; but other States (Brazil, Uruguay or El Salvador) did not agree to such a reduction of their capacity to decide the way in which the judiciary should deal with laws that are contrary to the American Convention and that have no legal effects.

2.3.1. *No "Conventional" Obligation to Follow the Jurisprudence of the Inter-American Court Beyond a Case Where a State is a Party to the Controversy*

There is an objection of some weight against the fact that the doctrine of conventionality control is grounded on the jurisprudence of the Court: Article 68.1 does not give support to the existence of an obligation for the States parties to the American Convention to follow the Court's jurisprudence as precedents. It is true that this Article creates an obligation for the States parties to the American Convention (1) "to comply with the judgment of the Court", (2) "in any case to which they (the States) are parties". But the language of this article suggests that the obligation to comply with the judgments of the Inter-American Court binds States as subjects of international law, only in those cases where they are parties to a dispute, and only with the purpose of ensuring the enjoyment of the right that was violated by the State, and in order to pay a fair compensation in case no remedy is possible.[77]

This means that a problem exists upon arguing that Article 68.1 supports the existence of an obligation on all domestic authorities to follow a doctrine created by the Court in a case against a third State. The ordinary meaning of Article 68.1 could lead to the conclusion that the obligations derived from a judgment of the Court must be fulfilled by States as legal entities (not by specific authorities, like the judiciary), only in cases where they are parties to a dispute (which means that the Court's judgments have no *erga omnes* effects), and only in the operative paragraphs (not in every consideration and reasoning made by the Court). This position is indeed supported by the practice of the ICJ, which decided in *Avena* that even when compliance with the judgment in that case was an obligation of results, the specific manner of complying with the judgment depended on the means chosen by the United States.[78]

This position follows the logic that was explained in the previous sections regarding the operation of the principle of indifference of the international legal order, applied this time to the mode of execution of judgments in the internal legal order. In this logic, it is up to the State to decide how to implement the judgments of an international court or tribunal, and which authorities are in charge of executing those judgments.[79] This position also follows the

---

77 *See generally*, Ezequiel Malarino, *Acerca de la Pretendida Obligatoriedad de la Jurisprudencia de los Órganos Interamericanos de Protección de Derechos Humanos para los Tribunales Judiciales Nacionales*, in SISTEMA INTERAMERICANO DE PROTECCIÓN DE LOS DERECHOS HUMANOS Y DERECHO PENAL INTERNACIONAL, p. 438 (Konrad-Adenauer-Stiftung, 2010).

78 *Request for Interpretation of the Judgment of 31 March in the Case concerning Avena and other Mexican Nationals (Mexico v. United States of America)*. Judgment of 19 Jan. 2009, §44.

79 *Id.*, §44; *see generally*, *Medellin v. Texas*, 552 U.S. 491 (2008), p. 8 (the Supreme Court of the United States established that: "no one disputes that the Avena decision – a decision that

"principle of relativity" (*principio de relatividad de las sentencias*) – to use the expression used in some civil law countries – in the sense that the judgments of the Inter-American Court have binding force only for the State that is involved in a dispute, and only to the extent necessary to remedy a concrete human right violation (as it was in certain manner suggested by the ICtHR itself in the *Advisory Opinion 14/94*).

This is indeed a position that limits the force of the Court's jurisprudence. Yet it might be closer to the ordinary meaning given to the terms of Article 68.1, with the general understanding about the non-existence of the doctrine of precedent in international law, and with the principle of sovereignty.[80] In other words, it is plausible to say that the obligation of the State "to comply with the judgment of the Court" is designed to function as an obligation of results, that has a limited scope defined by the concrete orders given by the Court in the operative paragraphs of a judgment. In this view, the powers given to the Court by the American Convention are not there to authorize the imposition of obligations for the States parties to modify or adopt new practices in their domestic legal systems, or to enforce those decisions as precedents by the State that were condemned in a particular procedure, or by other States that were not parties to the dispute.

The above-mentioned does not mean that States can decide whether or not to comply with the judgments of the Inter-American Court in cases where they are parties to a dispute, or that their domestic laws can be invoked as a justification not to comply with those judgments. States have an obligation of international law to comply with the judgment of the Inter-American Court (or of any other international court or tribunal that has jurisdiction on the State) notwithstanding any consideration of domestic law, as Sergio García Ramírez correctly pointed it out in his famous concurrent opinion in *Myrna*.[81] The judgments of an international court in the exercise of its contentious jurisdiction have a binding force, which means that they must be complied with as a matter of international law, and that States cannot claim their domestic law as justification for lack of compliance.

Consequently – from this perspective, based on positive international law and the principle of sovereignty – it is possible to argue that the binding character of the doctrine of conventionality control cannot be derived from the judgments

flows from the treaties by which the United States submitted to ICJ jurisdiction in regard to Vienna Convention disputes – constitutes an international law obligation on the part of the United States. But not all international law obligations automatically constitute binding federal law enforceable in United States courts.").

80 *See*, Statute of the International Court of Justice, Art. 38.1(d); *see also* Malcolm N. Shaw, International Law, *supra* n. 47, p. 103.

81 This is an obligation that comes from the operation of Art. 68.1 of the American Convention and Arts. 26 and 27 of the Vienna Convention.

of the Inter-American Court taken as precedents, not even if the Court says so constantly in its jurisprudence. The fundamental problem with arguing the opposite is that it is not possible to find a secondary rule of international law that establishes a legal duty for States to take the judgments of the Court as precedents, and therefore conventionality control – which is a creature of the Court's jurisprudence – cannot be considered as a legal obligation. From the perspective of positive international law, the judgments of the Court are limited by the principles of indifference and the principle of the relativity of the judgments, and the only mechanism to monitor compliance with these judgments is the "procedure for monitoring compliance".[82]

2.3.2. Logical Problems: Circularity in the Argument of the Inter-American Court

But someone may argue that it is possible to find this secondary rule precisely in the reasoning of paragraph 124 of *Almonacid*. The argument might look like this: State authorities must treat the jurisprudence of the Court as precedents because the Court established that obligation in *Almonacid* – and there is an obligation to comply with the judgments of the Court. So once the nature of the jurisprudence as a precedent was determined by the Inter-American Court, it follows that all State authorities must exercise conventionality control – that is a doctrine that is part of the Court's jurisprudence. But besides what has been mentioned throughout this chapter regarding the problem that represents arguing that Article 68.1 might be applicable for different cases even for the State that was condemned, this argument might face a serious logical opposition: it is circular.

The argument is circular because it grounds the obligation to exercise conventionality control in the obligation of all States to follow the Court's jurisprudence; but the obligation to follow the Court's jurisprudence is the result of the creation of the doctrine of conventionality control. This argument was developed by Ezequiel Malarino to question the existence of precedents

---

82 *See, Baena Ricardo et al. v. Panama*. Judgment, Inter-Am. Ct. H.R. (Ser. C) No. 105 (Nov. 28, 2003) §72. (Since *Baena Ricardo v. Panama* (2003) the Court has asserted that its authority to determine the international responsibility of the State for violations of the American Convention includes the power to administer justice. This power "encompasses monitory compliance with what has been decided", and to "establish and implement mechanisms or procedures for monitoring compliance with the judicial decisions, an activity that is inherent in its jurisdictional function."); *see generally* Sergio García Ramírez, *La Corte Interamericana de Derechos Humanos*, p. 72 (Purrúa, 2007); *see generally*, *Caesar v. Trinidad and Tobago*. Judgment, Inter-Am. Ct. H.R. (Ser. C) No. 123, (Mar. 11, 2005). Reasoned Concurrent Opinion of Manuel E. Ventura Robles (no para.).

in the Inter-American System, but it is also applicable to question the validity of conventionality control. The Argentinean scholar points out that in order to avoid a *petition principii* it will be necessary to find independent reasons to treat the decisions of the Court as precedents, and thus to ground the obligation of States to exercise conventionality control. In his view, the only reason given by the Court to assert the obligation of the States to follow its jurisprudence is that the Court is "the ultimate interpreter of the American Convention",[83] but he rejects this position as a valid reason because the fact that the Court is the final authority in the Inter-American System (Article 67 of the American Convention)[84] does not support the conclusion that domestic authorities have an obligation to enforce its judgments at the domestic level beyond the scope of Article 68.1.

Malarino argues that the position of the Court as the ultimate interpreter of the American Convention is not sufficient even to ground the notion that the Court's jurisprudence has the nature of a precedent at the international level, because the fact that a tribunal has the power to say what the law is in a particular case does not transform its criteria into binding rules for domestic courts or even for itself in future cases. This would happen only if there is an additional rule that establishes the binding character of precedents (*stare decisis et quieta non muovere*), and this rule does not exist in the Inter-American System. So, the Court confuses two questions that are conceptually different: the definitive character of its decisions and the binding character of its jurisprudence, and who is the final instance to determine what the law is at the international level and the domestic level. In this last sense he explains that: "the ICtHR is not the head of the national systems of administration of justice, not even regarding the interpretation of the ACHR, there is not a hierarchical relationship between the ICtHR and State tribunals."[85]

2.3.3. Problems of Legitimacy in the Position of the Inter-American Court

As a corollary to the third objection to conventionality control, it is possible to question the Court's legitimacy to create this doctrine through a decision in the exercise of its contentious jurisdiction; because by doing so the Court could be in violation of two fundamental principles of domestic law and

83 *See, Almonacid Arellano et al v. Chile, supra* n. 1, §124.

84 Organization of American States (OAS), American Convention on Human Rights, Nov. 22, 1969, O.A.S.T.S. No. 36, 1144, U.N.T.S. 123, Art. 67.

85 *See*, Ezequiel Malarino, *Acerca de la Pretendida Obligatoriedad de la Jurisprudencia de los Órganos Interamericanos de Protección de Derechos Humanos para los Tribunales Judiciales Nacionales*, in Sistema Interamericano de Protección de los Derechos Humanos y Derecho Penal Internacional, *supra* n. 77, pp. 439 and 440.

international law: the principles of constitutional supremacy and the principle of *pacta sunt servanda*. The first one would be violated because an extreme view of conventionality control implies that rules of constitutional law are no longer relevant to determine the hierarchical status of norms of IHRL in a domestic legal system; the second principle would be violated because States have never agreed to the obligations imposed by conventionality control. There is no doubt that these principles are so relevant for the international and domestic legal systems, that there is seriousness in asking the question about the Court's legitimacy and political prudence to create a doctrine that alters the way in which they operate.[86]

At the core of the critique about the Court's lack of legitimacy to create the doctrine of conventionality control might rest the view that this doctrine originated much more as a political choice of the judges rather than as a conclusion based on legal reasons. The doctrine of conventionality control presents a solution to the practical problem that constituted the existence of domestic laws or practices of domestic authorities that are contrary to the American Convention, and that produce violations of the State's obligations in terms of Articles 1.1 and 2. But one may argue that the problem is that the Court – in the process of fighting against human rights violations and the inefficiencies of domestic legal systems – diminished the State's freedom to decide important questions that are usually reserved as part of their sovereign capacity as subjects of international law, that were never accepted by an express agreement or by practice at the international level, and – therefore – that constitute political decisions until they are transformed into international law by treaty or custom.

Connected with the above-mentioned, it is also possible to argue that the origin of the doctrine of conventionality control is closely related to the political choices of Chile and Peru regarding the manner by which the government of these countries decided to deal with the existence of amnesty laws enacted by previous regimes.[87] By the time that *Almonacid* and *La Cantuta* reached the Court, the defense of both States was not arguing the legality of the amnesty laws that were enacted by Pinochet's or Fujimori's regimes, or claiming the right of their courts to enforce them. They agreed with the Inter-American Court's jurisprudence settled in *Barrios Altos* regarding the necessity to remove these laws from their legal systems and not defending its enforcement in domestic courts.[88] For this reason, it could be possible to say that the Court's judgments in these cases served the political purpose of those who wanted to remove the

86 *See generally*, Supreme Court of Justice of Argentina, M. 2333. XLII (Mazzeo, Julio Lilo *et al.*, Appeal for annulment and constitutional motion), Jul. 13, 2007. Dissenting Opinion of Judge Carlos Fayt, §§18, 30 and 31.

87 *See*, Luigi Crema, "Are Amnesties Still an Option? A Non-Policy Based Critique of the Inter-American Approach", *supra* n. 7, p. 51.

88 *See*, *Almonacid Arellano et al v. Chile*, *supra* n. 1, §85.

amnesty laws from their domestic legal systems, or to leave these laws without efficacy. If this is true, the doctrine of conventionality control emerged partly because of the attitudes of the States involved in the above-mentioned cases, which means also that the decision of these States had an impact on those States not parties to the case.

This critique was developed by Luigi Crema, who argues the lack of legitimacy in the Court's decision to declare the nullity *ab initio* of amnesty laws and to create the doctrine of conventionality control because ultimately: "the political opinion (not the law) exercised by a government through the intermediary of the Court becomes compulsory also for other States, even when other States decided to transition to democracy in a different (but maybe still effective) way."[89] If Crema's position is true for amnesty law cases that involved impunity for serious human rights violations (as happened in *Almonacid* and *La Cantuta*), with stronger reason it is also true that the legitimacy of the doctrine is diminished when it refers to other types of domestic laws that are not preceded by such a strong rejection of their legitimacy, and where there is no clear agreement within the international community on how to deal with these laws.

If there is a deficit in the legitimacy of the Court's political choice when the doctrine of conventionality control was created because only Chile and Peru "collaborated" with its creation, and because it attempted to serve as a tool to combat a particular kind of problem (impunity for crimes against humanity provoked by the operation of amnesty laws), this deficit of legitimacy increases in as much as the Court argues the obligation to exercise conventionality control (1) in cases where there are different circumstances regarding the emergence of amnesty laws (as has actually happened with the cases of *Gomes Lund* in Brazil, *Gelman* in Uruguay and *El Mozote* in El Salvador); (2) in cases where the law in question is not null *ab initio*; (3) where there is no strong jurisprudential support about the anti-conventionality of a law, or (4) when the State actually defends the legality of the law in question at the international procedure. Ignoring the differences might affect the efficacy of the Court's judgments, and might endanger the permanence of some States in the Inter-American System.

There is a problem of lack of legitimacy when the Inter-American Court reduces the freedom of States to decide questions that are political by definition (for instance when the Court declares the nullity of an amnesty law, or when it orders the adoption of new criminal offenses in the penal code), especially when there might be democratic consensus in the way that the government of a concrete State shall deal with problems that involve sensitive human rights questions that do not have a clear answer – this has been the source of criticism

---

89 *See*, Luigi Crema, "Are Amnesties Still an Option? A Non-Policy Based Critique of the Inter-American Approach", *supra* n. 7, p. 51.

of the position of the Court in *Gelman*.[90] For obvious reasons, this critique just becomes stronger when it is argued that the Court's jurisprudence has the force of a precedent that overrules any law or decision to the contrary taken at the domestic level, as an extreme version of conventionality control appears to sustain. This critique recalls the "counter-majoritarian" arguments against excessive exercise of authority by constitutional courts *vis-à-vis* the legislative power, but this time applied to the Inter-American Court *vis-à-vis* State legislatures and domestic judiciaries. This argument certainly becomes a relevant objection when the Court tries to act as a constitutional court – especially when it does it in areas that are not clearly defined in treaty law, and that have been a subject of political debate in the States parties to the Convention.

The critiques based on the lack of the Court's legitimacy to create the doctrine of conventionality control are relevant not only because they point out problems about its legal nature as an international institution, which in its extreme version affects democratic life at the domestic level. They also help to explain why the main source of opposition to the acceptance of the doctrine might come from those courts or other public authorities that refuse to follow the Court's jurisprudence – and thus that they refuse to exercise conventionality control – if that action would constitute a violation of the domestic constitution or domestic law. Another source of opposition could come from domestic authorities if they simply reject the doctrine as an obligation of international law owing to its detachment from the text of the American Convention, or because it is too intrusive in State affairs and therefore violates the principle of sovereignty. It might be the case that some domestic courts, or in general some States, by not finding valid legal reasons that explain why they need to follow the Court's jurisprudence and repeal or amend certain laws or exercise conventionality control, will simply reject the political choice made by the Court and will follow their own choice or that of the legislator.

Regarding this last point – and just as an example – it is pertinent to recall the position of the Supreme Court of Justice of Uruguay in Judgment No. 20 (2013). In this case it was decided that certain provisions of the Uruguayan criminal code, passed by Congress in compliance with the judgment of *Gelman*, were unconstitutional since they violated Articles 7 and 10 of the Constitution of Uruguay.[91] The Supreme Court decided not only to refuse to exercise conventionality control, but chose to follow its duty under the Constitution

---

90 *See generally*, Ezequiel Malarino, *Judicial Activism, Punitivism, and Supranationalisation: Illiberal Tendencies of the Inter-American Court of Human Rights*, *supra* n. 7, p. 687; Roberto Gargarella, *La democracia frente a los crimenes masivos: una reflexión a la luz del caso Gelman*, Revista Latinoamericana de Derecho Internacional (2015).

91 *See generally*, Supreme Court of Justice of Uruguay, Judgment No. 20 (*Excepción de Inconstitucionalidad Arts. 1, 2 y 3 de la Ley No. 18.831, IUE 2-109971/2011*), Feb. 22, 2013.

rather than give priority to the Inter-American Court's decision.[92] In a similar fashion, and precisely by what was perceived by the State of Venezuela as an illegitimate interpretation of the American Convention – although certainly framed in language charged with political and ideological components – Venezuela denounced the American Convention arguing that the Court had systematically violated basic principles of international law. These principles included the duty to respect the sovereignty of States and the principle of self-determination, since the Inter-American Court has made judgments that were inapplicable by pretending that the State modified its domestic legal system.[93]

In the same sense, the Inter-American Court faced opposition from the Constitutional Tribunal of the Dominican Republic (CTDR) after the decision in *Expelled Dominican and Haitians* (2014), where it was decided that judgment TC/0168/13 (issued by the CTDR) deprived the victims of several rights connected to their right to nationality.[94] The IACtHR considered that the decision of the CTDR violated Article 2 in connection with Articles 3, 18, 20 and 24 of the American Convention,[95] and therefore suggested that domestic authorities should exercise conventionality control regarding that judgment and any other provision that results in a violation of the rights of the Haitian population in the Dominican Republic.[96] The response to CTDR was judgment TC/0256/14, which declared unconstitutional the instrument accepting the jurisdiction of the Inter-American Court.[97] The reaction of the CTDR was subject to severe criticism by the Inter-American Commission and other relevant actors in civil society.[98]

More recently, the Supreme Court of Justice of Argentina (SCJAN) issued a ruling on February 17, 2017 regarding the implementation of the case of *Fontevecchia y D'Amico v. Argentina*, decided by the Inter-American Court on

---

92 *See generally*, Walter Carnota, *The Inter-American Court of Human Rights and Conventionality Control* (July 2012), p. 27, available at https://ssrn.com/abstract=2116599.

93 Letter of the Popular Minister of Foreign Affairs of the Bolivarian Republic of Venezuela to the Secretary General of the Organization of American States, Sept 6, 2012 (the State of Venezuela referred specifically to the decision in *Lopez Mendoza v. Venezuela* of 2011).

94 *See, Expelled Dominicans and Haitians v. Dominican Republic.* Preliminary Objections, Merits, Reparations and Costs Judgment, Inter-Am. Ct. H.R. (Ser. C) No. 282 (Aug. 28, 2014) §314.

95 *Id.* §325.

96 *Id.* §311 and 471.

97 Constitutional Tribunal of the Dominican Republic, Resolution TC/0256/14, Nov. 4, 2014.

98 *See*, Inter-American Commission on Human Rights. Press release of Nov. 6, 2014, available at http://www.oas.org/en/iachr/media_center/PReleases/2014/130.asp (last accessed Dec. 9, 2017); *see also* Silvia Ayuso, "La República Dominicana se desliga de la Corte Interamericana de DD HH", editorial note from *El País* from Nov. 6, 2014, available at http://internacional.elpais.com/internacional/2014/11/06/actualidad/1415230815_658290.html (last accessed Dec. 9, 2017).

November 29, 2011.[99] In this case, the ICtHR ordered the State to overturn a judicial decision in its entirety.[100] The executive power supported compliance with the order, but the SCJAN refused to do so. The latter reasoned that the IACtHR lacked the authority to order the overturning of a judgment, and that by doing so exceeded its powers under the American Convention.[101] This judgment was particularly surprising since Argentina has been one of the most "open" States in the region to the incorporation of IHRL in general, and to the decisions of the ICtHR in particular. It has also been historically supportive of the Inter-American System. Yet, as Jorge Contesse correctly points out, the decision of the SCJAN goes "to the core of one critical issue": it questions the notion that the ICtHR has the authority to "revoke" a judgment and thus that it can act as a "fourth instance".[102] The influence that this judgment might have in future cases in Argentina and in the region, and the persuasiveness and effectiveness of the ICtHR's response in its decision on judgment compliance of October 18, 2017 remains to be seen.[103]

Of course, the positions of Uruguay, Venezuela, the Dominican Republic and Argentina are different on various levels, especially regarding the suspicious attitude that Venezuela has had towards the Inter-American System, and the historical aspects that surround the migratory treatment of Haitians in the Dominican Republic. These facts make it more plausible to think that the denouncement of the American Convention in the case of Venezuela is motivated solely by political purposes, and that the decision in Dominican Republic was a defiant action that might change in the near future. But these examples are relevant because they show extreme cases of how the structural

---

99 *See, Case of Fontevecchia and D'Amico v. Argentina.* Merits, Reparations and Costs Judgment of Nov. 29, 2011. (Ser. C) No. 238.

100 *Id.* §105.

101 *See*, National Supreme Court of Justice, *Ministerio de Relaciones Exteriores y Culto s/ informe sentencia dictada en el caso "Fontevecchia y D'Amico vs. Argentin" por la Corte Interamericana de Derechos Humanos*, Feb. 14, 2017.

102 *See*, Jorge Contesse, *Judicial Backlash in Inter-American Human Rights Law?*, I-CONnect, available at http://www.iconnectblog.com/2017/03/judicial-backlash-interamerican/#_ftn3 (last accessed Dec. 9, 2017) (for a summary and an analysis of the SCJAN decision).

103 *See, Case of Fontevecchia and D'Amico v. Argentina. Monitoring Compliance with Judgment.* Order of the Inter-American Court of Human Rights of Oct. 18, 2017 (in a critical paragraph (para. 14), the Court explained that States cannot invoke their domestic law as justification for the non-compliance with judgments. For the Court, the question is not about the supremacy of international law over domestic law, but rather about the duty of the State to honor its international commitments to comply with the judgments. Yet the Court also took a rather conciliatory position by clarifying to Argentina that, in order to comply with the order of the Court in *Fontevecchia*, the State does not necessarily need to "overturn" a domestic judgment, but that it can choose the means to "leave without effects" (*dejar sin efectos*) that judgment (para. 16). The Court also pointed out that the Supreme Court of Justice has no authority to determine if the ICtHR exceeded its powers under the American Convention, since that is a question that needs to be determined by the Court itself (para. 26)).

principles that shape international law are still relevant both from a normative and political perspective, and therefore that the legitimacy of the decisions of the Inter-American Court – including those involving conventionality control – must appropriately consider the normative and structural constraints of the Inter-American System, as a subsidiary system governed by rules and principles of public international law.

3. STRUCTURAL ASSUMPTIONS THAT SUPPORT THE OBJECTIONS AGAINST THE DOCTRINE OF CONVENTIONALITY CONTROL

The critiques that have been elaborated against the validity of the doctrine of conventionality control confer the highest importance to two structural notions: first, that the consent of States as sovereigns is the most – if not the only – relevant factor to identify the origin and content of international obligations as recognized in treaties and custom, including those derived from IHRL; second, that there is a strict separation, in theory and practice, between the obligations that States have as subjects of international law, and the obligations that specific authorities have from international law. This approach might sound tedious and anachronistic to a human rights activist or a constitutional lawyer, but it should not surprise anyone. The critical role of consent as the key element to identify rights and obligations at the international level, and the notion that States have absolute freedom to decide how these rights and obligations are operational at the domestic level, are two assumptions that have shaped the understanding of public international law since its inception.[104]

The doctrine of conventionality control, by apparently not taking these structural assumptions seriously into consideration, enters into tension with several well-settled rules and principles of public international law. For this reason, this section briefly discusses the theories of monism and dualism, which have traditionally shaped the understanding of the relationship between international law and domestic law. Analyzing this "classic" topic in public

104 *See*, Hugo Grotious, *Prolegomena*, in ROBERT J. BECK, ANTHONY C. AREND AND ROBERT D. VANDER LUGT, *INTERNATIONAL RULES*, p. 42 (Oxford University Press, 1996) (positivists lawyers and judges might argue that it is still true what Hugo Grotious famously mentioned centuries ago, in the sense that: "so by mutual consent it has become possible that certain laws should originate as between States, or a great many States."); *see*, ANTHONY CLARK AREND, *LEGAL RULES AND INTERNATIONAL SOCIETY*, p. 61 (Oxford, 1999); *see*, *S.S. Lotus, (Fr. v. Turk.)* 1927 PCIJ, Ser. A, No. 10, at 18 (Sept. 7); *Military and Paramilitary Activities in and Against Nicaragua (Nicar. v. U.S.)*. Merits, 1986 I.C.J. 14 (Jun. 27), §269; *see generally*, Paolo G. Carozza, *The Problematic Applicability of Subsidiarity to International Law and Institutions*, 61(1) The American Journal of Jurisprudence, 55 (2016).

international law touches at the core of why conventionality control is so innovative and controversial if seen solely from the perspective of international law. It also opens the door to discuss how the binomial of monism-dualism, notwithstanding its extended use by international scholars,[105] constitutes an insufficient theoretical basis to explain and mediate the tension generated by the fact that international law is increasingly regulating and influencing more aspects of the life of nations and individuals, and the existence of still valid principles such as the equal sovereignty of States and constitutional self-determination.

3.1. THEORIES THAT EXPLAIN THE RELATIONSHIP BETWEEN INTERNATIONAL LAW AND DOMESTIC LEGAL SYSTEMS

3.1.1. Monism

Monism is a theory that has been developed and defended by prominent philosophers and international lawyers.[106] This theory holds that international law and domestic law are part of the same universal legal system, where the former is binding on all State authorities and hierarchically superior to the latter. The notion that international law (e.g. treaties, custom and general principles of law) is supreme to domestic law (e.g. constitutions, general laws and judicial decisions) implies that State authorities shall always prefer the enforcement of the rule of international law in the event of regulatory conflict, for example between a rule contained in a treaty and a constitution. The direct effect and the supremacy of international law requires that the legislative power guarantees that domestic law is in conformity with international law, that the executive power always prefers the enforcement of international law over domestic law, and that the judiciary decides its cases always in conformity with international law.[107]

For the theory of monism the State is not merely conceived as a legal person in the international arena, which means that: (1) international law is obligatory for

105 *See generally*, IAN BROWNLIE, *PRINCIPLES OF PUBLIC INTERNATIONAL LAW*, pp. 31–33 (Oxford University Press, 7th ed., 2008); MALCOLM N. SHAW, *INTERNATIONAL LAW*, *supra* n. 47, pp. 93–95; JEFFREY L. DUNOFF, STEVEN R. RATNER AND DAVID WIPPMAN, *INTERNATIONAL LAW. NORMS, ACTORS, PROCESS* pp. 243–244 (Aspen, 2010); Eduardo Jiménez Arrechaga, *La Convención Americana de Derechos Humanos como derecho interno*, 69–71 Boletín da Sociedade Brasileira de Direito Internacional 25–32 (1987–1989).

106 HANS KELSEN, *PRINCIPLES OF INTERNATIONAL LAW*, rev. and ed. by Robert W. Tucker, pp. 328–339, 551–589 (Holt, Rinehart and Winston, Inc., 2nd ed., 1966); *see also* HERSCH LAUTERPACHT (Ed.), *OPPENHEIM'S INTERNATIONAL LAW*, p. 38 (Longmans, Green and Co. Ltd., 5th ed., 1937).

107 *See*, JEFFREY L. DUNOFF, STEVEN R. RATNER AND DAVID WIPPMAN, *INTERNATIONAL LAW. NORMS, ACTORS, PROCESS*, *supra* n. 105, p. 244.

each State authority, and not only for the State as a subject of international law; (2) the rules and principles of international law do not require to be incorporated by a legislative act to be binding at the domestic level, which also implies the direct effect of international obligations once that they can be identified (e.g. by the signature, ratification and entry into force of a treaty); and (3) the validity of domestic law – in a formal and material sense – is subject to its compatibility with international law, since international law is hierarchically superior to domestic law, in similar sense that a constitution is superior to statutory law at the domestic level. This theory recognizes that there could exist normative contradictions between international law and domestic law, but also holds that these contradictions are present in all legal systems.[108]

The logical coherence and simplicity of the theory of monism (resulting from the use of formal methods of legal analysis) could support the position that the validity of State acts is conditional on their compatibility with international law, and therefore that international institutions – like the Inter-American Court – have the power to declare the international responsibility of States when their domestic law is incompatible with international law. Yet, despite the logical coherence of the theory of monism, and its ideological and practical convenience to advance the effectiveness of international law at the domestic level, there are norms and principles of international law and constitutional law that weaken some of its basic postulates. Contrary to what the theory of monism holds, the international practice shows that States have ample – if not absolute – spaces of freedom to determine the place of international law in their legal systems.[109]

The theory of dualism – the competing theory to monism, so to speak – is closer to the normative and political realities of international law, and perhaps for that reason it has had greater influence on the manner that the relationship between international law and domestic law is understood by scholars and practitioners alike.

3.1.2. Dualism

The theory of dualism holds that international law and domestic law are two separate legal systems, each supreme in their respective spheres of competence.[110]

---

108 *See*, Hersch Lauterpacht (Ed.), *Oppenheim's International Law*, *supra* n. 106, p. 38.

109 *See generally*, Héctor Fix-Zamudio, *El derecho internacional de los derechos humanos en las Constituciones latinoamericanas y en la Corte Interamericana de Derechos Humanos*, 1(1) Revista Latinoamericana de Derecho 141 (2004); *see generally*, Eduardo Jiménez de Aréchaga, *La Convención Americana de Derechos Humanos como derecho interno*, 69–71 Boletín da Sociedade Brasileira de Direito Internacional, 35–55 (1987–1989).

110 *See*, L. Oppenheim, *Introduction to Picciotto*, in Cyril M. Picciotto, *The Relation of International Law to the Law of England and to the Law of the United States*

The central postulate of this theory is that each legal system regulates different subject matters: the international regulates the conduct of the subjects of international law (for example, States and international organizations), while the domestic regulates the conduct of individuals and authorities within each State. From this distinction it follows that States have absolute freedom to define the manner in which international law is incorporated in their domestic legal systems, so international law does not have direct effect or supremacy at the domestic level (unless there is a rule of constitutional or treaty law that says so).[111] It is true that – in accordance with this theory – international obligations must be complied with in good faith, and that domestic law cannot serve as a justification for non-compliance with such obligations, but for dualism these rules are only valid in respect to the regulation of the conduct of States in their international relations.[112]

The theory of dualism has important normative consequences. It proposes a conceptual and practical separation between (1) the subjects of international law and domestic law (in international law the main and archetypal subject of law is the State, while in domestic law it is persons and the State); (2) between the sources of international law and domestic law (in international law the main sources are treaties, customary rules of international law and general principles of law, whereas in domestic law they are usually the constitution, statutory laws and the decisions of the highest courts and tribunals); and (3) between the canons of interpretation and enforcement of those sources of international law and domestic law. This observation is proven by State practice, since it seems to be clear that the possibility and the manner by which norms of international law are enforced in domestic legal systems (for example, in a petition of *amparo* before a judge in any Latin American State) has usually depended on secondary norms of constitutional or statutory law.[113] The following paragraphs refer to how dualism is manifested in the theory and practice of international law and international institutions in the three above-mentioned aspects.

---

of America, p. 10 (McBride, Nast & Co., 1915). (Lassa Oppenheimer explains that "International Law and Municipal Law are in fact two totally and essentially different bodies of law which have nothing in common except that they are both branches – both separate branches – of the tree of law.")

111 *See generally*, Ian Brownlie, *Principles of Public International Law*, *supra* n. 105, p. 32.

112 *See*, United Nations, Vienna Convention on the Law of Treaties, 23 May 1969, United Nations, Treaty Series, Vol. 1155, p. 331, Arts. 26 and 27; Jean Salmon, *Article 26*, in Olivier Corten and Pierre Klein (Eds.), *The Vienna Conventions on the Law of Treaties. A Commentary*, *supra* n. 46, pp. 660 and 685; Anite Schaus, *Article 27*, in Oliver Dörr and Kirsten Schmalenbach (Eds.), *Vienna Convention on the Law of Treaties. A Commentary*, p. 689 (Springer, 2012).

113 *See generally*, Antonio Cassese, *International Law*, pp. 214–217 (Oxford University Press, 2nd ed., 2005).

3.1.2.1. First Aspect: The Subjects of Law

Dualism understands that international law imposes rights and obligations on subjects of law considering them as independent units, which interact as equals in the international arena.[114] Ian Brownlie defines a legal person as an entity recognized by customary law capable of possessing rights and duties and of bringing international claims.[115] The more an entity has these capacities (recognition of legal personality, capacity to possess rights and duties and capacity of bringing claims) its legal personality increases. States are the normal type of legal person since they are the entity that complies better with these capacities. It is possible to say that States are the archetype of a legal person from the perspective of international law, so other entities may be considered legal persons as much as they acquire capacities similar to those that have been recognized to States, and as much as States accept this condition. Consequently, for instance, international organizations, agencies of States and special types of persons such as non-self-governing territories, entities *sui generis* and individuals,[116] are also considered subjects of law by customary international law, since they have certain similarities to States, and because States have accepted that they are indeed subjects of law.

The concept of legal personality is particularly important in international law. It allows the identification of a legal entity (i.e. a non-State actor) as a member of a category that defines certain qualities. One of the most important qualities that States have (and that no other legal entity has, in principle) is that that they have the right to engage in the law-making process, and they also have the capacity to recognize other entities with similar rights that they have "for the mere fact of being States".[117] Colin Warbrick explains that States may add rights and obligations to international law because they have legal personality, which at the same time is a characteristic that is inherent in the mere fact of State's existence: "so, we say 'Because X is a State, it may make treaties', not 'X may make treaties, so it is a State'."[118] This means that the existence of a State presupposes its capacity to make, modify or terminate international legal rules and principles through its consent or practice; it can also confer powers on other

---

[114] *See*, Anthony Clark Arend, *Legal Rules and International Society*, *supra* n. 104, p. 43; *see*, H.L.A. Hart, *The Concept of Law*, in Robert J. Beck, Anthony C. Arend, and Robert D. Vander Lugt, International Rules, *supra* n. 104, p. 82.

[115] *See*, Ian Brownlie, *Principles of Public International Law*, *supra* n. 105, p. 57.

[116] *Id.*, pp 58–65 (Brownlie in this sense establishes that to "classify an individual as a 'subject' of the law is unhelpful, since this may be seen to imply capacities that do not exist and does not avoid the task of distinguishing between the individual and other types of subjects").

[117] *See*, Collin Warbrick, *States and Recognition of International Law*, in Malcolm D. Evans (Ed.), *International Law*, p. 229 (Oxford University Press, 2nd ed., 2006).

[118] *Ibid.*

entities to enforce these rules or even to create new ones. Thus, no other entities have the kind of *inherent* powers that States have. Here it is relevant to recall the five "exclusive and general characteristics" of States due to the mere fact of their existence, as explained by James Crawford:

> (1) States have plenary competence to perform acts in the international sphere – make treaties and so on.
>
> (2) States are exclusively competent with respect to their internal affairs – 'exclusive' means plenary and not subject to control by other States.
>
> (3) States are not subject to international process without their consent.
>
> (4) States are regarded in international law as 'equal', it is its formal, not a moral or political, principle.
>
> (5) States are entitled to benefit from the *Lotus* presumption [that sovereign States are free to do as they wish as long as they do not contravene an explicit prohibition], especially that any derogation from the previous principles must be expressly established.[119]

In domestic legal systems the question of the subjects of law is obviously different, since State institutions are free to determine what entities (and under which conditions) are capable of possessing rights and duties, and therefore who has the power to create rules of law or to bring claims before domestic courts.[120] Regular classifications of the subjects of law include natural persons and juridical persons (which include State organs and public organizations), which have certain capacities, rights and duties depending on the particular branches of domestic law (i.e. depending on what the civil, criminal, administrative or constitutional law recognizes as a subject of law). In this manner, for instance, the Chilean Civil Code recognizes in Article 55 legal persons as "all individuals of the human species, no matter their age, sex, origin or condition", and in Article 545 it establishes that "a legal person is a fictitious person capable of exercising rights and acquire civil obligations, and of being judicially and extrajudicially represented". But a different State could certainly limit or expand what it considers to be a legal person as a matter of domestic law, as well as the rights and obligations that come with this recognition, depending on ideological or political considerations.

---

119 James Crawford, *The Creation of States in International Law*, pp. 40–41 (Oxford University Press, 2nd ed., 2006) (cited by Warbrick, at 242. The reference to the *Lotus* presumption is mine).

120 *See generally*, Eduardo Garcia Maynes, *Introducción al Estudio del Derecho*, p. 272 (Porrua, 13th ed., 1976).

3.1.2.2. Second Aspect: The Sources of Law

It is a common understanding among international lawyers and judges that the sources of international law are defined almost exclusively by rules of international law, both in its formal elements (the legal procedure and methods for the creation of norms) and its material elements (the content of those rules that are legally binding). The complete statement of the sources of international law is listed in Article 38.1 of the Statute of the International Court of Justice, which recognizes treaties, customary rules and general principles as the main sources of international law.[121] The intention of the drafters of the Statute was to give a hierarchical order to these sources, and the practice of the International Court of Justice has followed that view.[122] In a similar fashion, the particularities of how these sources of law come into life and interact among each other are a subject determined entirely by rules and principles of international law, particularly those established in the VCLT, and from the practice of international actors.[123] Seen from the perspective of international law, norms of domestic origin are regularly conceived as facts with no normative value at the international level.

In domestic legal systems the determination of the sources of law is entirely defined by rules of domestic law, both in its formal and material elements. In civil law countries there is a strong tradition that recognizes the legislative power as the supreme producer of laws. The legislative branch may delegate some power to the executive power, the administrative agencies of the State, or the judiciary, but in all cases domestic law (statutory or constitutional) is the one that regulates the process by which any agency creates rules of law. The material components of the law are, in general, constitutions, statutes, treaties, judicial decisions, administrative regulations and customs; books and articles by legal authors or judicial decisions (domestic or international) are usually excluded as sources of law. These sources are usually arranged in descending order of authority, so a statute prevails over contrary regulation, and a statute and a regulation prevail over an inconsistent custom.[124] In Mexico, for instance, the norms that determine the legislative process are established in

---

121 Statute of the International Court of Justice, as specified by Chapter XIV of the United Nations Charter, which established the ICJ, Art. 38.1.

122 *See*, Ian Brownlie, *Principles of Public International Law*, *supra* n. 105, p. 5; *see also* Judge Tanaka, Dissenting Opinion, *South West Africa Cases* (Second Phase), ICJ Reports (1966), 300.

123 *See*, Ian Brownlie, *Principles of Public International Law*, *supra* note 105, pp. 6–29; *see also* Anthony Clark Arend, *Legal Rules and International Society*, *supra* n. 104, pp. 45–58.

124 *See*, John Henry Merryman and Rogelio Pérez Perdomo, *The Civil Law Tradition*, p. 25 (Stanford University Press, 3rd ed., 2007).

Article 71 and 72 of the Constitution, and Articles 3 and 4 of the Civil Code for the Federal District.[125] What is relevant is that the determination of these sources – as well as their hierarchy – is a matter that depends exclusively on rules of domestic origin.

3.1.2.3. Third Aspect: The Interpretation of International Law at the Domestic Level

Dualism sustains that international law has its own normative canons of interpretation and its own normative content, that may or may not be similar to those of domestic legal systems, even in areas where both international and domestic law concur (such as human rights law). The substance of the canons of interpretation of treaties is defined at the international level in the VCLT (Articles 31–33), which has adopted the view that what matters the most when interpreting a treaty is the intention of the parties as expressed in the text.[126] There are several principles that are involved in the textual approach for the interpretation of treaties: the principle of ordinary meaning: "a treaty shall be interpreted in good faith and in accordance with the ordinary meaning to be given to the terms of the treaty";[127] the principle of integration: "the meaning must emerge in the context of the treaty as a whole and in the light of its object and purpose";[128] the principle of contemporaneity: "the language of the treaty must be interpreted in the light of the contemporaneous meaning of the terms".[129] Other means of interpretation – although supplementary – are also accepted by international law: the preparatory work of the treaty, the circumstances of its conclusion, and the subsequent practice of States or international organizations.[130]

The canons of interpretation of domestic law are defined by rules and principles of each domestic legal system. In civil law countries the interpretation of law tends to afford particular importance to the text of statutory law and the intention of the legislator, or to the objective meaning of the text in accordance with the object of the law, or in accordance with other rules of that legal system.[131] For instance, the first paragraph of Article 12 of the Italian Civil Code

---

125 *See*, Political Constitution of the United Mexican States, Feb. 5, 1917 (Mexico), Arts. 71 and 72; Civil Code of the Federal District, [C. civ.] (Mx.), Arts. 3 and 4.

126 *See*, Ian Brownlie, *Principles of Public International Law*, *supra* n. 105, p. 631; *see*, Vienna Convention on the Law of Treaties, *supra* n. 112, Art. 31.

127 Ian Brownlie, *Principles of Public International Law*, *supra* n. 105, p. 633.

128 *Ibid.*

129 *Ibid.*

130 *See*, Vienna Convention on the Law of Treaties, *supra* n. 112, Art. 32; *see*, Ian Brownlie, *Principles of Public International Law*, *supra* n. 105, p. 631.

131 *See*, Eduardo Garcia Maynes, *Introducción al Estudio del Derecho*, *supra* n. 120, p. 329.

establishes that: "in interpreting the statute, no other meaning can be attributed than that made clear by the actual significance of the words according to the connections between them, and by the intention of the legislature"; the second paragraph is the direction of the judge regarding the problem of lacunae, and it establishes that "if a controversy cannot be decided by a precise provision, consideration is given to provisions that regulate similar cases or analogous matters" and if the case still remains in doubt "it is decided according to general principles of the legal order of the State".[132] The same could be said about the interpretation of international law when seen from the perspective of a domestic legal system, which means that international law – understood as domestic law – shall be interpreted in accordance with canons of interpretation defined by domestic legal systems.[133]

3.2. AN "INSUPERABLE PARADOX": THE LOGICAL CONSEQUENCE OF THE THEORY OF DUALISM

The dualist understanding of the relationship between international law and domestic law has created, using the words of Humberto Sierra Porto, an "insuperable paradox".[134] On the one hand, international law is supreme in the international legal system, so States shall comply with international law in good faith, and are prohibited from invoking domestic law as a justification for not complying with it.[135] Still, on the other hand, in domestic legal systems, the supremacy of international law is relativized by the principle of constitutional supremacy, making the following scenarios of implementation possible: (1) supra-constitutional;[136] (2) constitutional;[137] (3) supra-legal;[138] and

132 II Codice Civile Italiano [C. civ.] (It.), Art. 12.

133 *See generally*, *Murray v. The Charming Betsey*, 6 U.S. 64 (U.S. 1804).

134 *See generally*, Humberto Sierra Porto, *La Constitución colombiana frente al control de convencionalidad*, Resource from the Library of the Inter-American Court of Human Rights, pp. 428–429 (2013).

135 *See generally*, Vienna Convention on the Law of Treaties, *supra* n. 112, Arts. 26 and 27; *see*, Jean Salmon, *Article 26*, in Olivier Corten and Pierre Klein (Eds.), *The Vienna Conventions on the Law of Treaties. A Commentary*, *supra* n. 112, pp. 676–678.

136 *See*, Political Constitution of the Republic of Guatemala, May 31, 1985 (Guatemala), Art. 46.

137 *See*, Constitution of Argentina, May 1, 1853 (Argentina), Art. 75; Political Constitution of the United Mexican States, Feb. 5, 1917 (Mexico), Arts. 1 and 133; Political Constitution of Colombia, Jul. 1991 (Colombia), Art. 93; Political Constitution of the Kingdom of the Netherlands, 2008 (Netherlands), Art. 91.

138 *See*, Constitution of the Republic of El Salvador, Dec. 15, 1983 (El Salvador), Art. 144; Political Constitution of France, Oct. 4, 1958 (France), Arts. 54 and 55; Political Constitution of Haiti, 1987 (Haiti), Arts. 276 and 276-2; U.S. Const. (United States), Art. VI.

(4) legal.[139] These scenarios depend on the political choices of the State authorities (especially congresses and the highest courts), since there is no rule of international law that requires uniformity regarding the hierarchy that international law must have when it is implemented in domestic legal systems. The text of the constitutions of Guatemala (supra-constitutional), Argentina (constitutional), France (supra-legal) and South Africa (legal) provide good examples of the plurality of the hierarchies that international law may acquire at the domestic level.

Political Constitution of the Republic of Guatemala

Article 46. Primacy of international law. It is established the general principle that human rights treaties and American Conventions accepted and ratified by Guatemala take precedence over domestic law.

Constitution of the Argentine Nation

Section 31.- This Constitution, the laws of the Nation enacted by Congress in pursuance thereof, and treaties with foreign powers, are the supreme law of the Nation; and the authorities of each province are bound thereby, notwithstanding any provision to the contrary included in the provincial laws or constitutions, except for the province of Buenos Aires, the treaties ratified after the Pact of November 11, 1859.

Section 75.- Congress is empowered:

22.- To approve or reject treaties concluded with other nations and international organizations, and concordats with the Holy See. Treaties and concordats have a higher hierarchy than laws.

The American Declaration of the Rights and Duties of Man; the Universal Declaration of Human Rights; the American Convention on Human Rights; the International Pact on Economic, Social and Cultural Rights; the International Pact on Civil and Political Rights and its empowering Protocol; the Convention on the Prevention and Punishment of Genocide; the International Convention on the Elimination of all Forms of Racial Discrimination; the Convention on the Elimination of all Forms of Discrimination against Woman; the Convention against Torture and other Cruel, Inhuman or Degrading Treatments or Punishments; the Convention on the Rights of the Child; in the full force of their provisions, they have constitutional hierarchy, do no repeal any section of the First Part of this Constitution and are to be understood as complementing the rights and guarantees recognized herein. They shall only be denounced, in such event, by the National Executive Power after the approval of two-thirds of all the members of each House.

---

139 *See*, Political Constitution of South Africa, Dec. 4, 1996 (South Africa), Arts. 231–233.

Constitution of France

Article 54. If the Constitutional Council, on a referral from the President of the Republic, from the Prime Minister, from the President of one or the other Houses, or from sixty Members of the National Assembly or sixty Senators, has held that an international undertaking contains a clause contrary to the Constitution, authorization to ratify or approve the international undertaking involved may be given only after amending the Constitution.

Article 55. Treaties or agreements duly ratified or approved shall, upon publication, prevail over Acts of Parliament, subject, with respect to each agreement or treaty, to its application by the other party.

Constitution of South Africa

Section 231. (4) Any international agreement becomes law in the Republic when it is enacted into law by national legislation; but a self-executing provision of an agreement that has been approved by Parliament is law in the Republic unless it is inconsistent with the

Section 232. Customary international law is law in the Republic unless it is inconsistent with the

Section 233. When interpreting any legislation, every court must prefer any reasonable interpretation of the legislation that is consistent with international law over any alternative interpretation that is inconsistent with international law.

This "insuperable paradox" has led to an apparently absurd conclusion: that there is uniformity and supremacy regarding the binding nature of international law when seen from the perspective of the international arena, but that at the same time there is some kind of radical pluralism in the obligatoriness of international law when seen from the perspective of the domestic arena.[140] And this is precisely the case. Dualism proposes that, even when it is possible to identify the existence of an international obligation for States (e.g. derived from a treaty clause or from the judgment of an international court), this does not necessarily mean that domestic authorities shall apply that norm or judgment directly at the domestic level, or that international law could serve as a basis for declaring the invalidity of domestic law to the contrary. It should be noted that this type of reasoning continues to be valid for most areas of international law, and that there are cases resolved by prestigious domestic courts that show the practical consequences that this view causes. Two emblematic examples are the

140 *See*, Héctor Fix-Zamudio, *El derecho internacional de los derechos humanos en las Constituciones latinoamericanas y en la Corte Interamericana de Derechos Humanos*, *supra* n. 109, p. 108.

judgment of the Supreme Court of Justice of the United States of America in the case of *Medellin v. Texas* (2008),[141] and – to a lesser extent – the judgment of the German Constitutional Court in the case of *Görgülü* (2004).[142]

What makes dualism relevant as a theory to understand the relationship between international law and domestic law is not the attractiveness and idealism of the ideas that support its basic postulates, but the fact that it finds an echo in several norms, principles and practices of international law and constitutional law. So even when dualism does not have the same amount of logical purity as monism, or because it would not have the same degree of efficacy in the incorporation of IHRL at the domestic level, it is not possible simply to disregard this theory as "old" or as something that it is "regressive" and therefore with no normative value. Doing that is closing the eyes to how international law actually works in one of its fundamental aspects from a descriptive and normative perspective, and makes unintelligible the critiques that are made by international lawyers and constitutional lawyers of the doctrine of conventionality control, or of any other legal institution created at a supranational level that tries to increase the efficacy of international law at the domestic level without the express consent of States.

3.3. REFLECTION ON THE SHORTCOMINGS OF DUALISM

However, developments in recent decades, both in theory and practice, at the international and domestic levels, show that there are areas of international law that do not fit in with the strict conceptual and practical separation between what is understood as exclusively "international" and exclusively "domestic". These areas deal with questions of public order, as they directly or indirectly involve the protection of human dignity and the construction of a more just and humane legal order. For this reason, it is not unreasonable to sustain that States must comply – both as an ethical and legal duty – with the obligations arising from *jus cogens* norms or from areas of law such as international humanitarian law (IHL), international criminal law (ICL) or international human rights law (IHRL), and that States cannot argue that the effectiveness of these areas of law absolutely depends on the place that constitutional law grants to international law in their domestic legal systems. This position makes reasonable to affirm that, at least to some extent, *jus cogens* norms, IHL, ICL and IHRL impose direct obligations on State authorities.

---

141 *Cf. Medellin v, Texas* 552 U.S. 491, 2008.

142 *Cf. Görgülü Case* 111 BVerfGE 307, 2004.

3.3.1. Jus Cogens *Norms*

The paradigmatic examples for the existence of norms that impose direct obligations on State authorities are the peremptory norms of international law (*jus cogens*).[143] These types of norms are defined in the VCLT as

> a norm accepted and recognized by the international community of States as a whole as a norm from which no derogation is permitted and which can be modified only by a subsequent norm of general international law having the same character.[144]

The substantive content of those norms is controversial, but at least includes the prohibition on the use of force,[145] the law of genocide, the principle of racial non-discrimination, crimes against humanity and the rules prohibiting trade of slaves and piracy.[146] In the *Barcelona Traction Case (Second Phase)* the ICJ drew a distinction between obligations of States arising *vis-à-vis* another State and obligations towards the international community.[147] *Jus cogens* norms belong to the second category. In the words of the ICJ:

> an essential distinction should be drawn between the obligations of a State towards the international community as a whole, and those arising vis-à-vis another State in the field of diplomatic protection. By their very nature the former are the concern of all States. In view of the importance of the rights involved, all States can be held to have a legal interest in their protection; they are obligations *erga omnes*.[148]

There is little controversy that a treaty concluded against a norm of *jus cogens* is void, since Article 53 of the VCLT states that "[a] treaty is void if, at the time of

---

143 *See generally*, Dinah Shelton, *Normative Hierarchy in International Law*, 100 Am. J. Int'l L. 291 (2006) (the author studies the origins and normative implications of *jus cogens* norms, explaining that those who find the source of *jus cogens* in State consent would limit the effects of these rules only to the law of treaties; on the other hand, those who assert the existence of "necessary" legal rules would agree on much broader consequences of *jus cogens*).

144 Vienna Convention on the Law of Treaties, *supra* n. 112, Art. 53.

145 *See, Military and Paramilitary Activities in and Against Nicaragua (Nicar. v. U.S.)*, Merits, 1986 I.C.J. 14 (June 27) §190.

146 Ian Brownlie, *Principles of Public International Law*, *supra* n. 105, p. 511; *see*, Report of the Study Group of the ILC on Fragmentation of International Law: difficulties arising from the diversification and expansion of International Law, *supra* n. 9, p. 21 (the ILC has identified as the most frequently cited examples of *jus cogens* "the prohibition of aggression, slave trade, genocide, racial discrimination apartheid and torture, as well as basic rules of international humanitarian law applicable in armed conflict, and the right to self-determination".)

147 *See, Barcelona Traction. Light and Power Company, Limited (Belgium v. Spain) Second Phase.* Judgment, 1970 I.C.J. (Feb. 5), §32 and 33; *see also* Responsibility of States for Internationally Wrongful Acts, Ybk ILC, 2001, Vol. II (Pt. II), Arts. 42 and 48.

148 *Barcelona Traction. Light and Power Company, Limited (Belgium v. Spain) Second Phase*, *supra* n. 147, §32 and 33.

its conclusion, it conflicts with a peremptory norm of general international law". Some scholars, and the practice of some tribunals, even suggest that all powers of the State are bound by *jus cogens* norms and that domestic law that violates these provisions is devoid of legal validity.[149] Some practice at the international level supports this proposition.

The International Military Tribunal in Nuremberg held Nazi officials responsible for acts not prohibited by domestic law at the time they were committed, and excluded as a defense that officials were acting under valid positive law. In this sense, Article 8 of the Nuremberg Charter provided that: "[t]he fact that the defendant acted pursuant to an order or his government or a superior shall not free him from responsibility." The responsibility of the Nazi officials presupposed that they were directly bound – as individual agents of the State – by the prohibition against committing "crimes against peace" and "crimes against humanity", and the existence of an incompatible domestic law was irrelevant in terms of complying with those prohibitions and in punishing the perpetrators of these crimes at the international level.[150]

In a similar spirit the International Criminal Court for the Former Yugoslavia established in the case of the *Prosecutor v. Anto Furundzija* that:

> The fact that torture is prohibited by a peremptory norm of international law has effects at the inter-State and individual levels. At the inter-State level, it serves to internationally delegitimize any legislative, administrative or judicial act authorizing torture. It would be senseless to argue, on the one hand that on account of the *jus cogens* value of the prohibition against torture, treaties or customary rules providing for torture would be null and void *ab initio*, and then be unmindful of a State say, taking national measures authorizing or condoning torture or absolving its perpetrators through an amnesty law.[151]

Jus cogens impose an ethical – and legal or "meta-legal" – duty for all States. The spirit that inspires the strong normative force of these types of norms can be seen in the criterion of the International Court of Justice (ICJ) in the *Advisory Opinion on the Reservations to the Convention on the Prevention and Punishment of the Crime of Genocide* (1950) where the ICJ considered the fact that the Convention on the Prevention and Punishment of the Crime of Genocide was

---

149 *See*, Mary Ellen O'Connell *Jus Cogens: International Law's Higher Ethical Norms*, in Donald Earl Childress, III (Ed.), *The Role of Ethics in International Law*, pp. 87–89 (Cambridge University Press, 2012); *see also* Erika de Wet, *The Prohibition of Torture as an International Norm of Jus Cogens and Its Implications for National and Customary Law* 15(1) Eur. J. Int'l L. 112 (2004).

150 *See generally*, Mary Ellen O'Connell, *Jus Cogens: International Law's Higher Ethical Norms*, in Donald Earl Childress, III (Ed.), *The Rolle of Ethics in International Law*, *supra* n. 149, pp. 87–89.

151 *Prosecutor v. Furundzija*, Case No. IT-95-17/1-T10, Judgment (1998), (Int'l Crim. Trib. For the Former Yugoslavia), §155–157.

adopted for "purely humanitarian and civilizing purposes", that had as its object "to safeguard the very existence of certain human groups", and "to confirm and endorse the elementary principles of morality", thus:

> In such a Convention the contracting States do not have any interests of their own; they merely have, one and all, a common interest, namely, the accomplishment of those high purposes which are the raison d'être of the Convention. Consequently, in a Convention of this type one cannot speak of individual advantages or disadvantages to States, or of the maintenance of a perfect contractual balance between rights and duties. The high ideals which inspired the Convention provide, by virtue of the common will of the parties, the foundation and measure of all its provisions.[152]

3.3.2. International Humanitarian Law and International Criminal Law

The shortcomings of dualism can also be observed in certain aspects of IHL and ICL. IHL imposes limits to the conduct of individuals and groups involved in an armed conflict. Its provisions apply to State agents, insurgent groups and individuals engaged in armed conflicts (including internal armed conflicts). This body of international norms confers rights and imposes duties for individuals.[153] So it is reasonable to suggest that once – for instance – a State becomes a party to the Geneva Convention and Additional Protocols, the obligation "to respect and to ensure respect for the present convention in all circumstances" imposes obligations not on the State as a legal abstraction, but on those specific persons involved directly or indirectly in an armed conflict.[154]

The understanding that the contracting parties not only have to "respect" but also "ensure respect" for the Convention was deliberate. It was distinct from the language of the Conventions of 1864[155] and 1906,[156] which almost in the same terms established that "[t]he implementing of the present Convention shall be ensured by the Commanders in Chief of the belligerent armies, following the instructions of their respective Governments and in accordance with the

---

152 *Reservations to the American Convention on the Prevention and Punishment of the Crime of Genocide*. Advisory Opinion, 1951 I.C.J. (May 28), at 12.

153 *See generally*, A.A. Cançado Trindade, *The Access of Individuals to International Justice* (Oxford University Press, 2011) (on the consideration that the evolution of IHL has "contributed decisively to the evidencing and reassertion of the constant contact of the individual with the international legal order.").

154 *See*, International Committee of the Red Cross (ICRC), Geneva Convention for the Amelioration of the Condition of the Wounded and Sick in Armed Forces in the Field (First Geneva Convention), 12 August 1949, 75 UNTS 31, Art. 1.

155 *See generally*, Convention for the Amelioration of the Condition of the Wounded in Armies in the Field. Geneva, 22 August 1864.

156 *See generally*, Convention for the Amelioration of the Condition of the Wounded and Sick in Armies in the Field. Geneva, 6 July 1906.

general principles set forth in the Convention". The language of Article 1 of the Geneva Conventions has the intention of strengthening the obligation of the parties to the Treaty, meaning that the obligations derived from it extend to all of those to whom the State has authority as well as to the representatives of that authority.[157] If this is true, then, for example, the prohibition against committing "murder of all kinds, mutilation, cruel treatment and torture" of persons not taking part in the hostilities during a non-international conflict, in accordance with common Article 3 of the Geneva Conventions, imposes obligations on each participant of the internal armed conflict independent of further provisions enacted by her superiors.

Before the adoption of common Article 3 of the Geneva Conventions, IHL did not regulate armed conflicts that were domestic in nature, like those between a State and insurgent forces, or between different political factions. It was understood that those conflicts were outside international regulation. But common Article 3 of the Geneva Conventions of 1949 changed that position to include regulation of conflicts not of an international character – although certainly with a more limited scope of regulation than conflicts with an international character.[158] In the Case of *Prosecutor v. Tadic*, the International Criminal Tribunal for the Former Yugoslavia (ICTY) acknowledged that traditional international law excluded any possible intrusion by other States – and by extension of international institutions – into the domestic jurisdiction of other States, being the regulation of civil struggles the object of domestic criminal law.[159] But the ICTY identified that the clear-cut distinction between the regulation of international and domestic conflicts has become "more and more blurred" because civil wars have become more frequent, internal conflicts have become more cruel, internal conflicts usually have an international dimension, and the human rights doctrine has created a greater conscience concerning the necessity of protecting human beings.[160] In the words of the Tribunal:

> Fourthly, the impetuous development and propagation in the international community of human rights doctrines, particularly after the adoption of the Universal Declaration of Human Rights in 1948, has brought about significant changes in international law … A State sovereignty oriented approach has been gradually supplanted by a human

157 *See*, Paul Des Gouttes, 'Commentaire de la Convention de Genève du 27 juillet 1929,' (Geneva, 1930), on Art. 25, pp 186 ff, available at https://www.icrc.org/applic/ihl/ihl.nsf/Comment.xsp?viewComments=LookUpCOMART&ArticleUNID=074D7AE3436CF248C12563CD00519E38 (last accessed Dec. 9, 2017).

158 *See*, ICRC, Commentary to Article 3 to the Convention (I) for the Amelioration of the Condition of the Wounded and Sick in Armed Forces in the Field, Geneva, August 12, 1949.

159 *See*, *Prosecutor v. Tadic*, Case No. IT-94-1-T, Judgment (1997), (Int'l Crim. Trib. For the Former Yugoslavia), §96.

160 *Id.* §97.

> rights-being-oriented approach. Gradually the maxim of Roman Law *hominum causa omne jus constitutum est* (all law is created for the benefit of human beings) has gained a firm foothold in the international community as well. It follows that in the area of armed conflict the distinction between interState wars and civil wars is losing its value as far as human beings are concerned.[161]

Whether or not it is an overstatement that international law has changed from a "State sovereignty approach" to a "human rights oriented-approach", what appears to be true is that IHL imposes obligations on those involved in domestic conflicts in a manner that was not conceivable before World War Two and the subsequent adoption of the 1949 Geneva Conventions. The international protection of human dignity has been at the core of the development of norms of IHL, which have blurred the strict – and artificial, we may say – separation between international law and domestic law in case of domestic armed conflicts. In this regard the ICTY noted in *Tadic* that many principles applicable to international armed conflicts have been extended to internal conflicts because "elementary considerations of humanity and common sense make it preposterous that the use by States prohibited in armed conflicts between themselves be allowed when States try to put down rebellion by their own nationals on their own territory".[162] The ICTY found a contradiction between considering that actions that are inhumane in an international conflict, are permitted in a civil strife. The ICTY ultimately concluded that under customary international law the crimes of Dusko Tadic "entail individual criminal responsibility regardless of whether they are committed in an internal or international armed conflict".[163]

The understanding that State authorities are directly obligated by certain rules of international law is at the core of the theory of ICL, which is the third area where the shortcomings of dualism can be observed. The development of this area of law is intimately connected with IHL since some of the crimes that are prohibited by ICL are also prohibited by IHL (i.e. the definition of "war crimes" comes from the conducts described as "grave breaches" of the Geneva Conventions of 1949),[164] and because the origins of ICL are essentially connected with criminal actions committed during World War Two.[165] Before the emergence of ICL, international law only addressed acts committed by governments when they occurred in their territories, and against citizens of another State. These acts fell

---

161 *Id.* §97.

162 *Id.* §119.

163 *Id.*, §119 ("What is inhuman, and consequently proscribed, in international wars, cannot but be inhuman and inadmissible in civil strife.")

164 *See*, Convention (I) for the Amelioration of the Condition of the Wounded and Sick in Armed Forces in the Field, Art. 50.

165 *See*, Jeffrey L. Dunoff, Steven R. Ratner and David Wippman, International Law. Norms, Actors, Process, *supra* n. 105, p. 490.

into two areas: the law of international responsibility for injury to aliens (which included the disruption of property interests and some attacks on aliens), and the violation of the customs of war. The consequence of the breach of these two areas of law was directed at the State and not to the specific individuals that committed the violation.[166]

Yet, with the adoption of the Nuremberg Charter, and the subsequent establishment of the International Military Tribunal, Nazi leaders were held accountable for crimes against peace, war crimes and crimes against humanity committed in their individual capacity or as members of organizations or groups or in both capacities.[167] The precedent of the Nuremberg trials established that certain wrongdoings committed at the domestic level are individually punishable as a matter of international law, so these wrongdoings may be prosecuted by domestic courts of third countries or by international criminal courts. In *United States v. Joseph Alstoetter et al.*, the defendants claimed protection under the principle of *nullum crimen sine lege*, since their actions were not violations of international law at the time they were committed. The Nuremberg Tribunal rejected this position arguing that crimes against peace, crimes against humanity and war crimes, were prohibited by customary international law even before the adoption of the Nuremberg Charter. The Tribunal recalled the decision on the cases against the leading Nazi officials in the sense that:

> In the first place, it is to be observed that the maxim *nullum crimen sine lege* is not a limitation of sovereignty, but is in general a principle of justice. To assert that it is unjust to punish those who in defiance of treaties and assurance have attacked neighboring States without warning is obviously untrue, for in such circumstances the attacker must know that he is doing wrong, and so far from it being unjust to punish him, it will be unjust if his wrong were allowed to go unpunished ...[168]

It is accepted that the prohibition of the above-mentioned crimes are part of general international law and that they provide sufficient ground to prosecute whoever is responsible for these crimes whenever a court has jurisdiction to do so.[169] The Constitution of the special criminal tribunals for the former Yugoslavia and for Rwanda, and the adoption of the Statute of the International Criminal Court

---

166 *See, Id.* p. 566; *see also Mavrommatis Palestine Concessions (Greece v. United Kingdom)*, 1924 P.C.I.J. Ser. A, No. 2 (Aug. 30), at 12.

167 *See*, United Nations, Agreement for the prosecution and punishment of the major war criminals of the European Axis ("London Agreement"), 8 August 1945, 82 U.N.T.C. 280, Art. 1.

168 *See, United States v. Joseph Alstoetter et al.* Law No. 10. 1946–1949, Vol. III (1951), cited in Jeffrey L. Dunoff, Steven R. Ratner, and David Wippman, *International Law. Norms, Actors, Process*, *supra* n. 105, p. 570.

169 *See*, Ybk ILC, 1950, ii, 374–378 (the ILC formulated the following crimes under international law: a. Crimes against peace; b. War crimes; and c. Crimes against humanity).

(Statute of the ICC or Rome Statute) leave no place to doubt that genocide, crimes against humanity, war crimes and the crime of aggression are types of conduct prohibited for individuals by contemporary international law. There is also evidence that these crimes open the door for the exercise of universal jurisdiction by domestic courts. In the *Case of A.G. of the Government of Israel v. Adolf Eichmann*, the Israeli courts concluded that the nature of the offenses committed by the Nazis in occupied territories justified the exercise of universal jurisdiction, since

> (1) the crimes ... [have] always borne the stamp of international crimes, banned by the law of nations and entailing individual criminal responsibility [and] (2) [i]t is the peculiarly universal character of these crimes that vests in every State the authority to punish anyone who participated in their commission.[170]

The development of ICL show that there are certain types of conduct punishable either by international courts on the basis of a treaty like the Statute of the ICC, or by domestic courts in the exercise of universal jurisdiction. However, the capacity to exercise jurisdiction under ICL is subject to strict limitations imposed by international law and domestic law, making prosecution at the international level an exception. For instance, the jurisdiction of the International Criminal Court (ICC) is only possible once a State becomes a party to the Rome Statute, or the Security Council refers a case under Chapter VII of the UN Charter. The ICC also leaves to the States parties the first responsibility to investigate and prosecute persons responsible for international crimes.[171] In a similar sense the exercise of universal jurisdiction has been exceptional and has proved to be problematic in cases that involve immunity of heads of States even when they have committed international crimes.[172] In this sense, the International Court of Justice established in the *Arrest Warrant Case* (*Democratic Republic of Congo v. Belgium*) that:

> The Court accordingly concludes that the functions of a minister of Foreign Affairs are such that, throughout the duration of his or her office, he or she when abroad enjoys full immunity from criminal jurisdiction and inviolability. That immunity and that inviolability protect the individual concerned against any act of authority of another State which would hinder him or her in the performance of her duty.[173]

---

170 District Court of Jerusalem, *A.G. of the Government of Israel v. Adolf Eichmann*, IRL 36, 5, 287, Dec. 11, 1961, §10.

171 *See*, United Nations General Assembly, Rome Statute of the International Criminal Court, Jul. 1, 2002, 2187 U.N.T.S. 90, Arts. 12, 13, 17 and 18.

172 *See*, House of Lords, *R. v. Bow Street Metropolitan Stipendiary Magistrate and Others, ex parte Pinochet Ugarte (No. 3)*, 2000 1 A.C. 147 (1998), judgment of Lord Browne-Wilkinson.

173 *Arrest Warrant (Democratic Republic of the Congo v. Belgium)*, 2000 I.C.J. (Apr. 11), §54.

Notwithstanding the limitations to the exercise of criminal jurisdiction at an extra-national level, what is relevant for this section is that the substantive prohibitions imposed by ICL certainly escape the view that international law has anything to do with the individual criminal responsibility of State authorities. Since the Nuremberg trials gave rise to the notion that once a crime has been defined at the international level, individuals – not States as abstract entities – are obligated not to commit war crimes or crimes against humanity, and the sanction for failing to do is for the individual and not necessarily just for the State. In this logic, domestic law cannot be raised as a justification for the commission of international crimes. State agents are obligated to comply with these norms independently of domestic law. Consequently, it is possible to affirm that in ICL the strict separation between domestic law and international law is almost non-existent as a matter of substance. In this point the words of Lord Browne-Wilkinson, in his opinion in the case of *R. v. Bow Street Metropolitan Stipendiary Magistrate and Others, ex parte Pinochet Ugarte*, are illustrative of the reality of ICL:

> Apart from the law of piracy, the concept of personal liability under international law for international crimes is of comparatively modern growth. The traditional subjects of international law are States not human beings. But consequent upon the war crime trials after the 1939–45 World War, the international community came to recognize that there could be criminal liability under international law for a class of crimes such as war crimes and crimes against humanity ... Ever since 1945, torture on a large scale has features as one of the crimes against humanity ...[174]

3.3.3. *International Human Rights Law*

IHRL follows the same logic as IHL and ICL, at least to a certain extent. IHRL is an area of "the tree of law" that recognizes rights for individuals that derive from sources of international law, and that recognizes an obligation for State authorities to respect and ensure those rights.[175] It is generally accepted that the provisions of the United Nations Charter (UN Charter) related to human rights, and the Universal Declaration of Human Rights (UDHR), reflected the consciousness that the protection of the dignity of all individuals in States territories was a matter of international law. Just as happened with the emergence of IHL and ICL, the notion that the protection of human rights was a concern of the international community resulted from the atrocities committed by several governments against their own people during World War Two.

---

174 House of Lords, *R. v. Bow Street Metropolitan Stipendiary Magistrate and Others, ex parte Pinochet Ugarte (No. 3)*, *supra* n. 172, judgment of Lord Browne-Wilkinson.

175 *See generally*, A.A. Cançado Trindade, *The Access of Individuals to International Justice* (Oxford University Press, 2011).

The reaction to the atrocities committed in this era changed the fundamental understanding that the relationship between the State and its citizens – including the protection of their fundamental rights – was a matter of exclusive competence of States or, as Joseph Goebbels mentioned before the League of Nations in 1933, when he was questioned about the treatment of Jews in Germany, that "a man is master in his own home".[176] Contrary to the tradition that draws a clear-cut distinction between what is "international" and what is "domestic", and that plainly rejects "intrusions" of international law into the relationship between the State and its citizens, the UN Charter recognizes as one of its purposes and principles "promoting and encouraging respect for human rights and for fundamental freedoms for all without distinction as to race, sex, language, or religion",[177] and the General Assembly of the United Nations proclaimed the UDHR:

> as a common standard of achievement for all peoples and all nations, to the end that every individual and every organ of society, keeping this Declaration constantly in mind, shall strive by teaching and education to promote respect for these rights and freedoms and by progressive measures, national and international, to secure their universal and effective recognition and observance, both among the peoples of Member States themselves and among the peoples of territories under their jurisdiction.[178]

It is true that the provisions of the UN Charter that referred to human rights and the UDHR did not impose positive legal obligations on States, owing to the programmatic nature of the provisions of the former and the non-binding character of the latter.[179] Thus, the effects of these provisions left intact the requirement that the existence of human rights obligations depends on their recognition in a treaty or a custom. It also left intact the freedom of States to decide in what manner – or if – they will incorporate the UDHR into their domestic legal systems.[180] Yet, the adoption of the International Covenant on Civil and Political Rights and the International Covenant on Social, Economic and Cultural Rights, as well as the relevant body of treaty law that has

---

176 *See*, Louis Henkin, *International Law: Politics, Values and Functions*, 216 Collected Courses of the Hague Academy of International Law, Vol. IV, p. 215 (Martinus Nijhoff Publishers, 1989); *see generally*, Robert Badinter, *International Criminal Justice: From Darkness to Light*, in Antonio Cassese, Paola Gaeta, and John R.W.D. Jones (Eds.), *The Rome Statute of the International Criminal Court: A Commentary* (Oxford University Press, 2002).

177 United Nations, Charter of the United Nations, 24 October 1945, 1 UNTS XVI, Art. 1.3 (other provisions related with the promotion and protection of human rights include the Preamble, Arts. 13, Art. 55, Art. 62, Art. 68 and Art. 76).

178 UN General Assembly, Universal Declaration of Human Rights, 10 December 1948, 217 A (III), Preamble.

179 *See generally*, UN Charter, Art. 13.

180 *See*, Louis Henkin, *International Law: Politics, Values and Functions*, *supra* n. 176, p. 215.

emerged in the last decades at a universal and regional level (including, of course, the American Convention), the debate about the existence of international legal obligations was settled a long time ago: States are obligated, as a matter of international law, to respect and ensure the human rights of persons subject to their jurisdiction to the extent that these rights are protected by international law.

Still, the existence of international obligations on human rights did not mean that IHRL is supreme to domestic law. For instance, Article 2 of the ICCPR establishes that each State "undertakes to take the necessary steps, in accordance with its constitutional processes and with the provisions of the present Covenant, to adopt such laws or other measures as may be necessary to give effect to the rights recognized in the present Covenant". This provision was originally interpreted by the Human Rights Committee (HRC) as a norm that "generally leaves it to the States parties concerned to choose their method of implementation in their territories within the framework set out in that Article".[181] The interpretation of the HRC has changed in recent years, although there is still a high recognition of the right of States to decide how to implement the rules of IHRL into their domestic legal systems. In this sense the HRC interpreted Article 2 in a manner that opens the door to sustain that one consequence of the recognition of human rights at the international level implies – at a certain level – the existence of concrete obligations for State authorities to respect them, independent of the domestic laws that are put in place for their implementation:

> The obligations of the Covenant in general and Article 2 in particular are binding on every State Party as a whole. All branches of government (executive, legislative and judicial), and other public or governmental authorities, at whatever level – national, regional or local – are in a position to engage the responsibility of the State Party. The executive branch that usually represents the State Party internationally, including before the Committee, may not point to the fact that an action incompatible with the provisions of the Covenant was carried out by another branch of government as a means of seeking to relieve the State Party from responsibility for the action and consequent incompatibility.[182]

The existence of this ample latitude for the incorporation of the UDHR – and one may say IHRL in general – is in part explained because the recognition of human rights at the international level was not intended "to create a single approved model for human rights for the entire world; the Declaration's architects

181 UN Human Rights Committee (HRC), CCPR General Comment No. 3: Article 2 (Implementation at the National Level), *supra* n. 35, §1.

182 UN Human Rights Committee (HRC), General Comment No. 31 [80], The nature of the general legal obligation imposed on States Parties to the Covenant, 26 May 2004, CCPR/C/21/Rev.1/Add.13, §4.

expected that the fertile principles of the Declaration could be brought to life in a legitimate variety of ways".[183] The UDHR is the beginning of the human rights era at the universal level, and was certainly a base for the creation of subsequent human rights instruments both in its spirit and in its content. In the words of the Vienna Declaration and Programme of Action (VDPA):

> [T]he Universal Declaration of Human Rights ... is the source of inspiration and has been the basis for the United Nations in making advances in standard setting as contained in the existing international human rights instruments, in particular the International Covenant on Civil and Political Rights and the International Covenant on Economic, Social and Cultural Rights.[184]

Positions such as that of the UN Human Rights Committee diminish the logic of a strict separation between what is considered "international" and what is considered "domestic", at least as it is sustained by the theory of dualism. The international community seems to consider that certain principles and rules established in human rights treaties have certain specificity, since they reaffirm values so important to the public order that the duty to protect them transcends some limits imposed by the dualistic vision – which, in essence, is a theory that recognizes and protects the sovereignty and the interests of States considered as independent entities. It is also possible to identify this tendency in the Inter-American System, since it has been recognized that some of the obligations recognized by the American Convention are self-executing under Articles 1.1 and 2 of the same Treaty.[185] This position implies that the American Convention must be enforced by all the authorities of the States party to Convention, which is also the genesis of the doctrine of conventionality control.

The theory of dualism is thus insufficient to explain the contemporary legal phenomenon for areas of law that have emerged since the second half of the twentieth century. This phenomenon has been and still is the object of relevant academic inquiry.[186] For instance, Paolo G. Carozza has pointed out how the

---

183 Mary Ann Glendon, *A World Made New*, p. 221 (Random House, 2001) ("Their idea was that each local tradition was enriched as it put the Declaration's principles into practice and that all countries would benefit from the resulting accumulation of experiences.").

184 UN General Assembly, Vienna Declaration and Programme of Action, 12 July 1993, A/CONF.157/23, Preamble.

185 *Cf.* Eduardo Jiménez Arrechaga, *La Convención Americana de Derechos Humanos como derecho interno*, *supra* n. 105, p. 32; A.A. Cançado Trindade, *El derecho internacional de los derechos humanos en el Siglo XXI*, pp. 283–285 (Editorial Jurídica de Chile, 2001).

186 *See generally*, Paolo G. Carozza, *Subsidiarity as a Structure Principle of International Law*, 97 Am. J. Int'l L. (2003); Armin Von Bogdandy, *Pluralism, direct effect, and the ultimate say: On the relationship between international and domestic constitutional law*, 6 Int'l J. Const. L. 397–401 (2008); Anne-Marie Slaughter and William Burke-White, *The Future of International Law Is Domestic (or, The European Way of Law)*, 47 Harv. Int'l L.J. 328–330 (2006); Laurence R. Helfner, *Redesigning the European Court of Human Rights: Embeddedness as a Deep Structural*

concept of sovereignty "tells us nothing about how to resolve [the] anxious dialectic between universal and particular", leaving us only with descriptions of the "transient powers of States in international affairs".[187] He proposes that the principle of subsidiarity provides "an alternative way of thinking about the relationship between States (and substate associations) and international order in matters of humans rights beyond the rigid and ultimately empty dichotomies of 'sovereignty'".[188] Subsidiarity is a theory that "values the freedom and integration of local culture without reducing the particularism to pure devolution and decentralization of authority; it affirms internationalism and intervention without the temptation for a super State or other centralized global authority".[189]

In a similar spirit, Armin Von Bogdandy has pointed out that the theories of monism and dualism are conceptually insufficient to understand the relationship between international law and domestic legal systems in particular areas of law (including IHRL), because "their arguments are rather hermetic, the core assertions are little developed, opposing views are simply dismissed as 'illogical', and they are not linked with the contemporary theoretical debate".[190] He argues that "only a theory of legal pluralism can account, descriptively and normatively, for the diversity within the legal realm, in general, and the links between domestic constitutions and international legal phenomena".[191] The theory of legal pluralism shall go hand in hand with the construction of doctrines of direct effect and consistent interpretation, which would allow political and judicial institutions to "couple" international law and constitutional law by balancing constitutional principles such as "international cooperation, democratic government, and subsidiarity".[192]

More recently, Eduardo Ferrer Mac-Gregor Poisot argued, from his perspective as judge of the Inter-American Court of Human Rights, that the practice of judicial dialogue – this is the practice of domestic and international

---

Principle of the European Human Rights Regime, 19 The European Journal of International Law 125–159 (2008); Francis G. Jacobs, *Judicial Dialogue and the Cross-Fertilization of Legal Systems: The European Court of Justice*, 38(3) Tex. Int'l L. J. 547 (2003); Eduardo Ferrer Mac-Gregor Poisot, *What Do We Mean When We Talk About Judicial Dialogue?: Reflections Of A Judge Of The Inter-American Court of Human Rights*, 30 Harv. Hum. Rts. J. 89 (2017) (these articles show different points of view on how should we understand the relationship between international law and domestic law). *See generally*, Pablo González-Domínguez, *Reshape of the Relationship Between International Law and Domestic Law on the Basis of the Principle of Subsidiarity*, XVIII Anuario Mexicano de Derecho Internacional 718 (2017).

187 Paolo G. Carozza, *Subsidiarity as a Structure Principle of International Law*, *supra* n. 186, p. 65.

188 *Id.* p. 66.

189 *Id.* p. 78.

190 Armin von Bogdandy, *Pluralism, direct effect and the ultimate say: on the relationship between international law and domestic constitutional law*, *supra* n. 186, p. 400.

191 *Id.* p. 398.

192 *Id.* p. 403.

courts using the reasoning of other domestic or international courts in order to construct a better interpretation of human rights norms – is a proper mechanism to coordinate the constant interaction between courts in different latitudes.[193] Judicial dialogue serves as a practical tool to promote integration and normative coherence in human rights questions on the basis of the advances that exist at the domestic and international levels.[194] This practical approach would strengthen an organic construction of human rights standards based on the *pro personae* principle, with international and domestic judges at the forefront of that project.[195] This project would ultimately and ideally open the door for the construction of a global judiciary that guarantees a homologous protection of human rights throughout the world, on the basis of a universal *Jus Constitutionale Commune*.[196]

Although with relevant theoretical differences that are not the object of study in this or any other chapter of the book, Carozza, Von Bogdandy, and Ferrer Mac-Gregor Poisot – to mention just two scholars and a judge who have recently worked on new ideas on this particular question – provide relevant legal analysis on how the understanding of the relationship between international law and domestic law (both in its monist or dualist version) is unsatisfactory to mediate the inherent tension that exists between affirming the existence of a unifying body of law in an increasingly globalized world, and the necessity to regulate the interaction between norms and actors of the international legal system with those at the domestic legal system. As showed in the previous paragraphs, this inherent tension is especially clear in several branches of "the tree" of international law that deal with questions of public order with which States must comply in order to protect the dignity of persons and groups.

True, it is indeed arbitrary to claim that, because these areas of law make more sense if they are interpreted from theoretical basis different from dualism, then the structural principles of general international law have changed as a normative and factual matter. The problem with arguing the latter is not about the convenience or the inconvenience of this or that new theory, but about the fact that the validity of theories is sanctioned by the behavior of those in power to create and enforce international law (in international law primarily by States). Because, as H.L.A. Hart explains, the statement of a public official (e.g. a judge) that a rule or a principle is valid, is an internal statement that responds to the recognition that the rule satisfies the test for "identifying what is to count as law in his court".[197] New theories in international law (such as those that sustain the

193 *See*, Eduardo Ferrer Mac-Gregor Poisot, *What Do We Mean When We Talk About Judicial Dialogue?: Reflections Of A Judge Of The Inter-American Court of Human Rights*, 30 Harv. Hum. Rts. J. 89 (2017).

194 *Id.*

195 *Id.*

196 *Id.* at conclusions.

197 H.L.A. Hart, The Concept of Law, p. 105 (Oxford University Press, 2nd ed., 1961).

direct effect and supremacy of the American Convention) need to be identified as legally binding in order to be effective to explain legal phenomena and to shape the legal practice. But on the basis of the same premise, which links the normative value of legal rules to sociological facts, it might also sound arbitrary to sustain that the values, principles and practices in the above-mentioned areas of law do not reflect the shortcomings of the orthodox view of dualism, and therefore it is reasonable to think that new approaches are indeed shaping our understanding of international law in the twenty-first century.

4. CONCLUSION

The most serious critiques of conventionality control could be directly or indirectly based on three notions: first, that there is no rule in the American Convention or in general international law that allows sustaining the self-executing nature of the Convention, which means that the obligation of domestic authorities to comply with Articles 1.1 and 2 depends on the existence of domestic rules of implementation. Second, that the open language of Article 2 does not allow to derive any specific measure that the States parties to the American Convention shall take to comply with Article 1.1; this means that there is no international legal obligation for States to adopt specific legislation or adopt specific practices (such as conventionality control) to guarantee the effectiveness of the Convention at the domestic level. Third, that the Inter-American Court does not have authority to specify the measures that States must take to comply with Article 2, and thus it cannot create the doctrine of conventionality control without acting *ultra vires*.

These critiques are the consequence of two structural notions: that the consent of States as sovereigns is the only relevant factor to identify the origin and content of international rights and obligations as contained in treaties and customs (this means that the IACtHR has no authority to create law, but only to interpret the law as agreed by States); and that there is a strict separation in theory and practice between the rights and obligations that States have as subjects of international law, and the obligations that specific authorities have at the domestic level from the existence of those rights and obligations. These structural notions underline the traditional understanding of international law, which makes the formulation of theories that justify the "intrusion" of international institutions over the traditional sphere of a State's competences difficult to sustain. And this might be especially true in the Inter-American System, where the principle of the prohibition of Inter-American institutions against intervening in matters that are within the domestic jurisdiction of States has been important long before the adoption of the American Convention.

Nevertheless, the emergence of *jus cogens* norms, IHL, ICL and IHRL has showed the limitations of the theory of dualism to explain modern legal phenomena in areas of law connected with the protection of human dignity. These areas deal with questions of public order whose protection is not motivated by mutual interests among States as sovereigns, but by the goal of protecting human dignity without discrimination, and the prosecution of those individuals responsible for the commission of international crimes. This means that the understanding of these areas of law on the exclusive basis of theories like dualism seems to be at odds with the realization of the "high purposes" that are their object and purpose. This position does not necessarily mean the acceptance of the theoretical postulates of radical monism, or the acceptance that the agreement of States is not relevant at all to understand rights and obligations derived from treaties. Yet these areas may open the door for new theories (such as the notion of legal pluralism) and new legal instruments (such as conventionality control) that close the gap between international law and domestic law.

CHAPTER 4

RECONSTRUCTING THE DOCTRINE OF CONVENTIONALITY CONTROL IN LIGHT OF THE PRINCIPLE OF SUBSIDIARITY

Principles and rules are intended to provide a thinking man with a frame of reference ... a rule or principle of this sort is a law for action, but not in its formal, definitive meaning; it represents only the spirit and sense of the law: in cases where the diversity of the real world cannot be contained within the rigid form of law, the application of principle allows for a greater latitude of judgment.
Carl Von Clausewitz
On War, 1832

1. INTRODUCTION

The critiques made of the doctrine of conventionality control could be rejected on the grounds that the interpretation of international human rights norms must be based on principles of justice, as understood by the Inter-American Court and the Inter-American Commission, rather than on the agreement of States as reflected in the text and the *travaux préparatoires* of the American Convention and other treaties of the Inter-American System. This position – which could be based on the ideas of prominent authors such as A.A. Cançado Trindade – would reflect a strong idealist and monist position that confines the relevance of the sovereignty of States only to the emergence of international obligations at a very abstract level (i.e. with the consent to be bound by a treaty and the acceptance of the jurisdiction of monitoring institutions), and would conceive international institutions (especially the ICtHR) as the ultimate authority to determine and expand the content of the Inter-American *Corpus Juris*, and of its own jurisdiction, as it considers best for the protection of human rights.[1]

1 *See generally*, A.A. Cançado Trindade, *Os Tribunais Internacionais e a Realizacao da Justica*, p. 49 (Renovar, 2015) (the author argues that the position of an international tribunal can only be based on principles of justice and not based on the will of States: "*Deste prisma, a postura básica de um tribunal internacional sópode ser principista, sem fazer concessoes indevidas ao voluntarismo estatal.*").

This notion would reflect the conviction that the interpretation of international human rights law (IHRL) must be based in considerations of humanity and not in the consent of States, and for that reason criticism based on positive international law has no place in the Inter-American System.[2]

This chapter rejects both views – the positivist, explained in the previous chapter, and the idealist, explained in the previous paragraph – as solid points of departure to criticize or to sustain the validity of the doctrine of conventionality control. The first one because it ignores that although human rights treaties are governed by norms and principles of general international law (with the centrality that the principle of sovereignty *still* has), it is also true that the norms and practices in IHRL are based on other principles that are specific to this area of law, and that are equally relevant from a normative perspective: dignity, subsidiarity, solidarity, equality and proportionality.[3] But, on the other hand, there is no doubt that the sovereignty of States (manifested primarily in the consent to be bound by treaties, but not only) is still a relevant component to understanding not just the origin of international rights and obligations, but also their normative content and their implications for domestic authorities. Ignoring both realities (that human rights treaties have specific characteristics, but that the consent of States is still critical to determine the content of those obligations) is misleading to an understanding of the regime of IHRL from a descriptive and a normative perspective.[4]

Accordingly, this chapter has a twofold purpose: responding to the criticism against conventionality control as explained in the previous chapter, and reconstructing this doctrine on the basis of the principle of subsidiarity – hence implicitly rejecting the extreme monism and idealism that is behind the "principle of integration".[5] The discussion becomes especially relevant after the

---

2 *See generally*, A.A. Cançado Trindade, *International Law for Humankind: Towards a Jus Gentium (II): General Course on Public International Law* (Martinus Nijhoff Publishers, 2005) (the authors call for a new mentality conducive to a new awareness that "International Law cannot longer, and does not longer, operate upon a strictly inter-State basis – a new mentality conducive to the international community assuming its responsibility for securing the survival as well as the welfare of mankind").

3 *See generally*, Dinah Shelton (Ed.), *The Oxford Handbook of International Human Rights Law* (Oxford University Press, 2013), pp. 345–469 (on a study of the structural principles of IHRL).

4 *See generally*, Gerald L. Neuman, *Import, Export, and Regional Consent in the Inter-American Court of Human Rights*, 19(1) Eur. J. Int'l L. 115 (2008) (the author concludes that although the rights embodied in human rights conventions have a supranational basis, they also have consensual and institutional aspects. This means that the substantial evolution of the regional human rights regime must not be independent of the regional community of states).

5 *See*, Ariel E. Dulitzky, *An Inter-American Constitutional Court? The Invention of conventionality control by the Inter-American Court of Human Rights* 50 Tex. Int'l L. J. 54 (2015) (The principle of integration conceives human rights treaties of the Inter-American System and the jurisprudence of the Inter-American Court as "an integral part of domestic legal systems at the highest possible level.").

Court linked, in the decision of *Santo Domingo Massacre v. Colombia* (2012),[6] and in the decision of *Andrade Salmón v. Bolivia* (2016),[7] the existence of conventionality control with the subsidiary or complementary nature of the Inter-American System. It is also relevant since the Court also linked, in the decision of the monitoring compliance with the judgment of *Fontevecchia and D'Amico v. Argentina* (2017), the content of the reparations ordered in concrete cases with the principle of subsidiarity or complementarity.[8] The introduction of this principle as a theoretical basis for the existence of conventionality control, and for the ordering of reparations in the jurisprudence of the Inter-American Court, opens the door for new discussions about the legal foundations and the implications that conventionality control might have in the future – both in the manner that it is developed and applied by the Inter-American Court, and in its implications for the authorities of the States parties to the American Convention.

In a nutshell, the chapter argues that interpreting the American Convention in the light of the principle of subsidiarity provides a valid justification for the existence of conventionality control, and provides a theoretical tool for understanding its normative implications in the present and future. The chapter holds that the principle of subsidiarity justifies the creation of this doctrine as the source of an international legal obligation for domestic authorities to exercise a consistent interpretation of domestic law and to avoid the enforcement of domestic laws that have been found anti-conventional by the Inter-American Court. Yet, that subsidiarity also allows an understanding of the normative limits of this doctrine in a way that does not neglect the legitimate spaces of freedom that States have (under Article 2 of the American Convention and general international law) to decide the meaning and normative force of the Inter-American *Corpus Juris* at the domestic level. This view would open the door to reasonably "regulate" the "intensity" of the obligations that emerge from the existence of conventionality control without violating international law.

---

6 *See, Santo Domingo Massacre v. Colombia.* Preliminary Objections, Merits and Reparations Judgment, Inter-Am. Ct. H.R. (Ser. C) No. 259 (Nov. 30, 2012) §142 (the Inter-American Court drew a clear connection between subsidiarity and conventionality control when it mentioned that "[t]hese ideas [those of the Preamble and the decision in *Jaramillo*] have been also incorporated in recent case law based on the opinion that all the organs and of a State Party to the Convention have the obligation to ensure "control of conformity with the Convention").

7 *See, Andrade Salmón v. Bolivia.* Merits, Reparations and Costs Judgment, Inter-Am. Ct. H.R. (Ser. C) No. 330 (Dec. 1, 2016) §93.

8 *Cf. Fontevecchia and D'Amico v. Argentina. Monitoring Compliance with Judgment.* Order of the Inter-American Court of Human Rights (Oct. 18, 2017) §32; *see generally, Vereda La Esperanza v. Colombia.* Preliminary Objections, Merits, Reparations and Costs Judgment, Inter-Am. Ct. H.R. (Ser. C) No. 341 (Aug. 31, 2017) §259–265; and *Dismissed Employees of Petroperú et al. v. Peru.* Preliminary Objections, Merits, Reparations and Costs Judgment, Inter-Am. Ct. H.R. (Ser. C) No. 344 (Nov. 23, 2017) §200–206.

In order to prove this thesis, Chapter 4 is divided in four sections. It starts by arguing that Article 2 must be interpreted as a norm that recognizes a high but not absolute freedom for States to decide how to implement the Inter-American *Corpus Juris* at the domestic level, which opens the door for the specification at the international level of doctrines like conventionality control. The principles of human dignity, subsidiarity, solidarity and good faith, require that States effectively advance the protection of human rights at the domestic level, which means that the freedom recognized by Article 2 must be understood as a freedom for States to choose the best manner to comply with the Inter-American *Corpus Juris*, and not as a blank check to do as they please, as a view based on sovereignty would logically lead to conclude. Taking the subsidiary nature of the Inter-American System seriously requires that the Inter-American Court intervene and order States to repair the causes of human rights violations at a structural level, in order to avoid future breaches of the American Convention. This "intervention" is justified when States systematically fail to comply with their international obligations owing to the existence of domestic laws or practices that are manifestly anti-conventional, and where the Court finds that States are incapable or unwilling to modify laws and practices that are the causes of human rights violations.

Consequently – the arguments continue in section 3 – conventionality control is justified because it constitutes a juridical instrument created to combat a particularly serious problem in Latin-America that some States proved to be incapable or unwilling to address: the impunity for perpetrators of serious human rights violations produced by the existence of amnesty laws and for the enforcement of those laws by the judiciary; both types of conduct (the creation and enforcement of amnesty laws) are a clear violation to the American Convention and other rules of international law. So, the validity of conventionality control is essentially connected with the necessity to assist States to be capable of guaranteeing the right of access to justice for victims of serious human rights violations and for their relatives, to assist States to fulfill their obligations to investigate and punish those State agents responsible for those violations, and to provide reparations for the victims and to avoid the existence of future victims. The importance of guaranteeing the right of access to justice and to fight against impunity is one of the main goals of the Inter-American System, and has legitimized the progressive approach of the Court in its jurisprudence on criminal law since *Velásquez Rodríguez v. Honduras*.[9]

---

9 *See*, Dinah Shelton, *The Promise of Regional Human Rights Systems*, in BURNS H. WESTON AND STEPHEN P. MARKS (EDS.), *THE FUTURE OF INTERNATIONAL HUMAN RIGHTS*, p. 366 (Transnational Press, 2000) (on the notion that the Inter-American System has been strongly concerned, since its inception, with democracy, the rule of law and the right to judicial protection, owing to the experience of repeated military coups in the region).

The same spirit, which is intimately connected with the historic struggles of Latin America, is at the core of the validity of the doctrine of conventionality control.

Yet, it is obvious that conventionality control acquired broader dimensions after it was included in paragraph 124 of *Almonacid*. In subsequent cases the Inter-American Court decided that conventionality control required domestic judges to "control" all types of domestic laws (*Dismissed Congressional Employees (Aguado-Alfaro) v. Peru*, *Boyce et al. v. Barbados* and *Expelled Dominican and Haitians v. Dominican Republic*), and that all domestic authorities must exercise conventionality control (*Cabrera Garcia and Montiel Flores v. Mexico* and *Gelman v. Uruguay*). The expansion of the normative elements of conventionality control opens the door for another type of discussion. Because one thing is creating a juridical instrument to assist States to fight against impunity for serious human rights violations in a concrete case, and another is creating a doctrine that – in its most extreme version – seeks to "constitutionalize" the Inter-American *Corpus Juris* at the expense of legal pluralism in Latin America. Section 4 argues that in order to sustain the validity of the doctrine of conventionality control as understood since *Aguado-Alfaro*, it is necessary to conceptually distinguish its normative force in cases where it constitutes a "guarantee of non-repetition" to avoid that the interpretation or enforcement of domestic law violates international law, and when it is referred to as a doctrine with general applicability for all the authorities of the States parties to the American Convention. In the first hypothesis conventionality control must be considered as part of the obligations of the State to comply with the judgments of the Inter-American Court, and in the second hypothesis it must be understood with the normative force of a "principle".

The distinction of conventionality control as a "guarantee of non-repetition" and as a "principle" would allow sustaining its nature as an obligation that must be complied with exactly as mandated by the Inter-American Court in specific cases (when it is conceived as a guarantee of non-repetition, for example for Mexican judges after *Radilla Pacheco v. Mexico*), and at the same would allow its understanding as a flexible mechanism that accommodates different legal systems (when it is conceived as a principle). This approach – the chapter concludes – is crucial to guarantee the validity and effectiveness of conventionality control as a doctrine created by the Inter-American Court in its jurisprudence (not by the States by consent), without encroaching the freedom of States in a way that violates the American Convention and that endangers the political stability of the Inter-American System. The flexibility of this understanding would allow conventionality control to become a juridical instrument that increases the effectiveness of the Inter-American *Corpus Juris* at the domestic level; it would promote the existence of true judicial dialogue among international and domestic institutions, and it would contribute for the existence of a *Jus Constitutionale Commune* for the region. This view would also avoid the imposition of a homogeneous understanding of human rights that hinders pluralism in Latin America, and which creates unnecessary political tensions between the States parties to the Convention and the Inter-American Court.

2. ARTICLE 2 AS A BASIS FOR CONVENTIONALITY CONTROL

2.1. THE EXISTENCE OF A HIGH BUT NOT ABSOLUTE FREEDOM FOR STATES TO DECIDE THE MEANS TO COMPLY WITH INTERNATIONAL OBLIGATIONS

It is now commonplace among scholars that conventionality control finds its normative basis in Article 2.[10] This article imposes an obligation for States: "to adopt, in accordance with their constitutional processes and the provisions of this Convention, such legislative or other measures as may be necessary to give effect to those rights or freedoms [protected by the Convention]."[11] The Inter-American Court has determined that this article requires States to undertake two kinds of actions:

> 85. ... the adoption of measures to suppress laws and practices of any kind that imply a violation of the guarantees established in the Convention, and also the adoption of laws and the implementation of practices leading to the effective observance of said guarantees.[12]

Conventionality control has been considered to be precisely the "measure" that State authorities – and especially judges – must take to "suppress", to "purge" (using Sergio García Ramírez's language) domestic laws that are anti-conventional.

The approach taken by the Court, since *Suárez Rosero v. Ecuador*,[13] could be criticized on the basis that this article was originally conceived with a "programmatic nature". The criticism is based on the idea that no specific obligation could be derived from Article 2, because: (1) of the lack of specificity

---

10 *See*, Nestor Pedro Sagües, *International obligations and "Conventionality Control"*, 8(1) Estudios Constitucionales, 122 (2010); Eduardo Ferrer Mac-Gregor Poisot, *Reflexiones sobre el control difuso de convencionalidad. A la luz del caso Cabrera Garcia y Montiel Flores v. México*, XLIV (131) Boletín Mexicano de Derecho Comparado (2011), §59.

11 Organization of American States, American Convention on Human Rights, Nov. 22, 1969, O.A.S.T.S. No. 36, 1144, U.N.T.S. 123, Art. 1.1.

12 *"The Last Temptation of Christ" v. Chile Case (Olmedo Bustos et al.)*. Judgment, Inter-Am. Ct. H.R. (Ser. C) No. 73 (Feb. 5, 2001) §85.

13 *See*, *Suárez Rosero v. Ecuador Case*. Judgment, Inter-Am. Ct. H.R. (Ser. C) No. 35 (Nov. 12, 1997) §98.

of this article about the kind of measures that must be taken by States to give effect to Article 1.1, and (2) this article establishes that the measures shall be taken by States: "in accordance with the constitutional processes and the provisions of [the] Convention".[14] This view, which is the basis for the most important critiques presented in the previous chapter against conventionality control, would consider that, although States shall take measures to ensure the effectiveness of the Convention, the specification of these measures is an exclusive competence of States in accordance with international law. In this view, States have the right, as sovereigns, to define how to implement the Convention in accordance with their domestic legal systems and the choices of their political and judicial institutions.

The Inter-American Court has implicitly and explicitly rejected this view.[15] It has considered that it is authorized to create structural changes in the laws and practices of the States parties to the Convention, Article 2 being one of the main normative vehicles to promote those changes. It seems that, in the Court's view, the goal of preventing future human rights violations, and the necessity to strengthen the effectiveness of the Inter-American *Corpus Juris* at the domestic level, have trumped strict notions that do not allow any intrusion of international institutions in the domestic affairs of States beyond what was originally agreed upon treaty law. So, the Court has constantly specified the kind of legislative measures that States shall take to increase the effectiveness of the Convention at the domestic level, in some cases with a great deal of specification. These measures have included the nullification of domestic laws, or the adoption of certain policies like conventionality control.[16] The question, of course, is if there is enough normative space in Article 2 for a reading like the one adopted by the Inter-American Court since *Suárez Rosero* and to this date.

---

14 *See generally*, Ariel E. Dulitzky, *El Impacto del Control de Convencionalidad. ¿Un Cambio de Paradigma en el Sistema Interamericano de Derechos Humanos?"* in José Sebastián Elías et al. (Eds.), *Tratado de los Derechos Constitucionales*, p. 341 (Abeledo, 2014).

15 *See generally, Caballero Delgado and Santana v. Colombia*. Reparations and costs (Art. 63(1) American Convention on Human Rights). Judgment, Inter-Am. Ct. H.R. (Ser. C) No. 31 (Jan. 29, 1997). Dissenting Opinion of A.A. Cançado Trindade, §6–9; *El Amparo v. Venezuela Case*. Reparations (Art. 63(1) American Convention on Human Rights) Judgment, Inter-Am. Ct. H.R. (Ser. C) No. 28 (Sep. 14, 1996). Dissenting Opinion of A.A. Cançado Trindade, §3; *Hilaire, Constantine and Benjamin et al. v. Trinidad and Tobago*. Merits, Reparations, and Costs Judgment, Inter-Am. Ct. H.R. (Ser. C) No. 94 (Jun. 21, 2002) §113; *Juvenile Reeducation Institute v. Paraguay*. Judgment, Inter-Am. Ct. H.R. (Ser. C) No. 112 (Sep. 2, 2004) §206; *Lori Berenson Mejía v. Peru*. Judgment, Inter-Am. Ct. H.R. (Ser. C) No. 119 (Nov. 25, 2004) §219; *Caesar v. Trinidad and Tobago*. Judgment, Inter-Am. Ct. H.R. (Ser. C) No. 123 (Mar. 11, 2005) §91.

16 *See, "The Last Temptation of Christ" v. Chile Case (Olmedo Bustos et al.), supra* n. 12, §63–73; *Barrios Altos v. Peru Case*. Judgment, Inter-Am. Ct. H.R. (Ser. C) No. 75 (Mar. 14, 2001), §44; *Almonacid Arellano et al v. Chile*. Preliminary Objections, Merits, Reparations and Costs Judgment, Inter-Am. Ct. H.R. (Ser. C) No. 154 (Sep. 26, 2006) §124.

From an understanding based on traditional notions of positive international law, as shown in Chapter 3, the answer is no: Article 2 does not allow the evaluation of domestic laws and practices or propose new doctrines like conventionality control. Yet, one valid way to sustain the legality of the approach taken by the Court since *Almonacid Arellano et al. v. Chile* is by conceiving that Article 2 recognizes a *high* but not *absolute* degree of freedom for States to decide how to implement the Convention at the domestic level. This approach is justified on the notion that a State's freedom to choose the means to comply with its international obligations must find its limits in the principle of good faith (Article 26 of the Vienna Convention), and in the specific obligations derived from the Inter-American *Corpus Juris* (Article 1.1 of the American Convention).[17] In a view that takes the international commitment of States to respect and ensure human dignity seriously, the existence of the right of States to decide the best way to comply with their obligations under international law must be understood as the freedom to implement treaties in good faith and in accordance with their political preferences and social context, and not as the right to do as they please regarding how or if to comply with those obligations.[18]

So when a State is fragrantly and systematically violating core aspects of the Inter-American *Corpus Juris* by maintaining or adopting domestic laws or practices manifestly anti-conventional, Article 2 should be interpreted as the basis to declare the international responsibility of the State, and to order the necessary measures to remedy the causes of human rights violations.[19] This type of approach would not constitute an "arbitrary" intervention in State affairs as – for instance – the European Court of Human Rights has implied regarding the scope of freedom that States have to comply with its judgments.[20]

---

17 *See generally*, Jean Salmon, *Article 26*, in Olivier Corten and Pierre Klein (Eds.), *The Vienna Conventions on the Law of Treaties. A Commentary*, Vol. I (Oxford University Press, 2011), pp. 677–678 (the author explains that the principle of good faith requires that the object of a treaty must be executed in a reasonable way and in a manner that its purpose can be achieved).

18 *See generally*, International Commission on Intervention and State Sovereignty, *The Responsibility to Protect: Report of the ICISS* (2001) 2.29 (the International Commission on Intervention and State Sovereignty mentioned that the core meaning of UN membership has shifted from "the final symbol of independent sovereign statehood and thus the seal of acceptance into the community of nations", to recognition of a State "as a responsible member of the community of nations").

19 *See, Tibi v. Ecuador*. Preliminary Objections, Merits, Reparations and Costs Judgment, Inter-Am. Ct. H.R. (Ser. C) No. 114 (Sep. 7, 2004). Concurrent Opinion of Sergio García Ramírez, §5. (It is the practical concern of avoiding future human rights violations that García Ramírez called in this concurrent opinion for the necessity that the standards created by the Court in its jurisprudence are followed by the States parties to the Convention.)

20 *See, Hirst v. United Kingdom*, Appl. No. 74025/01, Eur. Ct. H.R. (2005), §83 (in the words of the European Court: "... In cases where a systemic violation has been found the Court has, with a view to assisting the respondent State in fulfilling its obligations under Article 46, indicated the type of measure that might be taken to put an end to the situation found to exist ... In other

It would constitute an approach that responds to the subsidiary nature of the Inter-American System to the benefit of the protection of human dignity, but without violating the rights of States as the primary actors in the creation of conditions for the realization of rights. This view would certainly clash with an understanding of Article 2 seen solely from the perspective of the principle of sovereignty, but this is not the only relevant principle that should be considered in the understanding of the interpretation of IHRL.[21]

2.2. THE PRINCIPLE OF SUBSIDIARITY

The principle of subsidiarity is especially relevant in the understanding of the content and effects of international human rights norms at a structural level, and on the limits of monitoring institutions in interpreting and enforcing those norms.[22] This principle has been defined as

> a principle of justice that requires larger communities to protect the legitimate autonomy of smaller communities to provide them with assistance (*subsidium*) needed to fulfill their ends, and to coordinate and regulate their activities within the common good of a larger community, of which they are part and which is also necessary to the flourishing of their individual members.[23]

It calls for "non-interference with the activities of individuals or smaller groups when these are capable of the tasks appropriate to them, and assistance to

exceptional cases, the nature of the violation found may be such as to leave no real choice as to the measures required to remedy it and the Court may decide to indicate only one such measure …").

21 *See*, Dinah Shelton (Ed.), *The Oxford Handbook of International Human Rights Law*, *supra* n. 3, pp. 345–469.

22 *See*, Paolo G. Carozza, *Subsidiarity as a Structure Principle of International Law*, 97 Am. J. Int'l L. 79 2003 (the idea of subsidiarity as a "structural principle" implies that it is a relevant for the understanding of all the norms and institutions that deal with human rights at a universal and regional level); Dinah Shelton (Ed.), *The Oxford Handbook of International Human Rights Law*, *supra* n. 3, p. 4 (on the idea that subsidiarity is a principle that directs the role of international human rights law in relation to States in the international community); Yota Negishi, *The Subsidiarity Principle's Role in Allocating Competences Between Human Rights Courts and States Parties: the Hybrid Model of Centralized and Diffused Conventionality Control of Domestic Law*, in Armin Von Bogdandy, Mariela Morales Antoniazzi and Flavia Piovesan, *Ius Constitutionale Commune na América Latina. Volume III. Diálogos Jurisdicionais e Controle de Convencionalidade* pp. 129–136 (Jurua Editora, 2016).

23 Paolo G. Carozza, *The Problematic Applicability of Subsidiarity to International Law and Institutions*, 61(1) The American Journal of Jurisprudence 53 (2016); *see generally*, John Finnis, *Limited Government*, in *Human Rights & Common Good. Collected Essays: Volume III*, p. 90 (Oxford University Press, 2011).

individual and lesser societies when these are appropriate or necessary tasks".[24] It constitutes a structural principle of IHRL, which means that it is intrinsic to the very existence of IHRL and shall be part of the interpretation of international norms and in the understanding of the competences and the jurisdiction of international monitoring institutions.[25] So it is not surprising that that the Preamble of the American Convention established that the Inter-American System "*reinforce[s] or complement[s]* the protection provided by the domestic law of the American states",[26] or that the Inter-American Court established in *Acevedo Jaramillo et al. v. Peru* that the State:

> 66. ... is the main guarantor of the human rights of the individual, so that, if an act that violates the said rights occurs, it is the State itself that has the obligation to decide the matter at the domestic level and, [as appropriate,] to make reparation, before having to respond before international instances, such as the inter-American system, which derives from the subsidiary nature of the international proceedings in relation to the national systems that guarantee human rights.[27]

From its procedural dimension – in IHRL – subsidiarity "describes a relationship between two institutions or norms, by which one supplements the other in appropriate circumstances".[28] From its substantive dimension subsidiarity proposes "a vision of the meaning of the social life of humanity, a common good towards the dignity of the social persons".[29] It provides criterion of judgement to understand and value the pluralism in the concrete determination of the meaning of human rights, understanding that accidents of society, politics and

---

24 Arthur Utz, The Principle of Subsidiarity and Contemporary Natural Law, 3 *Natural Law Forum* 177 (1958).

25 *See generally*, Protocol 15 amending the Convention for the Protection of Human Rights and Fundamental Freedoms, Strasbourg, 24 June 2013, Art. 1. (Protocol 15 to the European Convention on Human Rights recently added a new recital to Art. 1 establishing that: "The High Contracting Parties shall secure to everyone within their jurisdiction the rights and freedoms defined in Section I of this Convention. Affirming that the High Contracting Parties, in accordance with the principle of subsidiarity, have the primary responsibility to secure the rights and freedoms defined in this Convention and the Protocols thereto, and that in doing so they enjoy a margin of appreciation, subject to the supervisory jurisdiction of the European Court of Human Rights established by this Convention.")

26 Organization of American States, American Convention on Human Rights, Nov. 22, 1969, O.A.S.T.S. No. 36, 1144, U.N.T.S. 123, *supra* n. 10, Preamble (emphasis added).

27 *Acevedo Jaramillo et al. v. Peru.* Interpretation of the Judgment on Preliminary Objections, Merits, Reparations and Costs, Inter-Am. Ct. H.R. (Ser. C) No. 157 (Nov. 24, 2006) §66.

28 Gerald L. Neuman, *Subsidiarity*, in Dinah Shelton (Ed.), *The Oxford Handbook of International Human Rights Law*, *supra* n. 3, pp. 360; *see generally*, Paolo G. Carozza, *Subsidiarity as a Structure Principle of International Law*, *supra* n. 22, p. 66 (it is important to mention that for Carozza – different from Neuman – the principle of subsidiarity has not only a procedural aspect, but also a substantive aspect).

29 Paolo G. Carozza, *Subsidiarity as a Structure Principle of International Law*, *supra* n. 22, p. 68.

culture are relevant to transforming human rights into laws and practices of domestic institutions.[30] In this sense Paolo G. Carozza explains that

> [i]n each case, the balancing of the different aspects of the common good can be done in different ways, and every interpretation of the scope of a right involves some assessment of the reasonableness of balancing different specific aspects of the common good.[31]

Consequently, subsidiarity – seen as a principle that has both a procedural and a substantive dimension – recognizes a wide scope of freedom to apply norms of IHRL in ways consistent with the political, cultural and institutional structure of particular States.[32]

The subsidiarity nature of IHRL leads to the understanding that States shall take the necessary measures to respect and ensure human rights at the domestic level, the primary role of international monitoring institutions being to provide "guidance, monitoring, and back-up to domestic authorities but without replacing them".[33] It is the State, through the adoption of domestic laws and policies, and through the conduct of its authorities in the creation, interpretation and enforcement of domestic law, that the implementation and effectiveness of international norms shall be achieved. In this design, the role of international institutions is to assist States in the achievement of the effectiveness of IHRL through the articulation of standards, which might be binding depending on the institution and the procedure that gave origin to that standard: in some cases, the decisions of a monitoring body would have the force of a judgment, others of a recommendation, and others of a report made by a panel of experts.[34]

Gerald Neuman explains that the principle of subsidiary is manifested in IHRL in four doctrines: (1) the requirement of the exhaustion of local remedies; (2) the fourth instance doctrine; (3) the notion of remedial subsidiarity; and (4) the margin of appreciation.[35] These doctrines have the common denominator of conferring the primacy to State institutions regarding the protection of human

30 *Id.* p. 69.

31 *Id.* p. 72.

32 *Id.* p. 75.

33 Gerald L. Neuman, *Subsidiarity*, in Dinah Shelton (Ed.), *The Oxford Handbook of International Human Rights Law*, *supra* n. 3, p. 364.

34 *See generally*, American Convention on Human Rights, *supra* n. 10, Arts. 41 and 63 and 68.1 (Art. 41 reads as follows: "The main function of the Commission shall be to promote respect for and defense of human rights." Arts. 63 and 68.1, respectively, read as follows: "If the Court finds that there has been a violation of a right or freedom protected by this Convention, the Court shall rule that the injured party be ensured the enjoyment of his right or freedom that was violated" and "The States Parties to the Convention undertake to comply with the judgment of the Court in any case to which they are parties.").

35 Gerald L. Neuman, *Subsidiarity*, in Dinah Shelton (Ed.), *The Oxford Handbook of International Human Rights Law*, *supra* n. 3, pp. 369–377; Samantha Besson, *Subsidiarity in International Human Rights Law-What is Subsidiary about Human Rights*, 61(1) The American Journal of Jurisprudence 79–82 (2016).

rights in their territories, establishing a limit for international institutions to make pronouncements on the subject. They are, in a certain way, procedural doctrines that reflect deference to a State's independence and capacity to address the protection of human rights by their own means. The best example of how this deference is procedurally manifested is the rule of the exhaustion of local remedies, which "requires that a petitioner will not resort to an international institution until the petitioner has given the authorities of the State the opportunity to provide a remedy".[36] The best substantive example is the doctrine of the margin of appreciation, which entails "deference to determinations by national authorities regarding the compatibility of national measures with internationally protected rights".[37]

Subsidiarity allows explaining, from a descriptive and normative perspective, that international institutions assist States when they are not complying with their international obligations, or when the victims of human rights violations cannot find a remedy before domestic authorities, but without arrogating those tasks to themselves. For instance, the requirement of the exhaustion of local remedies finds its limits when there is no remedy provided by domestic law, when the victim has been denied access to that remedy, or when there has been an unwarranted delay in rendering a final judgment by domestic authorities. In this regard, Article 46.2 of the American Convention establishes that the requirement of the exhaustion of local remedies is not applicable when: "the domestic legislation … does not afford due process of law", when "the party … has been denied access to the remedies", and when "there has been unwarranted delay in rendering a final judgment under … the remedies".[38]

---

36 *Id.* p. 369; *see*, American Convention on Human Rights, *supra* n. 10, Art. 46.1:

> 1. Admission by the Commission of a petition or communication lodged in accordance with Articles 44 or 45 shall be subject to the following requirements: a. that the remedies under domestic law have been pursued and exhausted in accordance with generally recognized principles of international law.

European Convention on Human Rights, Art. 35.1:

> 1. The Court may only deal with the matter after all domestic remedies have been exhausted, according to the generally recognized rules of international law, and within a period of six months from the date on which the final decision was taken.;

International Covenant on Civil and Political Rights, Art. 41.c:

> Communications received under this Article shall be dealt with in accordance with the following procedure: (c) The Committee shall deal with a matter referred to it only after it has ascertained that all available domestic remedies have been invoked and exhausted in the matter, in conformity with the generally recognized principles of international law. This shall not be the rule where the application of the remedies is unreasonably prolonged.

37 Gerald L. Neuman, *Subsidiarity*, in DINAH SHELTON (ED.), *THE OXFORD HANDBOOK OF INTERNATIONAL HUMAN RIGHTS LAW*, *supra* n. 3, p. 375.

38 American Convention on Human Rights, *supra* n. 10, Art. 46.1 and 2.

Hence, it is possible to say that subsidiarity does not just have a "negative" face, that is a restriction for international institutions to intervene in States' spheres of authority, but also a "positive" face, which calls for action at the international level when action at the domestic level is not sufficient.[39] This aspect is obvious regarding the operation of procedural rules like those established in Articles 46.2 of the American Convention, but it has also impacted the manner by which courts and tribunals interpret these rules. The European Court of Human Rights (ECtHR) has considered that the rule of exhaustion of local remedies must be applied with "some degree of flexibility and without excessive formalism".[40] The practical impact of this view is that, when the ECtHR reviews preliminary objections about an applicant's failure to exhaust local remedies, it requires States that "the remedies in question must be sufficient certainly not only in theory but in practice, failing which they lack the requisite accessibility and necessity".[41]

The Inter-American Court has followed a similar flexible approach when evaluating the requirement of the exhaustion of local remedies, considering that this rule cannot impede the international protection offered by the Court in cases where there are States' policies and practices that impede the access of alleged victims to domestic remedies.[42] In *Velásquez*, the Court reasoned that the exceptions of Article 46.2 would be fully applicable in cases when it is proved that remedies are denied for trivial reasons, or without examination of the merits, or when there is proof of the existence of a policy ordered or tolerated by the State to impede certain persons from having access to domestic remedies. In these type of cases, resort to those remedies by the victims of human rights violations would become a "senseless formality", and for that reason they must be discharged of the obligation to exhaust domestic remedies, "since [the remedies] cannot fulfill their objective in that case".[43]

The principle of subsidiarity is distinct from the principle of sovereignty in the sense that it does not impose an absolute restriction of international law and international institutions to remain "at the boundaries of the State machinery" – recalling Roberto Argo's words (*see* Chapter 3, section 2.1) – when States are

39 *See*, Yota Negishi, *The Subsidiarity Principle's Role in Allocating Competences Between Human Rights Courts and States Parties: the Hybrid Model of Centralized and Diffused Conventionality Control of Domestic Law*, *supra* n. 22, pp. 134–136 (on an analysis of the negative and positive aspects of the principle of subsidiarity).

40 *Akdivar v. Turkey*. Appl. No. 21893/93, Eur. Ct. H.R. (1997), 203.

41 *See*, *Vernillo v. France*, Appl. No. 11889/85, Eur. Ct. H.R. (1991), §27.

42 *See generally*, *Velásquez Rodríguez v. Honduras*. Preliminary Objections, Inter-Am. Ct. H.R. (Ser. C) No. 1 (Jun. 26, 1987) §93.

43 *Id.* §68; *see*, Laurence Burgorgue-Larsen and Amaya Úbeda de Torres, *The Inter-American Court of Human Rights. Case Law and Commentary*, p. 138 (Oxford University Press, 2011).

failing to comply with their duty to ensure and respect, and specifically when they are failing to provide effective remedies for human rights violations.[44] The principle of subsidiarity certainly presupposes the primacy of State authorities in implementing and guaranteeing the protection of human rights at the domestic level, but it does not prohibit *a priori* the intervention of international institutions, nor does it call for a formalistic interpretation of rules like the exhaustion of local remedies. If IHRL was based on a strong view of the notion of sovereignty, it would be logically impossible to allow any intervention by international institutions in "domestic affairs", and the clauses of a treaty would need to be interpreted with a strict and formalistic connection with the text as a reflection of the consent of States. But this approach, although possible in theory, is at odds with the object and purpose of human rights treaties, and taken to its last consequences would transform the very notion of "IHRL" into a violation of the sovereignty of States.

In this sense Carozza has dealt extensively with the question of how a sovereign-oriented approach is insufficient to make sense of the structure of IHRL.[45] The approach based on sovereignty understands the relationship between international law and international institutions as two competing powers that resist each other, whereas subsidiarity makes

> possible and even necessary to say coherently that the system should *both* rely primarily on the most local body of giving meaning and effect to human rights *and* accord authority and responsibility to larger, more comprehensive bodies to intervene so as to assist in the realization of human rights.[46]

The measure of when assistance by international institutions is "necessary" is a legal and political question that must be addressed case-by-case, depending on the norms of a particular treaty, the powers of a particular monitoring body and the circumstances of a given case. But the principle of subsidiarity allows a reasonable interpretation of human rights instruments that combines intervention by international institutions and deference to State authorities.

The example provided by the European Court and the Inter-American Court regarding the interpretation of the rules for the exhaustion of local remedies shows how subsidiarity justifies a flexible understanding that trumps the empty limits placed by the principle of sovereignty and a formalistic understanding of human rights treaties. The example of the exhaustion of local remedies is

---

44 *See*, Sixth Report on State Responsibility by Mr. Roberto Argo, Special Rapporteur – the internationally wrongful act of the State, source of international responsibility (continued), Ybk ILC, 1977, Vol. II (1) A/CN.4/302 and Add.1, 2 & 3., §15.

45 Paolo G. Carozza, *Subsidiarity as a Structure Principle of International Law*, *supra* n. 22, p. 67.

46 *Ibid.*

valuable because it shows how subsidiarity serves both (1) to describe and justify the deference given to the State to remedy human rights violations by its own means; (2) and as a valid justification to interpret the rules that regulate the exceptions to the rule for the exhaustion of local remedies in a manner that better responds to the structure and the goals pursued by these rules, rather than simply accepting an approach that would give priority to the existence of formal structures at the domestic level in order to avoid assistance.[47]

2.3. ARTICLES 2 AND 63.1 IN THE LIGHT OF THE PRINCIPLE OF SUBSIDIARITY

Something similar happens with Article 2 of the American Convention. This article could certainly be read on the basis of sovereignty, which would lead to the conclusions about the illegality of evaluating the "conventionality" of any measure (legislative or other) adopted by the State to comply with its obligations under the Inter-American *Corpus Juris*.[48] Still, just as happens with the rules for exhaustion of local remedies, Article 2 makes more sense from a descriptive and a normative perspective if interpreted in the light of the principle of subsidiarity. In the light of this principle, the obligation of States "to adopt, in accordance with their constitutional processes and the provisions of [the] Convention, such legislative or other measures as may be necessary to give effect to [the] rights and freedoms [protected by the Convention]" would imply that the *primacy* (not the *exclusivity*) to define the type of "legislative or other measures" that shall be taken to guarantee the effectiveness of the Convention lies with State authorities; but it would also open new avenues for the understanding of the implications of this norm at the international level.

Interpreting Article 2 in the light of subsidiarity justifies that the Inter-American Court evaluates the conventionality of domestic laws and practices existing within the State when they are the cause of human rights violations. This approach would lead to the conclusion that the content of Article 2 does not reflect a blank check that justifies arbitrariness or negligence by States in the type of laws and policies adopted at the domestic level, as an interpretation based on sovereignty produces. On the contrary, subsidiarity recognizes that States have the freedom to decide the *best* manner to implement the Inter-American *Corpus Juris* at the domestic level in accordance with their domestic legal system

47 *See generally, Brewer Carías v. Venezuela*. Preliminary Objections, Inter-Am. Ct. H.R. (Ser. C) No. 278 (May 26, 2014). Joint Dissenting Opinion of Manuel E. Ventura and Eduardo Ferrer Mac-Gregor Poisot.

48 This was the position sustained in Ch. 3 of the book.

and practices, but that the Inter-American Court shall intervene ordering the State to correct the causes of human rights violations where it is clear that these violations are the result of laws or policies that the State is incapable or unwilling to modify. This principle also allows justifying that the Court, when it is necessary and justified depending on the circumstances of a case, orders measures with a high degree of specificity to correct the causes of those violations and to avoid future violations.[49]

This theoretical approach also opens the door to consider that the competence of the Court under Article 63.1 includes the power to order States to modify their laws and practices in grave circumstances.[50] The first paragraph of Article 63.1 confers competence to the Court to rule on violations of the rights and freedoms protected by the Convention, so that the injured party is allowed to enjoy his right and freedom that was violated. The second paragraph of this article establishes that: "it shall also rule, if appropriate, that the consequences of the measure or situation that constituted the breach of such right or freedom be remedied and that fair compensation be paid to the injured party." An interpretation of this article on the basis of sovereignty would lead to the conclusion that the Court has competence only to address concrete human rights violations and to order that the consequences of that violation be remedied, as appeared to be the approach followed by the Court in the *OC-14/94*. Whereas an approach based on subsidiarity reasonably opens the door for the Court to evaluate the causes of that violation of Article 2, and to order the State to remedy those causes in order to prevent future violations.[51]

It is true that this type of reading of Article 2 and of Article 63.1 could potentially open a "Pandora's box" regarding the understanding of the Court's power and attributions to evaluate the laws and policies that States take to give effect to the Inter-American *Corpus Juris*. The Court could consider itself as some kind of supreme legislator on human rights questions that can order States

49 *See generally*, Yota Negishi, *The Subsidiarity Principle's Role in Allocating Competences Between Human Rights Courts and States Parties: the Hybrid Model of Centralized and Diffused Conventionality Control of Domestic Law*, *supra* n. 22, p. 148.

50 Art. 63.1 establishes that:
1. If the Court finds that there has been a violation of a right or freedom protected by this Convention, the Court shall rule that the injured party be ensured the enjoyment of his right or freedom that was violated. It shall also rule, if appropriate, that the consequences of the measure or situation that constituted the breach of such right or freedom be remedied and that fair compensation be paid to the injured party.

51 *See generally*, Sergio García Ramírez, *La jurisprudencia de la Corte Interamericana de Derechos Humanos en material de reparaciones*, in La Corte Interamericana de Derechos Humanos. *Un Cuarto de Siglo: 1979–2004*, p. 11 (OEA-ICtHR, 2005); *see generally*, María Carmelina Londoño Lázaro, *Las garantias de no repetición en la jurisprudencia interamericana. Derecho internacional y cambios estructurales del Estado*, p. 203 (Universidad de la Sabana & Tirant lo Blanch, 2014).

to do as it pleases to ensure the protection of human rights, opening the door for arbitrariness and lack of legal certainty. But one could ask: does subsidiarity allow the Court to determine any measure that it considers appropriate to increase the effectiveness of the Inter-American *Corpus Juris*? Not at all. Subsidiarity is neither supremacy of international law and institutions over domestic law and institutions, nor a call for an unrestricted judicial activism. Subsidiarity requires seriousness and prudence when the Court evaluates the laws and practices of States under Article 2, and when it orders specific measures for the prevention of future human rights violations in concrete cases. Because the simplicity and emptiness behind the principle of sovereignty, and the idealist notion of supremacy and integration, violates the principle that "diversity [is] based not just in tolerance of difference but in a genuine pluralism in the understanding and pursuit of a unified good".[52]

The crucial question for the discussion in this chapter is if conventionality control, as an "other measure" under Article 2, is justifiable on the basis of the principle of subsidiarity.

If the premises presented above are valid, the question at this point is no longer if the specification of a new "measure" to increase the effectiveness of the Inter-American *Corpus Juris* constitutes *a priori* a violation of the rights of States as sovereigns, but if there are enough reasons that justify the existence of conventionality control as an obligation for State authorities when they face the existence of domestic laws or practices that are manifestly anti-conventional. In other words, the question is no longer whether a textual interpretation of Article 2 allows the derivation of specific obligations directly from its language (something that it is clear it does not, as the positivist critiques proved right); but (1) if the *subsidium* that the Court provided in *Almonacid*, and in subsequent cases, is legitimate under an interpretation of the Convention and the powers of the Court in the light of the principle of subsidiarity; and (2) what are the limits of the doctrine of conventionality control, seen as a general doctrine that aims to increase the effectiveness of the Inter-American *Corpus Juris* at the domestic level, mainly through the action of the judiciary?

This means that the legitimacy of conventionality control is to be found in other norms of the American Convention that, in connection with Article 2, justify the *determinatio* made by the Court since *Almonacid*. On this basis, the following section argues that Articles 1.1 and 25 of the Convention provide the substantive grounds that legitimize the existence of conventionality control as a "praetorian" creation of the Inter-American Court. In a nutshell, the section argues that conventionality control is justified by constituting a juridical instrument (an "other measure") for State authorities to comply with their obligation to ensure core aspects of human rights that have a relevant place in

52 Paolo G. Carozza, *Subsidiarity as a Structure Principle of International Law*, *supra* n. 22, p. 67.

the American Convention and in the Court's jurisprudence since *Velásquez*; the obligation to respect and ensure the rights and freedoms recognized in the American Convention; the duty to prevent, investigate and punish the perpetrators of serious human rights violations; and the obligation to provide access to justice, truth and reparation (qualified as non-derogable rights) for the victims of these violations and for their relatives.

3. THE SUBSTANCE BEHIND CONVENTIONALITY CONTROL

3.1. THE DUTY TO RESPECT AND ENSURE THE CORE OF HUMAN RIGHTS

The doctrine of conventionality control was created on the assumption that the American Convention has direct effect on State authorities by virtue of Article 1.1. This article establishes that: "the States parties to this Convention undertake to respect and ensure to all persons subject to their jurisdiction the free and full exercise of those rights and freedoms, without any discrimination …"[53] This assumption can be observed in paragraph 124 of *Almonacid*, where the Inter-American Court reasoned that even when "judges and courts are bond to respect the rule of law", once a State becomes party to a treaty like the American Convention "its judges, as part of the State, are also bound by such Convention".[54]

The Court did not explain why the American Convention has direct effect on domestic judges, but it appears that the reasoning in *Almonacid* is declarative and not constitutive. Conventionality control did not establish the direct effect of the American Convention, but it is a consequence of this condition. This means that judges shall not enforce domestic laws that violate the Convention under the doctrine of conventionality control *because* they have an obligation of international law to "respect" and "ensure" the rights and freedoms protected by the Treaty, specifically the right to access to justice, truth and reparation.

---

53 *See generally*, Eduardo Ferrer Mac-Gregor Poisot and Carlos Pelayo Möller, *Obligación de respetar los derechos*, in Christian Steiner and Patricia Uribe (Eds.), *Convención Americana sobre Derechos Humanos comentada*, p. 46 (Suprema Corte de Justicia & Konrad Adenauer Stiftung, 2014) (on the notion that the American Convention has a direct effect since: "this instrument does not constitute a 'programmatic norm' as some consider. The American Convention has *direct effect* ('*aplicación directa*') on all its dispositions when an American State has signed and ratified it.").

54 *See, Almonacid Arellano et al v. Chile, supra* n. 16, §124; *see generally*, Paolo G. Carozza, *The Problematic Applicability of Subsidiarity to International Law and Institutions*, 61(1) The American Journal of Jurisprudence 65 (2016) (the author explains that conventionality control requires "domestic authors of the state to give direct effect in their internal legal order to both the American Convention on Human Rights and to the case-law of the Inter-American Court").

The criterion in *Almonacid* pushes the logic of the Inter-American Court's jurisprudence regarding the normative content of Article 1.1 to its ultimate consequences. Since *Velázquez*, the Court has linked the duty to respect and ensure with the understanding that the protection of human rights required restrictions on the exercise of State power, since there are "certain inviolable attributes of the individual that cannot be legitimately restricted through the exercise of governmental power".[55] This meant that States had to ensure their actions were adequate in relation to the Convention in order to comply with their international human rights obligations.

The duty to respect requires a negative conduct, which is abstaining from violating any right protected by the Convention. The duty to ensure rights requires a positive conduct, since the State has an obligation to organize the governmental apparatus and all the structures through which State power is manifested, in such a manner that it is capable of juridically ensuring the exercise of human rights and to fulfill its duty to prevent, investigate and sanction all those responsible for human rights violations.[56] Héctor Gros Espiell, one of the first judges seated at the Court, reasoned in this sense that this obligation "presupposes the duty to prevent or do everything reasonably possible to prevent human rights violations of persons subject to the jurisdiction of the State by any person, public or private, individual or collective, natural or legal".[57]

Since *Velásquez*, the Inter-American Court has also consistently sustained that the duty to ensure requires not just the adoption of formal measures (i.e. the adoption of laws and policies), so the existence of rules of law and mechanisms for protection at the domestic level are not in themselves sufficient to make the fulfillment of the obligations imposed by Article 1.1 possible.[58] The obligation to ensure requires also a governmental "conduct" which allows the real – and effective – exercise of human rights.[59] The duty to ensure includes also the duty to "remove" the obstacles that impede the realization of human rights.[60]

---

55 *Velásquez Rodríguez v. Honduras*. Merits. Inter-Am. Ct. H.R. (Ser. C) No. 4 (Jul. 29, 1988) §156; *The Word "Laws" in Article 30 of the American Convention on Human Rights*. Advisory Opinion OC-6, Inter-Am. Ct. H.R. (Ser. A) No. 6 (May 9, 1986), §21.

56 *Velásquez Rodríguez v. Honduras*. Merits, *supra* n. 55, §166.

57 Héctor Gros Espiell, *La Convención Americana y la Convención Europea de Derechos Humanos. Análisis comparativo*, p. 65–66 (Editorial Jurídica de Chile, 1991).

58 *See, Gómez Paquiyauri Brothers v. Peru*. Judgment, Inter-Am. Ct. H.R. (Ser. C) No. 110 (Jul. 8, 2004) §72; *see also Five Pensioners v. Peru Case*. Judgment, Inter-Am. Ct. H.R. (Ser. C) No. 98 (Feb. 28, 2003) §163.

59 *See, Velásquez Rodríguez v. Honduras*. Merits, *supra* n. 55, §167; *see*, Cecilia Medina Quiroga, *La Convención Americana: Teoría y Jurisprudencia. Vida, Integridad Personal, Libertad Personal, Debido Proceso y Recurso Judicial*, p. 16 (Universidad de Chile & Facultad de Derecho & Centro de Derechos Humanos, 2003).

60 *See, Exceptions to the Exhaustion of Domestic Remedies (Arts. 46(1), 46(2)(a) and 46(2)(b), American Convention on Human Rights)*. Advisory Opinion OC-11, Inter-Am. Ct. H.R. (Ser. A) No. 11 (Aug. 10, 1990) §34.

Therefore, it is plausible to say that the general obligations of Article 1.1 are supposed to take effect not to the State conceived as an abstraction. They aim to affect the conduct of those who exercise public power, who must adapt their behavior in accordance with international law.[61]

The reading of Article 1.1 as a norm that requires State authorities in their respective sphere of power to "undertake to respect the rights and freedoms recognized herein and to ensure to all persons subject to their jurisdiction the free and full exercise of those rights and freedoms" is indeed the most logical way of reading a body of law that has as its object and purpose the protection of human rights against illegal intrusions of State power. Taking IHRL seriously requires that once that a human rights treaty comes into force, there must be recognized the existence of a correlative duty of each State authority to respect and ensure that treaty and the existence of domestic remedies to address violations of that treaty.[62] There must be a balance – on the one hand – between respecting the text of the Convention and its nature as a treaty governed by international law, and – on the other hand – the necessity to guarantee its effectiveness at the domestic level.

True, the abstract language with which human rights are formulated in treaty law – and the subsidiary nature of the Inter-American System – must certainly leave a wide scope of freedom for States to determine the specific characteristics of the laws and policies that would make human rights operative at the domestic level, and to determine who would be in charge of executing those obligations and in what manner. But it is reasonable to assume that once human rights treaties are binding for the State, its authorities have a legal obligation to respect and ensure the core of the human rights contained in those treaties.[63] At least this is the most coherent reading of provisions such as Article 1.1 of the American Convention. The core – the minimum – of human rights protection is defined by the agreement of States as established in the text of a treaty, and domestic law determines the specific features of that obligation and the manner by which these obligations must be fulfilled.[64]

---

61 *See*, Eduardo Jiménez de Aréchaga, *La Convención Americana de Derechos Humanos como derecho interno*, 69–71 Boletín da Sociedade Brasileira de Direito Internacional, 7 (1987–1989); *see also* A.A. Cançado Trindade, *El Derecho Internacional de los Derechos Humanos en el Siglo XXI*, pp. 283–285 (Editorial Jurídica de Chile, 2001).

62 *See generally*, UN Human Rights Committee (HRC), General Comment No. 31 [80], The nature of the general legal obligation imposed on States Parties to the Covenant, 26 May 2004, CCPR/C/21/Rev.1/Add.13, §6 (see the change in the criterion of the committee as mentioned in previous paragraphs).

63 *See generally*, Martin Scheinin, *Core Rights and Obligations*, in Dinah Shelton (Ed.), *The Oxford Handbook of International Human Rights Law*, *supra* n. 3, pp. 527–561.

64 *See generally*, Dinah Shelton and Ariel Gould, *Positive and Negative Obligations*, in Dinah Shelton (Ed.), *The Oxford Handbook of International Human Rights Law*, *supra* n. 3, pp. 527–561.

This idea of the existence of a "core" of human rights has been addressed in the discussion about limitations in human rights treaties. The Human Rights Committee has established that all or many human rights contain an essential core,[65] a concept that may be useful to reconcile the notion that there are aspects of human rights that should be protected equally by each authority because they are essential, and at the same time that States have the freedom to decide the peripheral aspects of a right and the manner to enforce it domestically in accordance with their laws and practices.[66] In this logic, the more it is possible to identify an irreducible core of some aspect of the rights protected by the Inter-American *Corpus Juris*, the stronger the notion that some laws are manifestly incompatible with Article 2, and that State authorities must execute specific types of conduct – such as conventionality control – to comply with Article 1.1. The process – and the methodology – for determining the core of human rights is certainly a project for years to come.

3.2. THE DUTY TO FIGHT AGAINST IMPUNITY

It is in this sense that the existence of the doctrine of conventionality control is connected with the obligation to ensure. Originally, conventionality control was conceived as a mechanism to set aside an anti-conventional piece of legislation, and in this manner avoid the international responsibility of the State for the failure to *prevent, investigate and punish* human rights violations and the violation of non-derogable rights.[67] Since *Velásquez*, the Court has sustained that the State has a legal duty:

> 174–175. ... to take reasonable steps to prevent human rights violations ... The duty to prevent includes all those means of a legal, political, administrative and cultural nature that promote the protection of human rights and ensure that any violations are

---

65 *See generally*, UN Human Rights Committee (HRC), CCPR General Comment No. 27: Article 12 (Freedom of Movement), 2 November 1999, CCPR/C/21/Rev.1/Add.9, §2; UN Human Rights Committee (HRC), General Comment No. 31 [80], The nature of the general legal obligation imposed on States Parties to the Covenant, 26 May 2004, CCPR/C/21/Rev.1/Add.13, §6; UN Human Rights Committee (HRC), General Comment No. 32: Article 14 (Right to equality before courts and tribunals and to fair trial), 23 August 2007, CCPR/C/GC/32, §18; Martin Scheinin, Core Rights and Obligations, in DINAH SHELTON (ED.), *THE OXFORD HANDBOOK OF INTERNATIONAL HUMAN RIGHTS LAW*, *supra* n. 3, p. 533.

66 *See generally*, UN Committee on Economic, Social and Cultural Rights (CESCR), General Comment No. 3: The Nature of States Parties' Obligations (Art. 2, Para. 1, of the Covenant), 14 December 1990, E/1991/23, §10.

67 For an understanding of the context and obligations that emerged from *Almonacid*, *see*, Douglass Cassel, *El fallo Almonacid de la CIDH, y las obligaciones que de allí emanan para el Estado de Chile*, in PAULINA VELOSO (ED.) *JUSTICIA, DERECHOS HUMANOS Y EL DECRETO LEY DE AMNISTÍA*, pp. 81–88 (PNDU, 2010).

> considered and treated as illegal acts, which as such, may lead to punishment of those responsible and the obligation to indemnify the victims for damages.[68]

As Douglass Cassel explains, the jurisprudence of the Court in its first two decades of existence was focused on putting an end to impunity in cases of serious human rights violations.[69]

This criterion has been particularly important in judgments against some States parties to the Convention, owing to the structural problems in the administration of justice and the necessity of involving State authorities – especially judges – in the protection of specific vulnerable groups[70] and in the fight against impunity for perpetrators of serious and systematic human rights violations.[71] Conventionality control is deeply connected with the fulfillment of these duties, by being a juridical instrument originally designed to "purge" elements of domestic law that impede the fight against impunity in cases where governments used amnesty laws to shield members of the military or police forces against criminal prosecutions. In this manner, conventionality control would allow judges to "initiate, ex officio and immediately, a genuine, impartial and effective investigation" that "must be carried out by all available legal means with the aim of determining the truth and the investigation, pursuit, capture, prosecution and punishment of the masterminds and perpetrators of the facts, particularly when State agents are or may be involved".[72]

The existence of practices and laws that were created specifically to avoid criminal investigations is a key element to understanding the approach taken by the Court in *Barrios Altos*, *Almonacid* and subsequent cases, both regarding the declaration of the nullity *ab initio* of amnesty laws, and regarding the creation of

---

68 *Velásquez Rodríguez v. Honduras. Merits, supra* n. 55, §174–175.

69 *See*, Douglass Cassel, *La Corte Interamericana de Derechos Humanos*, in VICTIMAS SIN MORDAZA. EL IMPACTO DEL SISTEMA INTERAMERICANO EN LA JUSTICIA TRANSICIONAL EN LATINOAMERICA: LOS CASOS DE ARGENTINA, GUATEMALA, EL SALVADOR Y PERÚ, p. 197 (Due Process of Law Foundation and Comisión de Derechos Humanos del Distrito Federal, 2007); *see also* Juan Mendez, *Lo que enseña la experiencia*, in VICTIMAS SIN MORDAZA. EL IMPACTO DEL SISTEMA INTERAMERICANO EN LA JUSTICIA TRANSICIONAL EN LATINOAMERICA: LOS CASOS DE ARGENTINA, GUATEMALA, EL SALVADOR Y PERÚ, p. 251 (Due Process of Law Foundation and Comisión de Derechos Humanos del Distrito Federal, 2007).

70 *See generally, González et al. ("Cotton Field") v. Mexico*. Preliminary Objection, Merits, Reparations and Costs Judgment, Inter-Am. Ct. H.R. (Ser. C) No. 205 (Nov. 16, 2009), §252; *Juridical Condition and Human Rights of the Child*. Advisory Opinion OC-17, Inter-Am. Ct. H.R. (Ser. A) No. 17 (Aug. 28, 2002), §53, 54, 60; Eduardo Ferrer Mac-Gregor Poisot and Carlos Pelayo Möller, *Obligación de respetar los derechos*, in CHRISTIAN STEINER AND PATRICIA URIBE (EDS.), *CONVENCIÓN AMERICANA SOBRE DERECHOS HUMANOS COMENTADA*, *supra* n. 53, pp. 50–51.

71 *See*, Cecilia Medina Quiroga, *Los 40 años de la Convención Americana sobre Derechos Humanos a la Luz de cierta jurisprudencia de la Corte Interamericana*, Anuario de Derechos Humanos, (2009), p. 26.

72 *Pueblo Bello Massacre v. Colombia*. Judgment, Inter-Am. Ct. H.R. (Ser. C) No. 140 (Jan. 31, 2006) §143.

the doctrine of conventionality control.[73] In these and similar cases the nullity of amnesty laws was decided because of the manifest incompatibility between these laws and the obligation to prevent, investigate and punish those responsible for serious human rights violations (in the first case a massacre in Peru, and in the second what was qualified as a crime against humanity in Chile), and in order to contribute to the construction of effective judicial guarantees at the domestic level, thus protecting the right of access to justice, truth and reparation for the victims and their relatives.[74]

The strong position that the Court has taken regarding the necessity to fight against impunity has never meant that State authorities must not follow domestic law in order to comply with the obligations of Article 1.1. It means – both in the context of *Velásquez* and in the context of the cases that defined conventionality control – that only in the case that a domestic law is contrary to the Convention, must State authorities use all their authority conferred by domestic law to avoid that the anti-conventional law in question produces its effects, and thus comply with Article 1.1. Consequently, conventionality control, in the logic of the analysis of this section, is constructed precisely on the basis that judges must use "all legal means available to combat [impunity]". In *Ticona Estrada v. Bolivia* (2008) the Court considered that

> 147. ... the State may not invoke any domestic law or provision to exonerate itself from the obligation to investigate and, if applicable, punish those responsible ... considering that this case deals with serious human rights violations, the State may not invoke the statute of limitations or any other principle that excuses it from taking responsibility, to decline its duty to investigate and punish those responsible.[75]

---

73 *See generally*, Santiago A. Canton, *Leyes de Amnistía*, in Victimas sin Mordaza. El impacto del sistema interamericano en la justicia transicional en Latinoamerica: los casos de Argentina, Guatemala, El Salvador y Perú, *supra* n. 69, p. 227 (the author explains that the criterion of the Inter-American System regarding amnesty laws has, as its main objective, the recovery of human dignity of the victims, and the rescue of an essential element to strengthen the rule of law: the fight against impunity); *see generally*, Pablo Saavedra Alessandri, *La respuesta de la jurisprudencia de la Corte Interamericana a las diversas formas de impunidad en casos de graves violaciones de derechos humanos y sus consecuencias*, in La Corte Interamericana de Derechos Humanos. Un Cuarto de Siglo: *1979–2004*, p. 388 (OEA-IctHR, 2005).

74 *See*, Douglass Cassel, *El fallo Almonacid de la CIDH, y las obligaciones que de allí emanan para el Estado de Chile*, in Paulina Veloso (Ed.), *Justicia, Derechos Humanos y el Decreto Ley de Amnistía*, *supra* n. 67, pp. 81–88; *see also* Laurence Burgorgue-Larsen and Amaya Úbeda de Torres, The Inter-American Court on Human Rights. Case Law and Commentary, *supra* n. 43, p. 356.

75 *Ticona Estrada v. Bolivia*. Merits, Reparations and Costs, Inter-Am. Ct. H.R. (Ser. C) No. 191 (Nov. 27, 2008) §147 (the Court cited as reference the cases of *Barrios Altos v. Peru*, *supra* n. 16, §41; *Almonacid Arellano et al v. Chile*, *supra* n. 16, §151; and *La Cantuta v. Peru*. Merits, Reparations and Costs, Judgment, Inter-Am. Ct. H.R. (Ser. C) No 162 (Nov. 29, 2006) §226).

3.3. THE DUTY TO ENSURE THE RIGHT OF ACCESS TO JUSTICE

Conventionality control is also intimately linked to the obligations derived from the right to judicial protection, which is a right recognized in Article 25 of the Convention.[76] This article establishes that:

> [e]veryone has the right to a simple and prompt recourse, or any other effective recourse, to a competent court or tribunal for protection against acts that violate his fundamental rights recognized by the constitution or laws of the State concerned or by this Convention, even though such a violation may have been committed by persons acting in the course of their official duties.[77]

The origin of this provision comes from the Mexican legislation of *amparo*, which was understood by the Court as an example of: "a simple and prompt remedy designed for the protection of all of the rights recognized by the constitutions and laws of the States Parties and by the Convention."[78]

There is a close connection between the general obligation of the State to ensure – as formulated in the American Convention, and developed since *Velásquez* – and the existence of a right to judicial protection.[79] In this regard, the Inter-American Commission has sustained that the duty to prevent human rights violations – which is also derived from the duty to ensure – requires the existence of adequate and effective judicial remedies that allow the enjoyment of rights.[80] In a similar fashion, the Court has sustained, for instance in *Ivcher Bronstein v. Peru* (1999), that the non-existence of effective judicial remedies constitute in itself a violation of the Convention, since judicial remedies: "must be truly appropriate to establish whether there has been a violation of human rights and to provide everything necessary to remedy it."[81]

---

76 The right of access to access to justice includes both the protection of Art. 8.1 and of Art. 25. In this section we have referred to Art. 25 because it is the access to a remedy that conventionality control aims to protect. For an analysis of the right of access to justice, *see*, Douglass Cassel, *La Corte Interamericana de Derechos Humanos*, in *Victimas sin Mordaza. El impacto del sistema interamericano en la justicia transicional en Latinoamerica: los casos de Argentina, Guatemala, El Salvador y Perú*, *supra* n. 69, p. 212.

77 American Convention on Human Rights, *supra* n. 10, Art. 25.

78 *Habeas Corpus in Emergency Situations (Arts. 27(2), 25(1) and 7(6) American Convention on Human Rights).* Advisory Opinion OC-8, Inter-Am. Ct. H.R. (Ser. A) No. 8 (Jan. 30, 1987) §32.

79 American Convention on Human Rights, *supra* n. 10, Art. 25.1; *see*, Cecilia Medina Quiroga, *La Convención Americana: Teoría y Jurisprudencia. Vida, Integridad Personal, Libertad Personal, Debido Proceso y Recurso Judicial*, *supra* n. 59, p. 19; *see also* Laurence Burgorgue-Larsen and Amaya Úbeda de Torres, *The Inter-American Court on Human Rights. Case Law and Commentary*, *supra* n. 43, p. 688.

80 IACHR, Report on Citizen Security, OEA/Ser.L/V/II. Doc. 57, Dec. 31, 2009, §35.

81 *See, Ivcher Bronstein v. Peru.* Judgment, Inter-Am. Ct. H.R. (Ser. C) No. 74, (Feb. 6, 2001), §136; *see also Cantoral Benavides v. Peru.* Judgment, Inter-Am. Ct. H.R. (Ser. C) No. 69 (Aug. 18, 2000) §164.

In the logic inaugurated in *Velásquez*, the obligation to establish adequate and effective remedies requires not just their formal existence in State laws, but also that State authorities perform actions in order to ensure the effectiveness of those remedies.[82] This is a fundamental aspect of subsidiarity from a procedural perspective, since judges are in a much better position than the Inter-American Court to protect individuals against acts that violate their human rights and to provide a remedy and adequate reparation for the damage caused.[83] In this sense, the access to an effective remedy has been appropriately considered "one of the fundamental pillars not only of the American Convention but of the very rule of law in a democratic society",[84] and requires not just the design and implementation of an effective remedy in domestic law, but that they also

> 235. … must be truly effective in establishing whether there has been a violation of human rights and in providing redress. [Because] a remedy that proves illusory because of the general conditions prevailing in the country, or even in the particular circumstances of a given case, cannot be considered effective.[85]

It is possible to observe that the origins and the subsequent use that the Court has made of conventionality control has been deeply connected with the necessity that domestic judges comply with their duty to ensure the right to a judicial remedy. Thus, conventionality control exists to allow that this right is not violated owing to the enforcement of anti-conventional laws that restrict or eliminate the capacity of judges to adequately perform their functions. This was perhaps the original idea of García Ramírez in *Almonacid*, since he apparently understood the judiciary as the adequate authority to "control" that these types of laws did not produce their effects.[86] This is the case not just for cases that involved the enforcement of amnesty laws, but also for cases that involved the enforcement of laws that restricted the access to judicial remedies in an arbitrary and disproportionate manner, and with cases that allowed military

---

82 *See*, *Velásquez Rodríguez v. Honduras*, *supra* n. 55, §166; *see*, Juana María Ibañez Rivas, *Artículo 25. Protección Judicial*, in Christian Steiner and Patricia Uribe (Eds.), *Convención Americana sobre Derechos Humanos comentada* (Suprema Corte de Justicia & Konrad Adenauer Stiftung, 2014), pp. 615–617 (for an analysis of the elements that integrate the right to an effective remedy).

83 *See*, Sergio García Ramírez, *The Relationship Between Inter-American Jurisdiction and States (National Systems): Some Pertinent Questions*, 1(1) Notre Dame Journal of International and Comparative Law 141 (2015).

84 *Castillo Petruzzi et al. v. Peru*. Judgment, Inter-Am. Ct. H.R. (Ser. C) No. 52 (May 30, 1999), §82.

85 *The "Street Children" Case (Villagrán Morales et al.)*. Judgment, Inter-Am. Ct. H.R. (Ser. C) No. 63 (Nov. 19, 1999), §235.

86 *See*, Sergio García Ramírez, *The Relationship Between Inter-American Jurisdiction and States (National Systems): Some Pertinent Questions*, *supra* n. 83, p. 23.

tribunals to exercise jurisdiction in cases that involved human rights violations committed by soldiers against civilians. Two cases are good to exemplify the above-mentioned approach.

In *Aguado Alfaro*, the Court determined that the prohibition against challenging the effects of Decree Law No. 25640 constituted a self-executing norm because those affected by its existence were impeded, *ab initio*, from challenging its effects before a court of law, a condition that constituted a limitation contrary to the letter and spirit of Articles 8 and 25 with regard to Articles 1.1 and 2 of the Convention.[87] The Court also considered that the context created by the existence of the Decree contributed to creating conditions for legal uncertainty that impeded those affected by the Decree from knowing which was the correct vehicle to challenge its enforcement.[88] However, the Court also found that that, in accordance with the Peruvian legislation, the Constitutional Court had the power not to enforce the particular provision that served as the basis to reject the recourses promoted by the victims at the domestic level. Consequently, the Court decided that the judges of the Constitutional Court should have used their powers under domestic law in order to avoid the enforcement of that law, and analyze the merits of the petition as a manner to guarantee the effectiveness of Articles 8 and 25 of the Convention.[89]

In *Radilla*, the Court found violations of Articles 8 and 25 in relation to Articles 1.1 and 2 of the Convention derived from the enforcement of Article 57 of the Code of Military Justice (CMJ) and Article 13 of the Political Constitution of Mexico. These articles served as a basis to deny that criminal judges addressed cases connected with crimes committed by members of the military forces, not connected with military discipline, and where civilians were the victims.[90] The jurisprudence of the Inter-American Court had already restricted the exercise of criminal military jurisdiction since *Castillo Petruzzi*, so the Court determined that Article 57 of the Code of Military Justice was partially incompatible with the American Convention and that it had to be modified to comply with the provisions of Article 2. It also found that through the exercise of conventionality control domestic judges should interpret Article 13 of the Constitution in order to confer on ordinary judges the jurisdiction of cases involving crimes committed by members of the military forces and where the victims were civilians, in order to ensure the protection of the right to due process and access to justice.[91]

---

87 *See, Dismissed Congressional Employees (Aguado-Alfaro et al.).* Preliminary Objections, Merits, Reparations and Costs Judgment, Inter-Am. Ct. H.R. (Ser. C) No. 158 (Nov. 24, 2006) §119.

88 *Id.* §108.

89 *Id.* §127.

90 *See, Radilla Pacheco v. Mexico.* Preliminary Objections, Merits, Reparations and Costs Judgment, Inter-Am. Ct. H.R. (Ser. C) No. 209 (Nov. 29, 2009) §280 to 282.

91 *Id.* §339 and 340.

Some judges of the Court have adopted similar approaches, connecting the obligation to exercise conventionality control as part of the obligation to guarantee access to an effective remedy for victims of human rights violations. A.A. Cançado Trindade commented that the obligation of judges to exercise conventionality control was intimately connected with the direct obligation that judges had to guarantee the right to access to justice.[92] For him, although not for the Court, except in *Goiburú*,[93] this right was also considered as a norm of *jus cogens* that required the establishment of a system of prompt local remedies and the effective application of these remedies, which imply the removal of obstacles that hinder the effectiveness of Articles 8.1 and 25 in connection with Articles 1.1 and 2 of the Convention.[94] Consequently, the right of access to justice required being protected by domestic judges through a harmonization of domestic law and international law, since the international and national legal systems are: "in constant interaction in the domain of the protection of the individual."[95]

Recently, Eduardo Ferrer Mac-Gregor Poisot has argued that Article 25 would lead to affirm that States must ensure the existence of judicial remedies that allow the protection of rights recognized by the Convention and the Constitution taken altogether.[96] This position implies the recognition of a "right to the guarantee of rights" (*derecho sustantivo a la garantía de los derechos*) on the basis of Article 25.1 in relation to Articles 1.1, 2, and 2(b),[97] that also implies the existence of a model for the exercise of conventionality control that allows the protection of human rights at the domestic level in accordance with the highest normative standard (whether domestic or international).[98] The obligation to ensure the effectiveness of a judicial remedy requires the existence of a model

---

92 *See, Dismissed Congressional Employees (Aguado-Alfaro et al.) v. Peru, supra* n. 87, Reasoned Concurrent Opinion of A.A. Cançado Trindade, §2 and 3.

93 *Goiburú et al. v. Paraguay Case.* Merits, Reparations and Costs Judgment, Inter-Am. Ct. H.R. (Ser. C) No. 153 (Sep. 22, 2006) §131:

Access to justice is a peremptory norm of international law and, as such, gives rise to obligations *erga omnes* for the States to adopt all necessary measures to ensure that such violations do not remain unpunished, either by exercising their jurisdiction to apply their domestic law and international law to prosecute and, when applicable, punish those responsible, or by collaborating with other States that do so or attempt to do so.

94 *Genie Lacayo v. Nicaragua Case, Interpretation of the Judgment*, Inter-Am. Ct. H.R. (Ser. C) No. 45 (Jan. 29, 1997). Dissenting Opinion of Judge A.A. Cançado Trindade, §21; *see* A.A. Cançado Trindade, *The Access of Individuals to International Justice* (Oxford University Press, 2011), p. 210.

95 *Dismissed Congressional Employees (Aguado-Alfaro et al.) v. Peru, supra* n. 87, Reasoned Concurrent Opinion of A.A. Cançado Trindade, §2 and 3.

96 *See, Liakat Ali Alibux v. Suriname.* Preliminary Objections, Merits, Reparations and Costs Judgment, Inter-Am. Ct. H.R. (Ser. C) No. 276 (Jan. 30, 2014). Concurrent Opinion of Eduardo Ferrer Mac-Gregor Poisot, §71–82.

97 *Id.* §71.

98 *Id.* §90.

of conventionality control that constitutes a "necessary measure" to guarantee the effectiveness of Article 25.[99] Consequently, in the view of the Mexican jurist,

> 133. ... the dimension of the *right to the guarantee of rights* is an integrating element of national and conventional fundamental rights, allowing a more extensive protection for persons at the domestic level, so they can claim their rights in a model of conventionality control.[100]

If conventionality control finds any basis in Article 25 it is by considering the strategic and normative importance that the effective realization of the right to judicial protection has for the effectiveness of the Convention at the domestic level, and for the subsequent construction of a rule of law in democratic societies. The importance that the existence of effective judicial remedies (like the Mexican *amparo*) has for the achievement of the object and purpose of the Convention, is what supports the obligation for domestic judges to ensure that – in as much as they have the power to do so – no domestic law hinders the effective access to justice for the victims of human rights violations or for their relatives. The notion that there is a right of access to justice that constitutes a norm of *jus cogens*, a position that implies the obligation to remove the laws that affect the effectiveness of this right, or the view that there is a *right to the guarantee of rights*, a position that implies that judicial remedies must be ensured through conventionality control, appears to follow a similar logic.

4. CONVENTIONALITY CONTROL IN LIGHT OF THE PRINCIPLE OF SUBSIDIARITY

4.1. THE CORE OF CONVENTIONALITY CONTROL

This chapter has sustained that the principle of subsidiarity justifies two practices of the Inter-American Court that are crucial to explain the existence and legal validity of the doctrine of conventionality control: (1) evaluating the compatibility between a specific State's laws and practices and the Inter-American *Corpus Juris* in the exercise of its contentious jurisdiction, and (2) ordering States to modify these laws and to adopt specific practices – like conventionality control – so State authorities can remedy the causes of human rights violations, and prevent future violations. Thus, it is on the basis of subsidiarity that conventionality control could be legitimately understood as an "other measure" to increase the effectiveness of the Inter-American *Corpus Juris* in case the State

---

99 *Id.* §91–94.

100 *Id.* §133.

failed to comply in good faith with its duties under Article 2, especially when the Court found the existence of laws that were manifestly anti-conventional. If this position is valid, then the critiques based on the notion that there is a radical separation between international law and domestic law must be rejected.

In this line of reasoning, it was also argued that the legitimacy of conventionality control requires the existence of reasons *external* to the content of Article 2 that justify the *determinatio* made by the Court since *Almonacid*, because Article 2 does not have a specific content and cannot be considered as a blank check for the Court to order "legislative and other measures" as it considers appropriate for the protection of human rights. In the case of conventionality control the reasons external to Article 2, but internal to the American Convention, that justify its creation can be found in a well-settled jurisprudence regarding Articles 1.1 and 25. The case law on these topics is intimately connected with core values of the Inter-American System (democracy, rule of law, and judicial remedy), and in the necessity to fight against impunity for perpetrators of serious human rights violations, particularly in cases that involved the existence and enforcement of amnesty laws that affected non-derogable rights: the right of access to justice, truth and reparation for the victims and their relatives.

This proposition may be supported by García Ramírez, who explained in his concurrent opinion in *La Cantuta v. Peru* that the criterion of the Court regarding amnesty laws includes the following notions that: (1) the obligation of Article 1.1 must prevail against obstacles of domestic law; (2) the consequent exile of impunity that could derive from those obstacles; (3) the duty of States to introduce the necessary measures to comply with Article 1.1 and to exile impunity; and (4) the freedom of States to decide how to suppress the norms that are the cause of impunity.[101] In my view, the original legal basis, as well as the reasons for the creation of conventionality control, cannot be conceptually separated from the evaluation made by the Court that judges have an international obligation to "introduce the necessary measures to comply with Article 1.1 and to exile impunity" in order to guarantee the rights of the victims and their relatives.

Yet, it is obvious that conventionality control had more far-reaching purposes than the fight against impunity and the protection of non-derogable rights in the context of transitional justice. The use of conventionality control in cases decided after *Almonacid* showed that this doctrine has had a much more ambitious purpose since its inception: functioning as a legal instrument that allowed judges, and in general all domestic authorities, especially after the decisions of *Cabrera* and *Gelman*, to guarantee the right of access to a judicial

101 *See, La Cantuta v. Peru, supra* n. 75, Reasoned Concurrent Opinion of Sergio García Ramírez, §4.

remedy against *any* law that violated *any* aspect of the Inter-American *Corpus Juris*, and as a way to guarantee that the jurisprudence of the Court would serve as a parameter for that evaluation. This is clear from the fact that conventionality control was used in *Aguado-Alfaro*, decided just two months after *Almonacid*, to remind judges of their duty to control the conventionality of a law that restricted the right to a judicial remedy in a manner manifestly incompatible with Article 25, but that was not related to a case involving the enforcement of an invalid amnesty law that violated non-derogable rights.

After *Almonacid*, conventionality control became a much more ambitious mechanism to increase the effectiveness of the Convention and the Court's jurisprudence through judicial action in cases not necessarily connected with transitional justice. However, although this might sound like an attractive approach, there is a normative problem with the view adopted by the Court since *Aguado-Alfaro*. Because if it is true that the validity of conventionality control is connected with the necessity to fight against impunity, then conventionality control lost part of its justification as a *subsidium*, as a "necessary measure" to ensure the effectiveness of the Convention, when it was no longer connected with the particular challenges presented by the extremity faced in cases like *Almonacid* and *La Cantuta*. These cases were preceded by a rich jurisprudence that served as the basis to declare the nullity of amnesty laws, and that justified the call for active action on the part of domestic judges to avoid future human rights violations in similar cases through the exercise of conventionality control.

This detachment does not necessarily mean that conventionality control is contrary to a reading of Article 2 on the basis of subsidiarity, but it certainly loses some of the legitimacy. So, one may legitimately ask: how can this doctrine still be compatible with the principle of subsidiarity, and in general with the American Convention and general international law, if it is detached from the concrete circumstances where it was created and which legitimized its existence in the first place? To answer this question, in this chapter's view, the first thing to say is that the validity of conventionality control on the basis of subsidiarity depends on our capacity to "regulate" the "intensity" of the obligations derived from this doctrine, and to determine appropriately the normative consequences that derive from a "flexible" version of conventionality control. Because one may argue that the obligation to exercise conventionality control is stronger when it is connected with a very concrete question, when it is referred to the judiciary, when the content of a domestic law or its interpretation by domestic judges is manifestly anti-conventional (and it has been qualified as such by the Court), when there are core aspects of human rights in peril due to the interpretation or enforcement of that law, when the acts committed by the State and which remained unpunished constituted serious human rights violations, and when there is a well-settled jurisprudence regarding a particular question involved in the case.

4.2. CONVENTIONALITY CONTROL AS A PRINCIPLE

The closer conventionality control remains to elements such as the above-mentioned, the stronger its nature as an "other measure" in terms of Article 2. Does this mean that conventionality control has no legal validity as a general doctrine, and that it shall only be understood as valid in connection with the particularities of cases of transitional justice similar to *Almonacid* and *La Cantuta*? Not necessarily. Certainly, the reasons that would make this doctrine legitimate under subsidiarity are weaker when it is understood as binding for the State authorities of all the States parties to the Convention, than in those cases where the Inter-American Court has declared the duty of domestic judges to interpret domestic law in a particular manner or to cease in the enforcement of a particular piece of legislation. In the first case (when conventionality control is seen as a doctrine with general applicability) the Court is "adding" new normative elements to the Convention, while in the second case (when it is connected with the existence of an anti-conventional interpretation or an anti-conventional law in a concrete case) it is establishing a practical tool to prevent future human rights violations in a concrete and defined set of circumstances.[102]

True, it is theoretically possible not to draw such a distinction. Someone may argue that – after *Almonacid* – the general obligations of the States in terms of Article 1.1 and 2 were transformed, to the extent that all the authorities of the States parties to the Convention shall enforce the Inter-American *Corpus Juris* against any domestic law to the contrary (including norms of constitutional hierarchy and the decision of their higher courts). The problem with this position is that it is so detached from the text of the American Convention and from general international law, that it would constitute a true act of judicial legislation that amends a fundamental aspect of the subsidiary structure of the Inter-American System – and actually it would go directly against subsidiarity by affirming the supremacy of international law and international institutions over domestic law and domestic institutions.[103] It also presents obvious practical

102 *See, Case of Fontevecchia and D'Amico v. Argentina. Monitoring Compliance with Judgment.* Order of the Inter-American Court of Human Rights of Oct. 18, 2017, §32 (the Court has linked the determination of certain types of reparations in concrete cases with the principle of complementarity or subsidiarity. In the Court's view, this principle has been applied by the Court to determine which reparations are necessary in specific cases in accordance with "objective and reasonable criteria" in a manner that complements – not substitutes – domestic jurisdictions); *see generally*, Samantha Besson, *Subsidiarity in International Human Rights Law-What is Subsidiary about Human Rights*, *supra* n. 35, p. 82–83 (on the view that the remedial means after a judgment issued by a Court is an extension of procedural and substantive subsidiarity).

103 *See generally*, Paolo G. Carozza, *The Anglo-Latin Divide and the Future of the Inter-American System of Human Rights*, 5(1) Notre Dame Journal of International and Comparative Law (2015) (on a reflection of how conventionality control has been used by the

problems, since the executive, legislative and judicial powers of the States parties to the American Convention would hardly accept that, after a decision of an international court in a case against Chile, they lost their say on how to implement all the substantive aspects of the Inter-American *Corpus Juris* at the domestic level.

Yet, there is another option to construct conventionality control that does not rely on such a radical monist view: distinguishing the normative force of conventionality control (1) when it is referred to as a "guarantee of non-repetition"; and (2) when it is referred to as a general doctrine (meaning that it is binding for all State authorities). This distinction would allow sustaining that – in the first case – State authorities shall exercise conventionality control owing to the obligations derived from Articles 63.1 and 68.1 in connection with Articles 2 and 1.1; and that – in the second case – conventionality control shall interact with other rules and principles at the domestic level. In the former case the obligation to exercise conventionality control shall be understood with the force of a legal obligation that admits no deviation, because it derives directly from an order of the Court in the exercise of its contentious jurisdiction; but in the latter case the obligation to exercise conventionality control shall be understood with the normative force of a "principle".

4.2.1. Principles as Sources of Legal Obligations

The reference to principles follows the famous distinction made by Ronald Dworkin in *Taking Rights Seriously*,[104] where he argues that when lawyers reason about legal rights and duties they make use of standards that do not necessarily work as rules – in the sense that the source of these rights and obligations are not exclusively the result of standards of behavior created by those that have authority on the basis of a secondary rule of recognition (i.e. rules enacted in a statute by congress or in a treaty agreed upon by States) – but that legal obligations can also be found in principles.[105] The American philosopher explains that rules and principles point to particular decisions about legal obligations in particular circumstances, but that they differ in the character of the direction they give: rules

---

Inter-American Court, in some cases, in a manner that reflects a very aggressive and hierarchical understanding of the American Convention, and how this goes against constitutional pluralism in Latin America).

104 *See*, Ronald Dworkin, *Taking Rights Seriously* (Harvard University Press, 1978), particularly chs II and III. (The analysis in this section does not pretend to exhaust the richness of Dworkin's arguments, nor on the enormous production of academic debate that has followed his ideas, and simply summarizes his basic thesis on the distinction between rules and principles.)

105 *Id.* p. 23.

are applicable in an all-or-nothing character, whereas principles state a reason in one direction but do not necessitate a particular decision.[106]

The flexibility of principles as valid legal standards does not come from their lack of legal value as sources of law, but because they have different moral and legal values makes them subject to balancing in a manner that rules do not allow.[107] Decision-making based on consideration of principle requires lawyers and judges to acknowledge and balance the content of principles that sometimes have different directions, which means that the application of a principle may not produce the same result in all similar cases. It might be that principles require a different conclusion in similar circumstances, depending on the relative weight of the principles involved in that case. In this context, it is the job of lawyers and judges to appropriately take into account the relative weight of different principles when they intersect.[108]

The view that principles are sources of rights and obligations – and therefore not just that rules are sources of law – allows to sustain that judges are applying binding legal standards when they base their decisions on principles and when the legal code does not provide an unequivocal answer that it is also just and fair. This view also allows sustaining that judges are not being arbitrary – they are not simply following their preferences – when a case is decided taking into account principles to reach a particular conclusion. Lawyers and judges that find in principles what is not determined in statutory law are not necessarily exercising arbitrariness, but instead they are looking to other normative elements to reach an appropriate conclusion.[109] This type of approach calls judges to make judicial decisions on the basis of standards that are not rules of law – formally speaking – but without displacing the existing rules of law by using principles.[110]

By adopting this approach Dworkin also departs from the positivist thesis that identifies the validity of a rule of law depending exclusively on the competence of the institution that created that rule, and in the procedure followed for the creation of that rule.[111] In a positivist understanding of the validity of sources of law, a rule of law can only exist if the institution that created it is acting in accordance with a secondary rule that defines its authority and the procedural requirements to recognize the validity of the creation of that rule.

106 *See*, Ronald Dworkin, *Taking Rights Seriously*, *supra* n. 104, pp. 22–24; on the distinction between rules and principles, *see also* Robert Alexy, 22 Constitutional Rights and Proportionality Revus (online) (2014), p. 52, available at http://journals.openedition.org/revus/2783 (Alexy defines rules as "definitive commands", and principles as "optimization requirements").

107 *See*, Davil Lay Williams, *Ronald Dworkin (1931–2013)*, in *Encyclopedia of Political Thought* (Wiley Publishing, 2014).

108 *See*, Ronald Dworkin, *Taking Rights Seriously*, *supra* n. 104, p. 34.

109 *Id.* p. 34.

110 *Id.* p. 37.

111 *Id.* p. 41.

But in Dworkin's understanding the validity of principles as sources of law lies in its appropriateness, and not solely on the fulfillment of formal requirements (like authority and procedure).[112] The legal force of principles is to be found in its fairness and on the institutional support that exists in a legal system since, "the more [institutional] support we find, the more weight we could find for a principle".[113]

The reference made to principles as a means to understand conventionality control is connected with three characteristics that were succinctly explained by H.L.A. Hart: first, that

> as a matter of degree: principles are, relatively to rules, broad, general, or unspecific, in the sense that often what would be regarded as a number of distinct rules can be exhibited as the exemplifications of a single principle;[114]

second, that principles,

> because they refer more or less explicitly to some purpose, goal, entitlement or value, are regarded from some point of view as desirable to maintain, or to adhere to, as so not only to provide and explanation or rationale of the rules which exemplify them, but as at least contributing to their justification;[115]

third, that principles

> differ from rules because they have a dimension of weight but not of validity, and hence it is that in conflict with other principle of greater weight, one principle may override and fail to determine a decision, but nonetheless will survive to be used in other cases where it may win in competition with some other principles of lesser weight.[116]

The above-mentioned serves the purpose to explain why the normative force of conventionality control – as a general doctrine – is better explained if it is conceived as a principle. This is because (1) the obligations derived from conventionality control are – and must be kept – broad, general and unspecific (domestic authorities must perform an interpretation in accordance with the Inter-American *Corpus Juris*, and cease in the enforcement of a rule if they have the capacity to do so if no consistent interpretation is possible); (2) its legitimacy as a source of obligations is based mainly on the fact that it is desirable as part of the legal system owing to the goal that it pursues (the effectiveness of human

---

112 *Ibid.*
113 *Ibid.*
114 *See*, H.L.A. Hart, The Concept of Law, p. 260 (Oxford University Press, 2nd ed., 1961).
115 *Ibid.*
116 *Ibid.*

rights at the domestic level and the strengthening of the subsidiarity of the Inter-American System); and (3) its practical application necessarily requires its interaction with other principles (mainly other rules of domestic law). This approach supports the distinction between conventionality control referred as a guarantee of non-repetition in specific cases, and conventionality control as a principle when seen as a general doctrine.

4.2.2. Conventionality Control as a Principle

The notion of conventionality control as a principle would have crucial implications for the operation of this doctrine in domestic legal systems. It would allow one to coherently understand conventionality control as a doctrine that heavily interacts with domestic legal systems (*see* Chapter 2, section 3.2 for a discussion on why there shall be a direct effect but not supremacy in the understanding of the American Convention), without necessarily assuming idealist notions of supremacy of international law as that proposed by the principle of integration.[117] Particularly, this approach would allow the affirmation that all domestic authorities have an obligation to interpret domestic law in accordance with the Inter-American *Corpus Juris*, and not to enforce that law if no conventional interpretation is possible and they have the authority to do so; yet this view would also allow sustaining that the particularities of how conventionality control operates in concrete circumstances is intimately connected with other rules and principles of constitutional law that exist in particular domestic legal systems, in this manner respecting the pluralism that is implied in Article 2.

Does this mean that, in this view, conventionality control does not impose real legal obligations? Not at all. If Dworkin is correct, principles are legal obligations that must be observed not because they will advance or secure an economic, political or social situation deemed desirable (as policies do), but because it is a requirement of justice or fairness.[118] Domestic authorities would be obligated to exercise conventionality control because of the justice that comes from interpreting domestic norms in accordance with the requirements of human dignity (expressed in the Inter-American *Corpus Juris*), and to cease in the enforcement of that law when they have the power to do so and no conventional interpretation is possible. Yet conventionality control would not be considered

117 *See generally*, Paolo G. Carozza, *The Anglo-Latin Divide and the Future of the Inter-American System of Human Rights*, *supra* n. 103, p. 155 (on the notion that the effectiveness of regional systems require that these systems come to terms "with the important differences among their members, mediating and harmonizing in order to construct a strong common whole".)

118 *See*, Ronald Dworkin, *Taking Rights Seriously*, *supra* n. 104, p. 22.

with the force of a rule until it is not legislated with an amendment to the American Convention, or with the adoption of a protocol. Until then, conventionality control – understood as a general doctrine – should be treated as a principle that heavily interacts with other rules and principles at the domestic level. This would allow conventionality control to coherently and legitimately take different "forms" in different States, depending on factors defined by domestic law and international law taken altogether.

This approach is coherent with the subsidiary nature of the Inter-American System, since it allows conventionality control to be legitimately used as guarantee of non-repetition to solve problems derived from the application of specific laws in particular cases decided by the Inter-American Court, but without transforming each one of those particular decisions into an "other measure" applicable to all other States as if they had been parties to the specific dispute – or as if States had agreed on a new rule of international law. The Court would avoid "amending" the American Convention with any decision established in its jurisprudence, which would give it more freedom to decide cases in accordance with the particularities of concrete situations, and more legitimacy when monitoring the compliance of those cases. At the same time, conventionality control could continue to be constructed as a general doctrine that serves as a vehicle (a "bridge") for the implementation of the Inter-American *Corpus Juris* at the domestic level, but without pretending to trump any consideration of domestic law as if the Inter-American Court constituted some kind of supreme legislator on human rights questions.

This approach also reduces the tension of the "counter-majoritarian" arguments against conventionality control, because this doctrine would not be considered as a vehicle to argue that the interpretations of the Inter-American Court have the normative force of a precedent that shall trump any consideration of domestic law in contrary. By considering conventionality control – as a general doctrine – with the normative force of a principle, the different elements of the Inter-American *Corpus Juris* that serve as parameters for conventionality control would constitute *one* relevant factor – not the *only* relevant factor – in the creation, interpretation and enforcement of domestic law; but this view naturally recognizes an ample space of freedom for domestic authorities (to the legislative, executive and judicial powers) to define the relevance of specific standards of the Inter-American *Corpus Juris* depending on the normative and factual factors that surround the solution of specific problems. It is necessary to acknowledge that arguments about the lack of democratic legitimacy of the Court's decisions will be always present; although the force of these arguments will be reduced as much as the Court remains closer to treaty law, and avoids adopting views too rigorous in questions that touch on sensitive political or ideological questions that allow different interpretations by reasonable people in different States.

Furthermore, this approach would increase the effectiveness of conventionality control "as an institution that allows all State authorities the adequate fulfillment of their obligations to respect and ensure".[119] Recognizing a high degree of flexibility on how conventionality control interacts with rules and principles at the domestic level would allow State authorities to accommodate the doctrine to the particularities of the domestic legal system and judicial culture, which is crucial for its effectiveness as a vehicle for the protection of human rights. Of course, this approach requires avoiding the temptation of constructing conventionality control as a vehicle for arguing the supremacy of the Inter-American *Corpus Juris* over any other consideration of domestic law, a position that could produce a political backlash or lead to inefficacy and injustice.[120] Conventionality control already has a great degree of flexibility in its design due to the inclusion of the "*Aguado-Alfaro* clause"; but this flexibility should be at the core of our understanding of conventionality control when seen as a general doctrine. This approach would make the doctrine of conventionality control meaningful and effective for domestic authorities.

Understanding conventionality control as a principle does not rely on idealistic and politically problematic notions of supremacy of international law and international institutions over domestic law and domestic institutions, opening the door to argue that it is through dialogue and accommodation that international law should be implemented at the domestic level. Borrowing the metaphor of García Ramírez – and perhaps with a different meaning to what the Mexican jurist thinks on this point – conventionality control, seen as a guarantee of non-repetition and as a principle, would better serve the "Latin American voyage" of human rights in the Americas.[121] How should conventionality control look on this view, and how should it interact with other rules and principles at the domestic level? This question requires deep elaboration and reflection, which cannot be fully covered in this section. The next paragraphs provide the first answer to this complex question, although the complete answer would require further serious thinking, discussion and writing by scholars of international law and constitutional law, as well as by the members of the Inter-American Court.

---

119 Eduardo Ferrer Mac-Gregor Poisot, *Control de Convencionalidad (sede interna)*, in Eduardo Ferrer Mac-Gregor Poisot, Fabiola Martínez Ramírez and Giovanni Figeroa Mejía (Eds.), *Diccionario de Derecho Procesal Constitucional y Convencional*, Vol. I, p. 236 (Poder Judicial de la Federación, Consejo de la Judicatura Federal, Universidad Nacional Autónoma de México & Instituto de Investigaciones Jurídicas, 2014).

120 *See generally*, Paolo G. Carozza, *Subsidiarity as a Structure Principle of International Law*, *supra* n. 22, p. 75 (on the notion that local discretion can be a means for absorbing human rights norms more deeply and consistently into society, "as opposed to painting human rights law over the surface without any deeper bond to internal traditions"); *see generally*, Nestor Pedro Sagües, *International Obligations and "Conventionality Control"*, *supra* n. 10, p. 124 (the Argentinian author – one of the main supporters of this doctrine – acknowledges the idea that "supremacy" that comes with some view of conventionality control could potentially be the "Achilles ankle" of conventionality control).

121 *See*, Sergio García Ramírez, *The Relationship Between Inter-American Jurisdiction and States (National Systems): Some Pertinent Questions*, *supra* n. 86, p. 117.

4.3. NORMATIVE FACTORS THAT "REGULATE" THE "INTENSITY" OF CONVENTIONALITY CONTROL

For the sake of clarity, it is convenient to insist on the main normative consequence of distinguishing the normative force of conventionality control as a "guarantee of non-repetition" and as a "principle". In the first hypothesis, conventionality control constitutes an obligation for State authorities to remedy the causes of human rights violations and to prevent future violations provoked by the existence and enforcement of specific pieces of legislation that have been found anti-conventional by the Inter-American Court in the exercise of its contentious jurisdiction (i.e. Decree Law 2.191 in *Almonacid*, or Article 57 of the Code of Military Justice in *Radilla*). In this hypothesis, the authority of the Court to order States to exercise conventionality control finds its basis in Article 63.1, and the obligation of States to comply with this order comes from Article 68.1 and – to a lesser extent – from Articles 2 and 1.1. In other words, in this hypothesis the Court is providing a *subsidium* for State authorities so they have clear guidance on how to interpret, or a mandate not to enforce, a domestic law that has been proven to be in clear violation of substantive elements of the Inter-American *Corpus Juris.*[122]

But in the second hypothesis the situation is different. Conventionality control is conceived as an integral part of Article 2. In this hypothesis the Inter-American Court is "developing" the content of the general obligations of the States parties to the American Convention (particularly of Article 2), acting in this manner as some kind of judicial legislator. Yet, the Court has not been vested with the power to create law, at least not in the same manner that States have that power.[123] So it is reasonable to assume that the standards developed by the Court as the "ultimate interpreter of the American Convention" have a different normative value from those agreed upon by the express consent of States, or those that have an uncontroversial conventional basis (like the reparations ordered for specific cases). This does not necessarily mean that the decisions of the Court are deprived of any normative value beyond specific cases,[124]

---

122 *See generally*, Oswaldo Ruiz-Chiriboga, *The Conventionality Control: Examples of (Un)successful Experiences in Latin America*, 3(1–2) Inter-American and European Human Rights Journal 203 (2010) (on the notion that the obligations for State authorities to carry out conventionality control vary depending on whether or not the Court has evaluated a particular domestic law, and has created an obligation not to enforce that law or those with a similar content).

123 *See generally*, Collin Warbrick, *States and Recognition of International Law*, in Malcolm D. Evans (Ed.), *International Law*, p. 229 (Oxford University Press, 2nd ed., 2006) (on the notion that States have the power to create law "for the mere fact of being States").

124 *See generally*, Ian Brownlie, *Principles of Public International Law*, p. 19 (Oxford University Press, 7th ed., 2008).

but these standards shall certainly be considered with a different "texture" than norms contained in treaties. This is why this chapter has qualified the normative force of conventionality control – when seen as a general doctrine created by the Court – with the normative force of a principle.

This distinction has crucial normative consequences: in the first hypothesis, conventionality control must be exercised by domestic authorities notwithstanding domestic law to the contrary, because the State cannot invoke norms of its domestic legal system as a justification not to comply with a judgment of the Inter-American Court – as is clear from Articles 68.1 of the Convention and 27 of the Vienna Convention, and as was pointed out by García Ramírez in his concurrent opinion in *Myrna*. Nevertheless, in the second hypothesis, the normative consequences and the operation of conventionality control by domestic authorities shall be intimately connected with the rules and principles of domestic law, because Article 2 recognizes an ample space of freedom for States to decide how to incorporate the Inter-American *Corpus Juris* into their domestic legal systems. Consequently, conceiving conventionality control with the normative force of a principle leads to the conclusion that, although this doctrine constitutes an autonomous source of obligations for domestic authorities, its operation shall have different "intensities" or "degrees" in different States.

The next question is somewhat obvious: which are the factors that define how conventionality control, conceived as a principle, "couples" with domestic legal systems, and what would be the practical consequences of this approach?

Without the intention of being exhaustive, and considering what has been mentioned here and in other chapters about the nature of the American Convention as a treaty governed by international law, it is reasonable to sustain that three factors "regulate" the "intensity" of conventionality control in specific States parties to the Convention: (1) the competences of domestic authorities and the procedural regulations for the substantiation of legal remedies, since the definition of the powers and attributions of domestic authorities is an exclusive competence of States, and since the formalities of judicial processes are necessary for the proper administration of justice;[125] (2) the constitutional hierarchy recognized to the Inter-American *Corpus Juris*, and the hermeneutical clauses to solve conflicts of rights, as they reflect values such as the rule of law, self-determination and democracy;[126] and (3) the legitimate choices of State authorities when interpreting and enforcing international human rights law in concrete cases, since human rights are designed to solve problems within

125 *See*, Sergio García Ramírez, *The Conventional Internal Control Court*, V(28) IUS Revista del Instituto de Ciencias Jurídicas de Puebla 152 (2011).

126 *See generally*, David Feldman, *Monism, Dualism and Constitutional Legitimacy*, 20 Australian Yearbook of International Law 106–109 (1999).

given political communities, which means that there must be a natural space for pluralism in the interpretation and incorporation of human rights standards.[127]

4.3.1. The Competences of Domestic Authorities and the Procedural Regulations that Shape the Judicial Process

The first of the elements that regulates the intensity of conventionality control are the "respective competences and the corresponding procedural regulations", as has been defined by the Inter-American Court in the "*Aguado-Alfaro* clause".[128] As mentioned in a previous section (*see* Chapter 2, section 2.4 for a full analysis on this topic), this clause is the solution that the Court found to draw a line between the obligation of domestic authorities to exercise conventionality control *ex officio*, but without "authorizing" them to act beyond the powers conferred by domestic law, and without opening the door to the disregard of the procedural regulations that shape the judicial process.[129] So conventionality control is based on the notion that States have the freedom to decide how to organize the powers and attributions of domestic authorities (for instance if there is a diffuse or concentrated system of judicial review), and on the type of formalities for the admissibility and substantiation of legal remedies (which are determined entirely by domestic law).[130] In this sense, the Court recently reasoned in *Liakat Ali Alibux v. Suriname* (2014) that:

> 124. Finally, in relation to the arguments of the representative and the Commission (*supra* paras. 112 and 113) on the violation of the right to judicial protection due to the absence of a Constitutional Court, although the Court recognizes the importance of such bodies as protectors of constitutional mandates and fundamental rights, the American Convention does not impose a specific model for the regulation of issues of constitutionality and control for conformity [*sic*] with the Convention. In this sense, the Court recalls that the obligation to monitor the compliance between domestic legislation and the American Convention is delegated to all bodies of the State, including its judges and other mechanisms related to the administration of justice at all levels.[131]

Hence, it is possible to say that a judge – or any other domestic authority – that has attributions and powers to exercise judicial review – or not to enforce a

---

127 *See generally*, Paolo G. Carozza, *Subsidiarity as a Structure Principle of International Law*, *supra* n. 22, p. 67.

128 *See*, *Dismissed Congressional Employees (Aguado-Alfaro et al.) v. Peru*, *supra* n. 87, §128.

129 *See*, Sergio García Ramírez, *The Conventional Internal Control Court*, *supra* n. 125, p. 151.

130 *See*, María Carmelina Londoño Lázaro, *The Legality Principle and the Conventionality Control: Confluences and Developments in the Inter-American Court of Human Rights*, 128 Boletin Mexicano de Derecho Comparado (2010).

131 *Liakat Ali Abux v. Surinam*, *supra* n. 96, §124.

domestic law – has a more intense obligation to exercise conventionality control than a judge who has fewer attributions and/or where procedural regulations are stricter.[132] So in a State like Mexico, with its mixed system of judicial review, and with the broad judicial protection of human rights provided by the *amparo* action,[133] more authorities (especially federal judges when deciding *amparo* petitions) would have the obligation to exercise conventionality control with higher intensity than in a State like Costa Rica, with its concentrated system of judicial review, and with the exclusive jurisdiction of the Constitutional Chamber of the Supreme Court to decide *habeas corpus* and *amparo* petitions.[134] The only two caveats that might limit the freedom recognized by the "*Aguado-Alfaro* clause" is that there shall be at least one court that is able to control the conventionality of domestic laws,[135] and that the procedural regulations that shape judicial processes must be consistent with the Inter-American *Corpus Juris*.[136]

In this sense, following the analysis of Allan R. Brewer-Carías on the centrality that the *amparo* action has for the protection of human rights in Latin America, on the connection between *amparo* actions and judicial review (diffuse or concentrated), and on the obligations that emerge from Article 25 of the American Convention,[137] it is reasonable to argue that the intensity of conventionality control – at least on what concerns the members of the judiciary – naturally follows the regulation that *amparo* has in different States parties to the Convention. This is of course only one piece of the puzzle on how conventionality control operates in different domestic legal systems considering the content of the "*Aguado-Alfaro* clause", since *amparo* is not the only legal remedy to control laws and acts of the State; yet it is a piece that opens the door for further studies on how conventionality control shall operate in different States. These studies

---

132 *See generally, Cabrera Garcia and Montiel Flores v. Mexico.* Preliminary Objections, Merits, Reparations and Costs Judgment, Inter-Am. Ct. H.R. (Ser. C) No. 220 (Nov. 26, 2010). Reasoned Concurrent Opinion of Judge Eduardo Ferrer Mac-Gregor Poisot; *see also*, Nestor Pedro Sagües, *International obligations and "Conventionality Control"*, *supra* n. 10, p. 121; *see*, Sergio García Ramírez, *The Conventional Internal Control Court*, *supra* n. 125, pp. 151–152.

133 *See generally*, HÉCTOR FIX-ZAMUDIO, *ENSAYOS SOBRE EL DERECHO DE AMPARO* (Porrúa, 2003) (for an explanation of the multipurpose judicial use of *amparo* in the Mexican legal system).

134 *See*, Rubén Hernández Valle, *El recurso de amparo en Costa Rica*, in HÉCTOR FIX-ZAMUDIO AND EDUARDO FERRER MAC-GREGORT POISOT, *EL DERECHO DE AMPARO EN EL MUNDO*, pp. 257–304 (UNAM & Porrúa, 2006).

135 *See, Cabrera Garcia and Montiel Flores v. Mexico*, *supra* n. 132. Reasoned Concurrent Opinion of Eduardo Ferrer Mac-Gregor Poisot, §35.

136 *See*, Sergio García Ramírez, *The Conventional Internal Control Court*, *supra* n. 125, p. 149.

137 *See generally*, ALLAN R. BREWER-CARÍAS, *CONSTITUTIONAL PROTECTION OF HUMAN RIGHTS IN LATIN AMERICA. A COMPARATIVE STUDY OF AMPARO PROCEEDINGS*, p. 83 and 87–162 (Cambridge University Press, 2009) (on the connection between the form of judicial review and *amparo* in Latin America, on a comparative study of *amparo* regulations in Latin America, and on an analysis of the history and normative components of Art. 25 of the American Convention).

would require a State-by-State analysis in order to explain how conventionality control "couples" with the regulation of legal remedies in place (especially with those that regulate *amparo* actions), since there is no obligation for homogeneity regarding the legal remedies that States shall put in place for the protection of human rights.[138]

4.3.2. The Constitutional Hierarchy of the Inter-American Corpus Juris

The second element that "regulates" the "intensity" of conventionality control at the domestic level comes from the norms of constitutional law that determine the hierarchy of the Inter-American *Corpus Juris* in specific domestic legal systems. Conceiving the normative force of conventionality control as a principle – and therefore rejecting the radical monist view that the Inter-American *Corpus Juris* is supreme as a matter of international law – supports the view that the obligation of domestic authorities to exercise conventionality control must be understood in the light of the relevant rules of constitutional law that define the place and operation of the Inter-American *Corpus Juris* at the domestic level. This happens because Article 2 of the American Convention confers ample spaces of freedom for States to determine how its provisions will have effect at the domestic level,[139] since the duty of States to undertake the "legislative" and "other measures" to give effect to the rights and freedoms protected by the American Convention must be fulfilled "in accordance with the constitutional processes and the provisions of [the] Convention" (*see* Chapter 2, section 3.2 for the reasons that sustain this position).[140]

Therefore, the American Convention – and other human rights treaties in the Inter-American System – must be "taken into account" (using the language of *Almonacid*) as parameters for conventionality control depending on their level of recognition as domestic law. They could be located above the constitution, as is the case of Guatemala;[141] at the level of the constitution, as is the case of Argentina,[142] Mexico[143] or Peru;[144] or above statutory law but below the

---

138 *See*, American Convention on Human Rights, *supra* n. 10, Art. 25 b.

139 *See*, Dinah Shelton and Paolo G. Carozza, *Regional Protection of Human Rights*, p. 113 (Oxford University Press, 2013).

140 *See*, American Convention on Human Rights, *supra* n. 10, Art. 2.

141 *See* Political Constitution of the Republic of Guatemala, May 31, 1985 (Guatemala), Art. 46

142 *See*, Constitution of Argentina, May 1, 1853 (Argentina), Art. 75; Political Constitution of the United Mexican States, Feb. 5, 1917 (Mexico), Arts. 1 and 133; Political Constitution of Colombia, Jul. 1991 (Colombia), Art. 93; Political Constitution of the Netherlands, Art. 91.

143 *See*, Political Constitution of the United Mexican States, *supra* n. 142, Art. 1.

144 *See*, Political Constitution of Peru, Dec. 29, 1993 (Peru), Art. 55, and Fourth Final and Transitory Provision.

constitution, as is the case of El Salvador[145] or Chile.[146] By the same logic, the jurisprudence of the Inter-American Court must be "taken into account" depending on how it has been incorporated in domestic legal systems. It could constitute a source of constitutional law, as is the case of Costa Rica after the decision of its Supreme Court of Justice in judgment 2313-95,[147] or the case of Mexico after the decision of its Supreme Court of Justice in the *Contradicción de tesis 293/2011*;[148] or it may be considered as a "relevant hermeneutical criterion" for establishing the meaning of constitutional rights, as is the case of Colombia after judgment *C-010/00* (*see* Chapter 2, section 3.2 to observe several examples on how the different elements of the Inter-American *Corpus Juris* have been incorporated in different Latin-American countries).[149]

This type of approach is no novelty. Some prestigious constitutional courts in Europe have found flexible ways to confer a special status in constitutional law to the European Convention on Human Rights (ECHR) and to the jurisprudence of the ECtHR, but without asserting the supremacy of these decisions. For instance, the Italian Constitutional Court (ItCC) has decided that – as a matter of constitutional law – the catalog of rights recognized by the Italian Constitution and the European Convention "are integrated into one another, mutually completing each other in their interpretation".[150] This understanding has opened the door for the ItCC to increasingly and seriously consider the jurisprudence of the ECtHR when it is deciding cases subject to its jurisdiction; but at the same time it has keep intact its jurisdiction over any conflict between national legislation and the ECHR as interpreted by the ECtHR.[151] In this sense, in the "twin judgments" 348/2007 and 349/2007, the ItCC decided that the signature and ratification of the ECHR require that no legislative act abrogate any of its provisions;[152] but it also established that the ECHR and the jurisprudence of

145 *See*, Constitution of the Republic of El Salvador, Dec. 15, 1983 (El Salvador), Art. 144; Political Constitution of France, Oct. 4, 1958 (France), Arts. 54 and 55; Political Constitution of Haiti, 1987 (Haiti), Arts. 276 and 276-2; U.S. Const. (United States), Art. VI.

146 *See*, Political Constitution of the Republic of Chile, Mar. 11, 1981 (Chile), Arts. 5 and 93.

147 *See*, Constitutional Chamber of the Supreme Court of Justice of Costa Rica, Opinion 2313-95 (Case File 0421-S-90) May 9, 1995, §VII.

148 Supreme Court of Justice of the Nation (Mexico), File 293/2011 (*contradicción de tesis*), Sep. 3, 2013.

149 Constitutional Court of Colombia, Judgment C-010/00, Jan. 19, 2000, §6.

150 Judgment 388/1999 in Vittoria Barsotti, Paolo G. Carozza, Marta Cartabia and Andrea Simoncini, *Italian Constitutional Justice in Global Context* (Oxford University Press, 2015).

151 *Ibid.*

152 Italian Constitutional Court, Judgment 348/2007 and 349/2007 in Vittoria Barsotti, Paolo G. Carozza, Marta Cartabia and Andrea Simoncini, *Italian Constitutional Justice in Global Context*, *supra* n.150.

the ECtHR are standards of judicial review of national legislation insofar as its provisions conform with the Constitution:

> The arguments set out above do not imply that the ECHR, as interpreted by the Strasburg Court, acquire the force of constitutional law and is therefore immune to assessments by this Court of its constitutional legitimacy. It is precisely because the provision in question supplement a constitutional principle, whilst always retaining a lower status, that it is necessary that they respect the Constitution. [T]he complete effectiveness of interposed rules is conditional on their compatibility with the Italian constitutional order, which cannot be modified by external sources.[153]

This approach is also present in the jurisprudence of the Federal Constitutional Court of Germany (FCCG) – which has interpreted the Basic Law's commitment to an "open State" in a manner that does not trivialize the sovereignty of the German State and its Constitution.[154] In *Görgülü* (2004), the FCCG established that the decisions of the ECtHR do not automatically displace existing rules of domestic law. So in cases where Germany is found in violation of the ECHR, domestic authorities have an obligation to "take (sufficiently) into account" the judgment of the ECtHR in order to "end a continuing violation of the Convention and to create a situation that complies with the Convention".[155] But – the FCCG reasoned – the judgments of the ECtHR have "limited substantive *res judicata*", meaning that its decisions "merely give the States that are not involved an occasion to examine their domestic legal systems and ... to orient themselves in line with the relevant jurisprudence of the European Court".[156] In the opinion of some scholars, the position sustained in *Görgülü* – although it asserts the supremacy of the Basic Law – opened a door for the FCCG to align its own jurisprudence to the decisions of the ECtHR though hermeneutical means.[157]

---

153 *Ibid.*

154 *See generally*, Basic Law of Germany, May 23, 1949 (Germany), Arts. 24(1) and (2), 24(3), 26 and 59(2). On the provisions that reflect the openness of the State to international law and cooperation, *see*, Donald P. Kommers and Russell A. Miller, *The Constitutional Jurisprudence of the Federal Republic of Germany*, p. 302 (Duke, 3rd ed., 2012) (for an analysis of the "Jurisprudence of the Open State").

155 Constitutional Court of Germany, 111 BVerfGE 307 (*Görgülü*), Feb. 26, 2004 (the duty to comply with the judgment of the European Court, however, must be done in accordance with the "state actors' jurisdiction and it does not exempt them from giving full respect to controlling domestic laws and acts"); *see*, Donald P. Kommers and Russell A. Miller, *The Constitutional Jurisprudence of the Federal Republic of Germany*, *supra* n. 154, p. 320.

156 111 BVerfGE 307 (*Görgülü*), *supra* n.155.

157 *See*, Donald P. Kommers and Russell A. Miller, *The Constitutional Jurisprudence of the Federal Republic of Germany*, *supra* n. 154, p. 324; *see generally*, Christian Tomuschat, *The Effects of the Judgments of the European Court of Human Rights According*

The reasons why States have the right to control the normative force of international law in their domestic legal systems go beyond legal technicalities.[158] The protection of values such as self-determination, democracy and accountability is relevant to justify the recognition of the freedom of States to protect their political life from excessive interference from international institutions, which are not subject to the political, democratic and constitutional checks that domestic institutions have under the principle of separation of powers and the rule of law. Thus, it is reasonable to assume that the different branches of the executive, legislative and judicial powers in different States parties to the American Convention retain the capacity to determine how the different elements of the Inter-American *Corpus Juris* would operate in their own constitutional systems, in the case of Latin America even after the creation of the doctrine of conventionality control. The deficit of democratic legitimacy and political control of the different organs of the Organization of American States make it particularly problematic to simply accept radical monist approaches on the relationship between international law and international institutions, and domestic law and domestic institutions.

For these reasons, the operation of conventionality control may be legitimately different in – let's say – Panama than in Mexico, since both States have different systems of judicial review and different rules of incorporation of IHRL. Panama has no system of diffuse judicial review and treaty norms do not have, in general, constitutional hierarchy.[159] Whereas Mexico has a system of diffuse judicial review, the Constitution recognizes the constitutional hierarchy of international human rights norms, and the Supreme Court of Justice of the Mexican Nation has considered the jurisprudence of the Inter-American Court binding for all domestic judges.[160] As mentioned in Chapter 2, these differences *do matter* at a normative level, because there is no rule of the American Convention or in general international law that requires homogeneity regarding the level

to the German Constitutional Court, 11 German Law Journal 529 (2010) (the author severely criticized the *Görgülü* judgment; yet, he also considered that this decision positioned the Constitutional Court as the guardian of the international commitments of Germany, and in cases decided after *Görgülü*, the Constitutional Court has shown its willingness to integrate its own jurisprudence with that of the ECtHR).

158 *See*, David Feldman, *Monism, Dualism and Constitutional Legitimacy*, *supra* n. 126, pp. 106–109; *see generally*, Paolo G. Carozza, *The Anglo-Latin Divide and the Future of the Inter-American System of Human Rights*, *supra* n. 103, p. 101.

159 *See generally*, Political Constitution of the Republic of Panama, Oct. 11, 1972 (Panama), Arts. 165 and 203; *see also* Allan R. Brewer-Carías, *El Sistema Panameño de control concentrado de la constitucionalidad, en el derecho comparado*, Paper presented in the *Segundas Jornadas de Derecho Procesal Jorge P.* (1995), p. 5. Available at: http://allanbrewercarias.net/Content/449725d9-f1cb-474b-8ab2-41efb849fea2/Content/I.1.513.pdf.

160 *See*, Supreme Court of Justice of the Nation (Mexico), Apr. 25, 2014, P./J. 21/2014 (*tesis aislada*).

of recognition that States confer on sources of IHRL.[161] Consequently, the understanding of the "intensity" of conventionality control should legitimately depend on the "openness" that constitutional law recognizes to the Inter-American *Corpus Juris* in each State.

4.3.3. The "Openness" of International Human Rights Law

The third aspect that "regulates" the "intensity" of conventionality control has a substantive nature, because reading IHRL in the light of the principle of subsidiarity leads to the conclusion that human rights norms and principles protect *both* the dignity of the person *and* the plurality of human cultures.[162] So this third aspect is not based on the existence of formal rules of law, as those that define the competences of domestic authorities to exercise judicial review, the procedural regulations that shape the judicial process in *amparo* trials, the hierarchical rules of constitutional law that determine the place of IHRL at the domestic level, or the hermeneutical rules to solve conflicts of rights of international or constitutional origin. This aspect responds to a view of IHRL as the source of universal norms and principles that in most cases acquire their concrete meaning in particular historical, social and political circumstances. Thus – as a matter of principle, not just of political realities – the content of human rights norms might be legitimately distinct in different times and regions of the world, and in different States at one particular time in history or in one particular region.[163]

The notion that human rights could have different meanings in different States and at different times might appear at odds with the notion that they are "universal" and "inalienable". Yet, this view should not surprise anyone that is familiar with the history and nature of IHRL. The Universal Declaration of Human Rights (which is the cornerstone of IHRL) was conceived as a document that proclaimed "a common standard of achievement for all people and all nations, to the end that every individual and every organ of society ... secure

---

161 The American Convention leaves freedom for States to define the competences of domestic authorities, the procedural regulations for the substantiation of legal remedies, the constitutional hierarchy recognized to human rights treaties and to the jurisprudence of the Inter-American Court seen as a precedent, and the hermeneutical clauses to solve conflicts of rights.

162 *See*, Paolo G. Carozza, *Subsidiarity as a Structure Principle of International Law*, *supra* n. 22, p. 40.

163 *Id.* p. 46; *see also* Clifford Kossel, *Global Community and Subsidiarity*, 8 Communio: Int'l Cath. Rev. 37 (1981), 48 (on the notion that adherence to the principle of subsidiarity results in the existence of a pluralistic society, thus avoiding the essence of social totalitarianism: that lesser associations are abolished or reduced to mere agencies of the higher in order to produce a monolithic view of society).

their universal and effective recognition and observance".[164] Still, the Declaration did not intend to "create a single approved model for human rights for the entire world; the Declaration's articles expected that the fertile principles of the Declaration could be brought to life in a legitimate variety of ways".[165] One of the main theoretical reasons for this design is that persons are not isolated, or in necessary opposition with each other, or with the State. They are situated within a social and political context, which is an essential component for the understanding of the demands of justice for each *and* everyone.[166] In the words of Carozza:

> Even if an abstract notion like a "human right" can reasonably be said to be necessary to the realization of the common good in all societies, the specification of that concept of "right" will depend on varying conceptions of who the holders of the right and the correlative duty are, or on the conditions under which the right claim is lost or waived, and so on. Thus, even when a right can properly be termed fundamental and universal, it may still, and probably will, differ in its instantiation in positive law in a given context.[167]

The experience of the twentieth century proved to us that human rights only have a real meaning within specific political communities. Hannah Arendt, in *The Origins of Totalitarianism*, reflected on how the Rights of Man – conceived by the French Declaration of the Rights of Man and Citizen as "inalienable", in the sense that they were supposed to be independent of history and social conditions – proved to be an illusion the moment human beings lacked their own government and no other institution was left to protect them.[168] Stateless people experienced, in their own lives, how the Rights of Man are unenforceable whenever people are no longer citizens of any State, since not belonging to any political community deprived them of their place in the world rather than "emancipating" them from the chains of society and the State.[169] This extremity, the Jewish thinker argues, made humanity aware of the existence of the "right to have rights", meaning the right "to live in a framework where one is judged

---

164 UN General Assembly, Universal Declaration of Human Rights, 10 December 1948, 217 A (III), Preamble.

165 Mary Ann Glendon, *A World Made New*, p. 221 (Random House, 2001) ("Their idea was that each local tradition was enriched as it put the Declaration's principles into practice and that all countries would benefit from the resulting accumulation of experiences.").

166 *See*, John Finnis, *Natural Law and Natural Rights*, p. 214 (Oxford University Press, 2nd ed., 2011) (on the notion that the Universal Declaration of Human Rights is a "way of sketching the *outlines of the common good*, the various aspects of individual well being in community").

167 Paolo G. Carozza, *Subsidiarity as a Structure Principle of International Law*, *supra* n. 22, p. 66.

168 Hannah Arendt, *The Origins of Totalitarianism* (1951) in Peter Baehr (Ed.) *The Portable Hannah Arendt*, p. 32 (Penguin, 2003).

169 *Id.* p. 36.

by one's actions and opinions and a right to belong to some kind of political community".[170]

Arendt's reflection certainly shows how important the existence of national and supranational mechanisms of protection for human rights are; but her reflections might have deep theoretical implications. They show that – all things considered – human rights spring from "within the nation" as much as they come from concepts such as the "human race" or the "sovereignty of the earth".[171] The experience of stateless persons proved that there is "nothing sacred in the abstract nakedness of being human", and for that reason the general formulations of human rights clauses must be conceived as a manner to solve problems within given communities.[172] This reflection – inspired by the tragic reality of those that lived "without a nation" in Nazi Germany – supports the view that a sound understanding of human rights must be able to coherently solve the following paradox: that these rights are universal and inalienable, but that they acquire their concrete meaning in a social, cultural and political context – where the actions of men and women acquire their true meaning.[173]

This approach could sound speculative and dangerous for "the recognition of the inherent dignity and for the equal and inalienable rights of all members of the human family".[174] But there are good reasons to consider that interpreting the content of human rights norms *within* a social and political context is a better way to describe – and understand – the logic of IHRL from a descriptive and normative perspective. The first reason is the different degrees of "openness" in the language of human rights norms, which leave different latitudes for their interpretation and implementation by domestic and international institutions.[175] So it is no coincidence that the rights that protect individuals from aggressions and that assure fair procedures (i.e. the right to life, the right to be free of torture, or the right to a fair trial) have a categorical force and provide for greater detailed regulations (some of them are even "absolute" and not subject to any limitation) than the rights of people in civil society (i.e. the right to privacy, the right to freedom of religion, or the right of assembly) or than the social and economic rights (which shall be realized in accordance with the "organization and resources of each State").[176]

---

170 *Id.* p. 37 (the author defines human rights as the general characteristic of the human condition, which no tyrant can take away, since its loss constitutes an attack on the most essential characteristics of human life).

171 *Id.* p. 39.

172 *Id.* p. 40.

173 *See generally*, Marta Cartabia, "The Age of 'New Rights'", Strauss Institute Working Paper 03/10 (2010) (on the notion that treating the holder of rights as a real person requires locating that person in a context made of personal, social, cultural and relational conditions).

174 Universal Declaration on Human Rights, *supra* n. 164, Preamble.

175 *See*, Paolo G. Carozza, *Subsidiarity as a Structure Principle of International Law*, *supra* n. 22, p. 60.

176 *See generally*, Mary Ann Glendon, *A World Made New*, *supra* n. 165, pp. 173–191 (the author explains how the Universal Declaration of Human Rights had a structure that

This characteristic of international human rights norms has allowed the establishment of strict limits on State conduct on questions that humanity has considered a clear violation of human dignity in all circumstances, and at the same time has allowed flexibility on those issues that could be legitimately understood in a plurality of ways by different cultures.[177] Thus – for instance – the Inter-American *Corpus Juris* recognizes a great level of protection of the Right to Humane Treatment (Article 5) by prohibiting any act of torture,[178] by not permitting any limitation or derogation of Article 5,[179] by developing the prohibition of torture with a great deal of specification in the Inter-American Convention to Prevent and Punish Torture,[180] and in the abundant jurisprudence of the Inter-American Court on this subject.[181] But the same cannot be said about the Right to Freedom of Thought and Expression (Article 13), whose terms are much more open to interpretation, that has not been expanded by any other treaty adopted in the Organization of American States, and that can be potentially derogated or subject to limitations.[182]

The second reason comes precisely from the existence of limitation and derogation clauses in treaties. The existence of these clauses reflects that only some – and not all – human rights are absolute, in the sense that most rights are interconnected with the values and the needs of social and political life.[183] Notions such as "public safety", "order", "health" or "morals" – which are terms usually referred in the limitation clauses of human rights treaties – exist to allow governments to protect common benefits in which all members of society participate.[184] So the capacity of governments to protect these common

responded to the necessity to speak in general terms owing to the uneasy relationship among freedom, equality and social security, and because it was necessary to guarantee that the treaty could be interpreted and implemented in a legitimate variety of ways).

177 This means that the more categorical the language of a treaty, the less freedom for a State exists; and the more open the language of the treaty, the less freedom for international monitoring institutions exists.

178 *See*, American Convention on Human Rights, *supra* n. 10, Art. 5.

179 *Id.* Art. 27.2.

180 *See generally*, Organization of American States (OAS), Inter-American Convention to Prevent and Punish Torture, 9 December 1985, OAS Treaty Series, No. 67, Adopted at Cartagena de Indias, Colombia, on 9 December 1985, at the fifteenth regular session of the General Assembly.

181 *See generally, Velásquez Rodríguez v. Honduras* (1988), to *J. v. Peru* (2013). (The Court has dealt with questions of torture in at least 60 cases in the exercise of its contentious jurisdiction, which represented, until 2013, 35% of its case law).

182 *See*, American Convention on Human Rights, *supra* n. 10, Arts. 13 and 27.1 and 27.2.

183 *See generally*, John Finnis, *Natural Law and Natural Rights*, *supra* n. 166, p. 214 (following Finnis, the limitation and derogation clauses should not be understood as aspects that act *against* human rights and in favor of the "general welfare", but that this type of limitations – when reasonable and just – are necessary owing to the fact that men are social by nature).

184 *Id.* p. 216.

benefits – and therefore to draw boundaries for individual rights – is justified because the common good requires the existence of an environment that is physically and morally healthy, and where the weak can live without fear of being abused. The creation of this environment sometimes requires governments to impose limits on the exercise of individual rights and freedoms, without this meaning a denial of their universality or inalienability.[185] It is in this restricted sense that it is possible to say that the common good is not only connected with an unqualified expansion of the rights and freedom of individuals, as if men and woman lived in some kind of island.[186] In the words of John Finnis:

> On the one hand, we should not say that human rights, or their exercise, are subject to the common good; for the maintenance of human rights is a fundamental component of the common good. On the other hand, we can appropriately say that most human rights are subject or limited by each and by other *aspects* of the common good, aspects which could probably be subsumed under a very broad conception of human rights but which are fittingly indicated (one could hardly say, *described*) by expressions such as "public morality", "public health", and "public order".[187]

Thus – for instance – Article 13 of the American Convention recognizes a broad protection to the freedom of thought and expression, which includes a prohibition to prior censorship.[188] But – different from Article 5 of the same treaty – it also recognizes that the exercise of freedom of expression has limits, and that it could be subject to the imposition of liability to the extent necessary to ensure the protection of "national security", "public order", "public health" or "morals".[189] It also establishes a narrow exception to the prohibition of prior censorship for the "moral" protection of childhood and adolescence,[190] and Article 27 authorizes the derogation of Article 13 in times of war, public danger, or other emergencies that threaten the "independence" or "security" of a State.[191] So the possibility for States parties to the American Convention to impose liability, or to limit freedom of expression in order to protect common benefits such as the "public order", "public health" or "morals", is that States have the right – and the duty – to legislate and enforce human rights in the context of the multiple aspects of the common good.

---

185 *Id.* p. 217.

186 *See generally*, Marta Cartabia, "The Age of 'New Rights'", *supra* n. 173, pp. 20 and 42 (the fact that the modern liberal tradition marked a new stage of human rights, and eventually dominated the legal and political discourse, does not imply that the only possible construction of rights is that which is solely based on an understanding of man as solitary and antagonistic, aiming at assuring self-preservation and security in a land of wolves).

187 John Finnis, *Natural Law and Natural Rights*, *supra* n. 166, p. 218.

188 *See*, American Convention on Human Rights, *supra* n. 10, Art. 13.1.

189 *Id.* Art. 13.2.b.

190 *Id.* Art. 13.4.

191 *Id.* Art. 27.1.

These considerations are relevant to understanding every aspect of the norms and principles of IHRL, including those of the Inter-American *Corpus Juris*;[192] thus, they should also be considered relevant to conceptualizing the different aspects of conventionality control at a theoretical level. This means that the "regulation" of the "intensity" of the obligation of domestic authorities to exercise conventionality control "taking into account" the different elements of the Inter-American *Corpus Juris* should be influenced by the specific regulation of the right that is involved in a particular case. Conventionality control in the light of subsidiarity would require State authorities to seriously evaluate the language used in particular provisions of the American Convention and any other treaty, and in the possibilities that the treaty offers to establish limitations and derogations of specific rights in order to protect aspects of the common good that have a social nature (such as the "security", "order", "health" or "morals" of a society). This approach would allow one to distinguish those cases where international standards must trump any consideration of domestic law or culture, and those where these standards allow more freedom for congress or the judiciary at the domestic level to legislate or to decide cases in a legitimate variety of ways.

So – for instance – the "intensity" of the obligation of a judge to exercise conventionality control "taking into account" the elements of the Inter-American *Corpus Juris* that prohibit torture should be considered – *prima facie* – higher than the obligation to take into consideration the regulations on freedom of expression. If a domestic law of a State party to the American Convention authorizes certain practices that would constitute acts of torture, on the basis that these practices are necessary for the protection of the "public order" or the "security" of the State or society, then a judge must do as much as is legally possible – including exercising conventionality control with a "high intensity" – not to enforce that law. But if a domestic law of the same State party authorizes the government to censor the projection of certain types of movies or TV shows in order to protect the "morals" of childhood or adolescence, then the same judge would have to seriously consider the legislator's reasons to permit censorship, or the authority's reasons to censor the projection of a movie; the law or the act of censorship might be disproportionate and thus anti-conventional, but it might also be valid since it protects morals as understood in a specific political community.

From this approach it follows that the "intensity" of the obligation of domestic authorities to "take into account" the jurisprudence of the Inter-American Court

192 *See generally*, Dinah Shelton, *The Promise of Regional Human Rights Systems*, in Burns H. Weston and Stephen P. Marks, (Eds.), *The Future of International Human Rights*, *supra* n. 9, p. 366 (on the notion that regional human rights systems grew out of inspiration from the human rights provisions of the UN Charter and the Universal Declaration on Human Rights).

should also be different owing to substantive – not just formal – considerations. Domestic authorities, when "taking into account" the jurisprudence of the ICtHR as a parameter for conventionality control, should evaluate the specific facts involved in a case and the nature of the right that was violated. Because it is not the same thing to ask domestic authorities to control the conventionality of domestic laws following the standards developed in the case law on forced disappearance,[193] the death penalty,[194] or amnesty laws,[195] which are lines of jurisprudence connected with serious violations of human dignity, and that also reflect the difficult struggles of Latin American governments to maintain democracy and the rule of law; than it is to ask domestic authorities to control the conventionality of domestic laws following the standards developed in the case law on the right to life of the unborn,[196] the criteria for limitations on the right to freedom of expression,[197] or the right to be elected,[198] which are questions intimately connected with the moral, social and political life of the different States parties to the Convention.

Why make these distinctions and not simply accept that all aspects of the Court's decisions have the same normative force as the Convention? One reason is because it is not possible to always assume that because a State departs from the Court's criterion on a question that admits different interpretations by reasonable people, that departure necessarily means that a domestic institution is acting against human rights and the common good. Actually, it might be the exact opposite, and State authorities might have good reasons not to interpret certain rights in the manner that the Court did in a particular case. This is true especially in those areas that involve relevant institutional, moral and political questions that are subject to different ideological positions (e.g. questions connected with economic, social and cultural rights, sexual and reproductive rights, or indigenous rights). For instance, one may ask if it is necessary for a State to always follow the Court's criterion developed in *Expelled Dominicans and Haitians* (2014) regarding the implications of the right to nationality. In this case the Court established that the right to nationality requires States – before denying nationality on the basis of *jus soli* and expelling a person that has the status of an illegal immigrant – must demonstrate that this person has

193 *See generally, Velásquez Rodríguez v. Honduras, supra* n. 55.

194 *See generally, Boyce et al. v. Barbados*. Preliminary Objection, Merits, Reparations and Costs Judgment, Inter-Am. Ct. H.R. (Ser. C) No. 158 (Nov. 20, 2007).

195 *See generally, Almonacid Arellano et al. v. Chile, supra* n. 16.

196 *See generally, Artavia Murillo et al. (in vitro fertilization) v. Costa Rica*. Preliminary Objections, Merits, Reparations and Costs Judgment, Inter-Am. Ct. H.R. (Ser. C) No. 257 (Nov. 28, 2012).

197 *See generally, "The Last Temptation of Christ" v. Chile Case (Olmedo Bustos et al.), supra* n. 12.

198 *See generally, Manuel Cepeda Vargas v. Colombia*. Preliminary Objections, Merits, Reparations and Costs Judgment, Inter-Am. Ct. H.R. (Ser. C) No. 213 (May 26, 2010).

a real chance to be recognized as a national of another State on the basis of *jus sanguini*.[199]

This criterion made sense since the Court found that there is a context of discrimination against Haitians in the Dominican Republic, which is manifested in the difficulty for Haitians to obtain documents for identification and the chance to use them, and in a systematic pattern of expulsions that targets Haitians.[200] Yet, this standard would not necessarily be reasonable for other States that do not target specific populations, and that do not have analogous historical and complex circumstances such as those that the Dominican Republic has had with the treatment of Haitians living in its territory.[201] In fact, the context of this case is what justifies the expansive approach taken by the Court in its interpretation of Article 20 of the Convention, even when this right has an open language and confers a great deal of freedom for States on questions connected with the recognition and loss of nationality. Still, most States do not have similar conditions, which means that imposing the duty for all migratory authorities to comply with the standards developed by the Court in the *Expelled Dominicans and Haitians* as a matter of law might impose duties for States to modify their migratory laws in a manner that is not practical nor even just.

Another reason is that accepting that any decision of the Court must trump any consideration adopted by domestic authorities constitutes an attempt to concentrate an unprecedented amount of authority on an institution conformed by seven persons and their staff. The judges and the lawyers that draft the decisions – no matter how well-trained and honest they are – have their own views about the law, as well as their own ideological convictions and political or professional interests.[202] So the assumption that any decision taken by the Court shall trump any consideration of domestic law to the contrary, would mean that the agreement among four people could potentially define fundamental aspects of the political, social and moral life of the sometimes very diverse States in Latin America – with its almost 600 million people living in 26 different countries.

---

199 *See generally, Expelled Dominicans and Haitians v. Dominican Republic.* Preliminary Objections, Merits, Reparations and Costs Judgment, Inter-Am. Ct. H.R. (Ser. C) No. 282 (Aug. 28, 2014) §290–298.

200 *Id.* §171.

201 *See generally*, Roxanna Altholz and Laurel E. Fletcher, "The Dominican Republic Must Stop Executions of Haitians", *New York Times* (July 5, 2015), available at https://www.nytimes.com/2015/07/06/opinion/the-dominican-republic-must-stop-expulsions-of-haitians.html.

202 *See generally*, Dinah Shelton, *The Rules and Reality of Petition Procedures in the Inter-American Human Rights System*, 5(1) Notre Dame Journal of International and Comparative Law 10 (2015) (on how some structural aspects of the functioning of the Inter-American Commission on Human Rights leads to illegitimacy of its decisions. Some of the critiques of the author could be similarly applied to the Inter-American Court, especially on the different levels of involvement of judges in actually deciding critical aspects of the decisions of the Court).

This position assumes some kind of infallibility and impartiality that the Court as an institution governed by humans cannot achieve, especially considering the complicated and controversial cases that sometimes are subject to its jurisdiction.[203] So here, in the realm of factual reality, the necessity to find limits to the normative force of the decisions of the Inter-American Court confirms the political and philosophical problem that long ago caused Plato to say: "Not man, but a god, must be the measure of all things."[204]

This does not mean that the decisions of the Court should be considered with absolutely no normative force beyond the cases connected with serious violations to human dignity. As has been argued in this chapter, what is necessary is to conceptually "regulate" the "intensity" of the obligation of State authorities to "take into account" the jurisprudence of the Court in cases where the State is not a party to the dispute, and for this purpose to accept that there must exist a margin of appreciation for State authorities - based *both* on formal and substantive considerations - to decide how to exercise conventionality control on the basis of the case law of the Court.[205] Since there is no legal obligation to consider the jurisprudence of the Court as the source of general rules of international law, it shall be through dialogue and accommodation that domestic authorities, and especially domestic courts, should bring to life the human rights standards developed by international institutions (mainly the Court, but also the Commission and other specialized bodies of the Organization of American States). But domestic authorities should keep their capacity to evaluate the particularities of the case at hand to decide - all things considered - the appropriateness of following the standards developed by these institutions in specific cases.

Recognizing the existence of ample spaces of freedom for State authorities to decide how to "take into account" the different elements of the Inter-American *Corpus Juris* would allow the doctrine of conventionality control to

---

[203] *See generally*, *Brewer Carías v. Venezuela*, *supra* n. 47; *Artavia Murillo et al. (in vitro fertilization) v. Costa Rica*, *supra* n. 196; *Case of Granier et al. (Radio Caracas Television) v. Venezuela*. Preliminary Objections, Merits, Reparations and Costs Judgment, Inter-Am. Ct. H.R. (Ser. C) No. 293 (Jun. 22, 2015); *Gender Identity, and equality and non-discrimination with regard to same-sex couples. State obligations in relation to change of name, gender identity, and rights from a relationship between same-sex couples (interpretation and scope of Articles 1(1), 3, 7, 11(2), 13, 17, 18 and 24, in relation to Article 1, of the American Convention on Human Rights*. Advisory Opinion OC-24, Inter-Am. Ct. H.R. (Ser. A) No. 14 (Nov. 24, 2017).

[204] *See*, Hannah Arendt, *The Origins of Totalitarianism* (1951), *supra* n. 168, p. 40.

[205] *See generally*, Pablo Contreras, *Conventionality Control, International Deference, and National Discretion in the Inter-American Court of Human Rights Case Law*, 20(2) Revista Ius et Praxis, 235–254 (2014) (the author argues that the understanding of the different degrees of discretion that domestic authorities enjoy to comply with their international obligations require a connection to be made between the doctrine of conventionality control and the doctrine of the margin of appreciation and the principle of proportionality).

become a vehicle for the construction of a Latin American *Jus Constitutionale Commune*.[206] The metaphor of the *Jus Commune* recalls a medieval reality of past European unity – before the emergence of modern States in the seventeenth century – that allowed the development and application of a transnational body of law created by jurists. This body of law was "born out of the complex dialogue that these jurists set up between the facts of contemporary life and the rules laid down in the texts of ancient Rome";[207] it searched for universal solutions founded on reason – on an ideal of justice – and yet it was a "pluralistic endeavor" that allowed absorption by very diverse local traditions.[208] So the unity provided by the *Jus Commune* was not based on a rigid monism that qualifies the validity and operation of the law in hierarchical terms (as legal positivism and idealism do); but on the notion that universal notions of justice coexist and interact in a legitimate variety of ways in different political communities, depending on degrees of recognition and on the specific circumstances of these communities.[209]

The doctrine of conventionality control – reconstructed in the light of the principle of subsidiarity – could constitute a flexible juridical instrument for domestic authorities to enforce and give concrete meaning to the rights and freedoms recognized by the Inter-American *Corpus Juris*, but without hindering legal pluralism in the States parties to the American Convention. Conventionality control, seen with the normative force of a principle, would help States to find their own voice in human rights questions in accordance with their history, culture and legal tradition; at the same time, it would allow States (especially courts) to listen to the voice of the Inter-American Court and other constitutional traditions in Latin America and other regions, without surrendering their legitimate space of freedom recognized by Article 2 of the American Convention. It is in this context that the practice of judicial dialogue, and the use of comparative constitutional law, would nurture a better understanding of the requirements of human dignity, and would contribute to the creation of a Latin American

---

206 *See generally, Cabrera Garcia and Montiel Flores v. Mexico, supra* n. 132. Reasoned Concurrent Opinion of Eduardo Ferrer Mac-Gregor Poisot, §88 (on the notion that an authentic "jurisprudential dialogue" between national and international judges will become the standard for the enforcement of human rights in the twenty-first century, and the point of conversion in human rights for the establishment of a *Jus Constitutionale Commune* in the Americas).

207 Paolo Grossi, *A History of European Law*. Trans. by Laurence Hooper 30 (Wiley-Blackwell, 2010); *see generally*, Paolo G. Carozza, *"My Friend is a Stranger": The Death Penalty and the Global Ius Commune of Human Rights* 81 Tex. L. Rev. 1037–1038 (2002–2003).

208 *See*, Paolo Grossi, *A History of European Law*, *supra* n. 207, p. 33; *see generally*, Paolo G. Carozza, *From Conquest to Constitutions: Retrieving a Latin American Tradition of the Idea of Human Rights*, 25 Human Rights Quarterly 294–295 (2003) (on the understanding that the requirements of dignity, freedom and community cannot be separated from the understanding and protection of human rights).

209 *Id.* 34; Paolo G. Carozza, *"My Friend is a Stranger": The Death Penalty and the Global Ius Commune of Human Rights*, *supra* n. 207, pp. 1039–1040.

Jus Constitutionale Commune that "seeks to preserve and protect the recognition of human dignity in a changing, independent, yet pluralistic world".[210]

5. CONCLUSION

This chapter has presented an alternative view to the foundations of the doctrine of conventionality control based on the principle of subsidiarity, hence departing from the idealistic view that conceived conventionality control as a doctrine based on the "principle of integration". On the basis of subsidiarity, the chapter has responded to the criticism based on orthodox views of public international law, and it has allowed a reconstruction of the normative consequences of conventionality control when the Inter-American Court is (1) addressing structural problems that require international intervention in concrete cases; and (2) when it is seen as a juridical instrument with general applicability for all the States parties to the American Convention.

Subsidiarity opens the door to argue that Article 2 recognizes a *high* but not *absolute* freedom for States to decide how to implement the American Convention and the jurisprudence of the Court. This means that the "legislative or other measures" chosen by States to comply with their international obligations find their limit in the principle of good faith and in the core of human rights as defined in the Inter-American *Corpus Juris*. Hence, when the Inter-American Court finds the existence of structural causes of human rights violations in concrete cases (i.e. anti-conventional interpretations, laws or practices), and when the State has proven to be incapable or unwilling to modify these structural causes, the Court shall legitimately intervene and order States to modify the laws and practices that produce those human rights violations. In those types of cases the Court is authorized to provide a *subsidium* that responds to the specific problems faced by a State, and this *subsidium* should not be considered *a priori* a violation to State's sovereignty.

The doctrine of conventionality control was created in *Almonacid* precisely as a *subsidium* to assist Chile to ensure core values of the American Convention and the jurisprudence of the Court since *Velásquez* – such as the protection of democracy, the rule of law, the fight against impunity and the protection of non-derogable rights. In *Almonacid*, the Court legitimately tackled a structural problem – produced by the existence and enforcement of amnesty law 2.191 – when it asked judges not to enforce a law that obstructed the investigation and punishment of perpetrators of a crime against humanity, and that was the

210 *See*, Paolo G. Carozza, *"My Friend is a Stranger": The Death Penalty and the Global Ius Commune of Human Rights*, *supra* n. 207, pp. 1084.

cause of the violation of the right of access to justice, truth and reparation of the relatives of Mr. Almonacid. Thus, it is possible to say that the necessity to empower the Chilean judiciary to fight against impunity in a particularly grave set of circumstances (the existence of a self-amnesty law null *ab initio*), and to ensure non-derogable rights of the relatives of Mr. Almonacid, is at the core of the existence of conventionality control.

Yet, it is evident that conventionality control acquired far-reaching purposes after the decision of *Aguado-Alfaro*, becoming a much more ambitious legal instrument to increase the effectiveness of the Inter-American *Corpus Juris* at the domestic level. The detachment of the set of circumstances that justified the *subsidium* provided by the Court in *Almonacid* does not necessarily mean that the doctrine of conventionality control must be rejected, although it requires a distinction to be made between its normative force at two levels: (1) when it is referred to as a "guarantee of non-repetition" to avoid the enforcement of anti-conventional laws (especially those that are null *ab initio*); and (2) when it is referred to as a doctrine with general applicability to increase the effectiveness of the Inter-American *Corpus Juris* at the domestic level. In the first case conventionality control is valid as much as it is possible to find structural problems that justify the Court's intervention (i.e. in *La Cantuta* or *Radilla*), which means that domestic authorities shall exercise conventionality control exactly as mandated by the Court; and in the second case conventionality control shall be understood with the normative force of a "principle" that heavily interacts with other rules and principles at the domestic level.

Conventionality control – understood as a principle – allows its incorporation to domestic legal systems without disregarding *a priori* the constitutional and statutory rules and principles that determine the competences of domestic authorities to exercise judicial review, the relevant procedural regulations that shape judicial processes, the hierarchy recognized to the American Convention and the jurisprudence of the Inter-American Court at the domestic level, the hermeneutical clauses for the solution of conflicts of rights of international and domestic origin, and the legitimate space of freedom that States have to determine the protection of human rights in their territory. This approach also allows the Court to avoid "amending" the American Convention with each decision in the exercise of its contentious or advisory jurisdiction, preserving its freedom to tackle extreme circumstances with a higher intervention but without compromising the stability of its own case law or its political strength. Finally, this view would allow State authorities to comply more effectively with the requirements of conventionality control, since it would respect rules and practices already exist at the domestic level.

In a few words, the principle of subsidiarity provides a strong justification for the existence of the doctrine of conventionality control. It allows making historical and normative sense of a doctrine that was created in a "praetorian" manner to fight against structural problems in Latin America, but which subsequently was expanded to increase the effectiveness of the Inter-American *Corpus Juris* in the region. The principle of subsidiarity allows one to coherently distinguish the normative force of conventionality control – in a manner that increases its legal validity and efficacy – as a juridical instrument to tackle specific problems (like the existence of anti-conventional laws that are also null *ab initio*), and as a general doctrine to guarantee a better protection of human rights in the States parties to the Convention. The approach developed in this chapter is a much safer path for the success of this doctrine as a vehicle for the effective implementation of the Inter-American *Corpus Juris* at the domestic level, for the maintenance of the institutional integrity of the Court as an international body of supervision, and for the development of a judicial dialogue and of a *Jus Constitutionale Commune* in the region.

GENERAL CONCLUSIONS

1. THE COURT AND ITS CIRCUMSTANCES

In the foreword to *Decisive Moments in History*, Stefan Zweig reflected on how unforgettable moments in history are linked to facts that precede human actions in crucial moments, for "all excitement needs time for preparation, and every real event must undergo development".[1] Zweig's reflection applies to those moments of humanity that radically change the course of history (as those brilliantly narrated in his book), yet it also applies to those unforgettable moments that occur in the lives of individuals, societies and governments. Since from time to time, among the vast number of insignificant and mundane things that occur in life, myriad events come together in narrows spans of time, allowing individuals to take actions that – even unknown to them – alter the course of history in concrete contexts. At the risk of sounding a bit too dramatic, this might be what happened in the year 2006 in the context of the Inter-American System of Human Rights, when the Inter-American Court of Human Rights created the doctrine of conventionality control in the case of *Almonacid Arellano and others v. Chile*.

The creation of this doctrine was precisely the result of a decision made by individuals searching for practical solutions to concrete problems, but who were also acting in a propitious context, and with ambitious future goals in mind. Paraphrasing José Ortega y Gasset, the inclusion of paragraph 124 in *Almonacid*, and its use in subsequent cases, was the result of "the Court and its circumstances".[2] Because the doctrine of conventionality control might never have been included in the body of the decision in *Almonacid*; or it might have passed as an extravagant occurrence of one its judges and a trusted clerk; or it might have been used only in cases of transitional justice against Chile and Peru, and then abandoned. But none of these things happened, and now conventionality control is a well-settled doctrine in the Court's case law. Why was this doctrine created and why is it still in use? To the extent that this book allows us to determine, the emergence and normative strength of conventionality control is intimately connected with four main factors.

1 Stefan Zweig, *Decisive Moments in History*, Preface pp. 5–6 (Ariadne Press, 1941).

2 José Ortega y Gasset, *Meditaciones del Quijote* (1914) (the phrase, in Spanish, reads as follows: "*Yo soy yo y mi circunstancia, y si no la salvo a ella no me salvo yo*").

First, conventionality control was created in the context of several transformations of constitutional law that have occurred in Latin America over the last decades.[3] Conventionality control was not created in a vacuum. The Inter-American Court noticed the phenomenon of the "constitutionalization of international law", and particularly how the mechanisms of protection by means of "constitutional guarantees" (*garantías constitucionales*) had been progressively expanded in order to protect human rights as enshrined in international treaties.[4] This phenomenon had progressively allowed for a more harmonious understanding of the relationship between the law and institutions of the Inter-American System, and the law and institutions of the States parties to the American Convention.[5] Hence, the doctrine of conventionality control was created, and found legitimacy, in the context of "the trend towards the 'constitutionalization' or 'nationalization' of 'international human rights law' and particularly the acceptance of conventional jurisprudence as a 'hermeneutic' element and for the 'control' of domestic regulations by the domestic courts themselves".[6]

Secondly, Conventionality control was created in connection with the Inter-American Court's progressive understanding of the normative force of Article 2 of the American Convention, and of its own remedial powers as an international tribunal.[7] Departing from previous jurisprudential criterion,[8]

---

3 *See*, Héctor Fix-Zamudio, *El derecho internacional de los derechos humanos en las Constituciones latinoamericanas y en la Corte Interamericana de Derechos Humanos*, 1 Revista Latinoamericana de Derecho 141 (2004); Rodrigo Uprimny, *The Recent Transformation of Constitutional Law in Latin America: Trends and Challenges* 89 Tex. L. Rev. 1587 (2010–2011); Laurence Burgorgue-Larsen, *Chronicle of a Fashionable Theory in Latin America. Decoding the Doctrinal Discourse of Conventionality Control*, in Yves Haeck, Oswaldo Ruiz-Chiriboga, and Clara Burbano-Herrera (Eds.), The Inter-American Court of Human Rights: Theory and Practice, Present and Future, p. 664 (Intersentia, 2015).

4 *See, Cabrera Garcia and Montiel Flores v. Mexico.* Preliminary Objections, Merits, Reparations and Costs Judgment, Inter-Am. Ct. H.R. (Ser. C) No. 220 (Nov. 26, 2010). Reasoned Concurrent Opinion of Judge Eduardo Ferrer Mac-Gregor Poisot, §21.

5 *See*, Sergio García Ramírez, *The Relationship Between Inter-American Jurisdiction and States (National Systems): Some Pertinent Questions*, 1(1) Notre Dame Journal of International and Comparative Law 125 (2015).

6 *Cabrera Garcia and Montiel Flores v. Mexico, supra* n. 4. Reasoned Concurrent Opinion of Eduardo Ferrer Mac-Gregor Poisot, §29.

7 *See generally, Caballero Delgado and Santana v. Colombia.* Reparations and Costs (Art. 63(1) American Convention on Human Rights). Judgment, Inter-Am. Ct. H.R. (Ser. C) No. 31 (Jan. 29, 1997). Dissenting Opinion of Judge A.A. Cançado Trindade, §6–9; *El Amparo v. Venezuela.* Judgment, Inter-Am. Ct. H.R. (Ser. C) No. 19 (Sep. 14, 1996). Dissenting Opinion of Judge A.A. Cançado Trindade, §3; Laurence Burgorgue-Larsen and Amaya Úbeda de Torres, The Inter-American Court on Human Rights. Case Law and Commentary 243–269 (Oxford University Press, 2011).

8 *See, International Responsibility for the Promulgation and Enforcement of Laws in Violation of the Convention (Arts. 1 and 2 American Convention on Human Rights).* Advisory Opinion OC-14/94 (Ser. A) No. 14 (Dec. 9, 1994) §49; *see also El Amparo v. Venezuela.* Judgment Inter-Am. Ct. H.R. (Ser. C) No. 19 (Jan. 18, 1995) §60.

since *Suárez Rosero v. Ecuador* (1997), the Inter-American Court started the practice of evaluating *in abstracto*, and in the exercise of its contentious jurisdiction, the compatibility between domestic laws and the American Convention.[9] This practice reached new heights when the Court declared the nullity *ab initio* of an amnesty law in the landmark case of *Barrios Altos v. Peru* (2001),[10] and when it ordered States to amend or annul norms (even those with constitutional hierarchy) that were found anti-conventional, as happened in *"The Last Temptation of Christ" (Olmedo Bustos) v. Chile* (2001).[11] So the creation of conventionality control constituted the last step taken on the basis of two assumptions: that Article 2 has a strong normative force, and that the Inter-American Court is in position to specify the "other measures" that States shall take to give effect to Article 1.1.[12]

Thirdly, conventionality control was created in the concrete set of circumstances that surrounded the decision in *Almonacid*. This case was a "point" in the line of jurisprudence that dealt with one of the most radical challenges faced by the Inter-American System since its creation: the existence and enforcement of amnesty laws that allowed impunity for perpetrators of serious human rights violations, and which gave rise to violations of the rights to access to justice, truth and reparation of the victims of those violations and for their relatives.[13] The extremity of the injustices produced by the existence and enforcement of these types of laws led the Inter-American Court to declare their nullity *ab initio* after *Barrios Altos*. The same spirit, which is intimately connected with the historic struggles of Latin America in the fight against impunity, and for the maintenance and consolidation of the rule of law in democratic regimes, is at the core of the creation and validity of the doctrine of conventionality control.[14]

Fourthly, conventionality control reflects the ideals and personal convictions of Sergio García Ramírez, the President of the Inter-American Court in 2006.[15]

---

9 *See, Suárez Rosero v. Ecuador Case.* Judgment, Inter-Am. Ct. H.R. (Ser. C) No. 35 (Nov. 12, 1997) §98.

10 *See, Barrios Altos v. Peru Case.* Judgment, Inter-Am. Ct. H.R. (Ser. C) No. 75 (Mar. 14, 2001) §44.

11 *See, "The Last Temptation of Christ" v. Chile Case (Olmedo Bustos et al.).* Judgment, Inter-Am. Ct. H.R. (Ser. C) No. 73 (Feb. 5, 2001) §90.

12 *See, Almonacid Arellano et al v. Chile.* Preliminary Objections, Merits, Reparations and Costs Judgment, Inter-Am. Ct. H.R. (Ser. C) No. 154 (Sep. 26, 2006) §123–124.

13 *See generally,* Dinah Shelton and Paolo G. Carozza, *Regional Protection of Human Rights*, pp. 923–942 (Oxford University Press, 2013).

14 *See generally,* Douglass Cassel, *El fallo Almonacid de la CIDH, y las obligaciones que de allí emanan para el Estado de Chile*, in Paulina Veloso (Ed.), *Justicia, Derechos Humanos y el Decreto Ley de Amnistía*, p. 87 (PNUD, 2010).

15 *See,* Sergio García Ramírez, *The Conventional Internal Control Court*, V(28) IUS Revista del Instituto de Ciencias Jurídicas de Puebla, Mexico 123–159 (2011); Sergio García Ramírez, *The Relationship Between Inter-American Jurisdiction and States (National Systems): Some Pertinent Questions*, *supra* n. 5.

He is the "father" - so to speak - of the idea of conventionality control. This idea finds its nominal and conceptual origins in his concurrent opinion in *Myrna Mack Chang v. Guatemala* (2003), where he reasoned that States must comply with their international obligations "as a whole".[16] By this he meant that domestic law provisions could not be invoked as a valid justification for lack of compliance with the judgments of the Inter-American Court.[17] This notion latter developed into the doctrine of (domestic) conventionality control, constituting an innovative means to reduce the gap between the duty of judges to apply domestic law and their duty to respect and ensure the rights protected by the American Convention.[18] Judges are the primordial guarantors of human rights, and conventionality control was a means of empowering them to comply with this duty notwithstanding the existence of domestic law to the contrary.[19]

The Mexican jurist recently captured the spirit that interconnects these factors in his description of conventionality control as part of the "Latin American Voyage" of human rights in the Inter-American System: "the nations of the Americas have made and are making their own voyage into the wind, from a certain point of departure, towards the common destiny of humanity: the arrival port that implies the definitive reign of human rights."[20] Conventionality control constitutes the last stage (chronologically speaking) of the efforts taken by the Inter-American Court both to mitigate the conflict between the national and the international realm of human rights, and to increase the effectiveness of the mechanisms of protection of the American Convention at the domestic level. Thus, this doctrine is the result of the ideas and actions of an international judicial institution navigating in the context of the "up's and down's, vicissitudes, advances and setbacks of the American voyage, and in the complex of relations between the international organs (especially the Court) and the national systems".[21]

2. THE ESSENCE OF CONVENTIONALITY CONTROL

During the last 12 years the Inter-American Court has progressively defined the content of conventionality control in more than 25 cases and in three

---

16 *See generally, Myrna Mack Chang v. Guatemala Case.* Judgment, Inter-Am. Ct. H.R. (Ser. C) No. 101 (Nov. 25, 2003). Concurrent Opinion of Sergio García Ramírez, §27.

17 *Id.* §26–32.

18 *See, La Cantuta v. Peru.* Merits, Reparations and Costs Judgment, Inter-Am. Ct. H.R. (Ser. C) No 162, (Nov. 29, 2006). Concurrent Opinion of Sergio García Ramírez, §8; *Dismissed Congressional Employees (Aguado-Alfaro et al.).* Preliminary Objections, Merits, Reparations and Costs Judgment, Inter-Am. Ct. H.R. (Ser. C) No. 158 (Nov. 24, 2006). Reasoned Concurrent Opinion of Sergio García Ramírez, §8.

19 *See*, Sergio García Ramírez, *The Relationship Between Inter-American Jurisdiction and States (National Systems): Some Pertinent Questions*, *supra* n. 5, p. 140.

20 *Id.* p. 119.

21 *Id.* p. 6.

Advisory Opinions. For this reason, a proper understanding of conventionality control cannot be made in the abstract, as if it were a finished doctrine created in *Almonacid*, or just by looking at the last decision where this doctrine is mentioned. It is necessary to evaluate all the cases that are part of the line of jurisprudence on conventionality control, with an emphasis on those that have added or refined aspects of this doctrine.[22] Accordingly, nine cases and two Advisory Opinions are particularly relevant to the conceptual understanding of conventionality control: *Almonacid*, *Dismissed Congressional Employees (Aguado-Alfaro) v. Peru* (2006), *Boyce and others v. Barbados* (2007), *Heliodoro Portugal v. Panama* (2008), *Radilla Pacheco v. Mexico* (2009), *Cabrera Garcia and Montiel Flores v. Mexico* (2010), *Gelman v. Uruguay* (2011), *Massacre of Santo Domingo v. Colombia* (2012), the *Resolution of Compliance with Gelman v. Uruguay Case* (2013), the *Advisory Opinion OC-21/14* (2014) and the *Advisory Opinion OC-22/16* (2016) and *Andrade Salmón v. Bolivia* (2016).

The analytical evaluation of the line of jurisprudence on conventionality control, and especially of the above-mentioned cases, allows for an understanding of the essential characteristics of this doctrine that were synthesized in a definition recently elaborated by Eduardo Ferrer Mac-Gregor Poisot. In accordance with the current Mexican judge, conventionality control is an

> International obligation in charge of all State authorities to the San José Pact to interpret any domestic legal norm (constitution, statutory law, decree law, regulation, etc.) in accordance with the American Convention and, in general, with the *Inter-American Corpus Juris*, which is integrated by the American Convention on Human Rights, the jurisprudence of the Court, and other binding human rights instruments; if there is clear incompatibility between the domestic legal standard and the *Corpus Juris*, State authorities should refrain from enforcing domestic legal standards to prevent violations of internationally protected human rights. State authorities must exercise control conventionality control *ex officio*, but always acting within their respective competences and the corresponding procedural regulations.[23]

This definition reflects the most recent developments in the Inter-American Court's jurisprudence on this subject, and for that reason it should be

---

22 *See*, Claudio Nash Rojas, *Control de Convencionalidad. Cuadernillo de la Corte Interamericana de Derechos Humanos No. 7* (Inter-American Court of Human Rights & Ministerio de Relaciones Exteriores de Dinamarca, 2015) and Silvia Serrano Guzmán, *El control de convencionalidad en la jurisprudencia de la Corte Interamericana de Derechos Humanos* (Comisión Nacional de los Derechos Humanos, 2013).

23 Eduardo Ferrer Mac-Gregor Poisot, *Control de Convencionalidad (sede interna)*, in Eduardo Ferrer Mac-Gregor Poisot, Fabiola Martínez Ramírez, and Giovanni Figeroa Mejía (Eds.), *Diccionario de Derecho Procesal Constitucional y Convencional*, Vol. I, p. 233 (Poder Judicial de la Federación, Consejo de la Judicatura Federal, Universidad Nacional Autónoma de México & Instituto de Investigaciones Jurídicas, 2014).

considered authoritative. It also distinguishes the essential components of conventionality control that can be systematized in the following manner.

Nature of the obligation. Conventionality control constitutes an international legal obligation based on Articles 1.1, 2 and 29 of the American Convention, and on Articles 26 and 27 of the Vienna Convention on the Law of Treaties. In the Court's theory, domestic authorities are directly bound by the American Convention, which means that they are obligated – as a matter of international law, not of domestic law – to observe that all the effects of the Inter-American *Corpus Juris* are not adversely affected by the enforcement of domestic laws that are contrary to its content, object and purpose.[24] This means that the interpretation and enforcement of domestic law shall be consistent with the international human rights obligations of the State.[25] The duty of State authorities to respect and ensure the rights recognized in the American Convention (Article 1.1), and the duty to adopt the legislative and other measures to ensure the rights and freedoms protected by the American Convention (Article 2), requires all domestic authorities to exercise conventionality control. This obligation is strengthened by the duty to comply with treaties in good faith (*pacta sunt servanda*), and the prohibition against invoking the provisions of domestic law as justification for the failure to perform a treaty (Articles 26 and 27 of the VCLT).[26]

Subjects of the obligation. The obligation to exercise conventionality control is primarily directed at the judiciary, owing to the crucial role that judges play in the protection of the right of access to justice and the rule of law in a democratic State.[27] But since *Cabrera* and *Gelman*, conventionality control has been constructed as an obligation for all State authorities, regardless of whether or not they belong to the executive, legislative or judicial power. This idea takes to its ultimate consequences the notion that the general obligations of States – in terms of Articles 1.1 and 2, and as interpreted since *Velásquez Rodríguez v. Honduras* (1988) – affect it "as a whole".[28] Because if all State authorities have a direct obligation to respect and ensure the rights and freedoms protected by the Inter-American *Corpus Juris*; and these obligations require domestic authorities to take the other measures necessary to achieve the effectiveness of the Inter-American *Corpus Juris*, and conventionality control is a valid other measure

24 *See, Almonacid Arellano et al. v. Chile, supra* n. 12, §123–124.

25 *Andrade Salmón v. Bolivia.* Merits, Reparations and Costs Judgment, Inter-Am. Ct. H.R. (Ser. C) No. 330 (Dec. 1, 2016), §93.

26 *See, Cabrera Garcia and Montiel Flores v. Mexico, supra* n. 4. Reasoned Concurrent Opinion of Judge Eduardo Ferrer Mac-Gregor Poisot, §59.

27 *See generally, Castillo Petruzzi et al. v. Peru.* Judgment, Inter-Am. Ct. H.R. (Ser. C) No. 52 (May 30, 1999) §82.

28 *See, Velásquez Rodríguez v. Honduras.* Merits, Inter-Am. Ct. H.R. (Ser. C) No. 4, 164 (Jul. 29, 1988) §166; *Myrna Mack Chang v. Guatemala, supra* n. 16. Reasoned Concurrent Opinion of Sergio García Ramírez, §27.

in terms of Article 2, then all State authorities must exercise conventionality control in order to comply with their duties under Article 1.1 and general international law.

Object of the obligation. The specific actions required by conventionality control have a core and a periphery. The core of conventionality control are those actions essential to conventionality control as a general doctrine: (1) the obligation to perform a consistent interpretation between domestic laws and the Inter-American *Corpus Juris*; and (2) the obligation to avoid the enforcement of domestic laws that cannot be interpreted in accordance with the Inter-American *Corpus Juris*. The periphery of conventionality control are those actions that have been connected with the exercise of conventionality control in very concrete sets of circumstances: (3) the obligation of judges to fill legal lacunae in criminal law, specifically in order to prosecute those responsible for the crime of forced disappearance of persons (i.e. *Heliodoro*);[29] (4) the obligation of legislators to avoid the enactment of statutory laws contrary to the Inter-American *Corpus Juris*, even when they are backed by popular support (i.e. *Gelman*);[30] and (5) the obligation of the judiciary to ensure the effectiveness of the judgments of the Inter-American Court in cases where the State is a party to the controversy (i.e. *Resolution of Compliance with Gelman*).[31]

Special features of the obligation. Conventionality control must be exercised by all domestic authorities "*ex officio* between domestic norms and the American Convention, evidently in the context of their respective spheres of competence and the corresponding procedural regulations".[32] The obligation to exercise conventionality control *ex officio* is an aspect of the principle of *iura novit curia*, to the extent that all domestic authorities, especially judges, shall take a strong pro victim approach and enforce the rules and principles of the Inter-American *Corpus Juris* whether the parties have invoked it or not.[33] But this is not a call for unrestricted judicial activism. Domestic authorities shall exercise conventionality control in the sphere of authority conferred to them by domestic law, and they must respect the procedural regulations that shape the judicial process.[34] So conventionality control is designed to couple with the powers and attributions of domestic authorities, and with the procedural regulations already in place in the laws of different States parties to the American Convention.

29 *See, Heliodoro Portugal v. Panama.* Preliminary Objections, Merits, Reparations and Costs Judgment, Inter-Am. Ct. H.R. (Ser. C) No. 186 (Aug. 12, 2008), §180.

30 *See, Gelman v. Uruguay.* Preliminary Objections, Merits, Reparations and Costs Judgment, Inter-Am. Ct. H.R. (Ser. C) No. 221 (Feb. 24, 2011) §239.

31 *Id.* Resolution for Monitoring Compliance, §68.

32 *Dismissed Congressional Employees (Aguado-Alfaro et al.) v. Peru, supra* n. 18, §128.

33 *See, Cabrera Garcia and Montiel Flores v. Mexico, supra* n. 4. Reasoned Concurrent Opinion of Eduardo Ferrer Mac-Gregor Poisot, §42.

34 *See*, Sergio García Ramírez, *The Conventional Internal Control Court, supra* n. 15, p. 141.

Parameters of conventionality control. Domestic authorities must exercise conventionality control on the basis of the Inter-American *Corpus Juris*. The Inter-American *Corpus Juris* is a term that, in its broadest meaning, constitutes "a set of instruments of international human rights law of varied content and juridical effects".[35] It includes the American Convention, treaties with similar nature, the interpretations of treaties made by the Inter-American Court in the exercise of its contentious, advisory, preventive and monitoring jurisdiction, and other instruments of soft law such as the American Declaration of the Rights and Duties of Man, or the decisions of the Inter-American Commission.[36] There has not been much discussion on how the different normative force of these instruments – as sources of international law, and not of constitutional law – are relevant factors in domestic authorities' exercise of conventionality control. Yet it is reasonable to assume that these differences *do matter*, so domestic authorities shall "take into consideration" the norms and principles of the Inter-American *Corpus Juris* depending on how binding they are for States as a matter of international law and constitutional law taken altogether.

3. A CONTROVERSIAL DOCTRINE OF INTERNATIONAL LAW

Notwithstanding the enormous jurisprudential and academic production on conventionality control, little has been said about its controversial nature as an international legal institution.[37] The lack of discussion on this point perhaps reflects an implicit embracing of the idea that the Inter-American System is a "self-contained regime", whose rules and principles of operation function independently of general international law. If this approach is right, then the validity of the decisions of the Inter-American Court cannot be tested by external standards to those of the Inter-American System. This theoretical point

35 *The Right to Information on Consular Assistance in the Framework of the Guarantees of the due Process of Law*. Advisory Opinion OC-16, Inter-Am. Ct. H.R. (Ser. A) No. 16 (Oct. 1, 1999), §115.

36 *See, Dismissed Congressional Employees (Aguado-Alfaro et al.) v. Peru*, *supra* n. 18, Reasoned Concurrent Opinion of Sergio García Ramírez, §2.

37 *See*, Ariel E. Dulitzky, *An Inter-American Constitutional Court? The Invention of conventionality control by the Inter-American Court of Human Rights*, 50 Tex. Int'l L. J. 57 (2015); Cristina Binder, *The Prohibition of Amnesties by the Inter-American Court of Human Rights*, 12 German Law Journal 1216 (2011); Luigi Crema, "Are Amnesties Still an Option? A Non-Policy Based Critique of the Inter-American Approach", Center for Civil and Human Rights, University of Notre Dame, Working Paper Series # 6, pp. 50–51 (2013); Guillermo Enrique Estrada Adán, *Una Visión del Control de Convencionalidad desde el Derecho Internacional*, in Maria Leoba Castaneda Rivas, *Homenaje al Maestro Edmundo Elías Musi* (Porrúa, 2013); Ezequiel Malarino, *Judicial Activism, Punitivism, and Supranationalisation: Illiberal Tendencies of the Inter-American Court of Human Rights*, 12 International Criminal Law Review 665–695 (2012).

of departure is certainly possible, although it is contrary to the accepted view that regional human rights systems are and should be structurally connected with the rules and principles of positive international law.[38] If there is a normative connection between general international law and the Inter-American System, then the fact that conventionality control is consolidated in the jurisprudence of the Inter-American Court is not sufficient reason to affirm the validity of its legal grounds or normative components.

In fact, four serious objections could be formulated against conventionality control if it is seen from an orthodox interpretation of positive international law.

First, conventionality control cannot be considered an "other measure" in terms of Article 2. This position is based on a reading of Article 2 that pays special attention to the ordinary meaning of its terms which do not specify the type of "legislative and other measures" that States shall take to ensure the effectiveness of the American Convention.[39] Using the language of the International Law Commission, it is possible to say that Article 2 imposes "obligations of results" and not "obligations of specific conduct", which means that States have complete freedom to decide the legislative and other measures necessary to give effect to the American Convention.[40] This position finds some support in the preparatory works of the American Convention, where some States agreed to the inclusion of Article 2 on the basis that they kept the exclusive competence to decide how to put the American Convention into effects[41] The first decisions of the Inter-American Court also support this conclusion, since there was an understanding that the jurisdiction of the Court was "intended to protect the rights and freedoms of specific individuals, not to resolve abstract questions".[42]

Secondly, Articles 26 and 27 of the Vienna Convention do not support the theory that domestic authorities shall exercise conventionality control. These rules reaffirm that treaties must be performed in good faith, and that the binding force of a treaty is determined solely by international law.[43] But these rules are

---

38 *See*, Report of the Study Group of the ILC on Fragmentation of International Law: difficulties arising from the diversification and expansion of International Law, Doc. No. A/CN4/L.682 (April 13, 2006).

39 Organization of American States, American Convention on Human Rights, Nov. 22, 1969, O.A.S.T.S. No. 36, 1144, U.N.T.S. 123, Art. 2.

40 *See generally*, Sixth Report on State Responsibility by Mr. Roberto Argo, Special Rapporteur – the internationally wrongful act of the State, source of international responsibility (continued), Ybk ILC, 1977, Vol. II (1) A/CN.4/302 and Add.1, 2 & 3., §17.

41 *See*, Inter-American Specialized Conference on Human Rights, San José, Costa Rica, Nov. 7–22, 1969, Proceedings and Documents, OEA.Ser.K/XVI/1.2, 1978, Doc. 5, at 38.

42 *International Responsibility for the Promulgation and Enforcement of Laws in Violation of the Convention (Arts. 1 and 2 American Convention on Human Rights).* Advisory Opinion OC-14, Inter-Am. Ct. H.R. (Ser. A) No. 14 (Dec. 9, 1994) §49.

43 *See*, Olivier Corten and Pierre Klein (Eds.), *The Vienna Conventions on the Law of Treaties. A Commentary*, Vol. I, pp. 659–701 (Oxford University Press, 2011); Oliver Dörr and Kirsten Schmalenbach (Eds.), *Vienna Convention on the Law of Treaties. A Commentary*, pp. 427–453 (Springer, 2012).

not absolute, nor do they operate in isolation from other rules and principles of general international law. They exist in relation to the rights of States as sovereigns, including the right to decide the extent to which States are bound by norms of international origin (i.e. they keep the right to establish reservations and declarations), and the right to decide the way in which international obligations shall be implemented at the domestic level (which implies that international law is not supreme to constitutional law).[44] So it is not possible to autonomously derive from Articles 26 and 27 alone that domestic authorities shall enforce international law without implementation, or that they shall prefer international law over domestic law.

Thirdly, the obligatoriness of conventionality control cannot be justified from the binding force of the Inter-American Court's jurisprudence, because the doctrine of precedent does not exist in international law. There is no norm in the American Convention or in general international law that obliges the authorities of the States parties to the American Convention to consider the interpretations of the Inter-American Court as precedents.[45] The judgments of international courts and tribunals are subject to the principles of relativity and indifference, namely that judgments are binding just for specific cases and that States are free to decide how to comply with these judgments. This weakens the argument that a doctrine created as the result of an interpretation of Article 2 could be the source of international legal obligations beyond specific cases. Furthermore, there is a problem of political legitimacy and logical coherency in arguing that, through conventionality control (which is a jurisprudential creation), the jurisprudence of the Inter-American Court now has the normative force of a precedent.[46]

These critiques are the consequence of two structural notions that have defined the theory and practice of international law since its inception: that the consent of States as sovereigns is the most relevant factor to identify the origin and content of international rights and obligations, as established in treaties and custom;[47] and that there is a strict separation between the rights and obligations of States as subjects of international law (as legal persons) and the obligations

---

44 *See generally, Request for Interpretation of the Judgment of 31 March in the Case concerning Avena and other Mexican Nationals (Mexico v. United States of America).* Judgment, 2009 I.C.J. (Jan. 19), §44.

45 *See*, Ezequiel Malarino, *Acerca de la Pretendida Obligatoriedad de la Jurisprudencia de los Órganos Interamericanos de Protección de Derechos Humanos para los Tribunales Judiciales Nacionales*, in *Sistema Interamericano de Protección de los Derechos Humanos y Derecho Penal* Internacional, p. 438 (Konrad-Adenauer-Stiftung, 2010).

46 *See*, Luigi Crema, "Are Amnesties Still an Option? A Non-Policy Based Critique of the Inter-American Approach", *supra* n. 37, p. 51.

47 *See generally, S.S. Lotus, (France v. Turkey)* 1927 P.C.I.J., Ser. A, No. 10, at 18 (Sep. 7); *Military and Paramilitary Activities in and Against Nicaragua (Nicar. v. U.S.).* Merits, 1986 I.C.J. 14 (Jun. 27), §269; Hugo Grotious, *Prolegomena*, in Robert J. Beck, Anthony C. Arend and Robert D. Vander Lugt, *International Rules*, p. 42 (Oxford University Press, 1996).

of specific authorities in those States to protect those rights and obligations.[48] These structural notions, which underline the traditional understanding of the content and effects of international norms, prevent international institutions from formulating theories that may constitute an intrusion into the traditional sphere of the State's competences. And this might be especially true in the Inter-American System, which upheld the principle of the prohibition of the OAS to intervene in matters that are within the domestic jurisdiction of States long before the adoption of the American Convention.

4. A NEW APPROACH BASED ON THE PRINCIPLE OF SUBSIDIARITY

But interpreting the American Convention in light of the principle of subsidiarity serves as a valid justification for the existence of the doctrine of conventionality control. It provides a theoretical ground to answer the criticism based on positive international law, but it also avoids the temptation of adopting radical monist views that claim the supremacy of international law and international institutions over domestic law and domestic institutions.[49] The principle of subsidiarity can be defined as

> a principle of justice that requires larger communities to protect the legitimate autonomy of smaller communities to provide them with assistance (*subsidium*) needed to fulfill their ends, and to coordinate and regulate their activities within the common good of a larger community, of which they are part and which is also necessary to the flourishing of their individual members.[50]

It also constitutes a structural principle of international human rights law.[51] This principle is implicitly established in the Preamble of the American Convention, which justifies the existence of an international system for the protection of human rights as "reinforcing or complementing the protection provided by the domestic law of the American states".[52] The Inter-American

48 Ian Brownlie, *Principles of Public International Law*, p. 32 (Oxford University Press, 7th ed., 2008).

49 *See generally*, A.A. Cançado Trindade, *Os Tribunais Internacionais e a Realizacao da Justica*, p. 49 (RENOVAR, 2015).

50 Paolo G. Carozza, *The Problematic Applicability of Subsidiarity to International Law and Institutions*, 61(1) The American Journal of Jurisprudence 53 (2016); *see generally*, John Finnis, *Limited Government*, in *Human Rights & Common Good. Collected Essays: Volume III*, p. 90 (Oxford University Press, 2011).

51 *Id.*; Dinah Shelton (Ed.), *The Oxford Handbook of International Human Rights Law*, p. 4 (Oxford University Press, 2013).

52 American Convention on Human Rights, *supra* n. 39, Preamble.

Court has also referred to it, for instance in *Acevedo Jaramillo et. al v. Peru*, in order to explain that the State:

> 66. … is the main guarantor of the human rights of the individual, so that, if an act that violates the said rights occurs, it is the State itself that has the obligation to decide the matter at the domestic level and, [as appropriate,] to make reparation, before having to respond before international instances, such as the inter-American system, which derives from the subsidiary nature of the international proceedings in relation to the national systems that guarantee human rights.[53]

The Court has referred succinctly to the relationship between conventionality control and the principle of complementarity or subsidiarity in the recent cases of *Santo Domingo Massacre* and *Andrade Salmón*. True, the Court has not developed in depth the normative consequences of this new approach, but – as has been argued in this book – subsidiarity opens the door to justify the creation of this doctrine and to shape its form in the future. On the basis of this principle, Article 2 can be legitimately interpreted as a norm that grants a *high* but not an *absolute* freedom for States to decide how to implement the Inter-American *Corpus Juris* at the domestic level. This means that the freedom of States to choose the "legislative and other measures" to ensure the effectiveness of human rights finds its limit in the principle of good faith and in the core of human rights as protected in the Inter-American System. So when the Inter-American Court identifies structural causes of human rights violations in concrete cases (i.e. when it finds the existence of anti-conventional interpretations or laws that are the causes of human rights violations), and when the State has proved to be incapable or unwilling to modify these structural causes (i.e. as happened with Chile in *Almonacid* or with Peru in *La Cantuta*), the Court shall legitimately intervene, on the basis of Articles 2 and 63.1, and order States to modify the interpretation or the content of concrete interpretations, laws or practices that are the cause of those human rights violations. In these types of cases the Inter-American Court is authorized to provide a *subsidium* that responds to the specific challenges faced by specific States.

The creation of the doctrine of conventionality control in *Almonacid* is justified precisely because it constituted a *subsidium* to assist Chile in an extreme circumstance that affected core values of the Inter-American System (such as the protection of democracy, the rule of law and the fight against impunity), and which the Chilean authorities were unable to solve by their own means. In *Almonacid*, the Court legitimately tackled a structural problem by declaring the nullity *ab initio* of Decree Law 2.191, and by asking domestic judges to

---

53 *Acevedo Jaramillo et al. v. Peru*. Interpretation of the Judgment on Preliminary Objections, Merits, Reparations and Costs, Inter-Am. Ct. H.R. (Ser. C) No. 157 (Nov. 24, 2006) §66.

exercise conventionality control, in order to avoid future violations of the right to access to justice, truth and reparation of other victims of serious human rights violations committed during the dictatorship. So, the creation of the doctrine of conventionality control is justified owing to the particular grave set of circumstances that surrounded *Almonacid*, and owing to the necessity to prevent new acts of injustice derived from the existence and enforcement of Decree Law 2.191.

Conventionality control acquired far-reaching purposes after the decision of *Aguado-Alfaro*, when the Court started to conceive conventionality control as a doctrine with general applicability. The detachment of the set of circumstances that justified the *subsidium* provided by the Court in *Almonacid* does not necessarily mean that conventionality control must be rejected as an aim to increase the effective application of international human rights standards. Nevertheless, its normative force must be distinguished on two levels: (1) when it is referred to as a "guarantee of non-repetition" to avoid the enforcement of anti-conventional laws (especially those that are null *ab initio*); and (2) when it is referred to as a doctrine with general applicability to increase the effectiveness of the Inter-American *Corpus Juris* at the domestic level. In the first case the use of conventionality control is valid as much as it is possible to find structural problems that justify the Court's mandate for domestic authorities to set aside a specific interpretation, law or practice in the exact terms of a particular judgment; and in the second case conventionality control shall be understood with the normative force of a "principle" that heavily interacts with rules and principles at the domestic level.

There are important normative consequences for distinguishing the normative force of conventionality control as a guarantee of non-repetition and as a principle. In the first hypothesis, conventionality control obliges all State authorities to remedy the causes of human rights violations provoked by the existence, interpretation and enforcement of specific pieces of legislation found anti-conventional by the Court in the exercise of its contentious jurisdiction (i.e. Decree Law 2.191 in *Almonacid*, or Article 57 of the Code of Military Justice and Article 13 of the Constitution in *Radilla*). In this hypothesis, the authority of the Inter-American Court to order States to exercise conventionality control finds its basis in Article 63.1 and 2; and the obligation of States to comply with this order comes from Article 68.1 in connection with Articles 2 and 1.1. In short, the Inter-American Court is providing a *subsidium* for State authorities so they have clear guidance on how to interpret or a mandate not to enforce a domestic law proved to be the cause of human rights violations.

But in the second hypothesis the situation is different. Here conventionality control is considered an integral part of Article 2. In this hypothesis the Inter-American Court is developing the content of the general obligations of the States parties to the American Convention, and so acts as a kind of judicial legislator. Yet the Court has not been vested with the power to create law, at least not in the same manner that States have been.[54] So it is reasonable to assume that the standards developed by the Court through its jurisprudence, including the doctrine of conventionality control, have a different normative value from those agreed upon by the express consent of States, or those that have an uncontroversial conventional basis (like the reparations ordered by the Court in specific cases). This does not necessarily mean that the decisions of the Inter-American Court are deprived of any normative value beyond specific cases,[55] but these standards should certainly be considered to have a different texture from the norms contained in treaties. This is why conventionality control must be considered to have the normative force of a principle when it is seen as a general doctrine.

This distinction has crucial consequences. In the first hypothesis, conventionality control must be exercised by domestic authorities notwithstanding domestic law in contrary, because the State cannot invoke the norms of its domestic legal system in order not to comply with an Inter-American Court's judgment, as is clear from Articles 68.1 of the Convention and 26 and 27 of the Vienna Convention. Nevertheless, in the second hypothesis the normative value and the operation of conventionality control at the domestic level shall be intimately connected with procedural and substantive rules and principles of domestic law. This happens because Article 2 grants States ample freedom to decide how to implement the Inter-American *Corpus Juris* through domestic law, policies and judicial decisions. Consequently, when conventionality control is considered to have the normative force of a principle, its operation as a general doctrine shall have different "intensities" in different States.

At least three elements shall "regulate" the "intensity" of conventionality control at the domestic level.

The first are the respective competences and the corresponding procedural regulations recognized by State law, as they have been clearly defined by the Court since *Aguado-Alfaro*.[56] This caveat to the operation of conventionality control comes from the Court's solution to oblige domestic authorities to exercise conventionality control *ex officio*, but not "authorize" them to act beyond the powers conferred by domestic law or open the way for the disregard of the procedural regulations that shape the judicial process.[57] Conventionality control is based on the notion that States have the freedom to decide how to organize the powers and attributions of domestic authorities (for instance, if there is a diffuse or concentrated system of judicial review), and on the type of formalities for the admissibility and substantiation of legal remedies (which are

---

54 *See*, Collin Warbrick, *States and Recognition of International Law*, in MALCOLM D. EVANS (ED.), *INTERNATIONAL LAW*, p. 229 (Oxford University Press, 2nd ed., 2006).

55 *See*, IAN BROWNLIE, *PRINCIPLES OF PUBLIC INTERNATIONAL LAW*, *supra* n. 48, p. 19.

56 *See*, *Dismissed Congressional Employees (Aguado-Alfaro et al.) v. Peru*, *supra* n. 18, §128.

57 *See*, Sergio García Ramírez, *The Conventional Internal Control Court*, *supra* n. 15, p. 151.

determined entirely by domestic law, and which are an essential component of a proper administration of justice).[58]

The second are the norms of constitutional and statutory law that affect the hierarchy and substance of the Inter-American *Corpus Juris* in specific domestic legal systems. Conceiving the normative force of this doctrine as a principle supports the view that the obligation of domestic authorities to exercise conventionality control must be understood in the light of the relevant rules of constitutional and statutory law that define the place and operation of the different elements of the Inter-American *Corpus Juris* (i.e. treaties and the jurisprudence of the Inter-American Court) at the domestic level. This happens because Article 2 confers ample freedom to determine how the provisions of the American Convention shall have effect at the domestic level.[59] Here it is important to remember that the duty of States to undertake the "legislative" and "other measures" needed to give effect to the rights and freedoms protected by the American Convention must be fulfilled "in accordance with the constitutional processes and the provisions of [the] Convention".[60]

The third are the specific regulations in the Inter-American *Corpus Juris* of the right involved in a particular case. Conventionality control in the light of the principle of subsidiarity would require State authorities to evaluate seriously the language used in particular provisions of the American Convention and of any other treaty, and in the possibilities that the treaty offers to establish limitations and derogations to specific rights in order to protect aspects of the common good that have a social nature (like the "security", "order", "health" or "morals" of a society). This approach would distinguish cases where international standards derived from treaties trump any consideration of domestic law or culture, and those cases where these standards allow more freedom for the legislative power or the judiciary at the domestic level to legislate or to decide cases in a legitimate variety of ways. Because asking domestic authorities to control the conventionality of domestic laws in accordance with the standards established in treaty law regarding the prohibition against torture (which is an absolute right), is different from asking them to do so in accordance with the standards regarding freedom of expression (which is a right that can be subject to limitations).

It also follows from this approach that substantive and not just formal considerations shall regulate the intensity of the obligation of domestic authorities to take into account the jurisprudence of the Inter-American Court. Domestic authorities, when taking into account the ICtHR's jurisprudence as a

---

58 *See*, María Carmelina Londoño Lázaro, *The Legality Principle and the Conventionality Control: Confluences and Developments in the Inter-American Court of Human Rights*, 128 Boletin Mexicano de Derecho Comparado 27 (2010).

59 *See*, Dinah Shelton and Paolo G. Carozza, *Regional Protection of Human Rights*, *supra* n. 13, p. 113.

60 American Convention on Human Rights, *supra* n. 39, Art. 2.

parameter for conventionality control, shall evaluate the specific facts involved in a case and the nature of the right that was violated in that case. Because asking domestic authorities to control the conventionality of domestic laws following the standards developed in the case law on forced disappearance,[61] which is a line of jurisprudence connected with serious and unquestionable violations to human dignity, is not the same thing as asking domestic authorities to control the conventionality of domestic laws following the standards developed in the case law on the right to life of the unborn,[62] which is a highly contested question that is intimately connected with the moral, social and political life of different States parties to the American Convention.

Conventionality control constructed in light of the principle of subsidiarity would actually preserve the Inter-American Court's freedom to tackle extreme circumstances with higher intervention, and it would justify the practice of ordering State authorities to exercise conventionality control as a "guarantee of non-repetition" in accordance with the standards developed in a particular case. But this view would avoid considering that the Inter-American Court is "amending" the American Convention with every decision taken in the exercise of its contentious or advisory jurisdiction. This approach would allow conventionality control to become a doctrine with general applicability that, as a matter of principle and not just of political reality, couples with domestic legal systems in a form that respects both the freedom of States to decide how the different elements of the Inter-American *Corpus Juris* operate at the domestic level, and the freedom of domestic authorities (especially judges) to decide how specific rights are interpreted and enforced attending to the factual and legal circumstances of concrete cases.

Distinguishing between a "hard" and a "flexible" version of conventionality control would allow this doctrine to become a juridical instrument capable of solving structural problems identified by the Inter-American Court in concrete cases, increasing also the effectiveness of the Inter-American *Corpus Juris* at the domestic level without hindering legal pluralism, contributing to the judicial dialogue between domestic and international institutions in the Inter-American System, and generating the conditions for the construction of a *Jus Constitutionale Commune* that recognizes the complexity of the relationship between international human rights law and particular positive law in the region.[63]

---

61 *See, Velásquez Rodríguez v. Honduras Case, supra* n. 28.

62 *See, Artavia Murillo et al. (in vitro fertilization) v. Costa Rica.* Preliminary Objections, Merits, Reparations and Costs Judgment, Inter-Am. Ct. H.R. (Ser. C) No. 257 (Nov. 28, 2012).

63 *See generally,* Paolo G. Carozza, *Human Dignity and Judicial Interpretation of Human Rights,* 19 Eur. J. Int'l L. 933 (2008).

5. AN ONGOING CONVERSATION

This book is not – and does not pretend to be – the final word on conventionality control. It is part of an ongoing academic conversation about this topic, and in general about the principles and practices that shape the relationship between international human rights law and constitutional law in the context of the Inter-American System.[64] So there are still important questions that require further thinking and writing by international, constitutional and procedural law scholars, both from a theoretical and a practical standpoint.

From a theoretical standpoint, an issue that is still pending is the development of new categories that allow a better understanding and practice of how the law and institutions of the Inter-American System should interact with the law and institutions of the States parties to the American Convention. Scholars seem to agree on the insufficiencies of the theories of monism and dualism as categories to understand this relationship, but there is not yet a comprehensive alternative to these views. So, it is necessary to explore, develop and apply new theories that are sound, and that are connected to the normative and political realities of the Inter-American System. Paolo G. Carozza (who argues from the principle of subsidiarity a new way of thinking about the relationship between States and international institutions) or Armin Von Bogdandy (who argues that a theory of legal pluralism can account for the diversity and links between international law and domestic law) are good examples of the types of approaches that may serve as points of departure for this understanding.[65] Thinking critically and seriously about this theoretical question is certainly a project for years to come, but it is one that can help to solve some of the most important tensions that hinder the effective protection of human rights in the Inter-American System.

Here it is relevant to mention the suggestive concept of *Jus Constitutionale Commune* (or ICCAL, as it is also referred to by its creators).[66] This concept indicates "an original Latin American path of transformative constitutionalism" that integrates elements from various legal orders (both national and

---

64 *See generally*, Laurence Burgorgue-Larsen, *Chronicle of a Fashionable Theory in Latin America. Decoding the Doctrinal Discourse of Conventionality Control*, in Yves Haeck, Oswaldo Ruiz-Chiriboga and Clara Burbano-Herrera (Eds.), *The Inter-American Court of Human Rights: Theory and Practice, Present and Future*, pp. 663–675 (Intersentia, 2015) (for an analysis of the different "schools of thought" that exist on conventionality control).

65 *See generally*, Paolo G. Carozza, *Subsidiarity as a Structure Principle of International Law*, *supra* n. 50, p. 63; Armin Von Bogdandy, *Pluralism, direct effect, and the ultimate say: On the relationship between international and domestic constitutional law*, 6 Int'l J. Const. L. 397–401 (2008).

66 *See*, Armin Von Bogdandy et al., *Ius Constitutionale Commune en America Latina. A Regional Approach to Transformative Constitutionalism*, in Armin Von Bogdandy, et al., *Transformative Constitutionalism in Latin America. The Emergence of a New Ius Commune*, p. 4 (Oxford University Press, 2017).

international). From a normative perspective, ICCAL aims to expand the protection of human rights standards and to empower social actors.[67] Its theoretical basis and institutional support makes it a concept that has the potential to reshape the relationship between international law and constitutional law in the region, especially regarding human rights questions. Yet, the legitimacy and effectiveness of this concept might be connected with its capacity to evolve as an idea that advances the common good in the region (through the full realization of democracy, the rule of law and human rights) by truly recognizing, respecting and integrating the plurality of ideas, institutions, values, voices and cultures in the region. That will always remain one of the central challenges inscribed in international human rights law, both from a theoretical and a practical perspective.

Additionally, further studies are needed on how conventionality control should couple in specific domestic legal systems. If the theories of monism (which considers international law as supreme to domestic law) and dualism (which considers international law and constitutional law as two radically separated areas of law) are no longer valid frameworks for the understanding of the relationship between international law and domestic law in the Inter-American System, then the manner in which conventionality control operates in specific States cannot be defined exclusively from rules of international law, or exclusively from rules of constitutional law. This book has proposed a series of factors that shall regulate the intensity of conventionality control in concrete domestic legal systems, but it is still necessary to study in detail the rules of constitutional and procedural law that shape the operation of conventionality control in Argentina, Colombia, Mexico and all the other States parties to the American Convention. This is a work that needs to be done by scholars who have a deep knowledge of international human rights law, of the doctrine of conventionality control and of the substantive and procedural aspects of constitutional law that define how international law is incorporated in concrete States.

Furthermore, it is necessary to develop legal standards that distinguish cases where the Inter-American Court shall declare the anti-conventionality of interpretations, laws or practices from those cases where it shall only declare the violation of specific rights of the American Convention and the duty to repair. If the hypothesis of this book is correct, the strength of the obligation of domestic authorities to exercise conventionality control in specific cases follows the level of anti-conventionality of concrete interpretations, laws or practices at the domestic level (as happened in *Almonacid* with Decree Law 2.191, or in *Radilla* with Article 57 of the Code of Military Justice), and the level of fairness and precision in the Court's *determinatio* of the type of actions that States must undertake as guarantees of non-repetition. But the Court shall develop

---

67 *Ibid.*

parameters that define when it will exercise "concentrated conventionality control" on domestic laws and practices, and therefore when it would order State authorities to amend or repeal laws and/or to exercise conventionality control as a guarantee of non-repetition; and when it will stay at the "boundaries of domestic law" by granting a margin of appreciation for States (so they can freely decide how to deal with their laws and practices at the domestic level in order to avoid future human rights violations).

It is not yet totally clear how conventionality control serves as a vehicle for the existence of a multilevel dialogue among judicial and political institutions, and for the creation of a *Jus Constitutionale Commune* for the region. This book has provided a theoretical construct for conventionality control that is flexible enough to improve the dialogue between the Inter-American Court and the authorities of the States parties to the American Convention (especially among judicial institutions), all whom are institutions invested in the protection of human rights in the region. This dialogue could be the ground for a cross-fertilization of legal standards that allow for a better understanding of the requirements of human dignity, without hindering the legal pluralism that naturally comes from the coexistence of different States with their own history, culture and legal traditions. But the conceptual aspects of the idea of "judicial dialogue" and of "*Jus Constitutionale Commune*", and the specifics of the connections between these concepts in the context of the Inter-American System are still to be considered, discussed and put into practice by scholars, judges and practitioners at the national and the international levels.[68]

From a practical standpoint, the Inter-American Court shall adopt three practices in relation to the use of conventionality control in its jurisprudence. First, it shall privilege ordering State authorities – as part of their obligation to exercise conventionality control – to perform a consistent interpretation of domestic law rather than its non-enforcement. Secondly, it shall only establish the obligation of domestic authorities to exercise conventionality control as a guarantee of non-repetition in those cases where it finds the existence of interpretations, laws or practices that are *manifestly* anti-conventional, and it shall always provide good legal reasons for why a specific interpretation, piece

68 *See generally*, Eduardo Ferrer Mac-Gregor Poisot, *What Do We Mean When We Talk About Judicial Dialogue?: Reflections Of A Judge Of The Inter-American Court of Human Rights*, 30 Harv. Hum. Rts. J. 89 (2017); Eduardo Ferrer Mac-Gregor Poisot, *The Conventionality Control as a Core Mechanism of the Ius Constitutionale Commune*, in Armin Von Bogdandy, et al., *Transformative Constitutionalism in Latin America. The Emergence of a New Ius Commune*, *supra* n. 66; Armin Von Bogdandy, Héctor Fix-Fierro and Mariela Morales Antoniazzi (Eds.), *Ius Constitutionale Commune en América Latina. Rasgos, potencialidades y desafíos* (UNAM & Max-Planck Institute & Instituto Iberoamericano de Derecho Constitucional, 2014); Laurence Burgorgue-Larsen, *El diálogo Judicial* (Porrua, 2013); Paolo G. Carozza, *"My Friend is a Stranger": The Death Penalty and the Global Ius Commune of Human Rights* 81 Tex. L. Rev. (2002–2003).

of legislation or practice must be set aside by a particular State as a matter of international law (as happened in *Almonacid*, where the Court connected the nullity *ab initio* of the amnesty law with a prohibition of *jus cogens*).[69] Thirdly it shall elaborate a theoretical construct, based on a comprehensive understanding of the principle of subsidiarity, that justifies the inclusion of conventionality control as part of the general obligations that derive from Article 2. This approach would require drawing the specific connection between the obligation of States to adopt "legislative and other measures" to put into effect the rights and freedoms protected by the American Convention, and the obligation of domestic authorities to exercise conventionality control. This approach will clarify that the general obligation of Article 2 includes the adoption of four kinds of measures, not two:

- The elimination of any norms and practices that in any way violate the guarantees provided under the American Convention.
- The promulgation of norms and the development of practices conducive to the observance of those guarantees.
- The consistent interpretation of norms and the American Convention and the jurisprudence of the Inter-American Court.
- The non-enforcement of anti-conventional norms.

Also, the Inter-American Commission on Human Rights, other organs of the Organization of American States, civil society and State authorities, shall continue the process of improving domestic laws and practices through the political channels already in place in the different States parties to the American Convention. It is fundamental to keep in mind that the effectiveness of the different elements of the Inter-American *Corpus Juris* can be only achieved if they are transformed into laws, practices and policies developed and agreed by the relevant political and social actors at the domestic level. Conventionality control certainly empowers State authorities to give life to international standards mainly through interpretative means, making it a relevant doctrine for the protection of human rights – a "bridge", in García Ramírez's words. But the effectiveness of the different elements of the Inter-American *Corpus Juris* as reasons for action for judges of the peace, public prosecutors and police officers in small municipalities, requires human rights to be incorporated into the laws and practices of States.

Finally, the Inter-American Court and State authorities shall continue their dialogue, so that they are in a better position to decide the best manner to

---

69 *See generally*, Armin Von Bogdandy, *Ius Constitutionale Commune Latinoamericanum. Una aclaración conceptual*, in ARMIN VON BOGDANDY, HÉCTOR FIX-FIERRO AND MARIELA MORALES ANTONIAZZI (EDS.), *IUS CONSTITUTIONALE COMMUNE EN AMÉRICA LATINA. RASGOS, POTENCIALIDADES Y DESAFÍOS*, *supra* n. 68, pp. 13–14.

give meaning to, and implement, human rights in the region. Real dialogue requires not constructing human rights only in accordance with the view of a judicial elite at the international and/or domestic level, and of considering that the standards for the protection in the region shall result solely from the consensus among judicial elites. The Inter-American Court and the judiciaries at the domestic level definitely play a fundamental role in the protection of human rights in the States parties to the American Convention, especially considering the history of repeated intrusions of the executive power into the sphere of power of the judiciary in Latin America. But judges are not the only actors who have a legitimate voice in the definition of human rights standards and the mechanisms for their enforcement, both at the domestic and the international level. Many actors are relevant to the development and implementation of human rights, and their voices shall be heard in accordance with the political, judicial and academic channels already in place at the State level and at the level of the OAS.

BIBLIOGRAPHY

BOOKS

A.A. Cançado Trindade, *El Derecho Internacional de los Derechos Humanos en el Siglo XXI* (Editorial Jurídica de Chile, 2001).

——, *International Law for Mankind: Towards a Jus Gentium (II): General Course on Public International Law* (Martinus Nijhoff Publishers, 2005).

——, *Os Tribunais Internacionais e a Realizacao da Justica* (RENOVAR, 2015).

——, *The Access of Individuals to International Justice* (Oxford University Press, 2011).

Allan R. Brewer-Carías, *Constitutional Protection of Human Rights in Latin America. A Comparative Study of Amparo Proceedings* (Cambridge University Press, 2009).

Anthony Aust, *Modern Treaty Law and Practice* (Cambridge University Press, 2007).

Antonio Cassese, *International Law* (Oxford University Press, 2nd ed., 2005).

Antonio Cassese, Paola Gaeta and John R.W.D. Jones (Eds.), *The Rome Statute of the International Criminal Court: A Commentary* (Oxford University Press, 2002).

Anthony Clark Arend, *Legal Rules and International Society* (Oxford University Press, 1999).

Armin von Bogdandy, Eduardo Ferrer Mac-Gregor Poisot and Mariela Morales Antoniazzi, *La Justicia Constitucional y su Internacionalización: ¿Hacia un Ius Constitutionale Commune en América Latina?* Volume I-II (Instituto de Investigaciones Juridicas & Instituto Iberoamericano de Derecho Constitucional & Max Institut Fur Auslandishes Offentliches Rechts und Volkerrecht, 2010).

Armin Von Bogdandy, Héctor Fix Fierro and Mariela Morales Antoniazzi (Eds.), *Ius Constitutionale Commune en América Latina. Rasgos, potencialidades y desafíos* (UNAM & Max-Planck Institute & Instituto Iberoamericano de Derecho Constitucional, 2014).

Black's Law Dictionary (West Publishing Company, 8th ed., 2004).

Burns H. Weston and Stephen P. Marks (Eds.), *The Future of International Human Rights* (Transnational Publishers, 1999).

Cyril M. Picciotto, *The Relation of International Law to the Law of England and to the Law of the United States of America* (McBride, Nast & Co., 1915).

Cecilia Medina Quiroga, *La Convención Americana: Teoría y Jurisprudencia. Vida, Integridad Personal, Libertad Personal, Debido Proceso y Recurso Judicial* (Universidad de Chile & Facultad de Derecho & Centro de Derechos Humanos, 2003).

——, *The American Convention on Human Rights. Crucial Rights and their Theory and Practice* (Intersentia, 2016)

Christian Steiner and Patricia Uribe (Eds.), *Convención Americana sobre Derechos Humanos comentada* (Suprema Corte de Justicia & Konrad Adenauer Stiftung, 2014).

Claudio Nash Rojas, *Control de Convencionalidad. Cuadernillo de la Corte Interamericana de Derechos Humanos No. 7* (Inter-American Court of Human Rights & Ministerio de Relaciones Exteriores de Dinamarca, 2015).

——, *El Sistema Interamericano de Derechos Humanos en acción. Aciertos y Desafios* (Porrúa, 2009).

David J. Harris and Stephen Livingston (Eds.), *The Inter-American System of Human Rights* (Oxford University Press, 1998).

Dinah Shelton, *International Law and Domestic Legal Systems* (Oxford University Press, 2011).

—— (Ed.), *The Oxford Handbook of International Human Rights Law* (Oxford University Press, 2013).

Dinah Shelton and Paolo G. Carozza, *Regional Protection of Human Rights* (Oxford University Press, 2013).

Donald Earl Childress, III (Ed.), *The Role of Ethics in International Law* (Cambridge University Press, 2012).

Donald P. Kommers and Russell A. Miller, *The Constitutional Jurisprudence of the Federal Republic of Germany* (Duke, 3rd ed., 2012).

Eduardo Ferrer Mac-Gregor Poisot, *Panorámica del Derecho Procesal Constitucional y Convencional* (Marcial Pons, 2013).

—— (Ed.), *Derecho Procesal Constitucional*, Vol. II (Porrua, 4th ed., 2003).

—— (Ed.), *El Control Difuso de la Convencionalidad. Diálogo entre la Corte Interamericana y los Jueces Nacionales* (Funda, 2012).

Eduardo Ferrer Mac-Gregor Poisot and Alfonso Herrera Garcia (Eds.), *Diálogo Jurisprudencial en Derechos Humanos. Entre Tribunales Constitucionales y Cortes Internacionales* (Tirant Lo Blanch, 2013).

Eduardo Ferrer Mac-Gregor Poisot and Rubén Eduardo Sánchez Gil, *El nuevo juicio de amparo. Guía de la reforma constitucional y la nueva ley de amparo* (Porrúa, 2013).

Eduardo Ferrer Mac-Gregor Poisot, Fabiola Martínez Ramírez, and Giovanni Figeroa Mejía (Eds.), *Diccionario de Derecho Procesal Constitucional y Convencional*, Vol. I (Poder Judicial de la Federación, Consejo de la Judicatura Federal, Universidad Nacional Autónoma de México & Instituto de Investigaciones Jurídicas, 2014).

Eduardo Garcia Maynes, *Introducción al Estudio del Derecho* (Porrua, 13th ed., 1976).

Eduardo Gongora Mena, *Inter-American Judicial Constitutionalism: On the Constitutional Rank of Human Rights Treaties in Latin America through National and Inter-American Adjudication* (IIDH, 2011).

Eduardo Jimenez de Arréchaga, International Responsibility, *Manual of Public International Law* (Sorensen, 1968).

Ernesto Rey Cantor, *Control de la Convencionalidad de Leyes y Derechos Humanos* (Porrúa, 2008).

H.L.A. Hart, *The Concept of Law* (Oxford University Press, 2nd ed., 1961).

Hans Kelsen, *General Theory of the State and the Law*, trans. by Anders Wedberg (The Lawbook Exchange, 2007).

——, *Principles of International Law*, rev. and ed. by Robert W. Tucker (Holt, Rinehart and Winston, Inc., 2nd ed., 1966).

Héctor Fix-Zamudio, *Ensayos sobre el derecho de amparo* (Porrúa, 2003).

Héctor Gros Espiell, *La Convención Americana y la Convención Europea de Derechos Humanos. Análisis comparativo* (Editorial Jurídica de Chile, 1991).

Hersch Lauterpacht (Ed.), *Oppenheim's International Law* (Longmans, Green and Co. Ltd., 5th ed., 1937).

Ian Brownlie, *Principles of Public International Law* (Oxford University Press, 7th ed., 2008).

James Crawford, *The Creation of States in International Law* (Oxford University Press, 2nd ed., 2006).

Jeffrey L. Dunoff, Steven R. Ratner and David Wippman, *International Law. Norms, Actors, Process* (Aspen, 2010).

Jo M. Pasqualucci, *The Practice and Procedure of the Inter-American Court of Human Rights* (Cambridge University Press, 2nd ed., 2013).

John E. Noyes, Laura A. Dickinson and Mark W. Janis (Eds.), *International Law Stories* (Foundation Press, 2007).

John Finnis, *Human Rights & Common Good. Collected Essays: Volume III* (Oxford University Press, 2011).

——, *Natural Law and Natural Rights* (Oxford University Press, 2nd ed., 2011).

John Henry Merriman and Rogelio Pérez Perdomo, *The Civil Law Tradition* (Stanford University Press, 3rd ed., 2007).

José Ortega y Gasset, *Meditaciones del Quijote* (1914).

José Sebastián Elías et al (Eds.), *Tratado de los Derechos Constitucionales* (Abeledo, 2014).

La Corte Interamericana de Derechos Humanos. Un Cuarto de Siglo: 1979–2004 (OEA-ICtHR, 2005).

Laurence Burgorgue Larsen, *El diálogo Judicial* (Porrua, 2013).

Laurence Burgorgue-Larsen and Amaya Úbeda de Torres, The Inter-American Court of Human Rights. Case Law and Commentary (Oxford University Press, 2011).

Lord McNair, *The Law of Treaties* (Oxford University Press, 1986).

Louis Henkin, *International Law: Politics, Values and Functions*, 216 Collected Courses of the Hague Academy of International Law, Vol. IV (Martinus Nijhoff Publishers, 1989).

—— (Ed.) *The International Bill of Rights. The Covenant on Civil and Political Rights* (Columbia University Press, 1981).

Luis Andres Fajardo, *Implementación del Sistema Interamericano de Derechos Humanos en Colombia a través del bloque de constitucionalidad*. Serie Documentos de Investigación en Derecho No. 11 (Diké, 2010).

Malcolm D. Evans (Ed.), *International Law* (Oxford University Press, 2nd ed., 2006).

Malcolm N. Shaw, *International Law* (Cambridge University Press, 5th ed., 2003).

Marcos del Rosario (Ed.), *Supremacía Constitucional* (Porrúa, 2011).

Maria Leoba Castaneda Rivas, Homenaje al Maestro Edmundo Elías Musi (Porrúa, 2013).

María Carmelina Londoño Lázaro, *Las garantias de no repetición en la jurisprudencia interamericana. Derecho internacional y cambios estructurales del Estado* (Universidad de la Sabana & Tirant lo Blanch, 2014).
Mary Ann Glendon, *A World Made New* (Random House, 2001).
Michael T. Gibbons (Ed.), The Encyclopedia of Political Thought (Wiley Publishing, 2014).
Miguel Carbonell and Pedro Salazar (Eds.), *La Reforma Constitucional de Derechos Humanos. Un nuevo paradigma* (UNAM, 2011).
Olivier Corten and Pierre Klein (Eds.), *The Vienna Conventions on the Law of Treaties. A Commentary*, Vol. I (Oxford University Press, 2011).
Oliver Dörr and Kirsten Schmalenbach (Eds.) *Vienna Convention on the Law of Treaties. A Commentary* (Springer, 2012).
Onder Bakircioglu, *Self-Defense in International Law and Criminal Law: the Doctrine of Imminence* (Routledge, 2011).
Paolo Grossi, *A History of European Law*. Trans. by Laurence Hooper (Wiley-Blackwell, 2010).
Paulina Veloso (Ed.), *Justicia, Derechos Humanos y el Decreto Ley de Amnistía* (PNUD, 2010).
Robert J. Beck, Anthony C. Arend and Robert D. Vander Lugt, *International Rules* (Oxford University Press, 1996).
Rodrigo Uprimny Yepes, *Bloque de Constitucionalidad, Derechos Humanos y Proceso Penal* (Consejo Superior de la Judicatura Sala Administrativa & Escuela Judicial "Rodrigo Lara Bonilla" & Universidad Nacional de Colombia, 2008).
Ronald Dworkin, *Taking Rights Seriously* (Harvard University Press, 1978).
Sergio García Ramírez, *La Corte Interamericana de Derechos Humanos* (Purrúa, 2007).
Sergio García Ramírez and Mireya Castañeda (Eds.), *Recepción Nacional del Derecho Internacional de los Derechos Humanos y Admisión de la Competencia Contenciosa de la Corte Interamericana* (UNAM & IIJ & Minister of Foreign Affairs & Inter-American Court of Human Rights, 2009).
Silvia Serrano Guzmán, *El control de convencionalidad en la jurisprudencia de la Corte Interamericana de Derechos Humanos* (Comisión Nacional de los Derechos Humanos, 2013).
Sistema Interamericano de Protección de los Derechos Humanos y Derecho Penal Internacional (Konrad-Adenauer-Stiftung, 2010).
Stefan Zweig, *Decisive Moments in History* (Ariadne Press, 1941).
Susana Albanese (Ed.), *El control de convencionalidad* (Ediar, 2008).
Thomas Buergenthal, *Self-Executing and Non-self Executing Treaties in National and International Law* (Martinus Nijhoff Publishers, 1992).
Victimas sin Mordaza. El impacto del sistema interamericano en la justicia transicional en Latinoamerica: los casos de Argentina, Guatemala, El Salvador y Perú (Due Process of Law Foundation & Comisión de Derechos Humanos del Distrito Federal, 2007).
Vittoria Barsotti, Paolo G. Carozza, Marta Cartabia and Andrea Simoncini, *Italian Constitutional Justice in Global Context* (Oxford University Press, 2015).

BOOK CHAPTERS

A.A. Cançado Trindade, *La búsqueda de la realización de la justicia en la era de los Tribunales Internacionales*, in Eduardo Ferrer Mac-Gregor Poisot and Alfonso Herrera Garcia (Ed.), *Diálogo Jurisprudencial en Derechos Humanos. Entre Tribunales Constitucionales y Cortes Internacionales* (Tirant Lo Blanch, 2013).

——, *The Operation of the Inter-American Court of Human Rights*, in David J. Harris and Stephen Livingston (Eds.), *The Inter-American System of Human Rights* (Oxford University Press, 1998).

Annemie Schaus, *Article 27*, in Olivier Corten and Pierre Klein (Eds.), *The Vienna Conventions on the Law of Treaties. A Commentary*, Vol. I (Oxford University Press, 2011).

Ariel E. Dulitzky, *El Impacto del Control de Convencionalidad. ¿Un Cambio de Paradigma en el Sistema Interamericano de Derechos Humanos?* in José Sebastián Elías et al. (Eds.), *Tratado de los Derechos Constitucionales* (Abeledo, 2014).

Armin Von Bogdandy et al., *Ius Constitutionale Commune en America Latina. A Regional Approach to Transformative Constitutionalsm*, in Armin Von Bogdandy, et al., *Transformative Constitutionalism in Latin America. The Emergence of a New Ius Commune* (Oxford University Press, 2017).

Cecilia Medina Quiroga, *Las Obligaciones de los Estados bajo la Convención Americana sobre Derechos Humanos*, in *La Corte Interamericana de Derechos Humanos. Un Cuarto de Siglo: 1979–2004* (OEA-ICtHR, 2005).

Claudio Grossman, *The Velásquez Rodríguez Case: The Development of the Inter-American Human Rights System*, in John E. Noyes, Laura A. Dickinson and Mark W. Janis (Eds.), *International Law Stories* (Foundation Press, 2007).

Collin Warbrick, *States and Recognition of International Law*, in Malcolm D. Evans (Ed.), *International Law* (Oxford University Press, 2nd ed., 2006).

Davil Lay Williams, *Ronald Dworkin (1931–2013)*, in Michael T. Gibbons (Ed.), The Encyclopedia of Political Thought (Wiley Publishing, 2014).

Dinah Shelton, *The Promise of Regional Human Rights Systems*, in Burns H. Weston and Stephen P. Marks (Eds.), *The Future of International Human Rights* (Transnational Publishers, 1999).

Dinah Shelton and Ariel Gould, *Positive and Negative Obligations*, in Dinah Shelton (Ed.), *The Oxford Handbook of International Human Rights Law* (Oxford University Press, 2013).

Douglass Cassel, *El fallo Almonacid de la CIDH, y las obligaciones que de allí emanan para el Estado de Chile*, in Paulina Veloso (Ed.), *Justicia, Derechos Humanos y el Decreto Ley de Amnistía* (PNUD, 2010).

——, *La Corte Interamericana de Derechos Humanos*, in Victimas sin Mordaza. El impacto del sistema interamericano en la justicia transicional en Latinoamerica: los casos de Argentina, Guatemala, El Salvador y Perú (Due Process of Law Foundation & Comisión de Derechos Humanos del Distrito Federal, 2007).

Eduardo Ferrer Mac-Gregor Poisot, *Control de Convencionalidad (sede interna)*, in Eduardo Ferrer Mac-Gregor Poisot, Fabiola Martínez Ramírez and Giovanni Figeroa Mejía (Eds.), *Diccionario de Derecho Procesal Constitucional* y *Convencional*, Vol. I (Poder Judicial de la Federación, Consejo de la Judicatura Federal, Universidad Nacional Autónoma de México & Instituto de Investigaciones Jurídicas, 2014).

——, *Interpretación conforme y control difuso de convencionalidad. El nuevo paradigma del juez mexicano*, in Miguel Carbonell and Pedro Salazar (Eds.), *La Reforma Constitucional de Derechos Humanos. Un nuevo paradigma* (Porrúa, 2012).

——, *The Conventionality Control as a Core Mechanism of the Ius Constitutionale Commune*, in Armin Von Bogdandy, et al., *Transformative Constitutionalism in Latin America. The Emergence of a New Ius Commune* (Oxford University Press, 2017).

Eduardo Ferrer Mac-Gregor Poisot and Carlos Pelayo Möller, *Obligación de respetar los derechos*, in Christian Steiner and Patricia Uribe (Eds.), *Convención Americana sobre Derechos Humanos comentada* (Suprema Corte de Justicia & Konrad Adenauer Stiftung, 2014).

Elena I. Highton, *Sistema concentrado y difuso de control de constitucionalidad*, in Armin von Bogdandy, Eduardo Ferrer Mac-Gregor Poisot and Mariela Morales Antoniazzi, *La Justicia Constitucional y su Internacionalización: ¿Hacia un Ius Constitutionale Commune en América Latina?*, Vol. I (Instituto de Investigaciones Juridicas & Instituto Iberoamericano de Derecho Constitucional & Max Institut Fur Auslandishes Offentliches Rechts und Volkerrecht, 2010).

Ernesto Jiniesta, *Control de Convencionalidad Ejercido por los Tribunales y Salas Constitucionales*, in *El Control Difuso de la Convencionalidad. Diálogo entre la Corte Interamericana y los Jueces Nacionales* (Funda, 2012).

Ezequiel Malarino, *Acerca de la Pretendida Obligatoriedad de la Jurisprudencia de los Órganos Interamericanos de Protección de Derechos Humanos para los Tribunales Judiciales Nacionales*, in *Sistema Interamericano de Proteccion de los Derechos Humanos y Derecho Penal Internacional* (Konrad-Adenauer-Stiftung, 2010).

Gerald L. Neuman, *Subsidiarity*, in Dinah Shelton (Ed.), *The Oxford Handbook of International Human Rights Law* (Oxford University Press, 2013).

Guillermo Enrique Estrada Adán, *Una Visión del Control de Convencionalidad desde el Derecho Internacional*, in Maria Leoba Castaneda Rivas, *Homenaje al Maestro Edmundo Elías Musi* (Porrúa, 2013).

Hannah Arendt, *The Origins of Totalitarianism* (1951) in Peter Baehr (Ed.) *The Portable Hannah Arendt* (Penguin, 2003).

Hans Kelsen, *The Nature of International Law*, in Robert J. Beck, Anthony C. Arend and Robert D. Vander Lugt, *International Rules* (Oxford University Press, 1996).

Hugo Grotious, *Prolegomena*, in Robert J. Beck, Anthony C. Arend and Robert D. Vander Lugt, *International Rules* (Oxford University Press, 1996).

Jean Salmon, *Article 26*, in Olivier Corten and Pierre Klein (Eds.), *The Vienna Conventions on the Law of Treaties. A Commentary*, Vol. I (Oxford University Press, 2011).

John Finnis, *Limited Government*, in *Human Rights & Common Good. Collected Essays: Volume III*, 90 (Oxford University Press, 2011).

Jorge Rivero Evia, *Corpus Iuris Internacional*, in Eduardo Ferrer Mac-Gregor Poisot, Fabiola Martínez Ramírez and Giovanni Figeroa Mejía (Eds.), *Diccionario de Derecho Procesal Constitucional y Convencional*, Vol. I (Poder Judicial de la Federación, Consejo de la Judicatura Federal, Universidad Nacional Autónoma de México & Instituto de Investigaciones Jurídicas, 2014).

Jorge Ulises Tinoco, *La reforma y las normas de derechos humanos previstas en los tratados internacionales*, in MIGUEL CARBONELL AND PEDRO SALAZAR (EDS.), *LA REFORMA CONSTITUCIONAL DE DERECHOS HUMANOS. UN NUEVO PARADIGMA* (Porrúa, 2012).

Juan Carlos Hitters, *¿Son vinculantes los pronunciamientos de la Comisión y de la Corte Interamericana de Derechos Humanos? (Control de Constitucionalidad y Control de Convencionalidad)*, in EDUARDO FERRER MAC-GREGOR POISOT (EDS.), *EL CONTROL DIFUSO DE LA CONVENCIONALIDAD. DIÁLOGO ENTRE LA CORTE INTERAMERICANA Y LOS JUECES NACIONALES* (Funda, 2012).

Juan Mendez, *Lo que enseña la experiencia*, in *VICTIMAS SIN MORDAZA. EL IMPACTO DEL SISTEMA INTERAMERICANO EN LA JUSTICIA TRANSICIONAL EN LATINOAMERICA: LOS CASOS DE ARGENTINA, GUATEMALA, EL SALVADOR Y PERÚ* (Due Process of Law Foundation and Comisión de Derechos Humanos del Distrito Federal, 2007).

Juana María Ibañez Rivas, *Artículo 25. Protección Judicial*, in CHRISTIAN STEINER AND PATRICIA URIBE (EDS.), *CONVENCIÓN AMERICANA SOBRE DERECHOS HUMANOS COMENTADA* (Suprema Corte de Justicia & Konrad Adenauer Stiftung, 2014).

L. Oppenheim, *Introduction to Picciotto*, in CYRIL M. PICCIOTTO, *THE RELATION OF INTERNATIONAL LAW TO THE LAW OF ENGLAND AND TO THE LAW OF THE UNITED STATES OF AMERICA* (McBride, Nast & Co., 1915).

Laurence Burgorgue-Larsen, *Chronicle of a Fashionable Theory in Latin America. Decoding the Doctrinal Discourse of Conventionality Control*, in YVES HAECK, OSWALDO RUIZ-CHIRIBOGA AND CLARA BURBANO-HERRERA (EDS.), *THE INTER-AMERICAN COURT OF HUMAN RIGHTS: THEORY AND PRACTICE, PRESENT AND FUTURE* 676 (Intersentia, 2015).

——, *La Erradicación de la Impunidad: Claves para Desifrar la Política Jurisprudencial de la Corte Interamericana de Derechos Humanos*, in EDUARDO FERRER MAC-GREGOR POISOT (ED.), *EL CONTROL DIFUSO DE LA CONVENCIONALIDAD. DIÁLOGO ENTRE LA CORTE INTERAMERICANA Y LOS JUECES NACIONALES* (Funda, 2012).

Manuel Becerra, *La jerarquía de los tratados en el orden jurídico interno. Una vision desde la perspectiva del derecho internacional*, in SERGIO GARCÍA RAMÍREZ AND MIREYA CASTAÑEDA (EDS.), *RECEPCIÓN NACIONAL DEL DERECHO INTERNACIONAL DE LOS DERECHOS HUMANOS Y ADMISIÓN DE LA COMPETENCIA CONTENCIOSA DE LA CORTE INTERAMERICANA* (UNAM & IIJ & Minister of Foreign Affairs & Inter-American Court of Human Rights, 2009).

Marc Jacob, *La Función Sistémica del Precedente: Perspectivas del Derecho Internacional*, in ARMIN VON BOGDANDY, EDUARDO FERRER MAC-GREGOR POISOT AND MARIELA MORALES ANTONIAZZI, *LA JUSTICIA CONSTITUCIONAL Y SU INTERNACIONALIZACIÓN: ¿HACIA UN IUS CONSTITUTIONALE COMMUNE EN AMÉRICA LATINA?* VOLUME II (Instituto de Investigaciones Juridicas & Instituto Iberoamericano de Derecho Constitucional & Max Institut Fur Auslandishes Offentliches Rechts und Volkerrecht, 2010).

Martin Scheinin, *Core Rights and Obligations*, in DINAH SHELTON (ED.), *THE OXFORD HANDBOOK OF INTERNATIONAL HUMAN RIGHTS LAW* (Oxford University Press, 2013).

Mary Ellen O'Connell *Jus Cogens: International Law's Higher Ethical Norms*, in DONALD EARL CHILDRESS, III (ED.), *THE ROLE OF ETHICS IN INTERNATIONAL LAW* (Cambridge University Press, 2012).

Pablo Saavedra Alessandri, *La respuesta de la jurisprudencia de la Corte Interamericana a las diversas formas de impunidad en casos de graves violaciones de derechos humanos y sus consecuencias*, in *La Corte Interamericana de Derechos Humanos. Un Cuarto de Siglo: 1979–2004* (OEA-ICtHR, 2005).

Robert Badinter, *International Criminal Justice: From Darkness to Light*, in Antonio Cassese, Paola Gaeta and John RWD Jones (Eds.), *The Rome Statute of the International Criminal Court: A Commentary* (Oxford University Press, 2002).

Rodolfo Vigo, *Constitucionalización y Neoconstitucionalismo: algunos riesgos y algunas prevenciones*, in Marcos del Rosario (Ed.), *Supremacía Constitucional* (Porrúa, 2011).

Santiago A. Canton, *Leyes de Amnistía*, in Victimas sin Mordaza. El impacto del sistema interamericano en la justicia transicional en Latinoamerica: los casos de Argentina, Guatemala, El Salvador y Perú (Due Process of Law Foundation & Comisión de Derechos Humanos del Distrito Federal, 2007).

Sergio García Ramírez, *El Futuro del Sistema Interamericano de Protección de los Derechos Humanos*, in Eduardo Ferrer Mac-Gregor Poisot (Ed.), *Derecho Procesal Constitucional*, Vol. II (Porrua, 4th ed., 2003).

——, *La jurisprudencia de la Corte Interamericana de Derechos Humanos en material de reparaciones*, in *La Corte Interamericana de Derechos Humanos. Un Cuarto de Siglo: 1979–2004* (OEA-ICtHR, 2005).

Susana Albanese, *La internacionalización del derecho constitucional y constitucionalización del derecho internacional*, in Susana Albanese (Ed.), *El control de convencionalidad* (Ediar, 2008).

Vratislav Pechota, *The Development of the Covenant on Civil and Political Rights*, in Louis Henking (Ed.) *The International Bill of Rights. The Covenant on Civil and Political Rights* (Columbia University Press, 1981).

Yota Negishi, *The Subsidiarity Principle's Role in Allocating Competences Between Human Rights Courts and States Parties: the Hybrid Model of Centralized and Diffused Conventionality Control of Domestic Law*, in Armin Von Bogdandy, Mariela Morales Antoniazzi and Flavia Piovesan, *Ius Constitutionale Commune na América Latina. Volume III. Diálogos Jurisdicionais e Controle de Convencionalidade* (Jurua Editora, 2016).

ARTICLES

Alexei Julio Estrada, *Comentario al articulo "Control de convencionalidad interamericano: una mera aplicacion del derecho internacional", de Karlos Castilla*, Derecho del Estado no. 34, Universidad Externado de Colombia (2015).

Allan R. Brewer-Carías, *El Sistema Panameño de control concentrado de la constitucionalidad en el derecho comparado*, Paper presented in the *Segundas Jornadas de Derecho Procesal Jorge P.* (1995).

Andrés Gil Domínguez, *El bloque de la constitucionalidad federal y los informes de la Comisión Interamericana de Derechos Humanos*, II(58) Revista Argentina de Derecho Constitucional (2001).

Anne-Marie Slaughter and William Burke-White, *The Future of International Law Is Domestic (or, The European Way of Law)*, 47 Harv. Int'l L.J. (2006).

Ariel E. Dulitzky, *An Inter-American Constitutional Court? The Invention of conventionality control by the Inter-American Court of Human Rights*, 50 Tex. Int'l L. J. (2015).

Armin Von Bogdandy, *Pluralism, direct effect, and the ultimate say: On the relationship between international and domestic constitutional law*, 6 Int'l J. Const. L. (2008).

Arthur Utz, *The Principle of Subsidiarity and Contemporary Natural Law*, Natural Law Forum, Vol. 3 (1958).

Cecilia Medina Quiroga, *Los 40 años de la Convención Americana sobre Derechos Humanos a la Luz de cierta jurisprudencia de la Corte Interamericana*, Anuario de Derechos Humanos, (2009).

Christian Tomuschat, *The Effects of the Judgments of the European Court of Human Rights According to the German Constitutional Court*, 11 German Law Journal 529 (2010).

Clifford Kossel, *Global Community and Subsidiarity*, 8 Communio: Int'l Cath. Rev. 37 (1981).

Cristina Binder, *The Prohibition of Amnesties by the Inter-American Court of Human Rights*, 12 German Law Journal (2011).

David Feldman, *Monism, Dualism and Constitutional Legitimacy*, 20 Australian Yearbook of International Law 105 (1999).

Diego Garcia-Sayán, *The Inter-American Court and Constitutionalism in Latin-America*, 89 Tex. L. Rev. (2010–2011).

Dinah Shelton, *Normative Hierarchy in International Law*, 100 Am. J. Int'l L. (2006).

——, *The Rules and Reality of Petition Procedures in the Inter-American Human Rights System*, 5(1) Notre Dame Journal of International and Comparative Law: Vol. 5: Iss. 1 (2015).

Douglass Cassel, *Lessons from the Americas: Guidelines for International Responses to Amnesties for Atrocities*, 59 Law & Contemp. Probs. (1996).

Dunshee de Abranches, C.A. *Comparative Study of the United Nations Covenants on Civil and Political Rights and on Economic Social and Cultural Rights and of the Draft Inter-American Convention on Human Rights*, Inter-American Yearbook on Human Rights (1968).

Eduardo Ferrer Mac-Gregor Poisot, *Reflexiones sobre el control difuso de convencionalidad. A la luz del caso Cabrera Garcia y Montiel Flores vs. México*, XLIV (131) Boletín Mexicano de Derecho Comparado (2011).

——, *What Do We Mean When We Talk About Judicial Dialogue?: Reflections Of A Judge Of The Inter-American Court of Human Rights*, 30 Harv. Hum. Rts. J. 89 (2017).

Eduardo Ferrer Mac-Gregor Poisot and Pablo González-Domínguez, *Death Penalty, Amnesty Laws and Forced Disappearances: Three Topics of the Inter-American Corpus Juris in Criminal Law*, 5(1) Notre Dame Journal of International and Comparative Law (2015).

Eduardo Jiménez de Aréchaga, *La Convención Americana de Derechos Humanos como derecho interno*, Boletín da Sociedade Brasileira de Direito Internacional (1987–1989).

Erika de Wet, *The Prohibition of Torture as an International Norm of Jus Cogens and Its Implications for National and Customary Law*, 15(1) Eur. J. Int'l L. (2004).

Ezequiel Malarino, *Judicial Activism, Punitivism, and Supranationalisation: Illiberal Tendencies of the Inter-American Court of Human Rights*, 12 International Criminal Law Review (2012).

Francisco Fernandez-Segado, *El juez nacional como juez comunitario europeo de derecho común. Las transformaciones constitucionales dimanantes de ello*, 13 Revista Mexicana de Derecho Constitucional (2005).

Gerald L. Neuman, *Import, Export, and Regional Consent in the Inter-American Court of Human Rights*, 19(1) Eur. J. Int'l L. (2008).

Héctor Fix-Zamudio, *El derecho internacional de los derechos humanos en las Constituciones latinoamericanas y en la Corte Interamericana de Derechos Humanos*, XXV (75) Boletin Mexicano de Derecho Comparadom (1992).

——, *El derecho internacional de los derechos humanos en las Constituciones latinoamericanas y en la Corte Interamericana de Derechos Humanos*, 1(1) Revista Latinoamericana de Derecho (2004).

Humberto Sierra Porto, *La Constitución colombiana frente al control de convencionalidad*, Resource from the Library of the Inter-American Court of Human Rights (2013).

Jorge Contesse, *The final word? Constitutional dialogue and the Inter-American Court of Human Rights*, 15(2) International Journal of Constitutional Law (2017).

Juan Carlos Hitters, *Constitutional Control and Conventionality Control. Comparison (Criteria Established by the Inter-American Court of Human Rights)*, 7(2) Constitutional Studies (2009).

Luigi Crema, "Are Amnesties Still an Option? A Non-Policy Based Critique of the Inter-American Approach", Center for Civil and Human Rights, University of Notre Dame, Working Paper Series # 6 (2013).

Manuel Fernando Quinche-Ramirez, *El Control de Convencionalidad y el Sistema Colombiano*, 12 Revista Iberoamericana de Derecho Procesal Constitucional (2009).

María Carmelina Londoño Lázaro, *The Legality Principle and the Conventionality Control: Confluences and Developments in the Inter-American Court of Human Rights*, 128 Boletin Mexicano de Derecho Comparado (2010).

Marta Cartabia, "The Age of 'New Rights'", Strauss Institute Working Paper 03/10 (2010).

Michael S. Paulsen, *The Constitutional Power to Interpret International Law*, 118 Yale L.J. (2009).

Mirian Lorena Henríquez Viñas, *Hierarchy of Human Rights Treaties: Analysis Jurisprudential from the Method of Cases*, 6(2) Estudios Constitucionales (2008).

Nestor P. Sagües, *El "control de convencionalidad", en particular sobre las constituciones nacionales, La Ley*, Year LXXIII, No. 35 (2009).

——, *International obligations and "conventionality control"*, 8(1) Estudios Constitucionales1 (2010).

Oswaldo Ruiz-Chiriboga, *The Conventionality Control: Examples of (Un)successful Experiences in Latin America*, 3(1–2) Inter-American and European Human Rights Journal (2010).

Pablo Contreras, *Conventionality Control, International Deference, and National Discretion in the Inter-American Court of Human Rights Case Law*, 2 Revista Ius et Praxis 254 (2014).

Pablo González-Domínguez, *Reshape of the Relationship Between International Law and Domestic Law on the Basis of the Principle of Subsidiarity*, XVIII Anuario Mexicano de Derecho Internacional (2017).

Pablo González Domínguez and Christian González Chacón, *Dos visiones de la fuerza normativa del artículo 2 de la Convención Americana sobre Derechos Humanos*, 23 Revista Iberoamericana de Derecho Procesal Constitucional (2015).

Paolo G. Carozza, *From Conquest to Constitutions: Retrieving a Latin American Tradition of the Idea of Human Rights*, 25 Human Rights Quarterly (2003).

——, *Human Dignity and Judicial Interpretation of Human Rights*, 19 Eur. J. Int'l L. (2008).

——, *"My Friend is a Stranger": The Death Penalty and the Global Ius Commune of Human Rights*, 81 Tex. L. Rev. (2002–2003).

——, *Subsidiarity as a Structure Principle of International Law*, 97 Am. J. Int'l L. (2003).

——, *The Anglo-Latin Divide and the Future of the Inter-American System of Human Rights*, 5(1) Notre Dame Journal of International and Comparative Law (2015).

——, *The Problematic Applicability of Subsidiarity to International Law and Institutions*, 61(1) The American Journal of Jurisprudence (2016).

Paolo G. Carozza and Pablo González-Domínguez, *The final word? Constitutional dialogue and the Inter-American Court of Human Rights: A reply to Jorge Contesse*, 15(2) International Journal of Constitutional Law (2017).

Roberto Gargarella, *La democracia frente a los crimenes masivos: una reflexión a la luz del caso Gelman*, Revista Latinoamericana de Derecho Internacional (2015).

Rodrigo Uprimny, *The Recent Transformation of Constitutional Law in Latin America: Trends and Challenges*, 89 Tex. L. Rev. (2010–2011).

Roger P. Alford, *Subsidiarity and competition: decentralized enforcement of EU competition laws*, 27 Cornell International Law Journal (1994).

Samantha Besson, *Subsidiarity in International Human Rights Law-What is Subsidiary about Human Rights*, 61(1) The American Journal of Jurisprudence (2016).

Segio García Ramírez, *The Conventional Internal Control Court*, V(28) IUS Revista del Instituto de Ciencias Jurídicas de Puebla (2011).

——, *The Relationship Between Inter-American Jurisdiction and States (National Systems): Some Pertinent Questions*, Notre Dame Journal of International and Comparative Law 1(1) (2015).

Walter Carnota, *The Inter-American Court of Human Rights and Conventionality Control* (July 24, 2012).

OTHER SOURCES

Discurso pronunciado por el Juez Diego García Sayán en la inauguración del 48 periodo de sesiones de la Corte Interamericana de Derechos Humanos (held in Mexico City, Oct. 7–11, 2013).

Letter of the Popular Minister of Foreign Affairs of the Bolivarian Republic of Venezuela to the Secretary General of the Organization of American States, Sept 6, 2012.

Roxanna Altholz and Laurel E. Fletcher, "The Dominican Republic Must Stop Executions of Haitians", *New York Times* (Jul. 5, 2015).

Silvia Ayuso, « La República Dominicana se desliga de la Corte Interamericana de DD HH », editorial note from *El País*, (Nov. 6, 2014).

INDEX

Law and Cosmopolitan Values

In this series, the editors envisage monographs and collections of essays that address fundamental topics in law and globalisation, which range over doctrinal as well as normative questions of International and European law, human rights, justice and democracy. A main purpose of the series is to encourage scholarship that explores and transcends the categories and assumptions on which contemporary debates on globalization are conducted, and to stimulate reflection upon questions concerning the interplay between law, policy and principle. Recognizing that there is no occasion to distinguish sharply between theoretical and systematic work in the field from an analysis of law in context, the editors welcome studies from a wide variety of methodological traditions. Contributions to the series, inevitably crossing disciplinary lines, will be of interest to students, researchers and professionals in public law, international law, human rights law, political science, legal and political philosophy. Submissions of manuscripts by anyone who is working in the field are strongly encouraged.

Instructions to authors

Manuscripts can be forwarded to any member of the editorial board at any time.

If the entire manuscript or a minimum of 2 chapters are available then the author is required to submit a detailed table of contents and brief proposal (up to 3 pages) outlining methodology, likely public, and the contribution the book is or is likely to make. If no manuscript is available, then the proposal should, in addition to the above, contain summaries of all chapters (no longer than 10 pages).

Every contribution should be accompanied by a statement that it is the author's own original work, that it is not being considered for publication elsewhere, and that it does not constitute a substantial repetition of work published or to be published elsewhere.

Manuscripts that are deemed worthy of further consideration will be forwarded by the editors to a member of the advisory board or an external expert for a second review. Peer review reports are signed and should be detailed, describing and commenting on content, methodology, likely public, and the contribution the book makes or is likely to make. In case of disagreement between first and second reviews, the editorial board will ask a third reviewer for a further opinion.

It is expected that the reviewing process will not exceed 2 months in each case.

Related link:
http://lcv.intersentia.com

www.ingramcontent.com/pod-product-compliance
Ingram Content Group UK Ltd.
Pitfield, Milton Keynes, MK11 3LW, UK
UKHW051847100926
8556IPUK00005B/494